World Economic Problems and Policies

World Economic Problems and Policies

Edited by

Herbert V. Prochnow

HARPER & ROW, PUBLISHERS

New York, Evanston, and London

FIRST EDITION

LIBRARY OF CONGRESS CATALOG CARD NUMBER: 64–18107

MO

Contents

Preface

With each succeeding year, the world grows smaller. The nations are gradually being shaken into a more closely related community as machines weave the economic life of the world into a single fabric.

Striking achievements in communication and transportation are also giving us a new awareness of the economic and political problems of other peoples. Moreover, there is an increasing realization that economic, social, and political developments within one nation may profoundly affect all nations.

Consequently, men and women who wish to be well informed are seeking to understand and interpret major trends within individual nations and over large areas of the world where the problems are similar. There are difficult and perplexing questions, such as the balance of payments and the functioning of the world's monetary mechanisms, which concern all nations. There is a challenging development, such as the European Common Market, that has brought significant advantages to some nations, and perhaps to the entire free world in the cold war, but which has created problems for other nations. With the economic expansion of the Common Market have come such questions as British entry into the Market, the future of the European Free Trade Association, and the relationship of the former African colonies and other underdeveloped nations to the Market. There is also the vast problem of the course to be followed by the hundreds of millions of people of the less-developed nations as they struggle with poverty, disease, malnutrition, and the serious handicap of inadequate experience in self-government. These people are searching for the means of transforming primitive agricultural economies into complete modern industrial societies. They speak the language of urgency.

This volume undertakes to analyze thoughtfully a number of significant world economic problems and to assess realistically the policies that are being followed to solve these problems. Analyses are made also of underlying economic trends and their implications. These problems and trends are often of such magnitude and complexity that no one person is able to discuss all of them authoritatively. The book therefore brings to the discussion of these world economic problems and policies fifteen distinguished persons, each with a high degree of competence in a special field.

The contributing authors come from positions of distinction in the governments of a number of nations, from academic life, and from banking and business. Many of the authors discuss the economic problems and policies of their own countries or of related groups of countries. Each is particularly qualified by experience, study, and training to analyze his subject critically and constructively. Each one is responsible only for the chapter he has written, and he has been free to express his views without restriction. As a result, there are differences of opinion. The editor of this volume himself is not necessarily in agreement with the views of some of the contributing authors. However, in a discussion of problems of great importance, differences of viewpoint are perhaps inevitable and necessary if we are to have an understanding of the problems.

If this book gives the reader a better comprehension of the world economic problems and policies that may profoundly affect the future of our people and of all nations, it will have served its purpose.

H. V. P.

Evanston, Illinois
September 1964

Contributing Authors

KARL BLESSING: German banker and businessman. Commercial High School, Berlin. Reichsbank official, 1920–30; chief of section, Bank for International Settlements, Basle (1930–34); advisor to Dr. Schacht in the Reich Ministry for Economic Affairs, 1934–37; member of Reichsbank Directorate, 1937–39; dismissed by Hitler in consequence of the memorandum of the Reichsbank Directorate directed against the inflationary financing of German armament. President of the Deutsche Bundesbank since 1958. Author of *Die Verteidigung des Geldwertes*.

DAVID B. BOLEN: B.S. and M.S. University of Colorado, 1950; MPA Harvard University, 1960; vice consul, American Embassy, Monrovia, Liberia, 1950–52; economic officer, American Embassy, Karachi, Pakistan, 1952–54; international economist, Department of Commerce, 1955–57; international economist, Department of State, 1957–58; international relations officer in charge of Afghanistan affairs, 1958–59; chief, Economic Section, American Embassy, Accra, Ghana, 1960–62; staff assistant to the Assistant Secretary of State for African Affairs, 1962–64; officer-in-charge Nigerian affairs, Department of State 1964.

BARON PIERRE BONVOISIN: Chairman of the board of various banks and honorary chairman of the board of Banque de la Société Générale de Belgique; professor of money and banking, University of Louvain; chairman, Belgian-American Banking Corporation, New York; Belgian-American Bank and Trust Company, New York; Banque Belge Ltd., London; Banque Italo-Belge, Brussels; Crédit Foncier International, Brussels; Crédit Foncier de Belgique, Brussels; director, Banque de l'Union Parisienne, Paris; Banque Hypothécaire Franco-Argentine, Paris; Compagnie Bancaire, Paris; H. Albert de Bary & C⁰, N.V., Amsterdam; Angola Diamond Company, Lisbon; Compagnie Belge d'Assurances Générales, Brussels; Agence Maritime Internationale, Antwerp.

TORE BROWALDH: LL.M., Stockholm University, 1940; B.A. economics, 1942; assistant to Professor Gunnar Myrdal on government mission to study American postwar planning, 1943; financial attache, Swedish Legation, Washington, 1943; assistant secretary, The Royal Committee of Post-War Economic Planning, 1944–45; administrative secretary, The Industrial Institute for Economic and Social Research, 1944–45; secretary to Board of Management, Svenska Handelsbanken, 1946–49; director of the Economic, Social, Cultural and Refugee Department in the Secretariat General, Council of Europe, Strasbourg, 1949–51; executive vice president, The Confederation of Swedish Employers, 1951–54; president, Svenska Handelsbanken since 1955. Member of the boards of directors of several large Swedish corporations; chairman, Swedish Banks' Association, 1959–61. Author of *Management and Society*, 1961.

FELIPE HERRERA: B.A., Santiago, Chile, 1939; Master in Law and Social Sciences, University of Chile, 1946; Law Degree, University of Chile, 1947; postgraduate work in economics, University of London, England, 1950–51. Legal Department, Central Bank of Chile, 1943–47; lawyer for Central Bank of Chile and own law firm, 1947–52; Under-Secretary of Economy and Commerce, 1952; Minister of Finance of Chile, 1953; general manager, Central Bank of Chile, 1953–58; executive director of International Monetary Fund representing Argentina, Bolivia, Chile, Ecuador, Paraguay, and Uruguay, 1958–60; president of Inter-American Development Bank, 1960– . Part-time professor of economics, University of Chile, 1947–58. Received Great Cross for Distinguished Services from the Government of the Federal Republic of Germany, 1958.

ETIENNE HIRSCH: French civil engineer and administrator. Educated Écoles des Mines, Paris. Active in French chemical industry, 1924–40. Joined Free French forces, 1940; deputy director of armaments, 1945; president, French Supply Council, London; French representative temporary Economic Committee for Europe, 1945; head, technical division Commissariat-General au Plan, 1946–49; deputy commissioner general, 1949–52, commissioner general, 1952–59; participated in negotiations for ECSC, 1950–52; NATO Committee of Wise Men, 1951–52; president, Euratom commission, 1959–62; Commander Legion d'Honneur. President, Institut technique de Prevision economique et sociale, 1962– .

DAVID HOROWITZ: President, Bank of Israel, 1954– ; governor for Israel, International Bank for Reconstruction and Development.

Former lecturer, Tel-Aviv University; chairman, Board of Directors, Eliezer Kaplan School of Economics and Social Sciences; member, Board of Governors, Hebrew University, the Weizmann Institute of Science, Supreme Council for Education; director, Economic Department, Jewish Agency, 1935–48; member, Jewish Delegation to Lake Success, 1947; director-general, Ministry of Finance, 1948–52; author of several books on economics including *State in the Making,* 1953; *Kalkalat Israel,* 1954; and numerous articles dealing with Israel.

REINHARD KAMITZ: Realgymnasium, Hochschule fur Welthandel, diploma 1929; doctorate, 1934; [honorary professor of economics, political economy and finance, University of Vienna;] Research Staff, Austrian Institute for Cyclical Research, 1934–38; assistant professor, Hochschule fur Welthandel, 1939; senior lecturer, 1944–46 (political economy); Austrian Chamber of Commerce, 1939–48; director, Economic Department, Austrian Chamber of Commerce, 1948; deputy secretary general, Austrian Chamber of Commerce, 1950. Minister of Finance, 1952–60. President of the Austrian National Bank, 1960– . [Governor of the International Monetary Fund for Austria.] Various publications on monetary, financial, and economic subjects.

THORKIL KRISTENSEN: School of Commerce Certificate, 1916. Peoples College, Askov, 1920–21. University of Copenhagen, 1927. Lecturer, High School of Commerce, Aarhus, University of Copenhagen, 1927–38; professor, commercial and industrial economics, University of Aarhus, 1938–47; School of Advanced Commercial Studies, Copenhagen, since 1947. Member Danish parliament, 1945–60; minister of finance, 1945–47; 1950–53; member, finance committee, 1947–49, 1953–60; member, consultative assembly of Council of Europe, 1949–58; member, foreign affairs committee, 1953–60; president of Foreign Policy Association, 1948–60; member, assurance council, 1958–60. Secretary-General of the Organization for Economic Cooperation and Development, 1961– . Author and editor of many books including *European Markets—Plans and Prospects,* 1958, *The Economic World Balance,* 1960.

PAUL W. McCRACKEN: Student, William Penn College, 1937; M.A., Harvard, 1942, Ph.D., 1948; Faculty Foundation School, Berea College, Kentucky, 1937–40; economist, Department of Commerce, Washington, 1942–43; financial economist, director of research, Federal Reserve Bank of Minneapolis, 1943–48; associate professor, School of Business Administration, University of Michigan, 1948–50, professor, 1950– ; member,

Council Economic Advisers, Washington, 1956–59; director, Group Securities Incorporated. Member, American Economic Association, American Finance Association, American Statistics Association, Royal Economic Society. Author of *Hypothetical Projection of Commodity Expenditures; Northwest in Two Wars; Future of Northwest Bank Deposits; Rising Tide of Bank Lending.*

CHARLES MALIK: B.A., American University, Beirut, 1927; M.A., 1934; Ph.D., 1937, Harvard University; 40 honorary degrees from American, Canadian, and European universities and colleges. American Mission High School for Boys, Tripoli, Lebanon, 1920–23; American University of Beirut, 1923–27; graduate study, Harvard University, 1932–35; Travelling Fellowship from Harvard in Freiburg University, Germany, 1935–36. Instructor, American University of Beirut, 1927–29; Philosophy Department, Harvard University, 1936–37; instructor associate and professor, Department of Philosophy, American University of Beirut, 1937–47; Dean of Graduate Studies, 1955–58; E. K. Hall visiting professor, Dartmouth College, 1960; visiting professor, Summer School, Harvard University, 1960; professor, School of International Science, American University, Washington, D.C., 1961–62; professor of philosophy, American University, Beirut, 1962. Minister and ambassador of Lebanon to United States, 1945–55; chairman, delegation of Lebanon to General Assembly of the United Nations, 1956–58; president, Security Council of the United Nations, 1953, 1954; president, General Assembly of the United Nations, 1958–59. Author of many articles, essays, pamphlets, and books in both English and Arabic.

THOMAS C. MANN: B.A., LL.B., 1934, Baylor University; member of law firm, 1934–42; member, Texas and U.S. Supreme Court Bars; Department of State, 1942–47; foreign service officer, 1947–63. U.S. ambassador to El Salvador, 1955–57; assistant secretary of state for economic affairs, 1957–60; assistant secretary of state for Inter-American affairs, 1960–61; U.S. ambassador to Mexico, 1961–64; assistant secretary of state for Inter-American affairs, 1964– .

GAGANVIHARI L. MEHTA: M.A., University of Bombay, London School of Economics. Assistant editor, Bombay Chronicle, 1923–25; manager, Scindia Steam Navigation Co., Calcutta, 1928–47; president, Indian Chamber of Commerce and Industry, 1942–43; commissioner for Port of Calcutta, 1930–34, 1940–42, and 1946–47; Indian diplomat. Member of Indian Employers' Delegation, International Labour Conference, 1937;

member, Inland Transport Committee of ILO, 1947; member, Constituent Assembly of India, 1947; president, Indian Tariff Board, 1947–50; member, Planning Commission, 1950–52; chairman, Tariff Commission, January–August, 1952; Indian ambassador to U.S.A. and Mexico, 1952–58; and to Cuba, 1956–58; chairman, Hindustan Shipyard Ltd., 1958–62; the Industrial Credit and Investment Corporation of India, Ltd.; honorary LL.D., Rollins College, Florida, and Simpson College, Iowa; honorary Fellow, London School of Economics, 1958; Padma Vibhushan from President of India, 1959. Author of *From Wrong Angles, Perversities, The Conscience of a Nation, Understanding India.*

HERBERT V. PROCHNOW: B.A. Commerce, M.A., Economics, University of Wisconsin; Ph.D., Finance, Northwestern University; Honorary Doctor of Laws—Ripon College, University of Wisconsin, Northwestern University, Lake Forest College; Honorary Doctor of Letters, Millikin University; president and director, The First National Bank of Chicago; director, Summer Graduate School of Banking, University of Wisconsin since 1945; secretary, Federal Advisory Council of Federal Reserve System since 1945; president, Chicago Association of Commerce and Industry; consultant to the Secretary of State, 1955, 1957; Deputy Under Secretary of State for Economic Affairs, 1955–56; Alternate Governor for the United States of the International Bank and International Monetary Fund, 1955–56; member, U.S. Delegation to the Colombo Conference at Singapore, 1955; member and chairman, U.S. Delegation, General Agreement on Tariffs and Trade, Geneva, 1956; member, U.S. Delegation, Organization for European Economic Cooperation, Paris, 1956; formerly member of the faculty of Northwestern and Wisconsin Universities; author or editor of a number of books including *The Federal Reserve System, Practical Bank Credit, Great Stories from Great Lives, Term Loans and Theories of Bank Liquidity, American Financial Institutions, Determining the Business Outlook, The Public Speaker's Treasure Chest, A Dictionary of Wit, Wisdom and Satire.*

SIR LESLIE ROWAN: K.C.B., C.V.O., M.A., Cambridge University, England. Managing director, Vickers Limited; director, Barclays Bank, Legal and General Assurance Society, Limited; chairman of Council of Overseas Development Institute Limited. Entered Colonial Office, 1930; Treasury, 1933; assistant private secretary to Chancellor of Exchequer (Neville Chamberlain), 1934–37; assistant and later principal private

Those were dark and disillusioning days as men awakened from their wartime dreams and surveyed the dismal wreckage. There were few grounds for courage. And yet, as we now know, the raw materials of economic and social renewal were present in western Europe, waiting only to be given the leadership that was in less than two decades to make this one of the great areas of strength in the world.

At the outset of World War II in 1939, Soviet Russia was the only country in the world controlled by Communists. Then a relentless drift to socialism and communism began. Ten years later communism had swept over one-third of the world's population, one-fourth of the earth's surface, and numerous nations.

In 1945, in one of his less prophetic moments, Churchill declared, "I have not become His Majesty's First Minister to preside over the liquidation of the British Empire." But his successors were so to preside. During the nineteenth century and the first half of the twentieth, Britain, France, Belgium, Holland, and Portugal maintained order in a large part of Asia, the Middle East, and Africa. At the end of World War I, the Austro-Hungarian and Ottoman empires came to an end. By the end of World War II, the winds of political freedom were blowing fiercely through the corridors of all the old colonial empires. The pillars of reverence and loyalty were pulled down from under ruling groups that had provided the world with some stability. A world of clear landmarks was destroyed. Reasonable certainty in international affairs came to an end. Envies that had been restrained were set free. The last great empires were shattered, and forty new nations with almost one billion population—one-half the people of the noncommunist world—proclaimed their independence.

Among these new nations are some whose boundaries are not clearly established, many whose finances are in disorder and chaos, and a large number whose governments are on shaky foundations, with inexperienced leadership and illiterate masses lacking the qualifications for even the most elementary self-government. These millions do not always seem willing to follow the slow and painful road of the plodding generations of the past.

In the midst of these vast changes, the United States came to leadership as the world's major economic power. We may well scan the pages of history and ask, "How did the United States happen to become the world's leading economic power at this critical period in history?"

For many centuries, almost up to the beginning of the 1700s, living standards, social ideals, and political concepts for the masses of people were essentially similar over the world. In many respects, life in the early 1700s was not wholly unlike life two thousand years ago. Candles and oil lamps were used for light, fireplaces for heat, horses and sailing ships for travel. No message could be sent faster than a man could travel.

As recent as 1812, it took three months for the people as close as Kentucky to know who had been elected President of the United States in November. When Benjamin Franklin first took the stagecoach from Philadelphia to New York, he spent four days upon the journey. His driver spent his time knitting stockings as the coach jogged along. All trade by land between Boston and New York was carried on with two stagecoaches and eight horses, and in winter the trip took a week.

When the United States, shortly after its birth, sent its first representative to the British government, the captain of the sailing vessel in New York harbor told him to come aboard at once. He hurriedly bought a sack of flour, three hams, and a bag of potatoes, and arranged on ship for a sailor to cook his meals. He expected the ship to sail any hour, but it was five weeks before the ship left the harbor, and six weeks more before the representative of the government of the United States saw the coast of Great Britain.

However, in the middle of the 1700s, economic forces began to come into existence that were destined to change vitally the entire course of U.S. history. Unfortunately, these forces left great areas of the world untouched so that they now lag centuries behind the economic progress of other parts of the world. The regrettable fact is that while we all dwell on the same globe and use the same calendar, hundreds of millions of people are living centuries back in terms of economic, social, and political progress. For them, the world has stood still. In some countries, oxen slowly thresh grain by treading it under foot just as they did two thousand years ago. The women of Jericho go to the well for water and carry it in earthen jugs on their heads just as they did in the days of Abraham, Isaac, and Jacob.

One of the principal forces that enabled some parts of the world to take gigantic strides ahead was the Industrial Revolution, which began in Great Britain and spread to other countries, especially to the United States. The Industrial Revolution was ushered in by a number of unusual inventions, machines that replaced men in industry after industry.

The old-fashioned spinning wheel gave way to the cotton textile factory, and as early as 1840 the United States had 1,240 factories with over $2\frac{1}{4}$ million spindles in the cotton industry. Horses gave way to the new steam engine and to water power. In 1807, Robert Fulton's "Clermont" made the historic 160-mile trip up the Hudson River from New York to Albany in 32 hours. In 1838, the Atlantic Ocean was crossed for the first time by steam.

In 1830, Peter Cooper's little steam locomotive, the "Tom Thumb," proudly traveled 13 miles at an average speed of 6 miles an hour. At that time, there were only 23 miles of railroad, but by 1860, there were 30,000 miles, and by 1890, over 160,000 miles. By 1860, the U.S. factory system was firmly established. The United States had 140,000 manufacturing plants, and was producing more goods by machine than by hand. This was a major turning point. The foundations of a machine economy had been firmly laid.

The United States was making colossal strides in every field. The iron plow and the reaper were taking their toll from the prairies. New processes were revolutionizing the iron and steel industry. Typewriters, cash registers, arc lamps, electric lights, sewing machines, the telegraph, rotary presses, pneumatic tires, tank and refrigerator cars, air brakes, power shovels, electric locomotives in place of mules in mines, mechanical loaders, tractors and tractor-drawn farm equipment, automobiles, trucks, heavy industrial equipment, and airplanes are only a few illustrations of the striking mechanization and the new products that were remaking the U.S. economy and thrusting it dramatically forward in the world.

Great natural resources, a vast continent, insulation from major foreign wars for over a century, a rapidly expanding, hard-working population, and confidence that its economic system would reward men well gave enormous driving energy to the people of the United States.

Agriculture provides a remarkable example of mechanization in a single industry. George Washington was the President of a rural nation with at least 90 per cent of the people engaged in agricultural pursuits. By 1840, the iron plow had displaced the inefficient wooden plow. Then came the steel plow, along with the reaper, mower, hay rake, thresher, seed drill, corn planter, and cultivator, to bring amazing changes. By 1860, a U.S. farmer could produce his crops with one-third less labor than he required just twenty years earlier.

By 1880, only 44 per cent of the people were engaged in farming, which compares with about 48 per cent in Soviet Russia today. By 1900 about 36 per cent of the labor force in the United States was engaged in agriculture, in contrast to less than 10 per cent today.

Moreover, between 1850 and 1950, the work week on the farm declined from 70 to 45 hours. The increased use of science and equipment, including tractors, trucks, milking machines, and great combines, as well as fewer but larger farms, has vastly increased farm production.

In 1820, one farm worker in the United States produced sufficient food for four persons. Today he produces enough for twenty-four persons. In contrast, in Soviet Russia, one farm worker produces enough food for about two persons. Since 1932 the production of U.S. farms has increased by 50 per cent, but at the same time, the farm population has declined by more than 25 per cent. For at least twenty years the productivity of farm labor has risen at an average annual rate of more than twice the 2.2 per cent annual increase for the remainder of the U.S. economy. These are some of the striking achievements in agriculture that resulted from mechanization and heavy capital investment.

Thirty per cent of the people of Europe, 40 per cent or more of

South America, and as high as 70 to 80 per cent for large areas in Asia, Africa, and the Middle East are engaged in agriculture. Today, over one-half the people of the world still live in pre-industrial societies engaged in agriculture. Any nation in which a large percentage of the people must work solely to subsist will be greatly retarded in its industrial development.

The combined forces of mechanization, capital investment, technology, research, and science were great mainsprings that gave the U.S. economy a driving momentum. The foundations of U.S. society were laid by men who worked long hours and endured economic want so that they could save and invest and accelerate their economic progress.

By 1914 the United States stood at the threshold of world leadership. Then it emerged as victor in two world wars. Its ships, its planes, its machines, its investments are now in every part of the world. It has come to the pinnacle of world leadership in large part because its people had the opportunity to develop their nation under a government that gave them political freedom and encouraged initiative, enterprise, industry, thrift, and inventive genius. Freedom and achievement are not unrelated. The United States helped to make the idea of political freedom a great force that swept the world and created in only fifteen years over forty new nations with more than one billion people. The voices of Washington, Jefferson, Madison, and Lincoln have been heard by the new and emerging peoples in the most remote areas of the world.

Working hours are at their shortest, and leisure and its luxurious use are at the highest point in U.S. history. In terms of a dollar of constant value the total U.S. real national product has, on average, nearly doubled every twenty years. For practically the first time in history, the possible abolition of poverty has seemed within man's grasp.

Only a century ago, water and steam power furnished less than one-fourth of the energy needed in production. Men and animals provided 75 per cent, and men gave by far the larger part. Today, men are largely free from the hardest physical labor, and machines supply 98 per cent of all power for industry in the

United States. The average work week now is 40 hours compared to 60 hours in 1890. Moreover, the average factory worker receives an income that will buy almost twice as much as it did only a little over a generation ago. The average worker receives better wages, has shorter hours, produces more goods, and has more plant, equipment, and energy working for him than at any time in U.S. history. With less than 9 per cent of workers required to feed the people, 91 per cent are free to produce other goods and services to raise the standard of living. Until the late 1940s, more persons were engaged in production industries, such as manufacturing, construction, agriculture and mining, than in service industries. There are now 25 per cent more in service industries, such as retailing, transportation, finance, and utilities, than in production industries. Only one out of four of the U.S. labor force now works in factories. There has been gratifying progress in surmounting the age-old obstacles of poverty and ignorance.

Economic progress depends in a large measure on three factors: working, saving, and investing. Standards of living can rise and men can have more goods and services only when they produce more. There is no easy route to economic growth. Our standard of living improves only when the gross national product—the total goods and services produced each year—increases faster than the population. Physical labor may increase production somewhat, but the great expansion in production is made possible by machines. For example, in the 1950s, the output of U.S. manufacturing industries increased 40 per cent, with only a 9 per cent increase in employees.

To obtain machines and equipment a nation must save and invest. To induce men and women to save, adequate incentives must be given. It must be worth while to save. Nations whose fiscal policies result in inflation and the erosion of the value of the savings of the people, or nations in which taxation becomes excessive, destroy the incentive to save.

In 1900, the amount of U.S. capital invested per worker in manufacturing was $1,880. During the next forty years, this investment increased to $5,080. The investment is now estimated at

$15,000 or more per worker. During these sixty years, the average factory worker's weekly pay rose from $9 to over $90. These great benefits to the worker reflect, in a large measure, investments in machines by businesses encouraged by the possibility of profits. It is estimated that the average age of the U.S. plant is twenty-four years and that two-thirds of the machine tools are more than ten years old. Moreover, it is estimated that $150 billion of plant and equipment in the United States will become obsolete between now and 1970 and that $270 billion more will be needed to equip the millions of persons who will enter the labor force by 1970. These estimates give some idea of the vast amounts that will be required in business earnings and in savings if the people of the United States are to maintain their competitive position with other leading industrial nations.

With this perspective on U.S. historical development, consider some of the problems now confronting that country. It has excelled other countries in many technical and productive skills. Now it is aware that in only a few years the European Economic Community, or Common Market, of 175 million people has become a major economic force. Moreover, if the market ultimately embraces all or most of western Europe with its 300 million persons, it may become the world's greatest trade center and most powerful economic group. Its people are skilled. They are literate. They are increasingly equipped with the most modern machinery and plants. They are highly disciplined in work, saving, and investment. Across the Pacific in Japan, with its almost 100 million people, the United States is confronted also by industrial competition in world markets of a nation of extraordinary competency.

The U.S. market is still the largest in the world, but unless it can sell its goods and services abroad in increasing volume, it will be unable to buy the raw materials and goods it must import in the years ahead to keep its economy operating and expanding. In international trade, it will need a hard discipline in costs to keep the products of the United States competitive. It faces the economic competition not only of the great industrial nations of the free world, but also that of Soviet Russia and her satellites with their more than 300 million people.

The U.S. position of leadership has brought with it another responsibility neither anticipated nor sought. With the shattering of all the great empires following two world wars, forty new nations with a population of one billion have emerged. These people are engaged in a struggle against poverty and ignorance. They stir uneasily in their hopes and dreams. They constitute a continuing threat to the peace of the world, one that cannot be safely ignored. And yet, it is a serious question whether the United States with 190 million persons can solve problems of poverty, illiteracy, disease, inadequate tax systems, persistent inflation, and land reform for a thousand million people of the world. Six hundred million people with problems of this kind live in India, Pakistan, Indonesia, and Southeast Asia; over forty million, in the Middle East; 235 million, in Africa; and 214 million, in Latin America.

Can the United States assure that these nations, many of which are largely unprepared for self-government, do not endanger the peace of the world through revolutions and violence? Can it give educational facilities to hundreds of millions who are illiterate? Can it assure the necessary food to millions suffering from malnutrition, when per capita food production now in various areas is probably less than it was before World War II? Can it eliminate widespread disease in the underdeveloped nations and add even five years to the life expectancy of these people, many of whom live only thirty or forty years? Can it provide pure water supplies and systems of sanitation for hundreds of millions? Can it supply means of transportation, communication, and power to many countries that are almost completely without such facilities? There is not sufficient available capital in the entire world to accomplish these objectives within a reasonably short time. Under these conditions it is inevitable that the United States will face for many years a turbulent and politically unstable world.

Consider only Latin America, with its 214 million people living in an area about twice as large as the United States. It is estimated that by the end of this century, the population may be double that of the United States. This area is critical relative to U.S. security, particularly since the developments in Cuba. Many Latin American nations have had independence for well over a century. Nevertheless, there is widespread illiteracy, poverty, and disease. Per capita income has ceased growing in various areas. There is much discontent and restlessness. There is a reluctance to follow policies that encourage saving and investment. There is a flight of capital.

Over 60 per cent of the 62 million children of school age in Latin America do not attend any school. Approximately one-half of the 214 million people has bad water supplies. The large slum areas and shanty towns around the shadowy perimeters of many of the major cities are among the worst in the world. The average life expectancy is about forty-five years. Tax avoidance is widespread. One-half of the people cannot read or write. Many live at a bare subsistence level. In some countries a few families own 90 per cent of the arable land. Between 1956 and 1960, the per capita rate of increase in the gross national product was at the disappointing rate of about 1 per cent, which compares with approximately 2.7 per cent between 1945 and 1955. This decline in the rate of economic growth is undoubtedly one of the factors responsible for the present restlessness.

Can the United States make certain that no Latin American nation will follow the path of Cuba? Is there a reasonable assurance that the programs it is sponsoring in Latin America at a cost of $1 billion a year to U.S. taxpayers will provide economic and social improvement with tax and land reform, or are they destined to failure for which the United States will be blamed? No matter how well-intentioned the U.S. programs may be, they are almost certain to fail unless these nations themselves take steps to balance budgets, stabilize currencies, adopt adequate systems of taxation, and halt chronic inflation. U.S. capital, which constantly seeks opportunities for profitable investment, will not flow to countries whose fiscal and monetary policies are unsound, whose governments threaten expropriation, and whose investors themselves send their own capital to other countries for safekeeping.

It must be recognized that it is no easy task for governments in some Latin American countries, in their present stage of economic development and with widespread illiteracy and poverty, to follow middle-of-the-road policies that satisfy the radical elements, the military groups, the landowners of large tracts, and businessmen. As they soberly analyze their grave problems, the leaders of many of these countries feel impelled to adopt policies of expedience rather than wisdom.

In the vast area of the Far East, there are new nations with hundreds of millions of persons who have thrown off years of colonialism to obtain independence. There is poverty, disease, and illiteracy. There is no certainty that constitutional free government will prevail in these areas. There is only the certainty that the governments that do not strongly promote policies for the social and economic progress of the masses will be broken. These people want economic progress, and they want it as soon as possible. In the case of India, it is a serious question whether an underdeveloped country with a population of hundreds of millions of persons can solve the problems of mass poverty with a democratic form of government unless assistance in some form is forthcoming. One of the objectives of the free world is to assure the survival of democracy in its struggle with communism. The survival of democracy over the world may finally depend to a significant degree upon the economic and political systems adopted by the underdeveloped and newly independent nations, where most of the world's people live.

The people in the United States now have the highest standard of living of any people, and that nation has become one of the greatest economic powers in history. And yet it is confronted over the world with challenges of vast magnitude. These are not easy challenges. U.S. policies have no assurance of success. However, there are infinite sources of strength in the U.S. tradition of private enterprise and political liberty. It lies within its power to meet these challenges and to play fully its historical role in the free world if it brings to its problems those inherent qualities that made a people strong and a nation great.

World Economic Problems and Policies

CHAPTER 1

The United States Experience
in Economic Development

Thomas C. Mann

In judging economic systems, the important thing is not whether an economic theory is logical or whether its proponents have good intentions, but whether it produces results—whether, without destroying freedom, it creates prosperity or poverty for the people.

This is the yardstick by which all economic systems and policies will ultimately be judged. Whether a particular policy will promote or impede progress is often open to debate; for, unlike mathematics, economics is not an exact science. But whether a particular system or policy is, or is not, successful can be ultimately determined with great accuracy.

If we apply the test of achievement to the economy of the United States, there is abundant reason for satisfaction. As Walter Hallstein points out in his book, *United Europe:*

One of the aspects of the United States that impressed Alexis de Tocqueville, as it has impressed visitors from Europe to this day, was the extraordinary degree of prosperity that he saw around him. "No people in the world," he declared, "has made such rapid progress in trade and manufactures. . . . The Americans arrived but as yesterday on the territory which they inhabit, and they have already changed the whole order of Nature." In the century that followed, the speed of this progress became even more striking. Between 1900 and 1938, United States industrial production rose by 163 percent; by 1955, the gross national product per head of population in the United States stood at $2,353. . . .

Other nations have had more spectacular rates of economic growth for short periods of time, but no one can match this record of sustained growth and achievement over a long period of time. U.S. production today is the highest in the world, whether we measure it in terms of individual or national income.

The U.S. record of social achievement has been even more impressive. It has had a continuously rising curve of individual productivity, steadily increasing wages, and an unmatched domestic purchasing power created by the simple act of sharing growth with middle- and low-income families. Some economies today pay the capitalist a larger rate on his loans and investment than he can earn in the United States. But no economic system pays so well its workers in the factories and on the farms, its teachers, its professional class—all those who produce goods or render services. And no other system has been more successful in leveling off extremes of poverty and wealth, in achieving an equitable distribution of the national product, and in preventing the exploitation of man by man. The United States has already achieved a large degree of social justice, whereas socialists still talk about social justice as if it were a goal for the distant future.

All this has been accomplished in the United States without sacrificing freedom, either economic or political, and without creating divisive hatreds between classes. In comparison, socialist regimes, at a great cost in human lives and human misery, to say nothing of human liberties, have succeeded only in substituting for the old ruling classes a new privileged class of bureaucrats. Their people are, after all these years, still far from achieving the standard of living and individual income that the United States has enjoyed for decades.

It is a paradox of our times that, in spite of this record, so many people spend so much time lamenting the shortcomings of the U.S. economic and social systems. They apparently fail to understand the difference between theory and practice, between Utopian dreams and solid achievement. Many of them speak as if they were unaware of the great changes that have taken place in society since Karl Marx attacked the kind of capitalism that existed in Europe in the mid-1800s.

The progress made in the United States is, I suggest, attributable to certain broad economic principles, tested in practice for more than 175 years, which form the guidelines for the U.S. economic system and for its economic policies.

The first of these to be discussed here is economic freedom.

ECONOMIC FREEDOM

During the seventeenth and eighteenth centuries, when Europe was ruled by kings and the United States was a colony of England, the theory of mercantilism dominated European economic and political thought. Essentially, mercantilism taught that a state prospers by amassing gold. This could be brought about by a country's exporting more than it imported. Foreign trade, as well as domestic production, was therefore tightly and extensively controlled in order to make it possible for the country to maintain, on a bilateral basis, "favorable" balances of trade with each trading partner. To cite only one example of the degree of control exercised by government in those days, it is said that, between 1666 and 1730, the rules of the French government for the French textile industry alone filled two thousand printed pages.

When it became apparent that these controls were stifling production to the detriment of the living standards of the people—and we should not forget that mercantilism *did* fail—the pendulum swung naturally in the opposite direction.

Adam Smith, in his *Wealth of Nations,* spoke of "natural" liberty as including the right of people to be free in the economic as well as the political sense. Economic progress would come faster, Smith said, if governments were relieved of "the duty of superintending the industry of private people." This idea that political and economic freedom were interdependent was developed, in England at least, by other economists and philosophers and by distinguished lawyers such as Sir Henry Maine and Edward Coke. In essence, they feared the exploitation of man by the state even more than they feared the exploitation of man by man. Man, they reasoned, can better protect himself from the tyranny of an individual than from the tyranny of an all-powerful state.

In our own time, Ludwig Erhardt, the chief architect of the remarkable postwar recovery of West Germany, expressed the same idea in his book, *Prosperity Through Competition:*

This basic principle of freedom for the consumer must logically be counterbalanced by freedom for the producer to make and sell what he believes to be marketable, that is, what he has found, after studying individual needs, to be essential and likely to succeed. Freedom for the consumer and freedom to work must be explicitly recognized as inviolable basic rights of every citizen. Democracy and a free economy are as logically linked as are dictatorship and state controls.

The concept of economic freedom runs through the Declaration of Independence and the Constitution of the United States. To cite two illustrations: Although we are a group of sovereign states, no state may put obstacles in the way of interstate commerce; in the vernacular of today, the U.S. Constitution created a common market in which the free movement of capital goods and labor was guaranteed. On the other hand, the power of the federal government to regulate intrastate affairs was severely curtailed. Second, because it seemed logical that the right of the individual to the "pursuit of happiness," to which the Declaration referred, would be incomplete without economic as well as political freedom, the Fifth Amendment to the Constitution provided:

No person shall be—deprived of life, liberty or property without due process of law; nor shall private property be taken for public use without just compensation.

This does not mean, of course, to imply that Americans believe economic freedom should be unlimited. As James Madison pointed out, men are not angels. He wrote in the *Federalist Papers* about the danger of the tyranny of the majority:

A pure democracy can admit no cure for the mischiefs of faction— there is nothing to check the inducements to sacrifice the weaker party.

And because tyranny by the few over the many is also possible, the United States has adopted antitrust laws to prevent unfair trade practices. Similarly a limited number of U.S. industries that have monopolistic or other peculiar characteristics, such as railroads and public utilities, are regulated. There are other limitations to the principle of absolute economic freedom, notably with respect to research needed for production of military and space machines and nuclear energy. There are certain controls on shipping, telecommunications and aviation, and on the production of a limited number of agricultural commodities.

But it needs to be emphasized that these are the exceptions and not the rule. Virtually all U.S. industry and farms are privately owned. Individuals and corporations conduct their own research, improve their own designs, seek new and better ways to improve the quality of their product and to reduce its cost. The producer is free to make what he pleases and to fix the price of his product. The consumer is free to buy what he chooses. In the words of Smith, the U.S. government does not attempt to superintend "the industry of private people."

A free economy is not only consistent with, and indivisible from, principles of political freedom, but also serves the material end of promoting material progress. This is so because, as has so often been observed, freedom of choice by the individual unleashes individual ingenuity and inventiveness; this in turn gives a vitality and dynamism to the economy, which it could not otherwise have. John Chamberlain explains the principle in these words:

The virtue of a free system—i.e., competitive capitalism—is that it allows energy to flow uncoerced into a thousand and one different forms, expanding goods, services and jobs in myriad unpredictable ways.

Mr. Chamberlain has observed that economists did not plan or foresee the machines of the Industrial Revolution or Eli Whitney's cotton gin. No economist thought of Henry Ford's innovations in assembly-line production; his $5.00 daily wage to workers was, both in classical and socialist theory, an economic impossibility. New techniques for making marginal land productive and food plentiful disproved the gloomy predictions of Malthus and Ricardo, which for years were accepted as economic gospel. Even after the Industrial Revolution was well advanced, how many economists understood that, in free economies, innovations were to be continuing and self-perpetuating phenomena that would create vast numbers of jobs and for the first time in history place within the reach of the common man all the things he needs for a decent life? Even today, who can imagine the shape of things to come if man, the individual man, remains free to invent, to experiment, and to produce the things which the world needs?

And now a second principal tenet of the U.S. economic system is examined: High standards of living for the people can best be achieved in a competitive economy.

COMPETITION

Let us first consider the protectionist, the one who does not wish to compete. In the United States a minority of businessmen, who usually profess to believe in "private initiative" and competition for the other fellow, asserts that their businesses are an exception and need protection. Often they say that their only motive is the protection of the jobs of their employees or, perhaps, their only interest is that national "security" be maintained by denying foreign competitors access to our markets. The same rationale is expressed in different words in other countries.

To be sure, there are cases in which protection is justified and desirable; for example, in the case of an infant industry that has good prospects of becoming efficient and competitive if, for a limited period of time, it is given a reasonable degree of protection. There are other exceptions. As do most economic decisions, the problem in the end becomes one of scope and degree. But we need constantly to remind ourselves that the national economy and the people pay a high price for excessive protection. Protection to a small group of individuals who own a particular factory is, in economic terms, a subsidy to the owners, no matter what form it takes—whether it is a tariff, a quota, a licensing arrangement, or a cash subsidy.

If the subsidy is in the form of cash paid the producer, it is the taxpayer who foots the bill. If it takes other forms, it is paid by the consuming public through higher prices, usually for an inferior product, thereby lowering the real income of the people. Precisely the same thing occurs when the industry is state-owned, with the difference that in this case the higher prices for consumer goods can be considered as an indirect tax. If the prices are kept artificially low for social or other purposes, the consumer of the particular commodity gains, but it is the taxpayer who pays.

So, in these days when we are all talking so much about raising real income of the masses, the question may well be asked on social as well as on economic grounds: Who receives the subsidy? Who pays the subsidy? Will the protected industry really be able, within a reasonable period of time, to pay the people back by efficiently producing goods of high quality at low cost?

The answers to these questions clearly demonstrate that the consumer—and this includes every one of us because we all buy consumer goods—has a stake in keeping industry efficient and competitive. For whether we consumers are employers or employees, whether we work in a factory, on a farm, or in an office, the quantity and quality of the things our money will buy is at least as important to our standard of living and our *real* income as the number of dollars we earn.

And the same thing is doubly true of our wage earner. His real wages are reduced if he has to pay more for what he consumes. In addition, he loses his chance of a noninflationary wage increase, for the only noninflationary way to increase his wage is to increase his individual productivity. Productivity is increased more in efficient industries because they use the latest and best machines. It is no accident that in free competitive economies, the real wages of the worker are much higher than they are in economic systems that avoid competition.

If the consumer, the taxpayer, and the worker profit more, as individuals, in a competitive economic system, so does the economy as a whole. Henry Hazlitt reminds us that:

> Economics . . . is a science of recognizing *secondary* consequences. It is also a science of seeing *general* consequences. It is the science of tracing the effects of some proposed or existing policy not only on some *special* interest *in the short run* but on the *general* interest *in the long run.*

Experience of the United States proves the value to its economy of the free play of competitive forces. We may also learn from the experiences of other economies in which competition has been, or is being, restricted on the theory that "controlled" economies eliminate "waste" and make for a better utilization of resources. If we look at the experiences of others, we find that there are indeed a number of general and secondary consequences to restricting competition. The following paragraphs will briefly discuss a few of them.

First, industries that are protected from the spur of competition have no incentive to conduct research, to modernize their machines and methods of production, or to find ways to improve the productivity of the individual worker. The result is that the national industrial plant, not to mention wages, remains static while the competitive world passes it by on the road to more efficient production.

Second, protected industries can seldom compete abroad, and when too many industries become noncompetitive, the national industrial plant cannot earn foreign exchange. We may well ask ourselves whether monopoly trends, already discernible in some parts of the free world, will not in the end have the effect of tying some economies, perhaps permanently, to groups of high cost, inefficient industries.

One consequence of the inability to compete abroad is that as capital imports are reduced in developing countries, economic growth rates decline. Another is an inevitable discrimination against the exports of other countries, which are expected at the same time to continue to buy the exports of the discriminating country. Still other consequences are balance-of-payments and monetary stability problems, so common in the world today.

Third, a high degree of protectionism often goes hand in hand with the progressive expansion of the public sector and a corresponding contraction of and control over the private sector. This phenomenon, in turn, tends to undermine confidence, which so often translates itself into a reluctance on the part of the private sector to invest and which sometimes causes flights of capital. The end result again is a lowering of the growth rate and the creation of balance-of-payments and other problems.

Fourth, another demonstrable inhibitor restricting competition is that in controlled economies, inefficient industries are seldom allowed to go out of business. Usually the state takes over the business to prevent economic "waste." The same end result of government ownership can be achieved by the nationalization of an efficient, privately owned enterprise, for nationalistic or other reasons. And when the state becomes the owner of an inefficient business, the government usually ends up by having to protect it from competition of more efficient industries by giving it monopoly status or other special privileges. When these things occur, there are also a number of consequences: One is that the industry, which previously was privately owned and hence a taxpayer, often becomes instead a subsidy receiver. Indeed, it is becoming increasingly difficult to find industries in the free world that have been state-owned for an appreciable length of time and which pay taxes rather than receive subsidies; and each dollar lost in tax collections or paid out in subsidies means one dollar less available for economic development and social progress. Another demonstrable consequence of state ownership is that the state must provide large sums of money, not only for the purchase of already existing industries but for plant expansion as well. This, in turn, further reduces domestic resources available for other economic development and social projects in which private capital could not be expected to go.

There are, of course, other consequences of economic policies that do not recognize the value of competition to the nation and to the individual. Suffice it to say that the lessons learned from U.S. experience are substantially the same as those learned from the experiences of other economic systems: Wherever competition is suppressed or controlled, the result is high cost and low-quality production, to the detriment of both individual and national well being.

To be sure, these material sacrifices required of the individual and the nation might well be justified if there were reasonable prospects that inefficient industries would ultimately become competitive and efficient. And here is an important point of difference between the true liberal and the socialist. The liberal believes that competition best serves the national and individual interest for all the reasons stated here. The socialist believes that Marx's theory about the perfectibility of man will become a reality in the form of a completely selfless, dedicated man—a perfect man who lives in a perfect world in which there will be no more featherbedding, no more grafting, no more subordination of the requirements of efficient production to the conflicting and selfish interests of political parties and politicians. Liberals may despair of debating about the perfectibility of man and the comparative efficiency of privately owned and government-owned business, but they should not fear a comparison of the concrete achievements of the two economic systems.

A third tenet of the U.S. economic system is this: Individual incentive has economic value.

INDIVIDUAL INCENTIVE

Most people do not consider it a virtue to content themselves with what they already have. Most of us want to have a better life for ourselves and our children. It is this aspiration plus the activity it generates that has ever been the mainspring of progress, for progress and economic growth require human effort and the rate of progress and growth are related to the degree of human effort that people are willing to put into the job.

Some economic theories are premised on the notion that man is capable of being selfless, of subordinating his own self-interest and that of his family to a theoretical concept of what the general welfare is. "From each according to his abilities, to each according to his needs," is one statement of this doctrine.

The economic system of the United States rejects the notion that "you work for John and you may be sure he will attend to your needs," as impracticable and Utopian. Its citizens are as idealistic and as concerned about their fellow man as any people in history. But they also recognize the reality that man has a driving urge to satisfy his own needs and those of his family.

They therefore believe that society benefits from both the idealism and the self-interest of man—that man can best contribute to the general welfare through his efforts to provide for himself and his family. They therefore conclude that the profit motive is an indispensable element of economic progress and concern themselves with preventing excesses and man's exploitation by man.

The U.S. asserts that the validity of this thesis is proved by the comparison, for example, of the agricultural production in economic systems that have taken away the farmer's personal incentives to produce with the U.S. system, which provides guarantees to the farmer that his land is his to own, improve, develop and make productive, and pass on to his children.

This introduces the fourth and final tenet to be discussed in this chapter: Capital and the capitalist are essential and useful elements in the process of efficient production.

CAPITAL AND CAPITALIST:

Under all economic systems, national and individual incomes can be increased only when national production is increased. Economic development, or economic growth, is essentially the increase of national production plus the distribution of increased production on a broad scale so as to increase the purchasing power of the masses.

Under all economic systems, the rate of economic growth depends upon the extent to which a country (1) accumulates capital and (2) uses the accumulated capital, in combination with its natural and human resources, in the efficient production of goods and services.

If one looks at the free world today, he must come to the conclusion that the most important missing component in many of the economic development programs is risk capital and the managerial and technical skills that go with it. Those countries that have created internal conditions that attract the largest amounts of risk capital are those that have the highest sustained rates of economic growth. Conversely, those that discourage risk capital, and which must then necessarily depend too much on investments by the public sector, will in the long run have lower rates of economic growth.

Capital is scarce because, as Marshall points out:

. . . the *supply* of capital is controlled by the fact that, in order to accumulate it, men must act prospectively: they must "wait" and "save," they must sacrifice the present to the future.

Who are the savers that provide the capital component of economic development? In the United States today they are the millions of people who have refrained from consuming all their earnings and who have invested their savings directly or indirectly in productive enterprises that create jobs and produce goods for the people. Thus they contribute a scarce and essential component of the productive process that, within a few generations, accomplished more material progress for mankind than had been accomplished in the preceding thousand years.

It is true that the capitalist may make a profit until such time as a competitor makes a better product or becomes more efficient and hence able to sell at a cheaper price. But it is also true that in order to make a profit in a free competitive economy such as that in the United States, the investor must earn it by first making a new or a better product wanted by the people. To illustrate, some six hundred companies have been formed at one time or another in the United States to manufacture automobiles. Out of the fierce competition that prevails in this industry, not more than a dozen significant producers have survived. But the result is a better product at a lower price for the benefit of the consumer than would have been otherwise possible. Who can gainsay that the investor who has survived this degree of competition and who has, in the process, made available to the public a better and cheaper product, is not entitled to his reward just as are the managers, the technologists, the workers, and others who contribute to the productive process?

Of course profits can be excessive. In the early days of capitalism—the only kind of capitalism that Marx knew anything about—they sometimes were. But in the United States it has not seemed necessary to burn down the barn to kill the rat.

In the United States, taxes become progressively higher in proportion to earnings. It is this system of a progressive and cumulative tax on the income of the corporation and the individual, together with inheritance, estate, and gift taxes, that effectively and automatically prevents excessive profits. At the same time, the tax on income has provided the bulk of national tax revenues and has also been the chief instrument in the fair and orderly elimination of the extremes of poverty and wealth and in bringing about an equitable distribution of the national product, which is the essence of social justice.

There is another point about the profit system in a free economy that needs to be repeated more often: It is the fairest system yet devised for rewarding those who contribute to the public welfare. In socialistic systems, success and material rewards are usually dependent on political favor. But in the U.S. economic system, success or failure or profit or loss is decided in a very impersonal manner by the consuming public. The sole judge of whether a product "sells," and hence whether the investor earns a profit, is the anonymous consumer, and he makes his decision without pity and favoritism, and even in an unconscious manner, because he makes it on the basis of his own self-interest. How could there be a fairer judge or a more impartial standard?

It is therefore no accident that most of the highest positions in the U.S. competitive system are filled by those who have "worked their way up" on the basis of ability. And because of these same factors, the large corporations of the United States are no longer owned by a few. They are owned by the people who have invested their savings in the exercise of their own will and judgment. This is why U.S. capitalism is often called a "peoples' capitalism."

SUMMARY

The achievements of the U.S. economy are in large part due to its climate of freedom and of competition; to the value ascribed to both the capitalist and the worker, and to the absolute importance of teamwork between them and with the entrepreneur and the technologist; to the value its system ascribes to individual incentive and to the individual initiative that it produces; and because the rights of every person, whether he is a citizen or a foreigner, are effectively guaranteed by laws that are impartially administered.

CHAPTER 2

Economic Problems Confronting the Free World

Thorkil Kristensen

THE INTERNATIONAL CHARACTER OF ECONOMIC PROBLEMS
—RECENT EXPERIENCE OF INTERNATIONAL COOPERATION

The economic problems faced by a modern country are inevitably problems of an international character. It would be otherwise only if a country could succeed in cutting itself off completely from the outside world. But even those countries that have long taken the view that the progress of their economy should mainly be confined within national limits, with merely a sidelong glance at the outside world, have had to revise their concepts when confronted by the manifest interdependence of economic phenomena.

Take one example only of this interdependence: The U.S. crisis of 1929 was very rapidly followed by catastrophic consequences in Europe; the grave economic disorders then experienced by Germany and the general unemployment from which she suffered paved the way for the success of Hitlerism. The economic disequilibrium of the 1930s may thus rightly be regarded as one of the principal causes of the World War II. The unfortunate example given to the rest of the world by the Western nations from 1930 onwards, when each was trying to escape from the economic slump by its own resources, regardless of the problems of its neighbors (unwarranted devaluations, cuts in external credits, quantitative restrictions on trade, higher customs barriers, etc.), is there to show by contrast that the only way of facing common economic problems is to solve them on the basis of common interests rather than on the premise of a narrow and ineffective nationalism.

It is clear from experience that the measures taken by a country that disregards the fate of its neighbors will have no other effect except the export of unemployment, monetary crises, and economic slumps. There exists between all nations a physical solidarity that is the forerunner and foundation of their moral solidarity. The result of this indivisible solidarity is that it is impossible for any one of them to be rich and prosperous in isolation. A balance of payments crisis, for example, may be solved in three ways: the country in crisis may either increase its exports—and therefore be tempted to resort to devaluation—or it may cut down its imports and therefore build a wall of customs duties or quotas around its frontiers. In order to gain time for the successful conclusion of an appropriate internal economic and financial policy, it may call upon international cooperation, or in plain words, it may ask for foreign credits. If it is unwilling or unable to follow the latter course, the measures taken merely have the effect of restricting the market available to foreign countries. Lack of credits may divert the traditional channels of export trade as a result of the distortions introduced by devaluations, not to mention all the speculations to which such operations traditionally give rise.

In principle, under the gold standard, as under any other system that involves fixed parity between currencies, disequilibrium in the balance of payments should result in quasi-automatic correctives: In a deficit country, the private banks should be induced to buy foreign exchange from the central banks, to reduce their liquidities, and therefore their credits; the slowing down of economic activity would result in smaller imports and a new equilibrium should be established in consequence. But the national monetary authorities may decide to resort to deliberate expansion of credits, which counteract foreseeable natural evolution and tend to sustain the deficit. Only the adequate coordination of monetary policies between the central banks can then prevent grave distortion in trade and the erratic evolutions of the different currencies.

What is true of monetary cooperation is also true of trade cooperation. Customs disarmament may have adverse effects on an economically and technically backward country, and corrective steps must often be taken in connection with capital investments or the training of manpower. The fact remains that between economic growth and the intensification of trade, there are links clearly established by economic analysis as well as by more immediate experience. Lower costs and higher production in effect mean bigger markets. Since in the economic sphere everything is connected, whether it be economic growth, currency safeguards, trade policy, capital policy, labor policy, or the like, the need for international economic cooperation must be evident to all. And so we arrive at the conclusion, which is almost one of ethics and which is yet supported by the most highly technical considerations, that no nation can prosper in isolation. If you fail to export your prosperity, you will sooner or later be bound to import the economic poverty that surrounds you. The world is one.

Until World War II occurred, it had not been found possible to establish this economic cooperation on a thoroughly sound basis. During the war, English and U.S. economists recommended policies and mechanisms to the various allied governments for the purpose of restoring prosperity to the nations ruined by the war. Following the International Bretton Woods Conference in 1943, institutions like the International Bank for Reconstruction and Development and the International Monetary Fund were created to meet the problems of postwar economic reconstruction. The International Monetary Fund, the competent body for exchange restrictions, was given resources for the provision of short-term aid to member countries in difficulties.

The IBRD was created as a banking organization to allow better world-scale mobilization and distribution of the long-term capital needed for the reconstruction and development of the world.

Another organization was planned, this time a trade organization competent in the matter of quantitative restrictions and customs tariffs. This was to be the International Trade Organization planned by the Havana Charter of 1947. When it became clear that the International Trade Charter, which was worked out in great detail at the Havana Conferences of 1947–48, had little chance of being accepted, the General Agreement on Tariffs and Trade was adopted, with more modest ambitions.

These world-wide agencies have played an important part since the World War II in the establishment of concerted policies among the nations of the West in the economic field. But, mainly because of the inadequate resources of the Fund and of the Bank, their action has nevertheless proved to be insufficiently adapted to the difficult problems of the immediate postwar period, which the victors of 1945 did not ignore, but which they no doubt underestimated. The experts were mainly concerned to prevent the reappearance of the restrictive practices in the form of quotas, customs duties, and devaluation, which had marked the period between 1930 and 1938. Their main standard of reference, therefore, was the period of deflation that had dominated Europe and the United States before World War II. But they failed to make a correct assessment of the immense financial and monetary needs of postwar reconstruction. The necessary means of payment and the enormous credits that were essential were not within the reach of the established institutions.

It was then that the United States of America made the historic decision to extend a massive and direct contribution by loans and grants to the reconstruction of western Europe. The nations of western Europe did not seize the occasion merely to combine their respective demands upon the United States government; they offered to cooperate in every aspect of their economic policies. At the same time, the United States made it clear that since the whole of western Europe was suffering from an immense dollar deficit, the economic needs must be filled not only by U.S. aid but also by mutual assistance among the European countries themselves. The United States supplied the European nations with the goods or credits that they could not procure on the European scale, and within the framework of the Organization for European Economic Co-operation (OEEC), which came into being in 1948, an extremely fruitful cooperation was established among the western European countries. As a result, within ten years a vast program of liberalization of trade and invisible transactions was put into effect, together with a large multilateralization of payments, which reached its culmination in the general return of European currencies to external convertibility on December 27, 1958.

Originally created as an instrument for the distribution of U.S. aid, the OEEC not only carried out this program within five years, thus rendering unnecessary the continuance of this transitional aid, but also provided an outstanding example of the effectiveness of confronting free countries with their respective national policies.

The very success of the work undertaken within the OEEC made it essential to continue with the cooperation inaugurated between the nations of the West, in order to confirm and accelerate the recovery of the European economy far beyond the results already achieved. Outside the framework of cooperation between United States and western Europe, other problems appeared, which would have everything to gain from the permanent cooperation instituted in the OEEC. The progressive emancipation of the former European colonies laid increasing stress on the tragic position of nearly two thousand million people deprived of the very necessities of life, in contrast with the relative prosperity of the Western countries. With respect to these countries recently promoted to independence, the Western countries felt obliged to bring all their resources into play to help them emerge from underdevelopment and poverty. This was a new "Marshall Plan" to put into operation, but on a scale quite different, both in duration and in volume. U.S. aid to Europe had been relatively limited in its amount and in time because, from the outset, Europe had the advantage of its own wealth and, above all, of its own knowledge, so that it was able rapidly to reach its prewar level and then to pass it.

Nothing of the sort could be expected from the underdeveloped countries of Africa, Asia, and Latin America, where poverty was long standing, the cultural level low, and where the population was increasing by leaps and bounds and threatening to outdistance very rapidly all the efforts made for economic and social betterment. Thus, the problem became a long-term task, no doubt extending over several generations, to which the industrialized nations of the West must now harness themselves. Their only chance of achieving their aims is to pool their resources in men, capital, and knowledge in order to make it easier and quicker for such nations to get going, for these nations must in their turn be in the position sooner or later to pursue their development on their own. Only in this way can they attain their political maturity, since without economic independence, political independence is only a delusion.

In addition to these vast objectives assigned to the industrial countries of the West, the progressive, world-scale widening of the economy made it essential for them to adapt their respective policies in the matter both of economic growth combined with monetary stability and of the general expansion of trade.

The OEEC, reconstituted in 1961 as the OECD (Organization for Economic Co-operation and Development), enlarged by the accession of the United States and Canada (now full members of the organization) and soon to be strengthened by Japanese participation, offers a favorable framework for the different Western industrialized nations that desire to confront their economic policies within that organization and in cooperation with other international organizations. It is of the highest importance that the West should develop common ways of growth and trade and be of assistance to underdeveloped countries. The problems raised are difficult ones and cannot be dissociated.

COORDINATION OF ECONOMIC POLICIES OF INDUSTRIALIZED COUNTRIES

Even before coordinating their economic, monetary, and trade policies toward the underdeveloped countries, the Western countries must take great care to ensure the essential cooperation among themselves. Twentieth century economy in the international sphere remains essentially a market economy: The first thing to be taken into consideration is the need that is reflected in effective demand. The very mass of trade between the developed countries and the part played in world production by a very few of these countries make it essential to promote the progressive and balanced growth of these economies. Moreover, one of the main ways of ensuring the relative prosperity of the underdeveloped countries, whose economy largely rests upon the export of raw materials and tropical agricultural products toward the whole of the industrialized world, is to guarantee them regular markets. The harmonious growth of the different Western economies implies (1) monetary cooperation, and (2) the coordination of trade policies.

Monetary Cooperation

It is in fact only effective monetary cooperation that can allow general economic growth without jeopardizing financial stability. The inevitable short-term disequilibria in the balance of payments must be countered by mutual support in restoring equilibrium by means of appropriate internal policies. The members of the OEEC well understood this when, within the framework of the European Payments Union, they introduced procedure that linked credits to gold payments, together with the progressive liberalization of trade and invisible transactions, particularly by eliminating quotas. But at the end of 1958, when the transferable currency zone crowned its success by the general return to external convertibility, such cooperation became even more essential. New problems arose, since the persistent dollar gap of western Europe had given place to a deficit in the U.S. balance of payments under the influence of substantial military and economic aid to other nations and very considerable exports of capital, notwithstanding the constant trade surplus of the United States.

It was especially desirable, in different ways, to facilitate access to international liquidities by countries which, because of the key position of their currency and its constant use as a reserve currency, are more interested than others in the sound equilibrium of world money reserves. When the economic growth of a country is too fast, it is not unusual for it to be handicapped by a deficit in its balance of payments, owing to the excessive expansion of imports. Adequate international credits may allow the continuance of this growth at a more moderate rate while introducing a monetary discipline to prevent excessive economic activity that would ultimately prejudice all national economies.

The growth in international liquidity required by these credits could be provided by revaluing the price of gold, but the U.S. government, not without reason, will not accept this solution. It could also come from the issue of an international currency by the IMF, but this would give that body excessive powers of drawing upon the various national economies. A system of variable exchange rates would make these credits unnecessary, since the adjustment of the rates would automatically follow variations in trade. But it would completely disorganize the present equilibrium established on the basis of the fixed parity of currencies deposited with the International Monetary Fund.

We were therefore driven to accept the last conceivable solution, namely, the reciprocal grant of credits between the various monetary authorities. The reserves made available to the IMF were thus increased by 50 per cent in 1959. Further, mutual support has been arranged between the central banks, currency swap agreements have been concluded, and special bonds designated in the currency of the creditor country have been issued in favor of the benefiting country. It appears that these procedures of relatively limited but effective scope, are calculated to solve the problems raised. This is evident particularly when one recalls (as concluded by a recent report of the Bank for International Settlements) that the operation of the system of international payments depends less on the play of the mechanism itself than on the policies followed in the different countries. The Economic Policy Committee of the OECD, especially in its working party 3, which is concerned with the balance of international payments, enables the desirable confrontations in this connection to take place between the principal monetary powers.

It is to be hoped that these confrontations will make it possible to solve the essential problem raised by the persistent deficit in the U.S. balance of payments. In view of the responsibilities at present assumed by the United States, the long drain of private capital from that country, a drain that is directly responsible for U.S. balance-of-payments deficit, should be corrected because its continuance is a grave threat to world monetary stability.

Coordination of Trade Policies

But monetary cooperation is only one element in the economic cooperation that is necessary between nations. The coordination of trade policies is equally indispensable. The progress made by the European nations under the European Payments Union was reflected on the trade level by the progressive elimination of quotas, leaving only customs barriers in existence, but this program had to expand.

The return to currency convertibility in 1958 might have given the impression that Europe was orienting itself toward general free trade. In fact, an organization had been set up a little earlier, designed progressively to eliminate all customs barriers, though within the limits of a specifically circumscribed customs union. The six countries who signed the Treaty of Rome on March 25, 1957, agreed on a program for the total elimination within twelve or fifteen years of the customs barriers, which were handicapping their internal trade. During this gradual elimination, a customs cordon would be set up around themselves, in accordance with the GATT regulations, and this would afford protection no greater than the arithmetic mean of the earlier national customs protection. What will be the respective importance of this customs network and the barriers established around most industrial countries? The European Free Trade Association (EFTA), uniting Great Britain and Denmark, Norway, Sweden, Portugal, Switzerland, and Austria, is proceeding to progressive and reciprocal customs disarmament, but does not provide for any common customs barrier against the outer world. The enlargement that was at one time expected in the Common Market by the entry of new partners, the foremost among which was Great Britain, has not taken place; everyone remembers the Brussels breakdown.

An extreme liberalization of trade within the Atlantic community would certainly become real if the Trade Expansion Act passed by the U.S. Congress in September 1962, were followed up. The Act, passed in response to the appeal of the late President Kennedy, provides the possibility of a 50 per cent reduction in existing duties within the framework of reciprocal negotiations. During May 1963, negotiations at ministerial level took place at Geneva within the framework of the GATT. The methods of linear reduction of customs items advocated by the United States were confronted by the signers of the Rome treaty with the need (in their view) of cutting down the particularly high tariffs that the United States instituted to protect some of its industrial products. After difficult discussions, agreement was reached on the basis of global and uniform linear reductions, accompanied in certain special cases by more specific reductions. It will be a matter in the immediate future for the experts to determine these special cases and the criteria to be adopted for making these reductions.

Negotiations of these matters were resumed in 1964. It is to be hoped that agreement will be reached on the basis of a large customs disarmament. The economy of vast markets is the only one calculated to give consumers the greatest advantage from lower costs and natural conditions, but measures of adaption would be indispensable and sometimes painful, since the problems to be solved were and are not simple, especially in connection with agricultural trade.

Problems of Agriculture

Whatever may be the problems of adaptation in any particular branch of industry, they fade into insignificance when compared with the unknowns that are raised by agriculture. In theory, everything is, or should be, quite simple; thanks to the progress of agricultural science, the Western countries, which have enough purchasing power, can obtain all the products they desire. Because of their special geographical or historical position, some of them are able to supply at the best price, and in considerable quantities, excellent products in any sector whatever: cereals, vegetables, fruit, wines, and so forth. It might therefore be thought that each country would specialize in those crops specially suited to it for reasons of climate, soil, economic conditions, or the like. Theoretically, an immense free-trade system would be set up, within which each country would supply the products that were most suitable to it. An accelerated evolution would make it possible to cut down to a minimum the population employed in agriculture; output would increase in proportion as each producer benefited from a more extensive zone, where he would be able to use the most modern scientific and technical farming methods. On the other hand, rapid industrialization would progressively absorb the countrymen who left the countryside. Judicious educational programs would make it possible to give adequate training to farmers, who might then be distributed harmoniously between the different sectors of activity, such as industry or services. The most technically and economically advanced countries are those where the active agricultural population is proportionately the smallest. An adequate distribution of tasks between the different industrial countries, especially through the medium of liberalization of trade, should therefore—in agriculture more than anywhere else—encourage over-all economic growth and the prosperity of all.

It goes without saying that the necessary trends in agriculture nevertheless imply specially worked out measures of adaptation. The resettlement of individuals calls for large-scale educational programs, mobility in employment and housing programs, and social welfare arrangements designed to make the process less painful. But all these advantages should be subordinate to a consistent policy of agricultural production. During the 1930s, however, the leading industrialized countries, including those which set most store upon economic liberalism, such as the United States, took steps to protect their farmers on the national plane. Usually for political reasons, the leaders of the industrialized countries, seeing the farmers threatened by the surpluses created by technical progress, introduced mechanisms that are often very complicated, but whose aim is identical; namely, to guarantee to the farmers the prices and markets that will enable them to stabilize and even to increase their incomes. By this very fact the necessary trend toward a reduction in the numbers employed in agriculture has been considerably hampered. In particular, for some commodities, production has grown without intermission, so that government silos store ever-increasing stocks for which disposal is difficult.

In the United States, guaranteed prices for agricultural products have resulted in considerable overproduction, especially of cereals and cotton. The immense area of reserve land in relation to limited population enables the United States to produce, as does Canada, enormous quantities of very good quality agricultural products at the cheapest price, which they subsequently try by every means to sell on the world markets. World cereal prices are thus very low and very much below the national prices maintained in many countries.

As early as the 1880s, some European countries began to protect their agriculture against competition from North America. This protection was reinforced during the crisis in the 1930s, and it continued after World War II, the result being that today both importing and exporting countries apply various systems of support, protection, or price guarantees. Consequently, production is not guided by effective demand in the usual way, and the tendency toward overproduction for certain commodities may well influence various international negotiations in a very unfortunate way if future policies are not considered with great care.

In general, the problem is this: Exporting countries tend to press for constant or increasing outlets, whereas importing countries may approach a state of self-sufficiency. In particular, the United States, and also Canada and a few other non-European countries, have large surpluses available for exports. In Europe, the main importing area, what room there will be for imports from other continents will to a large extent depend on the further evolution of the common agricultural policy of the Common Market. Since guaranteed prices in Germany are higher than, for example, in France, and French exports to Germany therefore are subject to a special duty, difficult trade problems exist today both within Europe and between the European Common Market and North America.

In the long run, there is no other solution than a gradual change in policies, both in exporting and importing countries. Prices must be determined so as to bring about a reasonable equilibrium between supply and demand. The farm population must be supported, where incomes are too low, but such support should be given to the persons in question and to their retraining for other activities rather than to the prices of products of which production already exceeds demand.

As mentioned below, some outlets can be found for certain farm products in less-developed countries, but this does not mean that Western countries can escape the necessary readjustments of their agricultural policies. These readjustments should be worked out through close cooperation among all Western countries, based on a realistic evaluation of the trends in the various markets.

ECONOMIC AND FINANCIAL ASSISTANCE TO UNDERDEVELOPED COUNTRIES

The Necessity of Assistance

Considerable differences in economic and social standards are apparent between the industrialized nations (western Europe, Japan, and North America) and the underdeveloped nations in Africa, Asia, and Latin America. The latter countries, representing more than 40 per cent of the world population, produce less than 20 per cent of world income. Their economic weaknesses are manifested in particular by the very high proportion of the population employed on "primary" activities, mainly agriculture, the low standards of literacy, nutrition, and public health of these countries, and the inadequate social and economic capital available to them. The insufficiency of capital is a great obstacle to their economic growth, which is also uneven.

There are few underdeveloped countries where the economy is stationary. Nevertheless, their income per head of population is still low, and the rapid increase in population absorbs a substantial part of the benefit of economic expansion for most of them.

The low level of income of the population of the underdeveloped zones seriously compromises their growth, since it reduces their capacity for savings, necessary for the provision of the equipment they require. A substantial part of their capital must, if possible, be raised internally. But imports of capital can, without any doubt, largely facilitate the ultimate getting under way of the less-developed countries. These countries should, after a certain time, be capable of self-sustained progress on their own, since external aid cannot be prolonged indefinitely.

Imports of foreign capital are already making a large contribution to the growth of underdeveloped countries. Thus, in most countries where the rate of progress in the real product is very rapid (more than 5 per cent a year), the national resources have been largely reinforced by foreign capital. The most striking examples are Israel, Venezuela, the Antilles, the Federation of Rhodesia and Nyasaland, Algeria, and Formosa. On the other hand, most countries where the rate of expansion has been slow have been those that have not received substantial foreign capital in relation to their size; this is the case of Indonesia, Sudan, Pakistan, Ceylon, and the United Arab Republic. The decisive importance to these underdeveloped countries of foreign capital is therefore beyond doubt.

The industrialized nations of the West are already making considerable efforts in relation to the underdeveloped countries. In 1962, nearly $8.4 billion were placed at their disposal. More than two-thirds of this figure, or $5.95 billion, came from official sources in the form of bilateral or multilateral contributions, the remainder being private capital exports. The public funds were mostly given in the form of grants, loans payable in local currency or loans repayable in more than five years, often on favorable terms. Although this financial aid is now tending to level off (it did not grow between 1961 and 1962), it should be further increased in the course of the next few years, thanks to the concerted action of the various Western industrial powers.

In this connection a special effort is being made through the Development Assistance Committee of the OECD. Here, the main Western nations discuss their aid programs and coordinate their policies. This coordination is essential because the giving of aid to underdeveloped countries is more easily accepted by the industrialized nations if it is fairly shared between them. National public opinion is still insufficiently informed of the magnitude of the needs, and tends to measure its aid by reference to the efforts of other countries. Only constant confrontation among the different donor countries can allow the continuous growth of aid and the adoption of more favorable conditions in its distribution. The considerable growth in the external debt of underdeveloped countries renders more advantageous loans particularly necessary.

The question is, moreover, not only to increase the amount of official and private aid, but also to make it more effective. The growth of an economy requires the establishment of supplementary equipment, which must be partly financed by capital imports because any deficit in the balance of payments would be likely to prevent any long-term growth. A judicious balance must be reached in the allocation of aid provided to the underdeveloped countries in order to avoid waste. The role of specific projects with a direct economic return and that of general growth plans must be carefully defined.

In its various forms, aid to underdeveloped countries should tend to the development of their economy, and primarily of their agriculture, which will for a long time provide the bulk of their national income. Next, it should facilitate their industrialization, and finally, encourage economic growth by the adoption of special measures designed to increase and facilitate their trade.

Food and Agriculture

In the case of agriculture, many underdeveloped countries have limited natural resources in proportion to their population, and all use relatively primitive techniques. Consequently, nutritional standards are often deplorably low, since most of these countries cannot afford to import large quantities of food.

This is a paradoxical situation, taking into account the surplus production in Western agriculture referred to above. Since the world population is increasing very fast and the poor countries have a much faster population growth than the industrial powers, it seems reasonable and indeed urgent to make it possible for the Western surplus to be transferred to the countries where the needs are. In fact it is not inconceivable that in the foreseeable future it will be necessary to mobilize all the cultivable land on the planet in order adequately to feed the population of the underdeveloped countries. Under Public Law 480, the United States is already disposing of part of its agricultural surpluses by grants, or on conditions very near outright grants, to India and other countries. No doubt the technique used by the United States could be improved and extended to the whole of the free industrialized world, which would be invited to supply the underdeveloped countries with the agricultural foodstuffs they need. For this purpose it is desirable to organize international cooperation for disposing of European and American surpluses in Africa, Asia, and Latin America. Both the FAO and the OECD have issued reports on this problem.

The aid to be given to these countries should, moreover, aim at their real economic development and should not merely consist of ensuring their subsistence by grants. Techniques that have proved themselves useful under the Marshall Plan exist for associating these gifts in kind with productive investment on the internal plane. The counterpart of Marshall aid served, as everybody knows, to finance massive investments whose effectiveness was supervised by the donor country. In the underdeveloped countries there is a great latent force, namely, human resources, partly unemployed or underemployed. Systems of a socialized character mobilize, sometimes by extreme methods, the underemployed masses of the agricultural sector. Similarly, food gifts could be associated with public works or sites for agricultural and industrial infrastructure. This procedure has been used with great success in Tunisia and Algeria, where major works are financed by the government authorities on the basis of surpluses supplied by the United States. It would no doubt be desirable to make these methods general. The problems raised by the distribution and cost of financing these surpluses on a world scale could be solved along the lines of the general action already taken in favor of the underdeveloped countries, especially by means of multilateral aid.

Nevertheless, if it is desired to give this agricultural aid a more liberal basis, it would be possible to conceive the establishment of a vast world market for agricultural products, the underdeveloped countries having recourse to this market on the basis of financial aid that would be given to them by the industrialized countries and which, without being closely tied, would nevertheless be subject to purchases of food. This suggestion combines the liberal perspective of the reconstitution of a world agricultural market with a utilization of aid that is in harmony with the interests of the donor as well as the beneficiary nations.

The beneficiary nations should, moreover, be most urgently invited to make the greatest possible efforts of self-help in this sphere of agriculture, not only by adopting modern techniques and applying them in their own countries, but above all by introducing major political, economic, and social reforms. Agrarian reforms are most frequently necessary, and the United States, under the Alliance for Progress, quite rightly made aid subject to the introduction of reforms of this kind in Latin America. Too often, in practice, landed proprietors possess immense lands in which they have no interest in improving on the economic plane. Often, absentee landlords use their agricultural profits for investment abroad. This use of profits for purposes alien to the economic progress of the country in question is to be regretted from every point of view. So, it is desirable that agricultural producers should be at the same time the owners of their land, and should thus be encouraged to promote the economic and technical development of their landed resources.

Industrialization of the Underdeveloped Countries

Nevertheless, however much progress may be made in the sphere of agriculture in the underdeveloped countries, this will not solve all the problems, particularly in view of the growth of population that is characteristic of these countries. Agricultural resources are in fact limited by nature itself; arable land is fairly narrowly confined and the progress of agricultural science cannot increase its productivity indefinitely. The economic growth of these countries is inseparable from their industrialization, and the specific role of the Western nations is to facilitate, especially by exports of capital, this passage to a more advanced stage of development.

It may be a good investment for Western countries insofar as they have an adequate market available and skilled executives, since the marginal return on capital tends to fall in the Western countries themselves because of the high cost of labor. Although considerable potential resources in the industrialized countries of the West are not exploited on the agricultural plane for want of markets, an extremely fruitful exchange could be made of the respective roles of the industrialized nations and the underdeveloped countries. During the nineteenth century, the industrial countries mainly exported their manufactures in exchange for the agricultural produce and raw materials from the underdeveloped countries, which at that period they often dominated politically. It is only an apparent paradox to think that the reverse flow of trade could now be instituted, the industrialized nations of the West exporting agricultural products against the industrial products which the underdeveloped countries would then be capable of selling them at low prices because of the low wage requirements of their labor. The British textile industries, especially around Manchester, have already felt the repercussion of the progress of similar industries created and developed in India and Hong Kong. The industrialization of low-wage countries, today Japan and Hong Kong, tomorrow Pakistan or Nigeria, should not cause any anxiety in the West, provided the necessary adaptation and desirable conversions are foreseen sufficiently far in advance. A division of labor could thus be introduced, the most highly developed of the economies reserving the most complicated and capital-intensive industries and leaving to the underdeveloped countries light industries that are more labor-intensive and require less technical skill and financial investment.

It is still necessary, if this process is to be extended, that technical and financial capital should establish itself without hesitation where there is abundant labor. But for some time, a certain stagnation has been noted in the flow of private capital to the underdeveloped countries. This stagnation relates to direct investment even more than to portfolio investments. The phenomenon is explained by the anxiety felt by a number of capitalists with regard to measures of expropriation and nationalization. These fears, which are often not without foundation, regrettably limit the exports of capital for which the underdeveloped countries have the greatest need. It is in the interest of the leaders of these countries to give adequate guarantees for investment of foreign capital in their industries. Draft conventions giving certain guarantees to private capitalists against government encroachments are at present under discussion within the OECD. Tax facilities together with provisions avoiding double taxation are likely to encourage further contributions of private capital.

The fact remains that the industrialization of these countries is possible only on a certain scale if the Western nations provide them with sufficient markets. The marginal return on capital invested in underdeveloped countries is in fact often jeopardized by the narrowness of the local market. Many of these countries are largely subsistence economies and are not in a position to enjoy sufficient purchasing power to cover their considerable needs. The increase in productivity allowed by foreign capital, and which may be very large because of the sometimes very primitive character of traditional economies, can bear fruit only if the industrialized nations of the West increasingly accompany their aid by adequate trade policies. An important ministerial resolution was adopted in this sense by the OECD in November 1962. Trade must increasingly supplement, if not replace, outright aid.

Trade Facilities to Be
Granted to Underdeveloped Countries

As we have seen, industrialization requires markets in the developed countries because of the narrowness of the local markets. But, as things are at present, the claims of the underdeveloped countries are more immediate; their foreign-exchange resources arise mainly from their industrial raw materials or their agricultural exports. They therefore urgently demand that the Western countries should reduce trade barriers progressively and without reciprocity, and that markets should be organized with a view to ensuring the stabilization of their foreign-exchange revenues in periods when the trend of raw material prices is against them. They also appeal for plans for financial compensation designed to guarantee them the foreign exchange necessary for their development in the event of a more or less extended reduction in their total export proceeds.

There are in fact two essential ways of meeting these demands. There are some who wish simply to abolish, as far as possible, customs barriers and to extend beyond the industrialized countries the measures of customs curtailment that have been discussed in the meetings between Europe and the United States. It is well known that discussions have been opened at the GATT on the basis of the "most favored nation" clause; in other words, third countries, including the underdeveloped countries, would derive immediate benefit from any concessions made between themselves by the Western countries. It has even been discussed whether a certain amount of preferences should be established in favor of all less-developed countries.

According to another school of thought, however, the virtues of free trade would not be enough to give the underdeveloped countries the necessary foreign-exchange resources. It would therefore be necessary to organize the markets for industrial raw materials and the main agricultural products, especially tropical products. The trend of prices for these commodities has been unfavorable to the producing countries for some years. These countries should, if possible, be in a position to count upon a rather stable income; and for that purpose world commodity agreements, even if they are limited to certain commodities such as coffee, cocoa, and oil seeds, would give them essential guarantees. Furthermore, it is desirable that the underdeveloped countries should be invited to join together to constitute vast economic zones on the model of those created in Europe; it is not natural that high customs duties should be exacted between the underdeveloped countries themselves.

The first school of thought maintains that direct aid is more valuable than artificial support, varying according to products, of the price of foodstuffs sold by the underdeveloped countries. The main argument from the other side is that more liberty and dignity is granted to the developing countries by guaranteeing somewhat fixed incomes than by controlling them closely through the medium of the aid that affluent countries are prepared to grant them.

The problem is thus largely political, but it is to be hoped that in one way or another, the Westerners will come to agreement among themselves so as to ensure the underdeveloped countries the ways and means of harmonious and stable growth. The effort will, in any event, be a long-term one, and the equalization of the conditions of life cannot be foreseen in the immediate future. Although many underdeveloped countries are making remarkable progress, their rate of growth considered as a whole has been less rapid in the immediate past than that of the industralized nations. According to recent estimates, their average, annual rate of growth was slightly less than 4 per cent during the 1950s, or less than 2 per cent per head of population, compared with an annual rate of growth per head of population of about 2.5 per cent in the Atlantic area and even more in the USSR and Japan. A great deal of the progress made by the underdeveloped countries is jeopardized by excessive population growth, but in this field, and in spite of the isolated example of Japan, it is difficult to take action; in any event, such action cannot be unilaterally imposed by the Western nations.

The world is becoming unified at an increasing pace, and especially the growing mass of knowledge created by scientific research will increasingly become the common property of mankind as a whole. It is difficult to measure at this stage the effects of the technical and intellectual assistance granted by the Western countries to the underdeveloped countries, but the link between economic development and the diffusion of knowledge is unquestionable. Even more than financial and technical capital, the underdeveloped countries need aid in the field of education and science. The essential thing is to create national elites capable of taking charge of the economic and cultural development of their own people. Through technical assistance, the Western nations can spread in Africa, Asia, and Latin America the knowledge and modes of thought that will be powerful trump cards in the service of economic growth.

The unification of the world will come about by the diffusion of culture and knowledge of a universal character. But recent history shows that the division of the world into several zones of civilization is inseparable from divisions of an economic or even a monetary character. The two great world wars were linked in evident manner to political and economic imperialisms which foreshadowed armed conflict. Henri Bergson, the French philosopher, drew a distinction between closed and open societies. The history of the twentieth century shows beyond all question that the closed society, founded on economic autarchy, purely national cultures, and inconvertible currency, leads to chaos. The hope of man in the present generation is to institute (in particular through the medium of monetary, economic, and trade cooperation) the basis of a truly ecumenical civilization, in which all the open societies of our time can take part on an equal footing.

CHAPTER 3

The Challenge of the Common Market

Etienne Hirsch

ECONOMIC IMPACT

In the Common Market treaty, many provisions were included in order to avoid economic and social disrupture which could be generated by the lifting of trade barriers between the member countries. No single country was to have the right to take unilaterally protective measures. But, on the one side, the treaty set a timetable for the removal of quotas and the reduction of tariffs, giving reasonable but limited time for adjustments. On the other side, the European Economic Community (EEC) could help governments prepare for the reconversion of enterprises unable to meet the competition and for the retraining of workers to new activities.

In fact, very little use had to be made of the latter provisions, and it soon became possible to go at a faster pace than provided for by the timetable. Things developed quicker and more smoothly than anticipated by the negotiators of the treaty, by the industrialists and the trade-unions, and by the professional economists. The latter considered that because the economies of the six member countries were not complementary, but largely in competition with each other, the advantages to be expected from a much larger market would come only after a long period re-

37

quired for the adaption of the pattern of production to such a new scale. Nobody really foresaw the magnitude of the potentialities opened by the new structures.

What happened was that, in their thinking and in their behavior, the entrepreneurs marched ahead of the actual developments. When it appeared that there would be a Common Market on the pattern already set by the coal and steel community, a large number of firms, without even waiting for the signing of the treaty, prepared to meet the expected competition. They engaged in a process of increasing productivity, of modernizing their equipment, of rationalizing their production, and of expanding their commercial structure in the other member countries. As a result, industrial production in the EEC increased at a very fast pace; adjustments, in an expanding economy, were easy and disturbances were reduced to a minimum.

During the first four years of the EEC, industrial production increased by 37 per cent. This figure is to be compared with 28 per cent in the United States (where the rate of growth of the population is much higher) and with 14 per cent in Great Britain. The gross national product increased by 21.5 per cent (United States, 19 per cent; United Kingdom, 11 per cent).

In spite of the sharp rise in productivity, the employment situation improved. In 1958 there was full employment in France and in the Netherlands, and some unemployment in Belgium; unemployment was important in Germany, and it was very large, as well as coupled with wide-scale underemployment in Italy. At present, there is everywhere full or overfull employment, with the exception of southern Italy, where both unemployment and underemployment have been appreciably reduced.

By July 1963, customs duties inside the EEC had been cut by 60 per cent for all industrial products and by 40 to 45 per cent for farm products. They will disappear by the end of 1967. The common external tariff, which applies to third countries, has not yet been put into force. But large steps have been made toward it through a reduction by 60 per cent of the difference between the national tariffs and the common tariff. In order to promote international trade, this difference has been calculated on the basis of an over-all reduction by 20 per cent of the common external tariff.

Although the dismantling of trade barriers was progressive, trade between the member countries increased tremendously, as shown by the following indexes (1958 = 100):

1959	124
1960	152
1961	171
1962	198

Expansion of trade between member countries was not at the expense of trade with outside countries; on the contrary, there was here also an expansion at a rate higher than the average of world trade. For the four first years of the Common Market, the increase amounted to 30 per cent for exports from the EEC to the rest of the world, and 36 per cent for imports. Third countries have therefore largely benefited by the prosperity of the Common Market. This is another evidence that real economic progress is not achieved at the expense of others, but only when it is beneficial to everyone.

These results are all the more significant because the Market is by far the largest import, and nearly the largest export, trade area in the world, as shown by the following figures, related to 1962 (1961 for U.S.S.R.) and expressed in millions of U.S. dollars:

	Community	U.K.	U.S.A.	U.S.S.R.
Imports from the rest of the world	$22,327	$12,578	$16,236	$5,832
Exports to the rest of the world	20,638	11,059	21,320	5,998

AGRICULTURE

In every country in the world, agriculture raises problems very different from those of industry. This was shown in particular when (ten years before the Common Market) Belgium, the Netherlands, and Luxemburg started a customs' union known as "BENELUX." Special provisions had to be made for agricultural products in order to avoid insuperable difficulties.

The main object is to devise a common agricultural policy in order to achieve greater efficiency and an increase in the standard of living of the rural community. It is obvious that such goals imply a large reduction in the size of the farm population. The process is well under way, and is helped by the industrial expansion that provides new employment opportunities. As an example, in France during the past eight years, the number of people active in agriculture has been reduced by one-quarter. But farmers still amount to 20 per cent of the total active population, which is more than double the percentage in the United States. This shows that, for a period of time, some protective measures are required to maintain an orderly process. An additional reason for such measures is that agricultural production is increasing very fast through technical progress, but that, contrary to what happens with industrial goods, the increase of the standard of living has only a small effect on the consumption of farm products, with exceptions such as meat and fruits. All this explains that integration has not developed so fast for agriculture as for industry.

REGIONAL DEVELOPMENT

Inside a large economic unit such as the European Economic Community, although the member countries are on similar levels of development, there are large differences between regions. Some are highly industrialized and enjoy rapid expansion and an increase in living standards. Others, on the contrary, have few or antiquated industries and offer no opportunities of employment for the population that is in excess in agriculture. This is the case in particular for the south of Italy and for Brittany in France.

According to all past experience, the normal effects of the free play of market forces tend not to reduce such differences but, on the contrary, to widen them. If tolerated, such a process would in the Common Market result in social inequity, in overcrowding of some of the urban areas, and also in very strong and damaging political tensions. In order to reverse the process, member governments are authorized by treaty to intervene. They can resort to a number of measures such as financial help, tax exemptions, and subsidies. In addition, help is provided by the EEC. The European Development Bank has as its first task the financing of projects that will improve the economic conditions in backward areas, such as transportation facilities and the creation of new industries.

As customs union proceeds at a quick pace and as trade barriers are removed, steps are being taken and new ones envisaged in order to achieve real economic union. The objective, a large market without obstacles, giving free room to competition, would obviously be defeated if restrictive trade practices and cartel agreements were allowed to survive. Antitrust regulations have been agreed upon and are being progressively enforced. Considering traditional European habits, this is by no means an easy achievement.

Competition must not be distorted through conflicting national policies. This applies in the very important field of tax policy. Taxes need not necessarily be identical, as shown for example in the United States, but it is essential that tax systems be harmonized in such a way that they have no influence on the free flow of goods inside the Common Market. This harmonization must come into force before customs duties have completely disappeared. Measures are being prepared by the Common Market commission, and thanks to the regular meetings of the six finance ministers, the first step contemplated is the harmonization of indirect taxation.

Such meetings and the recommendations of the commission provide a machinery for consultation on all policies or actions from individual governments that could affect the community. This applies to financial, monetary and budgetary policies, and to specific actions intended to influence the economic trend.

Monetary policy is of vital importance to the Common Market. Economic union, after the transition period, requires fixed exchange rates between participants, or at least variations kept between very narrow limits. This in fact amounts to monetary union. In addition, it is in the interest of the community to avoid tensions in the world monetary system based on gold and on two reserve currencies. A European reserve currency could provide a great contribution to international monetary cooperation and to the improvement of the present system. The Common Market commission has made concrete proposals toward these goals. The way would be prepared during the transition period by increased and regular consultations between governors of the central banks, and with the Monetary Committee of the community.

Economic union should not be considered as static. The setting up of a large market has promoted very rapid expansion. It is highly desirable that this impetus should not be allowed to dissipate. Policies should be developed that would facilitate and promote the fullest and best possible use of the resources of the community, and which would effect a continuing economic development at the highest possible rate compatible with the maintenance of stability.

Therefore, the Common Market commission has proposed to set up a "program" for the community, covering a period of four years. The concept of this program is very similar to the one of the French plan. The object is to provide governments and entrepreneurs with a guideline. It is not to embark on compulsory and authoritative procedures. The program should be prepared in close consultation with the main economic groups: industrialists, trade-unions, farmers.

With the exception of Germany, the member countries have national plans or programs. The spelling out of a program for the community would obviously be of great assistance to national planners. With the free flow of goods, of capital, and of workers inside the EEC, planning for one country has as a prerequisite certain assumptions concerning what will happen in the other member countries. A program for the community diminishes the uncertainties; it leads not only to coordination of national programs, but also to some revision of these programs.

GEOGRAPHICAL EXTENSION OF THE COMMUNITY

The Common Market is not restricted to the first six member countries. The treaty provides for possibilities of membership or association of other countries, subject to unanimous consent of the six.

Greece has been the first European country to ask to take advantage of these possibilities. Greece is still in a stage where the full obligations of membership would be dangerous for the development of her industries, and even for their survival. The formula agreed upon was that of association, with a transition period during which trade barriers between the Common Market and Greece would be progressively reduced. At the same time, Greece would receive financial help from the community in order to promote economic expansion. When the Greek economy becomes able to sustain full competition without protection, Greece will be a full member of the EEC.

Turkey presented a similar case more recently. Negotiations have resulted in a treaty of association, which was initialed in June 1963. But by far the most important problem was presented by Great Britain. Well before Robert Schuman's appeal, Great Britain had been invited to participate in the foundation of an integrated Europe. At that time, and later when the European coal and steel community, and again the economic and the atomic energy communities were established, Great Britain refused to join. It is not exaggerating to say that she even did her best to raise obstacles in the way to European integration. This was exemplified by the creation of the European Free Trade Association, known also as the "Outer Seven," with Norway, Sweden, Denmark, Switzerland, Austria, and Portugal as members in addition to Britain. This represented the traditional line of British foreign policy, opposed to unity on the European continent. The reversal of this traditional policy came suddenly when, in the middle of 1961, the British government applied for membership in the Common Market.

Such a change, which may be called revolutionary, was motivated by two reasons. The first one was the realization that economic growth in the Common Market was more than twice as fast as that in Britain, where unemployment was threatening and where time and again restrictive measures had to be applied in order to protect the balance of payments. The other reason was that, with a prosperous and developing united Europe at its doorstep, there was no future for special relations between Britain and the United States. If Britain maintained the legitimate ambition of exerting some influence on world affairs, she could not expect to do it through that channel, and obviously still less if she remained isolated.

Although it was clearly stated from the start that Britain accepted the contents of the Rome treaty as well as its long-term implications, the application for membership raised a number of new and delicate problems. The most important ones resulted from the special status of British agriculture, from the traditional ties of Britain with the Commonwealth, and from the new relations and commitments with the EFTA countries. When, by the end of January 1963, the President of France decided to interrupt the long, drawn-out negotiations, for reasons that had more to do with political than with economic motives, answers to a number of important problems had been found, but some of the problems remained unsolved, although none of them appeared insoluble.

A serious mistake was made by the British during the negotiations. It was to discuss at length both major and minor issues instead of leaving the latter to be solved in due time by the institutions of the community. This created uneasiness and ill will, which weakened the opposition to the decision of General de Gaulle to slam the door in the face of Britain.

Without any change of the political situation in France, and with a general election due in Britain by autumn 1964, there is no prospect for the immediate resumption of the negotiations between Britain and the Common Market. The situation is all the more unclear because a change of majority appears probable in Britain and the Labour party is divided on the issue of entering the Common Market. But it is to be expected that, after the elections and with the responsibilities of power, a Labour government will be compelled, by the same motives as the Conservative government, to apply for membership, and that pressure will be brought to bear on France by the five other member countries not to obstruct entry.

In the wake of Britain, other countries applied for membership or asked for the status of associates. The former are Ireland, Denmark, and Norway; the latter, the three neutral countries, Austria, Sweden, and Switzerland.

The difference between the two groups lies in the fact that although both desire to enjoy the benefits and are prepared to accept the rules of economic integration, the neutrals are not in a position to envisage the political implications of being full members of the community. Conversely, for the community to accept neutrals as full members would mean to renounce future political and military integration, to which economic integration has since the beginning been considered as a first step.

DEVELOPING COUNTRIES

The increase of the standard of living in the developing countries and the narrowing of the gap between them and the advanced countries present the most formidable economic and political challenge of our times.

In the Common Market treaty, provisions were made for the territories for which member countries held responsibilities. With their access to independent status, former colonial territories were no longer bound by the treaty. It was by their own free will that they entered with the EEC into an agreement providing for a status of association. The second agreement, covering the five-year period 1963–1967, was signed in July 1963.

The agreement has provisions both for aid and for trade. A development fund, to which all the Common Market countries contribute with public funds, provides grants and, for a minor part, loans on a very liberal basis. The total amount of $800 million for the five-year period is to be used both for social and economic development, and in particular for the diversification of production. This aid from the community is by no means exclusive of direct aid from the member countries to the associates. In the particular case of France, the contributions to the development fund are only a small percentage of the total amount devoted to aid for the underdeveloped countries.

Agreements concerning trade take into account the fact that colonial territories enjoyed a preferential treatment for the marketing of their products in the mother countries. It was felt that if such ties were severed, their economies would suffer great damage, with the risk of major disruptions. The system agreed upon provides that the associated countries will get the full benefit of all trade barrier reductions within the Common Market. This means that their products will have free access in the six member countries. But no reciprocity is requested from the associated countries. In order to facilitate industrialization, the agreement provides that they are entitled to protect their industries vis à vis the Common Market. As a consequence of these trade arrangements, the associated countries enjoy a preferential treatment in the Common Market. This has created in the other developing countries the fear that they have been discriminated against and that such a preference will work to their disadvantage. Although, thanks to the increased imports in the Common Market, the other developing countries have not in fact been penalized, the EEC has felt that due consideration should be given to their situation.

During the negotiations with Britain, the probem of the developing countries of the Commonwealth was considered in detail. Trade agreements were envisaged between the enlarged Common Market and countries such as India, Pakistan, and Ceylon, in order to take care of their interest in the export of cotton and jute manufactures and other industrial products. As for the Commonwealth countries in Africa and the Caribbean, it was planned to offer to extend to them the benefits of the agreement for association with the Common Market. In addition it was agreed that, at the end of 1963, the common external tariff would be nil for tea and for the tropical woods, and would be reduced by 40 per cent for coffee.

The problems of Latin-American countries, with the important exception of the above mentioned decisions, have not yet led to definite measures or to concrete agreements between the community and the interested countries, but it has been agreed that they will soon be the object of negotiations, with a positive approach from the side of the community, which is very conscious of its world-wide responsibilities. In the meantime, Latin-American exports to the Common Market have substantially increased as a result of the economic expansion in the community.

THE IMPACT IN THE WORLD

The impact of the Common Market on the world does not result only from its effect on world trade expansion. It goes further and deeper. A new pattern has been set for economic relations between countries. The example of European economic integration is being followed, if for the present only partially, by the Central and South American countries. In Africa, the newly independent states have begun to try and work together along similar lines.

Thinking within the Communist world is also being greatly influenced by the developments in western Europe. Since the start, it was understood that the Common Market, if at all successful, would strengthen the West by making it economically sounder, and would prove that the contradictions of capitalism were not insuperable. This explains the strong opposition that the creation of the community met from the Communist bloc. Now they have to accept it as a fact. In an article published in August 1962, Khrushchev draws the lesson. He shows what benefits result from competition and from a broader market. As a consequence, the organization for cooperation between the communist states, the COMECON, which had practically lost its existence, has been revived and has met probably more times in the past few months than in all the preceding years.

However important these developments, it is certain that the Common Market exerted the greatest influence on the United States. The postwar European recovery had been greatly facilitated and speeded up by the Marshall Plan. When it came to European integration, it was continuously and strongly favored by the U.S. administration, Republican as well as Democrat. Unification appealed to the sentimentality of the American people, and was rightly understood as the best means of strengthening the Western world. The economic progress achieved, thanks to the Common Market, and the impulse it exerted on world trade, led President Kennedy to the revolutionary steps embodied in the Trade Expansion Act. In that Act, two sets of measures of special importance to trade relations between the United States and the Common Market should be distinguished. One is the authority to decrease by 50 per cent any rate of duty. The other is the right in a trade agreement with the European Economic Community to exceed the basic 50 per cent limitation and to reduce tariffs to zero on industrial products within categories for which the United States and the EEC together account for 80 per cent or more of the aggregate world-export value. The tariff reduction achieved will be generalized in accordance with the "most-favored-nation" clause.

The new Act departs fundamentally from past procedures by the importance of tariff reductions authorized and by the fact that such reductions will not be limited to certain items, but will be applied across the board. In addition, the Act incorporates a very important new provision, inspired by the experience of the Common Market. Until the Trade Expansion Act became law, the imposition of increased import restrictions was the only remedy available to the President when it was found, on investigation, that increased imports resulting from a tariff concession were causing or threatening serious injury to a domestic industry. The new Act provides an alternative, a program of adjustment assistance to affected industries, firms, and workers, thus making it possible to provide relief to domestic interests without curtailing the opportunity of foreign producers to sell in the U.S. market.

The 80 per cent condition can be fulfilled only when Britain joins the Common Market, so that for the time being, only the tariff reduction by 50 per cent comes into consideration. Negotiations are to be held within the GATT beginning in the spring of 1964. Preparatory discussions between United States and Common Market representatives took place in May 1963.

A tariff reduction by 50 per cent raises a number of important problems, and the negotiations will no doubt be difficult; one of these problems has already created difficulties in the preliminary discussions. It arises from the fundamental difference in structure between the U.S. and the Common Market tariffs. On the average, the U.S. tariff is somewhat higher than the Common Market external tariff, but the difficulty does not lie there. Whereas Common Market duties are, within each large category of goods (raw materials, semifinished manufactures, manufactures), not wide apart from the average, duties in the U.S. tariff are very scattered. It is felt in Europe that a duty reduced, let us say from 50 to 25 per cent, still means a strong protection of the market, as is not the case for a duty reduced from 20 to 10 per cent. There is also the problem of the so-called nontariff protection, such as the U.S. escape clause and the U.S. antidumping legislation. It is feared in Europe that, whatever the reduction in customs duties, nontariff protection as it is practiced in the United States may nullify the effect of tariff reduction. This is considered as a standing threat to exporters who have been at pains to develop a successful market in the United States. There is no easy answer to such problems unless all parties agree not to take unilateral action without prior consultation, and accept some kind of arbitration if there is a dispute. This means in fact that a minimum of common institutions is required in order to see to it that all proceeds smoothly.

Agriculture raises especially difficult problems. Even in countries like the United States and Britain, where the farmers amount only to a relatively small percentage of the active population, there is a serious political problem. The situation is still more acute in continental Europe, where the percentage is much higher and where there is under way the steady but painful process of the reduction of the farm population. Too strong a pressure brought to bear by the United States in order to obtain in Europe a larger market for its farm surpluses would lead only to serious political strife, and would endanger the negotiations.

It is quite obvious that the problems of international trade cannot be approached for agriculture as they are for industry. One of the major challenges of our times is the need to deal with food surpluses when one third of the world population suffers from undernourishment and another third is on the verge of famine. In this situation, it is to be hoped that the tariff negotiations will provide the opportunity of considering and of discussing trade in the main agricultural products on a world-wide basis.

The European Economic Community means 175 million customers enjoying a per capita income somewhat above one-half of the income in the United States, but which is increasing at a rate higher than 3 per cent per annum. As indicated above, the Common Market is the largest importing area in the world, and the customs tariff is on the average somewhat below the U.S. tariff. This shows how important for the present and still more for the future the Common Market is for American exporters.

In selecting the lines for which trade offers the largest prospects, one has to take into account the differences between the U.S. and the Common Market economic conditions. Apart from the fact that the Common Market does not possess the large natural resources of the United States and depends largely on imports for most raw materials, the greatest difference lies in the lower cost of manpower in Europe. This difference, although decreasing as time goes on, is bound to remain for a long period. This means that, for manufactured goods, those in which the labor factor is the lowest in the United States are the most promising for export to the Common Market. In addition, there are, obviously, the new products being developed in the United States. The economic integration of Europe has given also a great impetus to American investments within the community. The incentive is a large and growing market, with labor costs lower than those in the United States. American industrial investments have contributed to the recovery and to the economic expansion of European countries, since they brought not only capital, which was scarce, but also new techniques and high productivity methods. Under present conditions, an over-all American investment policy in Europe has to take into account important factors, some related to the U.S. situation and others to the situation in Europe.

The U.S. balance of payments is such that an all-out investment policy abroad would add to the difficulties. If some brakes should be put on American investments abroad, there are political reasons in the present state of the world for giving priority to investments in the less-developed countries, although such investments may be less attractive than investments in the Common Market. An additional reason for restraint is the relatively high rate of unemployment in the United States; it would be against the interests of the U.S. economy to promote employment in Europe through American capital at the expense of employment in the United States.

Some caution and some restraints are also to be recommended in order to avoid the spreading of uneasiness in Europe about American investments. Too often the major policy decisions concerning the management of European branches or subsidiaries of American firms are reached in the United States. Such decisions are likely to ignore European traditions or emotions, especially in the field of labor problems. The closing down of a factory and the sudden turning out of the workers, for reasons that may be quite sensible in the over-all interest of the firm, are particularly resented when they are decided abroad. Difficulties of that kind can be avoided in associating U.S. capital with local firms and management. Restraint should be exercised in order to avoid market control or domination by U.S. interests in one particular branch, if such a branch is of importance to the European economy. There are fears that such a situation could materialize. It originates in the realization that U.S. firms are much larger than European firms. Thanks to the Common Market, there is a widespread movement toward specialization and concentration, but due to the short time period, it is only a beginning, and the differences in size remain tremendous. It is felt that U.S. firms are in a position to acquire practical control of important markets in Europe and in devoting to that end means that amount to a small proportion of their resources, but which are out of the reach of European firms.

The Common Market opens broad possibilities to U.S. business in the field of technical cooperation and the exchange of experience. Industrial research has been greatly expanded in recent years in Europe, and is in full swing. There are already some agreements for cooperation between European and U.S. firms, but their number and their scope could be greatly increased.

TOWARD THE UNITED STATES OF EUROPE

However important the economic problems, the foreign policy and defense problems play the leading part. Under present circumstances, with the existence of the two large world powers, no single European country, including Britain, whatever its traditions, has the means of exerting a real influence on world events. A united western Europe could, on the contrary, have a positive action and contribute to the consolidation of peace and freedom. The United States of Europe could set up the "partnership on equal basis" envisaged by the late President Kennedy in his 1962 Independence Day speech. The Common Market has created strong common interests between the member countries which, less than twenty years ago, were waging against each other the most ferocious war. These countries have set up supernational institutions to which they have already given part of their sovereign rights. Additional steps toward the United States of Europe are those of entrusting to these institutions further responsibilities and powers. This has been under discussion for a number of years. It is not surprising that with the inheritance of the past, many obstacles, mostly psychological, are being met, but gradual solutions are quite conceivable.

What length of time would such a process require? The answer is practically impossible to give. What can be said is that those who in 1950 participated in starting the whole process of European integration would have been tremendously encouraged if at that time they had known for certain that so much would be achieved in the short period of years.

CHAPTER 4

The European Free Trade Association

Tore Browaldh

HISTORY

Just as was the case with the EEC, the parallel organization in western Europe—The European Free Trade Association, or EFTA—was the outcome partly of inevitable historical trends, partly of the personal element in history. Those who created EFTA also sensed the strength of economic forces working toward integration and understood that history is impatient. But they came out with an interpretation of the future of Europe and of world trade which was different from the one conceived by the authors of the Rome treaty. EFTA is as a trade bloc less closely knit than the EEC, and its process of integration includes no political feature. From the beginning, it should be emphasized that EFTA as such never was looked upon as a self-sustained unit. It was created mainly in order to facilitate an agreement with the six signees for the creation of a larger free trade area. Some early statements even intimate the possibility of EFTA, the Commonwealth, and the United States negotiating together in order to achieve a more world-wide effect on tariffs by an agreement with the EEC.

To a great extent, EFTA was a logical projection of the work of the OEEC. That organization during the 1950s gradually succeeded in lifting quotas and other quantitative restrictions from the intra-European trade, and had accustomed the member countries to habits of close cooperation and consultation on a wide range of international economic problems. Its program for the 1960s included an attack on the remaining quotas and abolishment of tariffs on a regional basis. One effect of the gradual liberalization of trade within the OEEC area was to make the difference between high-and-low-tariff countries more pronounced. The elimination of quantitative trade restrictions was, understandably enough, felt much more by the low-tariff countries like Sweden, Holland, and Denmark than by France and Britain, where imports had to climb over high tariff walls. This problem of European tariff disparities resulted in two concrete proposals, presented independently of each other in 1953–1954. One was the French plan for a 30 per cent cut of tariffs between members of GATT, but granting low-tariff countries the right to reduce their tariffs by less than 30 per cent. The second project was presented by Professor Bertil Ohlin, within the Council of Europe, under the working name of "The Low Tariff Club." Its result would have been to make western Europe a single market.

However, the signing of the Rome treaty caused the two plans to be scrapped, and instead the idea of a free trade area embracing all the OEEC countries began to emerge. Negotiations were conducted within OEEC's so-called Maudling committee during 1957 and 1958, but broke down under dramatic circumstances in December 1958. The two official explanations for the failure of these discussions were first the assertion of the EEC members that the free trade area as proposed by the "outer eleven" would prove unworkable, and second, in the view of the six EEC members, that the scheme, if realized, would jeopardize the complete economic union that was the ultimate aim of the Rome treaty powers.

Four of the "outer eleven"—Greece, Iceland, Ireland, and Turkey—had shown only a mild interest in the free trade-area plan. However, the remaining seven[1] found it natural to con-

[1] Austria, Denmark, Norway, Portugal, Sweden, Switzerland, and the United Kingdom.

tinue discussions among themselves. Not only did they prefer to face the Common Market competition as members of a free trade area, but also they wanted to show the "six" that their concept was practicable and would work. The negotiations leading up to the formation of EFTA were characterized by a determination to succeed, and were conducted with a speed and efficiency that surprised many outside observers. Even though each national delegation contributed largely to the final outcome, it may be appropriate to mention especially Heathcoat-Amory and Reginald Maudling, and Gunnar Lange and Hubert de Besche, the British and Swedish ministers and their deputies, all of whom personally had large responsibility in the final shaping of the so-called Stockholm convention, which was initialed on November 20, 1959, and finally signed by the seven member governments on January 4, 1960.

On March 27, 1961, an agreement of association between EFTA and Finland was signed in Helsinki. This agreement generally follows the same lines as the convention with respect to trade arrangements with certain exceptions.

PRINCIPLES

The best way to describe the principles on which the EFTA convention is based is to make a comparison with the approach adopted by the Rome treaty. Even though both documents provide for the gradual abolishment of quantitative restrictions and tariffs within each area as well as the elimination of the protective element in excises and other taxes, there are striking differences.

The main difference between the EFTA convention and the Rome treaty can properly be said to be one of philosophy of outlook. The EFTA members have used the same pragmatic approach that was so typical of the work of the OEEC. The convention is characterized by flexibility and a minimum of organization, whereas the Rome treaty, with its much more ambitious aims in the field of economic and political integration, establishes a number of institutions and attempts to anticipate and provide specifically for every future issue. The very simple institutional setup of EFTA thus does not include bodies similar to the European commission, the Assembly, or the Court of Justice within the EEC. The Council of Ministers is the main organ of the EFTA, but may be assisted in its work by "standing committees." EFTA's secretariat in Geneva consists of only sixty-five persons, while the Economic Commission for Europe in Brussels has more than five thousand employees. The secretary-general of EFTA is Frank E. Figgures, formerly in the British Civil Service.

The council's terms of reference have no fixed limits. As the only institutional machinery established by the Convention, its functions are primarily to supervise the implementation and operation of the association. Thus, by unanimous vote, it can decide to make changes involving increased obligations for member states. Behind the elastic wording of certain articles on possible coordination of economic policies is the recognition of the fact that future developments may justify departures in new directions for EFTA. Among the more specific tasks of the council should be mentioned regular appraisals of how member states apply the rules of the convention. In particular, the council handles various matters of complaints, such as that free flow of trade has been obstructed (for instance, through restrictive business practices) or that diversion of trade has arisen, as discussed below. Furthermore, the council must examine all cases in which a member state claims that one of the escape clauses of the convention should be applied. These clauses aim at protecting a country that is suffering from payment difficulties or unemployment due to an increase in imports from other states.

On one point, the similarity between the EFTA convention and the Rome treaty is almost complete, namely, with respect to the timetable for reducing tariffs and lifting quota restrictions between member states. This is a logical corollary of the fact that the principal purpose of the EFTA is to facilitate bridging the gap between the Common Market and the "outer seven." EFTA members are pledged by the convention to abolish quotas and tariffs on industrial products at the latest by January 1, 1970. This target date has been successively brought forward, and the date for final elimination of tariffs on industrial goods is now December 31, 1966—one day in advance of the present revised deadline for the full abolition of tariffs among the six EEC countries.

Apart from these more general comments, certain other observations should be made concerning the difference between the Rome treaty and the EFTA convention. First, the aim of the EEC is to achieve economic integration and ultimately to proceed toward a political unification of the "six." In fact, the founding fathers of the Common Market seem to have looked upon the creation of a customs and economic union as a means to arrive at political integration rather than as an end in itself. EFTA, on the other hand, was designed to achieve, with a minimum of commitments, a wider free trade area that included both the EEC and other western European countries belonging to the OEEC. Secondly, each member state in EFTA is free to decide its tariffs against third countries. No attempt is made to establish a common tariff wall around EFTA, as is the case with EEC. In the European free trade area, each nation keeps its individual tariffs toward the outside world. This "commonwealth type of approach" (to quote a very appropriate term used by F. V. Meyer[2]) is very typical of the spirit of the convention. It means that the free flow of trade is stimulated, but that each member state retains its freedom of action in different respects, including that of changing its tariffs vis-à-vis with third countries.

However, there is this general limitation on its freedom: Its measures must not frustrate the benefits expected from the liberalization of trade. It is in keeping with this principle that the convention deals with the problem of "deflection of trade" resulting from differences in external tariffs. The risk for such diversion of trade is due to the fact that imports of certain goods to the EFTA area will tend to be channeled via the member state that applies the lowest tariff on this particular product. Moreover, manufacturing industries in a low-tariff country like Sweden may gain certain competitive advantages because they

[2] F. V. Meyer, *The European Free Trade Association*, Frederick A. Praeger, Inc., New York, 1960.

get imported raw materials and semimanufactured products at less costs than their competitors in other member states.

In order to avoid such effects of the free trade area, the EFTA convention stipulates that tariff reductions and other preferential treatments will apply only to goods that can be said to originate within the area. The basic rule defining the products that qualify for reduced rates of duty prescribes that materials stemming from the outside must not exceed 50 per cent of the export price. Goods produced in the EFTA area further qualify for EFTA tariff reductions if they have undergone certain manufacturing processes within the EFTA area. For most products the manufacturer can choose between the percentage and the process criterion, but in the case of textiles he can only qualify his products under the process rule. An important feature ensuring liberal origin rules in EFTA is the inclusion of a basic materials list, which is an extensive list of raw materials and semimanufactures not produced within EFTA but which are nonetheless considered to be of EFTA origin for the purposes of area tariff treatment. It was thought that these rules of origin would entail a lot of red tape and the creation of a bureaucracy for examining "the certificates of origin," proving that the 50 per cent rule really applied. Industry in the member states sometimes voiced this fear, and this risk was also one of the arguments used by the EEC negotiators when attempting to show that the larger European free trade area would not work. The EFTA system has now been in operation for nearly four years and no such negative consequences of the rules of origin have appeared. On the contrary, customs administrations have simplified formalities, and industry and trade have expressed satisfaction that goods at the ports of importation have been cleared so speedily. EFTA has thus been able to prove that a free trade area can function in spite of the fact that each member state keeps its original tariffs vis-à-vis with third countries.

The third main difference between the two trade systems is that the EFTA convention aims only at regional free trade in industrial goods and does not provide for the elimination of tariffs, quotas, and other barriers to trade in agricultural goods and fish. The Rome treaty, on the other hand, includes among the aims of the Common Market the shaping of a common agricultural policy and the liberalization of trade in agricultural products within the EEC. To some extent, this difference is due to structural dissimilarities between the two areas. The EEC countries are, as a rule, more self-sufficient in agricultural products, whereas in EFTA, some countries have large export surpluses, and others (in particular Britain) normally cover their import needs from non-EFTA areas.

It might also with some truth be asserted that the limitation of free trade to the industrial sector is yet an illustration to the pragmatic approach of the authors of the convention. In most western European countries, agriculture is regulated, production subsidized, and prices controlled. Within EFTA, only Denmark has a fully competitive agriculture. The other EFTA countries protect their agricultural production by various means; Sweden and Switzerland, partly because of their policy of neutrality. A prerequisite of independence is a certain degree of self-sufficiency with respect to food. To have made the attempt to include agricultural products in the free trade area would therefore have meant much longer and more complicated negotiations for the "outer seven," and it might be reasonably doubted whether the convention would then have come into existence at all. An interesting point in support of this reasoning are the protracted negotiations within the EEC over the common agricultural policy. On the other hand, EFTA could not completely disregard the important sector that contains agriculture and fishing. The Danish economy to a large extent depends on exports of food. Almost two-thirds of her total exports comes from this source. A similar problem presents itself for Norway, whose exports of fish are important, particularly to the British market. Therefore, the convention contains certain provisions that recognize the need for measures to facilitate expansion of trade in agricultural and fishing products. However, the means to achieve this end are not mentioned in the convention, but are instead included in a series of bilateral agreements running concurrently with the convention. It seems probable that EFTA in the future will give more attention to agriculture and fish.

A fourth difference between the two documents is that the

EFTA convention has no provisions corresponding to the arrangements for harmonizing social costs, taxes, and other conditions for competition. It is true that export subsidies are explicitly prohibited and that one article stipulates that nationalized industries must compete "fairly." In EFTA, a member state may, however, impose measures that to some extent discriminate against foreign firms, provided this less favorable treatment does not limit the advantages that freedom of trade would otherwise entail. A logical conclusion of EEC's ultimate aim of economic (and political) union, on the other hand, is that conditions for competition between companies in various member states must become more equal in all pertinent fields.

Two more differences should be brought out. One noticeable omission from the EFTA convention is detailed provisions for the free movement of capital and labor. The main reason for this is that the seven members of EFTA are also members of OECD, and have in general accepted the code of liberalization of this organization. The problem of right of establishment is dealt with in one article, which rules that individuals and companies of member countries should have freedom of establishment within the area, but only to the extent necessary to make free trade work.

Finally, the EFTA convention enables members to withdraw, subject only to twelve months' notice. The Treaty of Rome, on the contrary, recognizes no procedure for leaving the EEC.

STATISTICS

Before passing over to economic developments within EFTA during the three years of its existence, an attempt will be made to present a statistical picture of this region. Obviously, it is impossible to cram into a few tables so many pertinent figures that they can justifiably be said to give a well-rounded description of this area. Still the method has some merits, primarily that of brevity.

EFTA is, as a regional grouping, smaller and more geographically split than is the EEC. Moreover, EFTA is dominated by

Britain, which with respect to population, gross national product, and trade is significantly larger than any of her six partners, while three members of the EEC (France, Germany, and Italy) are more or less equal in size.

As is evident from Table 1, the economic strength of the

TABLE 1. EEC AND EFTA COMPARISON, 1962

	EFTA	EEC
Population, million inhabitants	91	173
Gross national product, billion dollars	125	210
GNP per capita, dollars	1,375	1,215
Steel production, million tons	28	73
Electric power production, billion kilowatts	265	313
Hard coal production, million tons	202	227
Exports, billion dollars	20	34
Exports per capita, dollars	227	200
Imports, billion dollars	25	36
Imports per capita, dollars	275	208

EFTA countries is greater than a mere comparison of population figures would imply. Though EFTA comprises only half the population of the "six," its gross national product is 60 per cent and its imports 70 per cent of EEC's corresponding figures. EFTA imports per capita are in fact about 30 per cent larger than that of EEC.

When examining Table 2, it should be recalled that the years 1960–1962 saw a gradual reduction of tariffs between the EFTA states of 40 per cent; and that on December 31, 1962, tariff barriers were cut to 50 per cent, and on December 31, 1963, to 40 per cent, of their level on June 30, 1960. There is thus a dynamic development behind the naked figures of trade in 1962. But this aspect of Table 2 will be dealt with in the next section of this chapter. Here the object is to bring out the structural differences in direction of trade between the various EFTA countries.

The first thing that strikes the eye is Austria's high degree of dependence on trade with the EEC. The Austrian case is exceptional, but both Britain and Switzerland seem to have their economies more geared toward EEC than toward their EFTA

TABLE 2. DIRECTION OF TRADE OF EFTA COUNTRIES IN 1962[a]

(*Exports [f.o.b.] and Imports [c.i.f.] in Millions of U.S. Dollars*)

	Imports from EEC	Exports to EEC	Trade Balance	Imports from EFTA	Exports to EFTA	Trade Balance	Total Imports	Total Exports	Total Trade Balance
Sweden	1.271	979	−292	902	1.127	+225	3.112	2.920	−192
Norway	520	268	−252	670	417	−253	1.655	973	−682
Denmark	825	452	−373	857	744	−113	2.117	1.625	−492
United Kingdom	2.013	2.261	+248	1.546	1.491	−55	12.578	11.059	−1.519
Switzerland	1.899	942	−957	398	396	−2	3.002	2.215	−787
Austria	927	645	−282	205	201	−4	1.552	1.263	−289
Portugal	218	86	−132	137	76	−61	587	367	−220
Finland	418	325	−93	393	336	−57	1.228	1.104	−124
EFTA	8.091	5.957	−2.134	5.106	4.787	−319	25.830	21.527	−4.303

SOURCE: *EFTA Trade Bulletin*, April 1963.

a A warning should be observed when trying to draw conclusions from the "trade balance" figures. Exports are assessed f.o.b, and imports are calculated on a c.i.f. basis.

partners. On the other hand, to the four Scandinavian countries, EFTA now represents a more interesting export market than does EEC, though it must be admitted that the differences between the two sets of figures are by no means large.

Table 3 shows a breakdown of the figures for EFTA's exports

TABLE 3. DIRECTION OF TRADE OF EFTA COUNTRIES IN 1962
(Exports [f.o.b.] in Millions of U.S. Dollars)

	Reporting Countries								
Exports to	Aus-tria	Den-mark	Nor-way	Portu-gal	Swe-den	Swit-zerland	United King-dom	Fin-land	EFTA
EFTA	201	744	417	76	1.127	396	1.491	336	4.787
EEC	645	452	268	86	979	942	2.261	325	5.957
Eastern Europe	188	76	38	6	154	58	369	245	1.133
U.S.A.	49	147	105	48	163	212	981	58	1.763
World	1.263	1.625	973	367	2.920	2.215	11.059	1.104	21.527

SOURCE: *EFTA Trade Bulletin,* April 1963.

to areas other than those of EFTA members and the EEC. The high percentage of Austrian and Finnish exports going toward eastern Europe is perhaps the most striking feature of the table. The explanation is obviously to be found in a combination of geographical and historical factors.

From Tables 2 and 3 it is evident how Britain dominates trade between the EFTA members. British exports and imports represent roughly 30 per cent of total intra-EFTA trade. It should be added that British tariffs are in general higher than those of its partners, which means that Britain with respect to tariff cuts, actually is giving more than it gains.

Looking at the composition of trade, it is striking that more than 25 per cent of Britain's imports from the rest of EFTA consists of food and that Denmark ships some 80 per cent of her food exports to that country. Another feature of intra-EFTA trade is that almost a third represents food, crude materials, mineral fuels, and lubricants and another third comprises machinery and transport.

Britain is also the biggest importer and exporter among the "seven." Almost 60 per cent of EFTA's total exports and imports concern that country. Second in size is Sweden, whose exports and imports roughly correspond to 13 per cent of the total figures.

One final conclusion stands out from the tables, namely, that both EFTA and the EEC are relatively unimportant to Britain. Of Britain's total exports in 1962, only 10 per cent went to the EFTA partners and 14 per cent to the EEC. Both figures are well below the average for the EFTA members.

ECONOMICS

A first question when dealing with the economics of a free trade area is whether this approach is as efficient a stimulus to economic development as a customs union of the EEC type.

In recent years many comparisons have been made between EFTA and EEC, relating to rate of growth of trade and economic performance in general. Most of these comparisons have stressed the more rapid increase in gross national product and in intra-area trade of the EEC; implicit in this reasoning has sometimes been the argument that EFTA has proved to be a less dynamic factor than the EEC.

Now it is a moot question whether these more spectacular gains are due to the different approach that the European Economic Community has chosen. A good case might in fact be made for the view that special factors were at work and would have stimulated growth within the EEC, irrespective of the existence of the European community.

In the same way, the less rapid gains of the EFTA area might be explained by the special problems harassing Britain, EFTA's dominating partner, during these years. This particular issue has recently been dealt with in a highly intelligent and readable book by Alexander Lamfallussy.[2]

During the past ten years, Britain has experienced special difficulties due to repeated pressures on her gold reserves. "Almost

---

[2] *The United Kingdom and the Six.* New York: The Macmillan Company, 1963.

every balance of payments problem has been met by increasing the bank rate, by clamping down on credits to business and by cutting down public investments. This does not create the kind of expansionist, dynamic atmosphere that business managers need to be able to compete on the world markets."[3] And the ensuing slowdown in Britain's economic growth must obviously affect also the rate of expansion in the rest of the EFTA area.

That the factors determining the less-rapid economic development in EFTA might be more than temporary is indicated in a study by Professor Ingvar Svennilson,[4] in which it is argued that the difference in the rate of growth between the two areas might continue. The study presents three alternative forecasts relating to the expected population and production trends between 1955 and 1975. According to the most "likely" one, industrial production will increase by 79 per cent within the EEC and by 51 per cent in EFTA. Population will rise by 5 per cent in EFTA compared with 9 per cent in the Common Market. Only in the field of service trades does Svennilson foresee a more rapid rate of increase in EFTA, namely, 77 per cent as against 73 per cent in the Common Market.

A second question relating to the economic achievement of EFTA is this: Has trade between member states been stimulated to the extent expected? At first sight, an examination of the trade figures of EFTA during the period 1960–1962 seems to support the opposite conclusion (Table 4). Trade between EFTA and the EEC has in fact during these years increased percentagewise more than trade between the EFTA states. And this increase occurred in spite of trade restrictions between the EFTA members having been gradually reduced during this period while the building of the outer tariff wall around the EEC had been started. This seeming contradiction can be explained primarily by the rapid industrial expansion and high economic activity in general that has been a characteristic feature of the EEC during this period.

[3] Tore Browaldh, "A Swedish View of Britain's Economy," *Three Banks' Review,* June 1963.
[4] "Perspektiv på Västeuropas utveckling 1955–1975" (Developments in Western Europe 1955–1975, Some Perspectives), Stockholm, 1960.

TABLE 4. TRADE OF EFTA (INCLUDING FINLAND) IN 1960 AND 1962
(Values, Percentage Shares and Visible Trade Balances)

Imports from and Exports to	Imports (c.i.f.)				Exports (f.o.b.)				Visible Trade Balance (Exports Minus Imports)	
	1960		1962		1960		1962		1960	1962
	U.S. $, Millions	Share, Per Cent	U.S. $, Millions	Share, Per Cent	U.S. $, Millions	Share, Per Cent	U.S. $, Millions	Share, Per Cent	U.S. $, Millions	U.S. $, Millions
EFTA	4,420	18.3	5,106	19.8	4,151	21.3	4,787	22.2	−268	−319
Austria	142	0.6	198	0.8	159	0.8	197	0.9	+17	−1
Denmark	651	2.7	745	2.9	566	2.9	720	3.3	−85	−25
Norway	421	1.7	449	1.7	549	2.8	661	3.1	+128	+212
Portugal	79	0.3	90	0.3	114	0.6	141	0.7	+36	+51
Sweden	1,048	4.3	1,228	4.8	748	3.8	900	4.2	−300	−328
Switzerland	365	1.5	435	1.7	276	1.4	402	1.9	−89	−33
United Kingdom	1,345	5.6	1,588	6.1	1,423	7.3	1,388	6.4	+78	−200
Finland	369	1.5	375	1.5	317	1.6	378	1.8	−52	+3
EEC	6,971	28.9	8,091	31.3	4,807	24.6	5,957	27.7	−2,165	−2,134
Germany F.R.	3,347	13.9	3,941	15.3	2,082	10.7	2,427	11.3	−1,265	−1,514
Belgium/Luxembourg	606	2.5	622	2.4	468	2.4	556	2.6	−139	−66
France	1,043	4.3	1,224	4.7	619	3.2	896	4.2	−424	−328

Italy	807	3.3	1,019	3.9	818	4.2	1,065	4.9	+11	+46
Netherlands	1,125	4.7	1,230	4.8	715	3.7	876	4.1	−409	−354
Greece	43	0.2	56	0.2	105	0.5	136	0.6	+62	+80
Eastern Europe	1,064	4.4	1,178	4.6	883	4.5	1,133	5.3	−181	−45
Other European Countries	803	3.3	907	3.5	797	4.1	1,026	4.8	−6	+119
Ireland	347	1.4	393	1.5	358	1.8	429	2.0	+11	+36
Spain	285	1.2	297	1.1	161	0.8	306	1.4	−125	+9
Turkey	55	0.2	75	0.3	83	0.4	93	0.4	+29	+18
Yugoslavia	85	0.4	101	0.4	116	0.6	113	0.5	+32	+12
Other	32	0.1	41	0.2	80	0.4	85	0.4	+47	+44
Western Hemisphere										
United States	2,708	11.2	2,450	9.5	1,641	8.4	1,763	8.2	−1,067	−687
Canada	1,206	5.0	1,131	4.4	694	3.6	636	3.0	−512	−495
Central and South America	1,674	6.9	1,662	6.4	1,308	6.7	1,214	5.6	−366	−448
Africa	1,547	6.4	1,591	6.2	1,771	9.1	1,689	7.8	+225	+98
Asia	2,597	10.8	2,644	10.2	2,261	11.6	2,233	10.4	−337	−411
Oceania	1,154	4.8	1,072	4.2	1,208	6.2	1,089	5.1	+53	+17
World	24,144	100.0	25,830	100.0	19,522	100.0	21,527	100.0	−4,623	−4,303

SOURCE: *EFTA Bulletin*, May 1963.

This has, of course, led to increased imports from the outside. But a psychological element has also come into play in trade relations between the two groups. In the summer of 1961 it became evident that EFTA was going to start negotiations with the EEC, aimed at bridging the gap between the two areas. Industry and commerce in EFTA in all probability reacted to this new turn of events by increased efforts to export to the EEC market, in anticipation of the time when (as was hoped) this area would be opened up for EFTA.

The more rapid rise in trade between EFTA and EEC should not hide the fact that the increase of trade within EFTA itself was also impressive during this period. Member exports to other EFTA nations increased by 10 per cent between 1960 and 1961 and by another 5 per cent in 1962. From an economist's point of view, it is interesting to note that EFTA trade also seemed to be affected during the initial period by anticipation of the expected changes in tariffs. Thus exports within EFTA rose by 17 per cent during the first half of 1960, compared with the corresponding period in 1959, even though the first tariff cut did not become effective until July 1, 1960.

The EFTA secretariat has made a very interesting analysis of the impact of tariff reductions on trade within the association. Certain conclusions from this study have been presented in an article by EFTA's assistant secretary-general, Knut Hammarskjöld.[5] Table 5 is taken from the quoted article. Even though, as is pointed out in the article, the figures must not be taken to represent a scientific measurement of the effects of the tariff cuts, they do indicate an interesting and consistent trend. In this connection it should be pointed out that during the period, tariff reductions amounted only to 30 per cent, whereas at present, tariff cuts are equal to 50 per cent.

It might be appropriate at this stage to return to the issue touched on at the beginning of this section, namely, to examine the indirect effects—apart from the stimulus to trade—of the formation of EFTA. The debate on EFTA and EEC has often

[5] "EFTA och framtiden" (EFTA and the Future), *Ekonomisk Revy,* April 1963, Stockholm.

TABLE 5. INCREASE IN IMPORTS OF CERTAIN "HIGH-TARIFF" GOODS
1959–1961 (In Percent)

	From EFTA Countries	From Third Countries
Austria	+129	+52
Denmark	+45	+39
Norway	+72	+39
Portugal	+20	+1
Switzerland[a]	+44	+14
United Kingdom	+34	+31
Sweden	+27	−18

SOURCE: *Ekonomisk Revy*, April 1963, Stockholm.
a No figures available for 1959.

claimed that these indirect gains of the creation of a large trade area were substantial. The classical gain from freer trade is, of course, the scope for economies of scale in production. But this argument must not be exaggerated. It might be asked how large a market must be in order to reap these rewards. Is Britain with its fifty million people too small to encourage efficient production? Why is it, then, that nations with much more limited markets (for instance, Holland, Switzerland, and Sweden) have been able to build up competitive export industries in the face of tariff walls and trade quotas while continuing to enjoy a high and rising standard of living? This is pointed out merely to emphasize that assessing the exact economic effects of a free trade area is a very tricky task, particularly when the perspective is as short as here. This does not imply, however, that the creation of a larger market is without substantial advantages.

Another effect of entry into a larger free trade area, which was strongly underlined by the Macmillan government in its justification of British membership in the Common Market, is to increase competition and thereby "weed out" inefficient firms, lower inflationary pressure, damp wage demands, and generally give the economy a stimulating jolt. Developments within EFTA make difficult any definite pronouncement that this particular effect has been achieved. It is true that, on the average, increases in consumer prices in the EFTA countries were lower during

1960–1962 than during the 1950s. However, this was a world-wide experience due to the relatively new phenomenon of over-capacity in many industries. Moreover, in 1962, Europe was beginning to feel the effects of the American recession. Secondly, the disturbing fact is that the trend in consumer prices during the first three years of the 1960s was upward, not downward (see Table 6). As regards wages, there did not seem to be much difference between the rate of increase during the first years of the 1960s and the preceding decade. (In the EEC countries, wage rises seemed to accelerate between 1960 and 1962.)

TABLE 6.   PERCENTAGE INCREASES IN COST OF LIVING AND WAGES

	Cost of Living			Wages		
	1959–60	1960–61	1961–62	1959–60	1960–61	1961–62
Denmark	1.1	3.4	6.9	6.9	12.4	10.9
Austria	1.8	3.6	4.4	9.3	8.5	6.5
Sweden	3.9	2.4	4.7	6.1	9.0	6.4
Switzerland	1.4	1.9	4.3	2.9	4.8	5.7
United Kingdom	1.0	3.4	4.2	8.6	6.4	3.7

SOURCE: *First National City Bank Monthly Economic Letter*, May, 1963.

It is even more difficult to assess to what extent the creation of EFTA has promoted competition and efficiency by causing inefficient firms to contract their activities. It is true that (for instance) some British paper mills announced their closing down in view of stronger competition from the integrated Scandinavian pulp and paper mills. But this was possibly the result of the world-wide overcapacity in the paper industry. And the number of firms that contracted their operations or were weeded out is remarkably small in most EFTA countries, in view of the fact that basic tariffs have by now been cut by 60 per cent. The main reason for this may have been that the full-employment policy, to which every government is pledged, mitigated the impact of more intense competition through the strong support from the demand side. In many instances the solution found by the small or less efficient firms seems to have been merger or close collaboration with other companies in the field, sometimes foreign-owned companies, rather than a contraction of operations or a closing down of the plant.

POLITICS

Even though the EFTA, as was stressed in the second section of this chapter, has only economic aims, the creation of EFTA nevertheless has had political repercussions. First of all, the attitude of the U.S. administration vis-à-vis that of EFTA has been dictated mainly by political-strategic considerations. Secondly, the facts that three members of EFTA (Austria, Sweden, and Switzerland) are neutral in one sense or other, and that Britain in forming the EFTA made the political problem of neutrality her own, entailed certain political implications for the negotiations between Britain and EEC.

There has never been any attempt on the part of the U.S. administration to hide its preference for the EEC solution to the EFTA approach. This was the logical corollary of a fifteen-year-old policy (what has been termed the "Grand Design"), aimed at creating a viable and politically stable "United States of Europe." Earlier elements of this policy for rebuilding war-torn Europe included the Marshall Plan, the setup of OEEC, and the economic support of the EPU system. Now the declared aim of the EEC—to create an integrated economic and political unit on the Continent of Europe and at the same time achieve a French-German rapprochement—fitted in with this long-term strategic thinking of the U.S. administration. Obviously, the United States found no place for EFTA in this pattern. Not only was the objective of EFTA limited to liberalizing trade between member states, while each retained its sovereignty in various respects, but the existence of EFTA also meant that the European Economic Community could not be strengthened by the entry of Britain. This accounted for the strong U.S. support of Britain's application for full membership in the EEC.

This lukewarm attitude of the United States toward EFTA can be best illustrated by the strong objections raised by the administration when a congressional conference dealt with the

Douglas-Reuss amendment to President Kennedy's Trade Expansion Bill.[6] This amendment would permit the administration to reduce tariffs down to zero on some twenty-six major groups of commodities, even if Britain did not enter the Common Market. As the bill was worded, there could be no effective tariff-cutting unless Britain really entered the Common Market. The deletion of this amendment implied that if EFTA continued to exist with Britain as one member, the United States would not be interested in making the world-wide and efficient attack on tariffs that was the original intention of the Trade Expansion Bill, one of the most important U.S. documents to appear after the end of World War II.

During the negotiations between Britain and EEC, the special position of the three neutral members of EFTA was brought out. The term *neutrality* in these three cases has different origins and different meanings, and definitions of the word are many. In this context, the concept is simply taken to mean that it is the declared aim of a country's foreign policy not to become involved in a future war. But it should be added that the neutrality of the three EFTA countries is not the same as "neutralism"; above all, their neutrality does not mean indifference to the great ideological conflicts of our age.

By its very definition, the state of neutrality can exist only in time of war. But neutrality casts a long shadow. The fact that a country is determined to stay neutral if war breaks out must also influence her foreign policy in peacetime. A prerequisite for a policy of neutrality is that the outside world have confidence in the power and will of the neutral state to assert this neutrality against a country that brings pressure to bear upon it or that is contemplating an armed aggression. Consequently, an efficient military and civilian defense organization is one of the most important instruments for a policy of neutrality. But neutrality restricts freedom of action in other ways, too. A neutral country cannot enter into coalitions nor can it sign treaties that imply commitments of a political nature. In the EEC, the member

6 Henry S. Reuss, "America Gets an Unexpected Break," *Harpers Magazine,* May 1963.

states have made a solemn declaration that their ultimate goal is to achieve political unity. This is the basic reason why the three neutral EFTA states did not apply for full membership when Britain decided to start negotiations with EEC, but instead asked to negotiate on terms for association with the Common Market.

The term *association* in this application is rather vague, and the EEC institutions have not made any official pronouncement on the implications of an associate membership. From the point of view of the three neutral states, the main difference between full membership and association was that an association agreement could be adapted to suit each country's particular foreign political situation. A neutral country has, for instance, to safeguard her freedom of action in the event of war. Although it might be willing to hand over, within certain limits, the right of making decisions to the supranational bodies of the EEC, it would have to retain its freedom of making trade agreements with countries outside the Common Market.

There must be no misunderstanding as to the object of such exceptions. They reflect only what a policy of neutrality inevitably requires. They do not imply that the three neutral countries wish to limit their participation in the great integrated market; nor do they imply that neutrals are opposed to shouldering obligations in the field of economic cooperation, at least those that go beyond the provisions embodied in the OECD charter and the EFTA convention.

Even though negotiations between the three neutral countries and the EEC did not take place before the breakdown, certain statements made by representatives of the Common Market and of the U.S. administration showed them to be unfavorable to the association of the neutrals. There were three main lines of argument presented. The first objection contended that a country that is not ready to shoulder the political obligations, which an active membership of the EEC entails, would not receive the economic advantages of the customs union. Here it may be pointed out that if a neutral country is not ready to accept the political obligations, neither will she share in the political rights. And there are certain substantial advantages. Moreover, the three neutrals would not be only at the receiving end in a possible association agreement. Their standards of living are high and the purchasing power of their markets would be an attractive feature to any exporting nation.

The second argument ran as follows: Neutrality is an out-of-date concept which reflects only the unwillingness of a nation to take a firm stand on the great issues of our time. This reaction seems to put the problem of the neutrality in a wrong perspective. Neutrality as such has a definite mission in today's world. World peace would suffer if the neutral nations of Europe were to disappear. Neutrality in Europe concerns perhaps the most vital problem in the world today: the cold war and the division of Europe into East and West. If we follow the line of demarcation between the West and the Soviet spheres, we find that it is only in Germany that East and West confront each other directly. How many times during the past ten years have headlines cried out the mounting tension in Berlin and the risk that troops might clash and thus start off another war? Compare this with the comparative stability that the north of Europe has enjoyed. It is no exaggeration to ascribe this stability to Finland's and Sweden's policy of neutrality.

The third argument presented was that progress toward complete economic integration would be slowed down if the Common Market were to permit association of countries that did not share its political philosophy. This reasoning can be dismissed by repeating that the three neutrals had declared themselves willing to cooperate actively in the work to create an integrated economic market in Europe.

FUTURE

Comments within EFTA on the breakdown of the negotiations between EEC and Britain tended to emphasize the political repercussions, both internally for the Macmillan government and externally for relations between France and the United States. The problem of what the economic implications of this event can be for EFTA members has been played down.

It should be recalled once more that the main objective of EFTA, besides liberalizing trade, was to strengthen the bargaining position for the forthcoming negotiations with the "six." And the ultimate goal of EFTA is still the creation of an outward-looking European free market, comprising both EEC and EFTA. The breakdown at Brussels served only to strengthen this aim, as was shown at the Geneva and Lisbon meetings of the EFTA ministers in February and May 1963, respectively. A prerequisite for attaining this aim is that the lowering of tariffs within EFTA must run parallel with the tariff reductions made by the EEC countries among themselves. It was no coincidence that the Council of Ministers decided at the Lisbon meeting to remove all import duties between EFTA members by December 31, 1966, the day before the EEC is to reach the same point.

However, it may very well be asked whether this coordination of the two timetables with respect to tariff cuts is sufficient to ensure a smooth alignment of the economic structures of the two groups. After all, the EEC is now embarking on the second stage of integration, in which problems of coordinating economic policies, of eliminating restrictive business practices, and of harmonizing taxes and social charges will require major decisions. None of these issues is explicitly dealt with in the EFTA convention, even though the council is free to take action on any of these problems if the benefits of free trade are otherwise frustrated. From this point of view, it may be significant that at the February meeting in Geneva, the Council of Ministers decided to investigate some of these areas. The final outcome of this decision may be to approach the EFTA convention (or rather its application) in principle somewhat to the corresponding articles in the Rome treaty. This is yet another piece of evidence of the desire of the EFTA countries to do everything in their power to prevent the widening of the split in Europe and to pave the way for the united European market which is their ultimate goal.

A passage in the official communiqué from the Lisbon meeting could be interpreted as a step toward a coordination of policies in the 1964 tariff negotiations within GATT. A further development toward a common commercial policy for all EFTA (which is the case with EEC) seems, however, rather improbable because it would go counter to the principle of neutrality embraced by three member states. The new impetus given to EFTA at the Lisbon meeting was also evident in the attention given to the Association's agricultural problems. First, certain agricultural goods would be moved over to the "industrial products section," which means that EFTA's present cuts in tariffs and quotas would automatically apply also to them. Moreover, through new bilateral agreements, Denmark and Portugal were granted concessions with respect to exports of certain agricultural products of other EFTA countries. Another subject that was not dealt with during EFTA's earlier existence was brought up at Lisbon, namely, the problem of freedom of capital movements. Those countries that had capital available for export agreed to consider opening their capital markets to other EFTA members.

EFTA undoubtedly seems to have embarked on a road that will lead her on to solutions that were not envisaged when the convention was initialed in Stockholm. The pragmatic and flexible approach of EFTA makes this possible without having to resort to the formal procedure of amending articles of the convention. But the Lisbon meeting also gave an indication that the "outer seven" might become the "outer six." The Austrian government expressed reservations over the central decision to liberalize all tariffs and other restrictions on trade in industrial goods within EFTA by the end of 1966. Behind this attitude was the wish of Austria to achieve an associate membership with the EEC. Since no one could tell to what extent the acceleration of tariff cuts decided at Lisbon might make Austria's negotiations with the EEC more difficult, the Council of Ministers stated that, "If as a result of negotiations with the EEC, Austria were embarrassed, she can count on our sympathetic consideration."[7] It is appropriate to add that the problem of neutrality, which was widely discussed during negotiations between Britain and EEC, might this time be brought to a head.

---

[7] Frank E. Figgures, secretary-general of EFTA, *EFTA Bulletin*, May 1963.

CHAPTER 5

Britain and the Common Market

Sir Leslie Rowan

When this chapter was started, the negotiations in Brussels between the European Economic Community and Britain were still in progress. As I finished it some months later, those talks had broken down on January 29, 1963, an outcome that was inevitable after De Gaulle's press conference of January 14.

POLICIES AFFECTING NEGOTIATION

The cessation of negotiations raises three questions:

1. Why were they broken off?
2. Should Britain try to leave the way open to negotiations at a later date?
3. What should be Britain's present policies?

There can be no doubt, from what was said by all concerned at the time, that the negotiations were broken off because one country out of the six, France, decided that this would best serve the interests of that country. The statements made by representatives of all other five countries and of Britain showed clearly that, whatever De Gaulle may have believed, his action was contrary to their interests, individual and collective.

77

Two main reasons are commonly given for the termination of the negotiations with Britain:

1. Little progress had been made because of Britain's inflexibility, and there lay ahead a long process of hard wrangling, with little prospect of success.
2. In any case, Britain was not ready to enter wholeheartedly into the economic, social, and political commitments of of the Treaty of Rome.

Both De Gaulle and his foreign minister gave another reason, which applied not only to Britain but also to any other country that might join the EEC. De Gaulle said:

The question is raised even more because, after England, other states who are, I repeat, tied to her in a free trade area for the same reasons as England, will wish to enter the Common Market.

But that would result in a very different Common Market, which would have to envisage building, one of Eleven, and then of Thirteen, and maybe of Eighteen—which would, without doubt, resemble very little the one built by the Six.

In the end, it would appear as a colossal Atlantic Community, dependent upon and under the direction of America, which would make short work of absorbing the European Community.

His foreign minister added on January 29:

Faced by critics on all sides who say that we want, we French, a little Europe, I will say once more that we are not trying to keep Europe small or large but to be sure that the Europe which we create is a Europe which is European. It is by that criterion which, in our view, these problems must be settled.

These two statements are of profound importance to the future; and will be examined later. In the meantime, consider the two main reasons given above, which apply to Britain.

The first reason is a matter more of fact than of opinion, which can be substantiated by reading the report of the European Commission, issued February 26, 1963, soon after the breakdown in Brussels, and entitled, "Report to the European Parliament on the State of the Negotiations with the U.K." Even the most casual reading of that report shows that (1) by no means all the difficulties arose because of British inability to state a clear position, and that (2) great progress had in fact been made in most complex negotiations. The report in no way suggests that, in the end, success was not to be attained, although it stresses that there were nevertheless formidable difficulties still to be surmounted. The reader who wishes to satisfy himself must read the report. He will then judge whether the following quotations give a fair impression:

Many points left in abeyance may be classified as of minor consequence. . . .

On the other hand, it is important not to minimize certain questions which were still unanswered (apart from the problem of relations with the E.F.T.A. countries, the terms of which were rather special).

Two special subjects are mentioned in the report, temperate foodstuffs and British agriculture:

With regard to temperate foodstuffs from the Commonwealth, although a solution had been put forward for cereals, its extension to certain other products might still have raised difficulties, even though the broad lines were already laid down.

Again, even though some measure of agreement had been reached as to the final stage regarding British Agriculture it would be a mistake to underestimate the importance for the Community of effective transitional arrangements ensuring the progressive integration of the economies of the Member States and the final establishment of a single market.

The Six themselves were still not agreed on the interpretation of the financial regulation, which can be looked upon as a very important element in the system for agriculture. . . .

It is not uninteresting to note that what was needed for a solution was in some cases mainly a move from the British Government, but that there were also cases in which the issue turned upon proposals to be drawn up by the Six themselves.

This brings us to reflect in more general terms upon the real difficulties in the negotiations. The question was not only one of reconciling British systems and commitments with the letter of the Treaty of Rome: it was rather one of reconciling them with a Community in the full surge of development. The British application for membership involved an obligation to accept not only the Treaty but the substantial advances made since the Treaty was signed. It was on these advances that discussion was sometimes most difficult. But the fact that in certain fields the content of the Treaty was still in a preliminary stage, and that, broadly speaking, the implementation of its various aspects was in an intermediary phase, may also be considered as having made matters more difficult for the negotiators. The problem was one of reconciling with Community arrangements the action taken to adjust the British system whilst paying due heed both to Great Britain's vital interests and to a Community system which itself lay largely in the future.

In many cases the right solutions could only be solutions which anticipated the future progress of the Community, for example in procedural matters, and which had at the same time the effect of leading the enlarged Community, probably sooner than originally intended, to start working out common policies.

The report finishes with the following paragraph:

The negotiations with the United Kingdom, because they brought these problems to the fore and in some cases considerably increased their scale, *compelled the Community, then, to come to grips with them sooner than it otherwise would have done. This process brought with it greater awareness of the responsibilities an enlarged Community would bear in the world.* Because of the United Kingdom's almost worldwide responsibilities, the question raised by the United Kingdom Delegation also made it vital for the Community to define without delay the main policy lines of such a large and powerful Common Market with regard to matters which, once Britain was a member, would have had a direct and crucial impact on the overall balance of the free world.

This is a most important statement, for the impact of the EEC on world policies for good or ill will depend greatly upon the attitudes it adopts to "the responsibilities it would bear in the world," not least in relation to the United States, the North Atlantic Alliance, and the developing countries. (These issues will be discussed later.) It is, at any rate, some gain if the negotiations with Britain heightened the community's awareness of these matters.

The second reason, Britain's alleged unreadiness to undertake wholeheartedly the commitments involved, needs more analysis, especially as we are essentially in the realm of opinion rather than fact. Perfide Albion dies slowly, even after two wars.

BRITAIN'S CONTRIBUTIONS TO ECONOMIC UNITY

There are two main aims that this writer would like to see as those of any European community, larger or smaller than the present six-member one. The first is to free movements of trade, finance, and people within its frontiers and to follow a liberal economic policy toward countries outside its frontiers. The second is to form a strong political and military unity, based on a healthy economy, to serve as one of the pillars that supports the whole Western structure. There will, hopefully, be little argument that the first aim is of cardinal importance to the whole concept, though one is bound to note that the members of the European Economic Community are by no means wholly agreed about it. This was shown in the negotiations most clearly by the great difficulties that arose over the level of tariffs on certain raw materials. There is clearly more argument about the second aim, for there are those who would wish to see a European community not as a pillar, inside and involved; not even as a buttress, involved but outside; not even as a bridge with links at both ends; but as a third and separate force, acting independently on its own. Britain has from the outset rejected this last concept; those who propound it, as De Gaulle does, pose a clear choice for all other members, a choice between France and the United States, or rather between two conflicting concepts of the role of Europe. To pose such a choice is both unwise and fraught with great dangers for more than the European community.

If then we can take as the two main aims of any European community on the one hand economic freedom within and liberal policies without, and on the other, politico-military unity as a pillar of the Western structure as a whole, to what extent can it be argued that in early 1963 Britain was unfitted or unwilling to undertake such obligations?

In seeking to answer these questions, one has to deal with two separate but interconnected matters:

1. The attitude of Britain in the postwar period to these general concepts.
2. Certain specific issues as they appeared at the time of the negotiations.

What then has been the British record, first in relation to the freeing of trade, finance, and movement, and second to the role of Europe in the Western structure?

Admittedly, Britain, with her responsibility for one of the two reserve currencies and for the system by which it serves world trade, has not the same liberty of action as countries whose currencies are either purely or largely domestic, and this includes all currencies of the Continent. But to argue either for this reason or because Britain did not in the initial stages join the negotiations that led up to the Treaty of Rome, that she was and is opposed to the policies of liberal trade and finance, is to fly in the face of the facts. Britain was by no means in the rear when the liberalization program was started under OEEC in the early 1950s; and it was Britain who initiated in 1952 the policy of "the collective approach to freer trade and payments." This policy was first set out by Britain at the Commonwealth Prime Ministers' Meeting in London in 1952 and agreed by them. It was then put to the United States and to the member countries of the OEEC. This writer recalls it well because he was the official responsible for arguing it. The timetable may have been slower than had been expected, but the main currencies were made convertible together; import restrictions were removed; tariffs were lowered; and trade and payments were freer in 1962 than in 1952 to a degree that would hardly have been thought realistic before the "collective approach" policy was developed. Thus Britain can claim not only to have taken, but also to have carried through, an initiative for the removal of barriers to trade and payments before EEC existed or began to develop a policy at all.

What then of the second main issue, Europe's role in the Western structure? Since World War II, the United States has done many things for Europe, which even the most ardent advocates of the North Atlantic Alliance would have, in 1945, thought impossible. These include the Marshall Plan, the U.S. commitment in NATO, the physical presence of their forces in Europe, the continuing military aid after the Marshall Plan, and so on. British policy has been consistently aimed at bringing the North Atlantic Alliance into greater and stronger unity, not in any sense of exclusivity, but in recognition that division here would be disastrous not merely to us, but to the free world as a whole. If this concept of keeping together the Atlantic Alliance should be a main aim of any European community, then it is not Britain but France that was at fault, for it is De Gaulle's policy that at present faces Germany in particular with a choice between Washington and Paris. Generally, therefore, British continuing policies are in tune with what is conceived to be the internal and external policy aims of the EEC.

The issues become real when one has to translate these general attitudes into answers to the specific problems that the negotiators raised. There were clearly four highly sensitive areas so far as Britain was concerned:

1. Britain's trading relations with the Commonwealth.
2. Sterling.
3. Home agriculture.
4. The longer-term issue of economic and political unification.

Can it be said that all or any one of these would have proved an insuperable obstacle to Britain's ability to become a full member of the EEC?

The Commonwealth trading relationship is a complex one. The real issue of the negotiations lay in the questions of Commonwealth free entry and preferences in the U.K. market, of Commonwealth access to the EEC, and of "associate status" for developing countries within the Commonwealth.

These matters are difficult to deal with briefly, but can most easily be seen if the component parts of the Commonwealth are taken separately and the issues are related to each country:

1. *Canada, Australia, and New Zealand.* Here the problems were basically temperate foodstuffs and raw materials. The difficulty rose from the fact that the agricultural policy of the EEC had for the most part not been formulated; without formulation of policy, which could not be done quickly, Britain could not get the necessary assurances for the Commonwealth.

This is one area of policy in which the United States and Canada, somewhat late, are becoming aware of the difficulties. Furthermore, these events illustrate that the argument, namely, that all Britain had to do was "to sign on the dotted line" and all would have been well, is much too facile and confuses rather than clarifies the problem.

2. *India, Pakistan, Ceylon.* Here the "six" showed themselves on the whole to be generous, and contemplated comprehensive trade agreements, one of the objectives of which was to "maintain, and if possible increase, foreign exchange earnings of these countries."

3. *The Others.* These comprise mainly the independent countries in Africa and the Caribbean, and the dependencies. Here, again, the offer of association was a satisfactory economic solution, if only some Commonwealth countries had not rejected it for political reasons. Even in these cases, there were prospects of helpful solutions.

4. *Hong Kong.* Here, negotiations had not made a great deal of progress at the time when the discussions broke off.

Thus, on the economic side, the Commonwealth problem was by no means insoluble as far as the United Kingdom was concerned. There were many problems still outstanding, but final solutions in some cases were dependent on decisions internal to EEC, which had not then been made.

Next was the issue of sterling, which if it did not play a large part in the negotiations, certainly played a very major part in public discussion. The argument ran on two lines: first, that the United Kingdom's internal position was so uncompetitive that the shock of competition in the Common Market would force a devaluation with all the disruption that would cause; second, that Britain has external liabilities (the sterling balances) so

large in relation to her convertible assets (gold and currency reserves) that they must endanger the stability of any community
of which Britain is part. Both arguments have some validity, and
their advocates can call in evidence the past. On the other hand,
no moment could have been better chosen under both heads; on
the internal side, inflation had been stemmed, long steps forward
had been taken in seeking planned growth (through the establishment of the National Economic Development Council, in
which all three main elements of the community are represented—government, employers, and trade-unions) and in seeking an acceptable incomes policy, and the government had
started a system of a five-year forward look at government expenditure. The British record, especially in its exports to the
EEC since the breakdown, has shown that Britain is by no
means uncompetitive.

Under the second head, the international position of sterling,
again the position was (and has since shown itself to be) strong.
Sterling has not been under real pressure. Furthermore, Britain
had just repaid the last of its drawings from the IMF and so had
those resources in full, in addition to the $1 billion standby
mutually arranged with the United States subsequently, to draw
upon to meet any immediate difficulties. It is debatable that
either entry into or failure to enter EEC would have the kind of
effect on sterling that so many pessimists forecast. The pessimists
forecast a devaluation in either event. For the reasons given here,
sterling was moving to a period of more continued strength. By
bringing into the EEC an international currency and the most
developed financial center in the world, London, Britain's access
would have been a strengthening rather than a weakening of the
community.

Third, there was the issue of British home agriculture. The
United States and Canada now realize that the solution of this
issue is not just the simple one of signing on the dotted line to
accept an already clearly established system within the EEC. As
far as the negotiations went, the position was that *first,* Britain
must undertake to change the basis of her whole system of agricultural support and to move from the dual-price system to the
single-price system of the EEC. Britain thought it reasonable and

fair to ask for a period of transition, in the course of which she could make this enormous change *gradually*. The "six," however, thought that Britain should make the change to the system (though not necessarily to the price levels) more or less overnight. *Second,* the common agricultural policy of the EEC, as far as it had been developed, was tailor-made to fit the requirements of the six member countries. Britain thought it only sensible that when Denmark, a very large exporter of certain commodities, and Britain, the largest importer in the world, joined the EEC, the common agricultural policy should be reviewed to see whether it still fitted the requirements of the enlarged Common Market. There was all too little thinking of what the interests of an enlarged community would be.

The report of the commission, quoted previously, recognizes that the negotiations forced upon the EEC (before they were really ready for them) decisions on matters of policy that had not been fully worked out. This admittedly involved difficulties for EEC negotiators. On the other hand, there was a good deal of evidence that when the community looked at the problems of enlarged membership and tried to work out their policy, they tended to look at them as problems of a community of the existing six members and not to think out what would be the interests of a community of eight or nine or ten. An illustration of this— though it does not relate to the development of their policy, but to arrangements that had been already made—is the trade in pig meat. The interests of a community with the major importer and the major exporter of pig meat inside the community must differ from the interests when one of or both those countries were outside the community; yet the "six" argued that what had been arranged had been arranged, and failed to consider whether they themselves might not wish to change it when they were part of a larger community.

MEMBERSHIP EFFECT ON THE COMMONWEALTH

The last and final issue, political and economic unification, is perhaps the most difficult, and that on which the truth is essentially subjective. Britain's problems would be much greater than those of the "six" because she would have at the same time to seek to maintain her Commonwealth link as well as her EFTA obligations. First, on the European issue, British ministers had given their pledge to accept fully the political and economic implications of the Treaty of Rome. The precise form in which these will evolve was and is by no means yet clear; the treaty contains certain specific provisions about majority voting in economic matters at certain dates. Britain accepted these. But beyond that, and the general aims, the systems and procedures remained to be evolved in consultation. Great damage has been done by rash assumptions that these systems will either involve complete integration in all spheres or will necessarily correspond to some existing form of federation or confederation. All this remains to be worked out; Britain said that she would in good faith join and seek to work it out.

Within the Commonwealth, the economic link would become weaker; the issue for Britain was whether this would weaken the political link as well. Herein lay the great challenge to Commonwealth statesmanship. But even here, the lessons of history were disregarded. Some twenty years ago, at the end of World War II, there was much talk about the end of Britain's Commonwealth. Yet, since then, only three countries have left it—Burma, Ireland, and South Africa. India, the first expected to leave, has remained as a member much respected by the rest of the Commonwealth. Present forms of Commonwealth association were certainly not remotely contemplated in 1945. For example, who could have forecast that the Commonwealth would in fact comprise republics; yet this is what it now does, without detriment to the Commonwealth link or weakening of the monarchy. These facts are relevant to present problems because they show the capacity of the Commonwealth to evolve systems together rather than to be disrupted by revolution.

In all these four issues, no one can give a judgment that can be proved. They are all matters of trust and faith. In the end, five countries of the EEC were ready to trust Britain; one was not. What is clear is that Britain's entry would have brought prob-

lems for the "six," for herself, for the Commonwealth, and for
EFTA. But it would have brought some great advantages in the
political, financial, military, and international fields, in all of
which Britain has sustained a remarkable stability as compared
with that of other European countries.

Politically, Britain has a great history of stability, in which the
monarchy has played and still plays a notable role. This is not
true in any of the three major countries in the EEC, namely,
France, Germany, and Italy. In this century alone, all have had
to change their political systems, and in one case (Germany and
the Nazis) with disastrous and costly effects.

Financially, Britain had two major contributions to make.
First, its tradition of firm currency, which is more than a financial fact. It is equally a symbol of social maturity that even a coin
as small as a single penny, though minted 150 or 200 years ago,
still has a recognizable if reduced purchasing power. In all other
countries mentioned, there has been at least one runaway inflation. Second, as mentioned, Britain could bring to Europe what
the Continent lacks, an international currency and a developed
financial market of the highest repute and the widest contacts.

The major challenge of the last half of this century will lie in
Britain's relationship with developing countries. Two-thirds of
the population of the developing countries (outside the Communist bloc) are members of the British Commonwealth of Nations, and Britain has direct, first-hand experience with their
problems. Britain's Commonwealth relationships may be difficult
to understand, but they are facts which add greatly to the strength
and stability of the free world.

In brief, therefore, the negotiations were broken off not because they risked failure but more because France felt they risked
success. Certainly the view that Britain was not ready to undertake the responsibilities of membership, economic and political,
does not appear valid. On the contrary, Britain could have
brought great advantages and strength to the EEC while receiving similar advantage and strength. But a contributory cause
was a lack of domestic understanding. Many people in Britain
adopted a totally unjustified line of argument: that Britain

would be "finished" economically, "excluded" from Europe in trade, and "disregarded" politically if she were not a member of EEC. This has never been true; this is not hindsight for this writer presented exactly this case in June 1962, at the meeting of the American Bankers Association in Rome at a time when there appeared to be a good chance of success. Those who argued in the defeatist way forgot the four contributions that Britain had to offer. They also forgot the history of the United States, which became the most perfect economic community over a hundred years ago; whose external economic policies until the 1930s were not notably liberal; and yet which has in recent years provided a major market for Britain's exports and has given the essential support for postwar reconstruction and the great international economic agencies, the IMF and the IBRD.

Thus a phase is ended, and Britain's problem now is to decide whether this break is final, and plan its affairs accordingly, or whether the way should be left open for negotiations at some later date. It is clear that no negotiations can begin again in the near future. the complexity of the problems calls for long preparation. This is, in the circumstances, no real loss because there should be no question of any further negotiations until there is a virtual certainty of success. One breakdown is bad enough; a second would be quite fatal to the cohesion of the West. This being so, two events must take place before even the preliminaries of negotiation can start. First, internal political affairs within Britain must be concluded insofar as the periodic elections are concerned. Second, De Gaulle must radically change his policy or have ceased to rule France; no British government would risk another negotiation with his veto overhanging it. Within these limits, the break should not be considered as final, and future negotiations should be encouraged. An absolute cut-off of Britain's access to the EEC could damage one or more of the major new dimensions of international policy, among which are:

1. In the military sphere, the obligations undertaken by the United States for Europe and the reality of her armed presence there.

2. In the economic sphere, the policy of countries to discuss and promote trade by reducing barriers, and to support international and regional institutions created to achieve this end; and to regard this as an essential foundation for the successful achievement of high levels of employment, to which every country is committed and which in many countries has been one of the greatest postwar achievements.

3. In the political sphere, the move toward closer unity, both within Europe and over the Atlantic area.

4. In the overseas field, the growing consciousness of the needs of the developing countries and of the importance to our own enlightened self-interest of ensuring to them the solid, self-sustaining economies that are the only real basis for their political independence.

5. The orderly evolution of Britain's policy of granting independence to former colonies.

6. The maintenance of sterling as a strong and respected international currency.

The breakdown of negotiations in Brussels does not prove that these aims are wrong or in need of modification. In fact what has happened reinforces them as desirable aims. One has only to ask a few simple questions to see the answers clearly. Is a phased withdrawal of U.S. troops from Europe what we want, even if all members of NATO still have the mutual treaty commitments to defend any member who is attacked? Such a commitment without the actual presence of U.S. forces in Europe in the 1930s would have been something for which every sane man would have thanked God every night; now, in the 1960s it is not enough. Do we wish to aim at less political cohesion in Europe or over the Atlantic? Do we think it wise or desirable to return to the 1930s when countries mostly talked apart and sought to protect their own position by raising, not lowering, barriers to trade; and when money was the master rather than the handmaiden of trade? Do we wish to make the decade of development a decade of lowering standards of life for two-thirds of the population of the world? Would the cause of peace and international understanding be advanced if the Commonwealth partnership no longer existed, an association where committed and uncommitted countries, rich and poor countries, countries of African, Asian, and European race and culture can consult and work together on a basis of equality and friendship? Would it benefit anybody, except perhaps the Communists, that this association should be dissolved or weakened? Or again, could it do anything other than damage international trade, and so weaken everyone, if one of the two international reserve and trading currencies ceased to play its international role or was severely impaired through devaluation? No new currency could spring up overnight to share the burden with the remaining international currency because the network of international banking agencies, the development of a large money market including a foreign exchange market, arrangements to provide large sums of foreign centers at short notice, and the confidence that would inspire foreigners to hold a currency as their reserve, are all developments that can take place only over a long period of time. Hence, would it not follow that if one of the two currencies lost its international status, the burden on the other would be infinitely increased? The answers must surely be clear, and with them the assertion that the six aims still stand.

Second, we need to look at these affairs against the perspective of history. A story is told of a conversation in the early part of the twentieth century between a European and a Chinese. The European extolled at great length the advantages of his own civilization, its long culture and great achievements, and then asked the Chinese, "What do you think were the main aftereffects of the French Revolution?" After a moment's reflection, the Chinese replied, "On the whole I think it is a bit too early to judge." We need not perhaps take such long views; we all hope that the fragilities of Europe, or at least of the three major countries in EEC, have been corrected. Indeed, the EEC itself is designed to that end, and its initial success has been great, internally at any rate, but it still has to prove itself in the long run.

These comments are not intended to damage others, but merely to point out that Britain, Europe, or the United States should not rush to conclusions after the breakdown in Brussels in the same way as some rushed to conclusions during the negotiations.

FUTURE POLICIES

As we consider all these very difficult issues, there is one other general thought that we should keep well in the forefront of our minds. In the 1930s, we were in general trying to deal with the problems of failure; in the 1950s and 1960s, so far at any rate, we have been dealing in the main with the problems of success. So far, and these words are emphasized, world trade has increased in every year but one; no recession has become a depression; Europe has been rebuilt; our great international and regional economic institutions have grown in status. In Britain it is preferable to have the problem of inflation with 2 per cent unemployed rather than the problem of 22 per cent unemployed and deflation, as was the case in 1931. It might be argued that we need success because the penalties of failure in the face of communism are so great. But nevertheless, in facing our current problems of failure, it is as well to remember that they have arisen from great success in the postwar years. In effect, then, the six British aims have merit and should not be discredited because of the Brussels breakdown.

What then in the light of this analysis should be Britain's policies? By far the most important single factor is the frame of mind in which Britain approaches the next phase. First it needs to rid itself of the pessimism that damaged the negotiations for EEC membership, and which in some measure contributed to their failure. Events have shown, even in the short time since the breakdown, that Britain has not suffered the damage forecast by many; close adherence to its aims should result in success. There is some time allowed for reflection, but there is no time for a vacuum. What then should Britain do now?

British domestic aims have not changed; primarily, these are to contain inflation, to increase competitiveness, to achieve a higher (but sustainable) rate of economic growth, and as a result of all these, to maintain the strength of sterling. All these are in course of realization. Inflation has ceased to be regarded as a political asset and is seen as a social and material evil; if negotiations with the EEC brought forward their realization of some of the problems between the EEC and the world, equally they brought home to business in Britain the need to become much more agressively competitive. It is not without significance that in the past two years British exports to EEC have increased proportionately more than to any other area. NEDC is projecting the concept of growth much more firmly into the public consciousness, and despite unofficial strikes and issues of work demarcation, the incomes policy is becoming a widely accepted need. For example, many European countries, especially France, Germany, and Italy, are in the early stages of a major series of wage increases that well outstrip productivity, but Britain has passed through that stage and therefore in the ensuing years will gain considerable advantage over some members of EEC with respect to this. All this adds to the strength of sterling.

Externally, three matters are of capital importance. First the EFTA must be strengthened. This was largely realized at the Lisbon meeting in May 1963, a meeting that contrasts sharply in its success and in the unity of its members with the Kennedy round in GATT and with the various meetings of the EEC ministers, whether on political, defense, or agriculture matters. It is now true to say that all the decisions to realize to the full the aims of EFTA have been taken. Of course its aims are limited, but they can be added to by consent so that the superstructure is well founded. It was also shown in Lisbon that one of the main difficulties of reconciling differing external tariffs and internal free trade, namely, the efficient working of certificates of origin, had been solved. Britain had long ago solved it in her relations with the Commonwealth, and Lisbon showed that this could be applied to a wider area. The point is of great importance because of the bearing it can have on relations between EFTA and other countries or areas with common tariffs and internal free trade.

One other factor is well worth noting in EFTA relations with other countries. The free trade-area principle of maintenance of individual national tariffs means that in no case need EFTA raise any barrier against other countries. But this must happen when a number of countries have to make the tariffs conform to a common average; and the extent to which the lower tariff members have to raise the tariffs depends upon how liberal is the interpretation of the common average. This is of special importance to the developing countries, who see their products to certain markets in EEC to be subject to an increasing tariff without any necessary assurance that the reducing tariffs in the other countries will make good any loss.

The second external matter of concern is the Commonwealth. When negotiations in Brussels ended, some major issues of the Commonwealth's free entry to the United Kingdom and of the access to the markets of EEC were still to be solved. It may well be that a reassessment will show that Britain accepted the possible changes in this position too lightly. The argument is not that Britain should find its future, economically, in a Commonwealth trading area. Rather, Britain should be able to find means of attaining its domestic and international aims without radically changing its Commonwealth trading relationship, as was implicit in the EEC negotiations. Perhaps in these negotiations, the abandonment of the principle of free entry into the United Kingdom for the products of (especially) Canada, Australia, and New Zealand has been too lightly treated. This system of free entry was in principle designed initially to cover raw materials and agricultural products. It has in fact been extended over the years to include many manufactures, an important but uncovenanted benefit to the rest of the Commonwealth. This is a really vital matter because the Commonwealth comprises some two-thirds of the total population of the underdeveloped countries outside the Communist bloc, and some 80 per cent of their imports into Britain are free of any duty or quota. Arrangements to cope with this were at least in prospect; but in issues of such importance, certainty is called for and should be secured in the future. To change the free-entry system is to change a great deal; to change it for the worse without assured compensatory advantages in other markets is to do great damage to one of Britain's main aims of policy.

Third, and finally, there is the role of the great economic international institutions, namely, the IMF, the IBRD, and the GATT. If internally full employment is the most significant difference between the 1930s and the 1960s, externally in the economic field there is no doubt where the main difference lies; it is in the willingness of countries to talk together to reduce barriers to trade and movement, and in the establishment of powerful institutions to help to this end. Of these, clearly, IMF, IBRD, and the GATT are outstanding. There have been signs, especially in relation to IMF, that some members of EEC wish to reduce rather than to enlarge the functions of these bodies, regarding them as unduly dominated by the United States. What is most astonishing about the use by the United States of its power, military and economic, since World War II has been its moderation, not its excess. Here, again, is a field in which Britain's role should be quite clear: It should not press for the curtailment of the strength and resources of these bodies, but for the enlargement of them. It should recognize not the limitations of their functions, but their scope, as for example in the use of the IMF for the settlement of the Indus waters dispute between India and Pakistan, a little heralded but outstanding achievement. In this, Britain can serve the interests not only of the rich countries but of the poor as well, for there is no doubt that the IMF has channeled resources to developing countries which would otherwise not have gone there, and has played and must continue to play through all its agencies a major role in the long task of ensuring that political independence of such countries is firmly established, as it can be only on sound and self-sustaining economic growth. Thus the position is reached that while the way to negotiations should be kept open, it would be wrong to take any rigid view about the manner in which negotiations should resume or that they resume at the point they reached in January 1963.

Britain is not alone, as history shows, in rejecting the view that there is only one method by which her national objectives can be attained in peace. She is perhaps more alone in showing that she has a capacity to endure, to evolve, and to attain her aims despite difficulties and dangers. From Britain's point of view, EFTA is now established firmly on the road to full realization of its aims, limited though they are; membership of EFTA does not involve any forced or forcible change in the Commonwealth relationship; both can accommodate themselves to the concept of the Kennedy round. Nothing in any of these relationships limits freedom of action toward the developing countries, as there would be, for example, in the concept of a common external tariff and in the position in the EEC of the former French colonies.

From the outset, a great danger about the EEC has been that it could become protectionist in its economic policies, and also exclusive in its political and military aims, as indeed the French policy is at the moment. This would be damaging in itself to the whole structure of the West and would be a precedent of the worst kind for others to follow. Proponents of British membership of EEC have argued that should such tendencies arise within EEC, they could much better be resisted by countries who are within EEC than by those outside. There is a great deal to be said for this line of thought. Nevertheless, it is necessary to strike a balance and to consider what the cost of membership, as interpreted by De Gaulle, would be in other fields of Britain's policy, such as the North Atlantic Alliance, the Commonwealth, the developing countries, the great international financial and economic institutions, and above all, the cohesion of the West in the face of communism.

For the United Kingdom, the De Gaulle interpretation would be very costly. This interpretation may change, but until it does, Britain's policy should be to declare again her aims, unchanged despite Brussels, and continue to pursue them resolutely. It should seek every chance to work in harmony with the EEC in the hope that friendly elements in the community will cooperate in the process. This policy should be followed throughout all the many bodies of which it is a member, such as the Commonwealth, NATO, EFTA, OECD, and the Western European Union. It should also recognize that there are other methods of advance except membership in the EEC, and that there are means of approach other than the economic. Future advances may be achieved more through military or political means than through the purely economic. Membership in EEC on terms that support rather than damage Britain's wider aims may still come about and may still prove the best method of advance, but it should not be accepted as the only method.

CHAPTER 6

Japan

Kiichiro Satoh

Before World War II

About a century ago, Japan took the first step forward toward economic development, or industrialization, partly as a result of the pressure put on her by Western powers to open her doors to foreigners for trade and domicile, and partly as a result of the consequent downfall of the Tokugawa Shogunate government, which adhered to the policy of isolation for almost three centuries.

The capitalistic system began to take shape after the Meiji restoration principally because of several new developments. Outstanding among them were: (1) the freedom of vocational choice through the abolition of the caste system; (2) the removal of restrictions on domestic travel simultaneously with the start of foreign trade; and (3) the recognition of the right of private property (such as land) and the right of transfer of ownership. Through the adoption of these new measures, the feudal system came to lose its foundation.

During this period, and particularly up to the time of the outbreak of World War I, Japan was endeavoring to extricate herself from an underdeveloped condition and achieve full-fledged industrialization. Japan in those days resembled some of the developing countries today who are struggling to attain the same end. Japan, however, was very fortunate in having been comparatively free from the ill effects of extraneous doctrines, because of the absence of powerful countries advocating ideologies other than capitalism, and also in having found the principal propelling force for her economic advance in a few financially strong Zaibatsu groups cooperating closely with the government. The outstanding features of government policy during these periods of development were (1) the compulsory education system, which contributed to Japan's high rate of literacy and its skilled labor force, and (2) the establishment of a banking system, which enabled her to mobilize her internal resources to the fullest extent at a later stage of economic development.

Owing to the belated start of her association with advanced countries, Japan had to industrialize rapidly so as to approach their levels. For this purpose, initiative on the part of the government was necessary. Thus, among the key industries sponsored under direct governmental supervision in those days were such industries as cotton spinning, shipbuilding, mining, telegraphy, steel making, and machinery. The government also embarked upon military gunpowder plants.

However, the all-out development policy naturally invited a sharp increase in currency circulation and the resultant advent of inflation. In 1881, therefore, the government had to adopt a retrenchment policy, and carried out a series of adjustment measures, including the transfer of governmental enterprises to private management. Inflation was thus somehow brought under control. The victory in the Sino-Japanese war enabled Japan to acquire new markets overseas. The textile industry was particularly strengthened, owing to its wholly owned mills established in China, and it remained as a leading export industry of Japan for many years.

About the turn of the twentieth century, heavy and chemical industries began to develop as a result of increasing military requirements. Progress in this direction was shown by the fact that heavy industry accounted for 6 per cent of the total industrial production of Japan in 1900. The ratio increased to 8 per cent in

1909, and further swelled to 13 per cent in 1919. In the interim, the production of steel and coal in Japan made a notable increase.

Japan took sides with the allied powers in World War I. Spurred by sky-rocketing exports in the wake of the war, Japanese industries enjoyed a boom, and Japan's industry expanded enormously. Because of its inexperience in handling such rapid growth, Japan eventually suffered a postwar depression. As countries in western Europe and the United States began to achieve more normal peacetime conditions, and their competitive power in world markets revived, Japanese products began to drop out of the international race, in quality as well as in price. As a consequence, exports came to a standstill while imports began to increase, and the consequent adverse trade balance was a chronic headache. Worse still, the Kanto area, embracing the capital city of Tokyo, was heavily damaged by a big earthquake in 1923, and the Japanese economy was virtually at a stalemate for the ensuing few years.

Moreover, in 1930, the government made a decision to go back on the gold standard, in an attempt to lower domestic prices to the international level. However, the move was premature and Japan lost a large volume of gold reserves by the outflow of capital, causing currency contraction in the domestic market, and the country felt the impact of a depression.

Thus, political discontent became more pronounced among those who suffered from the depression most, and they were joined by some military cliques. The Manchurian incident broke out in September 1931, and Japan was compelled to go off gold again by the end of the year. Thenceforward the economy of Japan was subjected to the so-called defense program, marking her entry into a type of controlled economy in every phase of business operations for about fifteen years. The wartime economy was overburdened by nonproductive activities and could not make any headway in technical development, with few exceptions. Thus, upon the termination of World War II, Japan found not only that most of her industrial equipment had been destroyed, but also that her engineering level lagged far behind the international standard, which had made notable progress during the war.

As stated above, the Japanese economy made rapid strides in every war in which she took part up to World War I. On the other hand, the increase in population was explosive, and industry was unable to absorb the swelling labor force. Thus, the agricultural population continued to account for nearly 50 per cent of the total population. The extreme scarcity of natural resources in Japan, in addition to the need of cotton and wool imports, was another handicap to the economic growth of Japan. As a result, her living standards in those days were perceptibly lower than that of advanced nations.

POSTWAR CONDITIONS

Rehabilitation

Let us first refer to the economic plight that confronted Japan immediately after the end of World War II. Before the war, Japan had a territory covering 670,000 square kilometers, but lost about 45 per cent of it through the defeat in the war. Japan also lost a so-called sphere of interest, Manchuria, together with its important raw material resources. National resources left on the mainland were also sharply reduced, owing to devastation inflicted on all facilities by the war, directly or indirectly. The total value of the loss of national resources caused by the war was estimated at about 134 billion yen, or roughly $33 billion (calculated on the basis of the prices at the time of the war's end). The damage ratio stood at 25 per cent in the case of nonmilitary assets, about 90 per cent in the case of military installations, and 41.5 per cent in the case of total national resources. In contrast, Japan's population kept on increasing because of the repatriation of soldiers, civil servants, and private citizens from the former territories and other overseas areas, in addition to the natural increase numbering 1,500,000 annually.

The democratization policy imposed by the allied forces simultaneously with the occupation of Japan was epochal in importance. It started with the promulgation of the new constitution, which stipulated defense incapability, the farm-land reform, the dissolution of feudalistic agricultural organizations, the enactment of labor laws for the protection of workers and trade-unions, the enforcement of the antimonopoly law, and the dissolution of the Zaibatsu, based on the Law for Deconcentration of Excessive Economic Power. Thus, democracy became the watchword of people in Japan after the war, and democratization programs were adopted one after another by the occupation regime. There is no denying, however, that these policies were originally aimed at disabling Japan from making a comeback as an industrial nation.

What troubled Japan as a defeated nation for a few years immediately after the war's termination was inflation. Deposits with banks failed to increase while loans swelled sharply. Accordingly, loans by the Bank of Japan bulged, and the note issue registered a sharp gain. As consumers in general were engrossed in buying daily necessities they had lost during the war, prices skyrocketed. The livelihood of wage earners was jeopardized and labor disputes instigated by left-wingers increased sharply. In order to cope with the situation, the government in February 1946 announced the so-called switchover from the old yen to the new yen and the freezing of deposits. These makeshift measures succeeded only in temporarily curbing the progress in inflation, and the currency volume began to increase again in September 1946. Continuous deficit financing further accentuated the tempo of runaway inflation.

It was in 1949 that the so-called Dodge line program was announced, with the object of terminating inflation for good. Minister Dodge's statement said in part: "The present state of the Japanese economy is not of the kind to be settled simply by financial manipulation or budgetary techniques. Stabilization is possible only by virtue of production rationalization, a balanced budget, and the promotion of trade and austerity." The program thus was aimed at stabilization in preference to recovery. In April 1949, accommodations by the Reconstruction Finance Bank were suspended, and the single exchange rate was established at 360 yen to a dollar instead of multiple rates ranging from 150 to over 600 to a dollar. The Japanese yen rate was left intact when the pound sterling was devalued in September 1949. As a result, Japanese price levels were higher than foreign prices, and exports failed to increase. Thus, it appeared that the so-called Dodge line program might fail. The outbreak of the Korean war rendered timely help.

Following the outbreak of the Korean war in June 1950, Japan's exports began to increase while the prices of export products made steep advances. In addition, special procurement orders for goods for the Korean operation by the allied forces were placed with Japanese manufacturers in rapid succession. The foreign currency reserves held by Japan, which stood at only $313 million at the end of June 1950, increased to $417 million at the close of December, and further swelled to $556 million by the end of March 1951. At the end of 1951, the reserves stood at $914 million. The Korean war thus served to contribute to Japan's business recovery, but at the same time, there arose again the signs of resurging inflation. In fact, following Japan's return to sovereignty through the peace treaty in 1952, the objective of a balanced budget seemed unattainable.

In 1953, domestic prices began to soar again as a result of a cold spell and flood damage. The inflationary trend became stronger in anticipation of the import curtailment resulting from the dwindling balance of foreign currency holdings. Under the circumstances, the government, backed by business people, adopted an anti-inflation policy based on the enforcement of the retrenchment budget and the adoption of a tight money program. Inflation was soon brought under control by the impact of recession.

Economic Growth and Trade Expansion

It is universally known that the Japanese economy after World War II expanded at an exceptionally fast rate compared to the economic growth of other nations. Japan's economic growth rate since World War II has averaged about 9 per cent per annum. This growth, however, was not particularly surprising because it was based on a recovery from a low level and came in the wake of complete economic frustration during the few years immediately after the war's termination. During the seven years from 1951 through 1957, the annual average economic growth rate in Japan was 8.9 per cent, which, together with the corresponding growth rate in West Germany, is generally accepted as a "postwar miracle."

The increasing rate of industrial production (mining and manufacturing inclusive), which barely reached 5 per cent per annum directly after the war's termination, has since continued at more than 8 per cent. The high rate of economic growth of Japan was due principally to the sharp expansion of private plant and equipment investments. This basic keynote was most conspicuously evident in 1956, when private investments for plant and equipment registered an increase as high as 80 per cent over the preceding year. This boom was called the greatest since the time of Jimmu (the first Emperor of Japan). Many factors were responsible for this unusual rate of economic growth. Outstanding stimuli causing expansion were the businessmen's desire to meet postwar demand and the keen competitive pursuit of technological innovation in order to catch up with advanced countries. The plentiful supply of skilled labor and the strong pressure of consumer demand, as well as timely supplies of credit from government agencies and private commercial banks, were other factors.

Here it may be proper to mention the market potentiality of a country like Japan, inhabited by more than 95 million people with good purchasing power. Almost all segments of industry could build large plants that were economical to operate and which had access to materials anywhere on a long shore line, which facilitated transportation.

Another cardinal factor that made the high economic growth rate possible was the increase in exports. During the period from 1952 through 1959, after the close of the stage of postwar recovery, Japanese export trade expanded at an annual rate of 14.5 per cent. In the years 1952 through 1961, the rate became as high as 12 per cent per annum.

The composition of Japan's trading markets at present may be broken down as follows:

1. Advanced countries (Japan exporting labor-intensive products and importing capital-intensive products).
2. Developing countries (Japan exporting capital-intensive products and importing labor-intensive products).
3. The Communist bloc (on the same pattern as in case 2).

It may thus be noted that the course of Japan's export trade is determined by the alternate action of the domestic economic trend and the international economic tendency. Let us take for example Japan's export trade with the United States before World War II. Before the war, raw silk was the virtual pillar of Japanese exports to the United States, but in 1963, textile products accounted for 10.8 per cent of the exports to the United States, with metal goods taking 22.2 per cent and machinery 18.0 per cent. Thus, Japanese exports to the United States have been more diversified, keeping pace with the change in the fundamental structure of the Japanese economy. Export products bound for the United States are still accounted for mostly by labor-intensive commodities. Even the machinery exported to the United States is largely durable consumer goods, not to be classified as full-fledged machinery. In Japan's total exports and imports, trade with the United States always accounts for about 30 per cent. The weight of the United States in Japan's trade became heavier after the war, balancing the loss of neighboring countries, notably Communist China, as major markets for Japan.

In contrast, Japan's trade with western Europe has been marking time under the impact of discriminating treatment to Japanese products. Average annual exports to the countries in the European Economic Community stand at around $1.00 per head (compared with the comparable average of $6.00 per head in exports to the United States). The future outlook of Japan's trade with western Europe, however, has become brighter, as more countries are ready to abolish the application of Article 35 under GATT.

The growth of Japan's exports to the developing countries has been rather slow, as these countries, because of foreign currency shortages, are asking for deferred payments for their purchase from abroad. In view of the trend of industrialization in the consumer goods field in developing countries, the possibility of increasing exports is becoming remote, other than that of more complex machinery and similar products, and hence the pattern of trade is likely to be modified to suit the needs of developing countries. Trade with the Communist bloc is still insignificant and accounts for only about 2 to 3 per cent of Japan's total exports.

The Japanese economy after the war was fostered under the protection of controlled imports. Now that Japan has been called upon to do her bit as a member of the free world, however, it has become necessary for this country to liberalize trade and exchange transactions. From about the time the countries in western Europe restored the convertibility of their currencies, business people in Japan envisaged the need to do the same on the part of Japan. The liberalization, which stood as low as 30 per cent in 1959, advanced to 44 per cent in 1960 and to 89 per cent in April 1963. Acceptance by Japan of the status of an Article 8 country under the charter of the International Monetary Fund allows further liberalization to take place.

Participation of Japan in the Organization for Economic Cooperation and Development (OECD) has been planned by the Japanese government to be coincidental with liberalization of capital transactions side by side with trade liberalization. As part of this liberalization program, Japan took steps in April 1963 to lift all restrictions on the remittance overseas of the principal of foreign investments in Japanese stocks.

Not only has the postwar mode of living of the urban population undergone swift change, but industry's needs for equipment also have changed and rationalization and modernization continue unabated. Under the circumstances, many opportunities are present for profitable foreign investment as is evidenced by the successful ventures in the past few years. We believe the Japanese economy, still young and expanding, has not in the least lost its vigor.

MAJOR PROBLEMS AT ISSUE

The Japanese economy, which recovered to the prewar level by
the first half of the 1950s, continues its remarkable growth. In
1961, Japan's national income reached about $39 billion, rank-
ing fifth in the free world and almost equal to that of France.
The gross national product (real income in goods and services)
was doubled during the seven years from fiscal 1955 through fiscal 1961, and the annual average growth rate was as high as 11
per cent. By virtue of the high economic growth, the per capita
national income also advanced from the 1952–1954 average of
$190 per annum to $341 in 1960 and to about $400 in 1961,
doubling in less than ten years. This increase ranks among the
highest in the world. However, the per capita national income is
still roughly only 50 per cent (or less) that of West Germany or
France.

The major indicators of the consumption level, such as the per
capita use of textiles, the ownership of television receivers, the
circulation of newspapers, and the number of movie-goers are already at the same level with their counterparts in advanced nations in Europe. The ownership of automobiles, however, is still
far lower, and the scarcity of so-called social capital investment,
such as housing and highways, is notable when compared with
other advanced nations.

As referred to elsewhere, the most important factor contributing to the remarkably high economic growth of Japan is found
in the extremely large capital investments in plant and equipment. The total volume of these capital investments in fiscal 1955
stood at $2,200 million, or only 10 per cent of the gross national
product. In the subsequent six years, however, such investments continued to expand at an annual rate of 32 per cent, and
they reached $11,200 million in fiscal 1961. In the same year, the
gross fixed assets formation, including housing construction and
public utilities investments, reached 35 per cent of the gross
national product. The comparable ratios in other countries are
about 15 per cent in Great Britain and the United States and
under 25 per cent in Italy and West Germany.

The continued and rapid increase in Japan's plant and equipment investments, even after the completion of postwar rehabilitation, was partially attributable to the effort of industry to catch up with the progress of current technological innovation. More fundamentally responsible, however, was the basic thinking among Japanese enterprisers that Japan would sooner or later be required to liberalize all trade and exchange, and that no time should be lost in regaining efficiency in order to cope with the intensified competition on the international market. Time after time, expansion of capacity in a particular industry was viewed with apprehension because of the possibility of overexpansion. But the expansion soon proved to be a timely move because the increase in demand far exceeded even the most optimistic estimates. Oil refineries, cold and hot steel strip mills, synthetic textiles, and other chemical plants are examples.

Meanwhile, there arose a problem of how to finance capital investment, which far exceeded industry's retained profits. The long-term capital market as such was almost nonexistent. As a result, the dependence of enterprises on bank loans intensified. In fiscal 1955, the ratios of internal (retained profits) and external financing (including funds raised through stock issues) were almost equally balanced. However, of investments aggregating $74,000 million during the period from fiscal 1955 through fiscal 1961, 40 per cent were from retained profits and 60 per cent represented funds from outside sources. Thus, the weight of external financing markedly increased. During the same period, 70 per cent of the external funds came from private monetary institutions, 20 per cent from new issues of stocks and bonds, and 10 per cent from the government. As the lion's share of the bonds was eventually purchased by private monetary institutions, the role played by these institutions has been extremely heavy.

The principal source of the funds supplied by the private monetary institutions was personal savings deposited with banks. The ratio of personal savings to the gross national product during the period from fiscal 1955 through fiscal 1962 was 12.5 per cent, far higher than the international average. The ratio of savings by wage earners, which stood as low as 2 per cent in 1951, gradually increased and reached 16 per cent in 1960, a level notably higher than the comparable figure of 8 per cent in the United States and about 3 per cent in Great Britain. The high personal savings rate in Japan, which is partially ascribable to the still undeveloped state of the social security system, may be considered traditional. It is an interesting fact that Japan, in the progress of the so-called consumption revolution, has been witnessing an annual increase in the personal savings rate while managing to elevate the level of personal consumption. The major part of personal savings was channeled to private monetary institutions as deposits because of the high credit standing of banks and the high rates of interest on deposits (for example, 5½ per cent on a one-year time deposit). Such deposits were mostly earmarked for loans to private enterprises and partially for purchases of bonds and stocks. Roughly speaking, 10 per cent of publicly owned stocks are in the hands of private commercial banks. In this manner, financing the high rate of growth of the economy was made possible without depending too much on foreign capital.

However, in spite of the increasing rate of savings, the demands of industry for credit sometimes exceeded the increase in the resources of banks. Hence, private monetary institutions, particularly commercial banks in big cities, were compelled to depend on borrowings from the Bank of Japan to raise part of the funds they supplied to enterprises. During the period from 1955 through 1962, loans by private monetary institutions increased by about $40,000 million. During the same period, loans from the Bank of Japan also rose by $2,800 million. This anomalous monetary structure, in which the grant of credit by private banks is in part covered by continued borrowings from the central bank, is criticized by some economists as an unsound practice. It should be remembered, however, that the Japanese government, unlike its British or United States counterparts, has had no budgetary deficit because the actual revenue has invariably exceeded the budget estimate. The budget has been more than balanced for the past few years. For this reason, banks carry few government bonds in their portfolios.

Although personal savings channeled through banks played

important roles in the remarkable economic growth of Japan, the encouragement of savings will continue to be a vital need for its further economic growth until it has reached a highly matured economic stage.

Let us consider the role of foreign capital. The ratio of loans to the industrial companies from overseas sources during the period from fiscal 1955 through fiscal 1962 was as low as about 4 per cent of the total external financing of capital investment. The major part of such foreign loans was earmarked chiefly for the four key industries of electric power, iron and steel, petroleum, and transportation. Hence, the weight of foreign capital in Japanese industries as a whole has been comparatively small. This was partly ascribable to the comparative rigor of Japanese restrictions on foreign capital investment. In view of the latest developments, such as Japan's entry into the Organization for Economic Cooperation and Development (OECD), as well as the increasing need of foreign capital for further economic growth and for assistance to developing countries, the Japanese government plans moderation of its restrictions on the import of foreign capital, including direct investments. Japan's overseas sales credit outstanding by exports on deferred payment terms reached $840 million as of the end of 1962. In Japan's induction of foreign capital so far, loans have been the principal formula. The effect of foreign investments in Japanese securities is still small.

Japan is not richly endowed in natural resources. Japan's population reached 95 million in 1962, whereas her territory is only 370,000 square meters. Therefore the population density is more than 250 per square kilometer. Considering the facts that Japan is extremely mountainous and that its arable land accounts for only 17.5 per cent of its territory, Japan ranks among the most densely populated countries in the world. Japan also is very poorly provided with underground resources such as iron, bauxite, and petroleum. The country is comparatively rich in coal resources, but mining conditions are extremely bad, and coking coal necessary for iron-steel making is produced only in small quantity. Animal and vegetable resources like raw cotton, wool, and crude rubber are nonexistent. Among the industrial nations of the world, Japan is the only country importing industrial salt from overseas sources. It lacks also adequate amounts of some cereals and sugar. It goes without saying that all these resources are indispensable for over-all economic growth. The high rate of economic growth of Japan has been made possible partly because of access to these raw materials from overseas after the war. The same need for imports is certain to continue in the future. Without heavy raw material imports, a satisfactory rate of economic growth is not possible. It is partly because of these facts that Japan advocates the promotion of free trade as a keynote of economic growth and wants to expand its national trade.

TABLE 1. JAPAN'S DEPENDENCE ON OVERSEAS SOURCES FOR KEY RAW MATERIALS

Material	1934–1936, Average, Per Cent	1960, Per Cent	1961, Per Cent
Rice	18.6	1.3	1.0
Wheat	24.4	63.6	59.6
Soybeans	64.0	77.5	75.0
Sugar	96.0	90.4	72.9
Coal	9.6	14.0	17.0
Crude oil	90.8	98.1	98.1
Iron ore	85.6	92.1	94.8
Phosphate rock	100.0	100.0	100.0
Bauxite	100.0	100.0	100.0
Raw cotton	100.0	100.0	100.0
Wool	100.0	100.0	100.0
Raw hides	67.5	53.7	55.3
Crude rubber	100.0	100.0	100.0
Salt	67.2	73.9	73.9

NOTE: Dependence rate $= \dfrac{\text{import volume}}{\text{domestic output} + \text{import volume}} \times 100.$

Although Japan is extremely poor in natural resources, its skilled or semiskilled labor force is still comparatively plentiful. Labor, therefore, is one of the major factors that supports the high rate of economic growth. The rate of population increase in Japan was around 1.3 per cent annually before the outbreak of World War II. Since the war, however, the birth rate has declined gradually, and the rate of population growth has gone down to the same level as that of other advanced nations in Europe, which is a rate of less than 1 per cent annually. The population of productive ages (fifteen years or more) has been increasing at a rate of about 2 per cent, or double the natural rate of increase, because of the decline of the death rate.

The employment structure comprises a large number of workers engaged in primary industries where per capita production is low, such as agriculture, forestry, fisheries. Until about 1950, nearly 50 per cent of the total number of the gainfully employed were in these primary industries. After 1950, some of these workers were absorbed by other fast-expanding sectors such as manufacturing and service businesses. They still account for over 30 per cent of the total number of the gainfully employed in 1961, the level being markedly higher than the comparable ratio of about 9 per cent in the United States and 4 per cent in Great Britain.

In advanced countries in Europe and America, it is understood that the scarcity of labor supply has been a major deterrent to economic growth. But in Japan, a reservoir of labor is sufficiently flexible to supply manpower through transfer to a higher productivity sector. Therefore, we may expect that a relatively high rate of economic growth is feasible until a state of full employment is reached, as in the case of the advanced countries in Europe.

It should also be noted that Japanese workers are capable of attaining and exercising certain high-level technical skills because the general level of education in this country stands relatively high compared to that of many nations. The educational program adopted since the Meiji era is a noteworthy achievement. The government has established a new program for further replenishing the supply of technicians by education, in order to cope with the intensification of the demand for technical skills.

Japan ranks fifth or sixth in the world in population. By virtue of the big market potentialities within the country, most modern Japanese industries that operate on a large scale will continue to prosper.

Parallel with the swift economic development and the progress

of trade liberalization, Japan's foreign trade has increased year
by year. In the past ten years, the amount of Japan's trade has
nearly trebled. In 1963, Japanese exports reached $5,452 million
(f.o.b.) and its imports attained $6,736 million (c.i.f.). The an-
nual average rate of increase from 1952 through 1963 stood at 15.6
per cent for exports and 10 per cent for imports, both far eclipsing the average rate of increase of a little over 4 per cent for the
export-import total of the free world during the same period. As
a result, Japan's share of the total exports and imports of the free
world advanced from 1.5 per cent in exports and 2.4 per cent in
imports in 1951 to 3.9 per cent and 4.3. per cent, respectively, in
1962. This is not, however, a particularly large share if compared
with the prewar (1938) equivalents of 5.3 per cent in exports and
4.5 per cent in imports.

Let us compare next the movement of Japan's trade in relation
to its national income; that is, from the standpoint of its dependence on trade. Japan's dependence on trade before World War
II (1934–1936 average) reached 22 to 23 per cent of GNP in
both exports and imports. Japan's postwar trade started with her
exports and imports at the low level of about 1 per cent each.
After the postwar reopening of trade, Japan's dependence on
trade increased at a swift pace until about 1950, but thereafter
slowed down. Dependence on exports stood at around 12 to 13
per cent. Dependence on imports stabilized at about 13 to 15 per
cent, except in 1951 and 1957 (because of the Korean War and the
Suez crisis, respectively). The fact that the dependence on trade
failed to increase in these years, despite the high rate of increase
of 11 to 12 per cent for both exports and imports, was due to the
equally high rate of increase of national income at 12 per cent
per annum.

In a fast-growing economy, the problem is always how to maintain equilibrium in the balance of international payments. The
rate by which imports grow is likely to exceed the rate by which
exports increase. In the case of Japan in recent years, however,
the rate of dependence on imports has been stabilized at about
13 to 15 per cent of GNP, which is markedly lower than the prewar level. The main reason may be found in the changing post-

war pattern of Japan's industrial structure. To put it more precisely, the cotton industry, which used to occupy a very important place in the prewar Japanese economy, began to recede, and the pivot of industry shifted to heavy and chemical industries, which produce far more added-value products. As a result, imports of raw cotton, the pillar of prewar imports, perceptibly decreased. By virtue of the growth of diversified industries, the imports of finished and semifinished products, such as ammonium sulfate, paper, pulp, iron and steel, and glass also declined. It should not be overlooked either that self-sufficiency in the rice crop, due to the progress in agricultural techniques, is also responsible for the decline in Japan's dependence on imports. On the other hand, the import of raw materials for the heavy and chemical industries (such as iron ore, coking coal, and petroleum), complex machinery for modernized equipment, and food for the increasing demand from dairy farming have all contributed to the increased dependence on imports. As a whole, however, factors working for the decline of this dependence have been stronger. Japan's dependence on exports is self-explanatory in that it must earn foreign exchange in order to pay for heavy import requirements.

Meanwhile, the importance of the domestic market increased steadily after World War II, owing to higher living standards which require diversified consumer goods. As a result, the rate of dependence on exports in manufacturing industries stabilized at a comparatively low level. In summary, the decline in Japan's dependence on exports has apparently been due to the lesser dependence on imports.

Productivity in Japan increased at a rate of 7.6 per cent annually from 1953 through 1959, thus eclipsing the 5.5 per cent annual increase in the rate of wages in the same period. The wage cost per unit of production declined at an annual rate of 1.8 per cent. During the same period, the wage cost increased in most advanced countries, such as Great Britain, West Germany, the United States, and France. How, then, will Japan's dependence on international trade fare in the future? The rate of Japan's dependence on imports will probably tend gradually upward. The major reasons are: (1) Japan decided to adopt the policy of total liberalization of trade as a principle by shifting to the status of an Article 11 country under the General Agreement on Tariffs and Trade (GATT) as of February 1963. As a consequence, the specialization of labor is bound to make further progress in Japan; (2) the hobbies and leisure pursuits of the Japanese people are destined to become more diversified, paralleling a further rise in consumer spending. Imports of consumer goods are therefore likely to increase; and (3) for the benefit of consumers, it will become necessary to replace by imports the domestically produced raw materials and food items whose prices are higher than the prices of these products in international trade. This step will also be essential for Japan's further cooperation with the developing countries.

Two major factors may contribute to the future decrease of imports: an advance in the rate of self-sufficiency in producing industrial products, due to further technological advances, and a decline in the consumption of imported raw materials for the production of manufactured products. These factors, however, are offset by the aforementioned opposite factors, which are likely to contribute to the rising tendency of imports. Under the "income doubling program" drafted by the Japanese government in 1960, the rate of dependence on imports in the fiscal year 1970 has been tentatively estimated at a little over 16 per cent; that is, between the average of 14.1 per cent in the base period (fiscal 1956 through 1958) and the prewar level of 23 per cent. This target is considered reasonably acceptable.

To achieve a balance in international payments, increasing imports should be offset by a corresponding increase in exports. The problem at issue is the fact that Japan's invisible trade balance stands in the red. Japan's payments overseas for technical know-how, royalties, and profits from foreign investments in Japan are large, while her income from foreign tourism is not necessarily high after Japanese spending for overseas travel has been deducted. Receipts of freight in international trade, which was a big source of invisible income in the prewar period, have now reversed and are falling short in spite of the fact that the country has rebuilt more than 7 million tons of merchant shipping since the end of World War II. Japan has already experienced a payments balance crisis on more than three occasions in the past. From the standpoint of planning the national economy, an increase in plant and equipment investment as large as that witnessed from 1955 through 1962 (an annual increase of 25.6 per cent) cannot be expected in the future. Under the circumstances, therefore, the significance of export trade as a cardinal stimulant to economic growth is clear.

What, then, is the future outlook of Japan's export trade? The growth of Japan's export trade after the war has been largely ascribable to the postwar recovery of her competitive power, based on an advantageous lower wage cost and increased productivity. There is no denying, however, that the efficacy of these incentives has been steadily waning. Now that some seventeen years have elapsed since the termination of the war, the postwar recovery urge has ceased to exist. The rising tempo of wages is threatening to eclipse the rising pace of labor productivity. In producing those products that are more labor-intensive, in which Japan used to specialize, her superiority is diminishing because of the advance of developing countries in the same fields.

On the other hand, by virtue of the fast progress of technological know-how, new export specialities have emerged from among metal products, machinery, electronics, and chemicals. For instance, in the limelight of Japan's export products in recent years, there are cameras, motor bicycles, ships, transistor radio receivers, television sets, synthetic fibers, automobiles, and industrial machinery. Japan's exports of steel products have also been increasing at an encouraging pace.

The ratio of "heavy and chemical industrial products," including the aforementioned articles in the total volume of Japanese exports, advanced to 40 per cent in 1952 from 21 per cent in 1938 and rose further to 47 per cent in 1961. This ratio is still low compared with that of other advanced industrial countries. For instance, the ratio had already passed 40 per cent in West Germany, Great Britain, and the United States before the war, and now stands at more than 50 per cent in these countries. Particu-

larly noteworthy is the high ratio of about 70 per cent attained
by Great Britain and West Germany, which suffer from the same
shortages of natural resources as Japan. Japan is hoping that her
export structure may steadily approach the British or West German pattern because of the increase of exports in heavy and
chemical products. On the basis of this possibility, the government, in its "income doubling program," has raised the estimated share of heavy and chemical products in the total volume
of exports in 1970 to more than 53 per cent.

In Japan's effort to increase her exports, discriminating import
restrictions by some advanced nations, such as the application of
Article 35 of GATT, have been presenting major problems. With
the progress of Japan's trade liberalization, however, such restrictions have been gradually moderated, a tendency highly encouraging to Japan's export trade. On the other hand, Japan needs to
increase its cooperation with the developing countries by purchasing their primary products and by extending loans in order
to strengthen the purchasing power of these countries.

There are still some problems that Japan must solve to continue her economic growth. The first problem is the need of
stabilizing prices. Wholesale prices in major Western countries
have been tending upward in recent years. In Japan, wholesale
prices have been comparatively stabilized since 1952. Chiefly responsible for the wholesale price stability in Japan are the increases
in manufacturing capacity and labor productivity. In contrast, the
consumer price index in Japan has been increasing almost at the
same pace as that in Western countries. This phenomenon may
be partially inevitable because wage levels in service professions,
small businesses, and agriculture, all closely affiliated with consumer spending and lower than normal levels, are being steadily
improved. The rise of consumer prices, however, may discourage
the practice of saving to which Japanese consumers in general are
traditionally attached. With a lower rate of savings, there may be
an eventual diminution in the financial resources required for
the future economic growth of Japan. Hence, it is considered
necessary to take proper measures to curb any sharp price increases in the future.

The second problem is the urgent need of replenishing Japan's social capital investment, including such projects as highways, harbors, water supplies, drainage, land conservation facilities, housing, and public parks. Compared with other advanced countries, Japan's replenishment of social capital is notably belated. The rate of increase in paved roads in Japan is less than one-third of the corresponding rate in the United States, France, and Italy. The ratio of public streets in the total area of a city is as low as 12 to 13 per cent in key cities such as Tokyo, Kyoto, and Yokohama, compared with 30 to 40 per cent in New York and Vienna and more than 20 per cent in Paris and London. The area of parks in Tokyo per capita is only about 10 to 20 per cent of that in Paris and New York. Japan also lies in the path of seasonal typhoons, and yearly flood damage is usually heavy.

In the process of postwar recovery, it was natural that investments would be concentrated on private plants and equipment directly contributive to production. But, if such investments in plants and equipment were to increase to a point where they created an imbalance with public investments, the deficiency in public facilities would restrict economic activity and also create difficult problems for industry. Hence, it is necessary in the future to build social capital step by step while paying close attention to the trend of business.

This chapter has studied the progress of the Japanese economy in relation to capital, natural resources, labor, and foreign trade. Although poor in natural resources and slow to enter the international trade arena, Japan has succeeded in achieving economic growth in the face of many obstacles. But her position has not fully matured, and both government and industry are eager to work for a further growth in the society of free nations. Japan's desire for world peace, the advancement of her economy by earnest endeavor, her technological progress and international cooperation, all augur continuance of her economic growth in the years to come.

CHAPTER 7

Latin America[1]

Felipe Herrera

THE SITUATION

In order to outline the Latin-American situation, one must recognize that there are profound differences between the countries of the region and even between different parts of a given country. The averages used in describing the Latin-American situation are, in many ways, only a mathematical abstraction that obscures the actual situation of a region characterized by unevenness and contrast. This unevenness is both a cause and effect of underdevelopment. The differences that can be readily appreciated in any highly developed country are even more marked in Latin America. Thus, for example, the difference between the level of per capita income in the poorest state of the United States, Mississippi, and the richest, Delaware, is 150 per cent. In some Latin-American countries the difference in per

[1] This chapter is not intended to be an exhaustive analysis of broad economic problems and policies. Its purposes are: (1) to describe the present situation of underdevelopment in Latin America by indicating, somewhat arbitrarily, a few of the many characteristics that, to a large extent, are applicable to all countries in the area; (2) to point out some of the factors involved in the economic *problem* of the area; (3) to venture some opinions concerning various possible *solutions;* and (4) to indicate the *role of the Inter-American Development Bank* in putting solutions into practice.

capita income between states or provinces is sometimes as high as 1000 or 1200 per cent.

It would be simple to continue indefinitely pointing out differences between the countries of Latin America, a region where diversity seems to be the rule rather than the exception. But it cannot be denied that beneath these differences is a common historical and cultural heritage manifested in a similarity of economic problems.

One characteristic of all Latin-American countries is a *high rate of population growth.* The population of the region increases each year at a rate of 2.6 per cent, the highest of any area in the world. In the United States the population grows at a rate of 1.7 per cent per year; in western Europe, 0.6 per cent; and in central Africa, 1.4 per cent. In 1850 Latin America had 33 million inhabitants; by 1962 it had 210 million. Twenty years earlier, the population of Latin America was already greater than that of the United States, and by 1955 it had surpassed the combined population of the United States and Canada. At this rate, Latin America will double its population in the next 27 years, whereas the United States will take 47 years; central Africa, 50 years; and Europe, 115 years.

One of the most interesting features of Latin America's population is the high percentage of young persons, which results in a high average rate of dependency. In 1960 more than 40 per cent of the population was less than fifteen years old. As a favorable development factor, it may be said that the massive incorporation of young persons into the labor force facilitates adaptation to economic change, but on the other hand, it also requires a continuous economic expansion to make possible full employment. Moreover, this spilling over of new generations into a region that is already facing deficits in housing and schools, sanitation, and hospitals, and which is characterized by primitive agricultural methods or inadequate food production, will undoubtedly retard development and make it necessary to adopt farsighted and vigorous measures so that the increasing social pressures will not have serious consequences.

It should be noted that the population explosion in Latin

America has effects completely different from those in any other region. This explosion is negative in that it forces the region to absorb investment and resources in meeting requirements that rise uncontrollably. But man himself is the first and foremost factor in progress if his efforts are coordinated within a technological, cultural, and sociological environment conducive to proper exploitation of natural resources. This is borne out by the experience of the United States and Europe after their rapid population increase in the nineteenth century.

In this connection it should be mentioned that six countries—Brazil, Argentina, Mexico, Venezuela, Colombia, and Chile, named in the order of their contribution—account for 87 per cent of the gross domestic product of Latin America and that these six countries have 76 per cent of the region's population. The other fourteen countries, with 24 per cent of the population, contribute 13 per cent of the gross domestic product.

Another population characteristic of the region is the high percentage of rural inhabitants. Despite the rapid rate of urbanization—unfortunately not always a direct result of industrialization—more than 50 per cent of the Latin-American population lives in the rural areas, which contrasts with 30 per cent in the United States and Canada. This high proportion of rural inhabitants is reflected in the distribution of active population among the various sectors of activity. From estimates based on the 1950 census, it may be assumed that 50 per cent of the population is engaged in farming, 1 per cent in mining, 16 per cent in industry, 4 per cent in construction, and 29 per cent in other activities. In comparing the distribution of the labor force with the contribution of the various sectors to the total gross product of the region, we arrive at another cause of disequilibrium that must be removed, both for economic and social reasons, namely, the extremely low productivity of this agricultural and livestock sector. Actually, 50 per cent of the active population is employed in the rural sector, but generates only 20 per cent of the gross domestic product. Per capita productivity is 3.8 times greater in industry and 15 times greater in mining and petroleum than in farming and cattle raising.

The *per capita gross product* also places the Latin-American countries in the underdeveloped category. In 1960 per capita income[2] was $366, or approximately one-eighth of what it was in the United States ($2,976), less than one-fifth of Canada's and very close to the Japanese per capita income ($376 in 1959). Here, too, there are notable differences between countries of the area. While Venezuela's gross per capita domestic product is more than $1,000 and Argentina's is about $600, Bolivia's is less than $100. More than 100 million Latin Americans exist at a bare subsistence level and exercise no effect on demand. As stated, this marginalism is largely the result of low productivity in the agricultural and livestock sector and of unequal distribution of the income structure, which must be improved not only for imperative reasons of social justice but also as a prerequisite for sustained and self-nourishing growth.

Another characteristic of the present social and economic situation in Latin America is the predominance, within the *social structure* of all the countries except Argentina and Uruguay, of "narrowly based pyramids" in which the middle classes are small in number and importance. In this context, social and economic contrasts are sharper and class differences or antagonisms more pronounced. According to available information, the Latin-American middle classes are less than 20 per cent of the total population. Furthermore, the middle class, particularly in its dependent groups, is not consolidated as such and has no class consciousness. The absence of a well-defined middle class not only weakens the stability of a society thus torn between two widely disparate and excessively antagonistic forces, but also hampers the necessary vertical mobility of a mass of population that is stirred by the demonstration effect, cohesively organized (at least in the urban sector), and struggling to rise in the social scale. The resulting sense of frustration is what underlies the explosiveness of the Latin-American social picture. In many countries, even in those where no important social revolution has taken place, the masses are bursting into the arenas of political power even before they are fully incorporated into the system of production and con-

2 Quoted in U.S. dollars.

sumption, where they might turn the "revolution of rising expectations" into a peaceful reality.

It must be stressed, however, that a highly positive element within the complex process of Latin-American development is the emergence of what has been termed the *entrepreneurial class,* composed of capable and dynamic businessmen who are seeking a new economic order more in tune with the technological and social exigencies of our times. Thanks to their forward thrust, we are witnessing the gradual disappearance of the entire scale of obsolete values and ineffectual production systems inherent in both the conservative oligarchies and the traditional type of improvised entrepreneur whose only asset was raw intuition or political protection and favor. Also, the appearance of responsible labor leaders, particularly in the urban proletariat, is bringing the workers into active participation in promoting economic and social development.

Another common characteristic of the Latin-American countries is the important role of *international trade* in their growth process. Actually, this trade is far more important than its volume would seem to indicate. In many cases the foreign trade of a developing country represents 20 per cent or more of its gross national product. In the United States, on the other hand, it accounts for only 8 per cent. Generally speaking, the dynamic sectors of a developing economy are those that are export-oriented. A large variety of essential articles cannot be produced economically because of the limitations of domestic markets; that is why such economies traditionally import many manufactured goods for consumption as well as production. These conditions give rise to dependence on foreign trade for two reasons: first, because exports are of prime importance in determining the degree of economic activity; and second, because exports are an essential means of obtaining the necessary foreign currency with which to pay for imports. We may even speak of a third reason for the dependence on foreign trade, since in many cases import and export duties are the chief source of the tax revenues required by a country to finance investments in the public sector. This is precisely the case in all countries of Latin America, where foreign trade is a basic element of economic life.

This extreme dependence on foreign trade accounts for the vulnerability of the Latin-American economy. As we shall see, the region's internal sector, as presently constituted, does not provide the necessary means for activating development, which can therefore be disrupted by outside forces beyond its control. Consequently, one of the many vicious deterrents involved in underdevelopment is the absence of independent means for rising above it. Underdevelopment is a manifestation of dependence.

The Problem

In the preceding section an attempt has been made to outline the Latin-American situation, describing some of its basic realities that are reflected to a greater or lesser degree in problems common throughout the region. This section will take up the causes of backwardness.

There are few leaders in Latin America today who question the need for deep and extensive change in the social and economic structure. There is a clear awareness that the chronic state of poverty is not inevitable and does not arise from a shortage of exploitable resources but from the persistence of obsolete systems of production and social organization. Without underestimating the importance of social, political, cultural, technological, and other factors whose effective interplay is essential to optimum utilization of available resources, this discussion will be limited to the problem arising from the structure of production and international trade. Unless this structure can be wisely reoriented, it will not be possible to start and accelerate a sustained process of economic and social development.

The two world wars and the great intervening depression not only destroyed a number of fallacious notions such as that of indefinite and automatic progress, but also brought into question a scale of values and concepts patiently elaborated by the optimistic thinkers of the nineteenth century. One concept that fell by the wayside was that of the international division of labor, according to which some countries were expected to specialize in the production and export of raw materials while others were to engage primarily in manufacturing and exporting more finished products. After the "preestablished harmony" of international trade had been shattered in the clash of arms, humanity began seeking other schemes to regulate international trade. This search led to truly revolutionary changes in the patterns of world trade. It is not necessary to stress the importance of such developments as the European Common Market, the European Economic Community, the COMECON of the socialist countries, or the United States Trade Expansion Act.

Latin-American countries have not been indifferent to the establishment of this international order, as witnessed by the bold attempt of the Central American countries to expand their limited geoeconomic horizons through the creation of a common market and by the promising actions already taken by the Latin-American Free Trade Association. It is not difficult to visualize, in the not too distant future, the existence of a formidable trade association as the expression of a philosophy of international cooperation, equally providing for the increasing prosperity of the highly industrialized countries and the legitimate progressive aspirations of the underdeveloped nations. The World Conference on Trade and Development has aroused the hope of many who consider it an opportunity to establish a new order in international trade. These expectations find fertile ground in the Latin-American countries, since one of the fundamental external causes of their stagnation lies in the unfavorable terms of their international trade.

First of all, it should be considered that Latin America has the lowest rate of commercial development of any region in the world. From 1953 to 1961, world trade rose by 70 per cent. In those years, the commerce of the industrialized countries increased by 85.3 per cent, that of the nonindustrialized countries by 30.7 per cent, and Latin America's by only 13.2 per cent. And what is worse, the outlook for the future, far from being promising, points to an even further reduction in Latin America's already declining share in world trade as a result of a possible loss of traditional markets.

The continuing decline in Latin America's trade is readily understandable if it is borne in mind that its exports are largely composed of primary products. In 1959 and 1960 the exports of seven Latin-American countries (Argentina, Brazil, Mexico, Chile, Peru, Colombia, and Venezuela), which accounted for 81 per cent of all Latin-American exports in those years, showed the following breakdown by principal categories: fuel, 34.6 per cent; other raw materials, 19.6 per cent; and foodstuffs, 34.4 per cent. One reason for the vulnerability of the region's exports is that the consumption of raw materials in the industrialized countries increases, not in direct proportion but in inverse ratio to their economic growth. This is the case in the United States, which receives 50 per cent of Latin America's exports and where the ratio between the consumption of raw materials and the gross national product declined from 8.19 per cent in 1926–1928 to 7.13 per cent in 1955–1957 and is expected to drop to 6.3 per cent by 1980.

The decreasing Latin-American share in international trade is also attributable to the low-income elasticity of the demand for raw materials, particularly foodstuffs. Western Europe, which absorbs 30 per cent of those exports, has contributed substantially to their decline through its zealous efforts to protect its agricultural production, by employing a variety of substitutes for natural raw materials, and by granting preferential treatment to African and Asian products. The slow rate of growth or actual decline of the raw materials market and the unfavorable supply and demand relationship are responsible for the fluctuations affecting the volume and value of trade in those products. From 1957 to 1961 the index of raw materials and foodstuff prices declined 12 per cent. As a result, the per capita value of Latin-American exports, at constant 1950 prices, dropped from $58 in 1930 to $39 in 1960. Statistics also reveal an unfavorable trend in the relationship between the prices of raw materials and those of manufactured goods. In the 1953–1959 period alone, terms of trade deteriorated by 21 per cent.

The harmful effects of these fluctuations vary according to the term on which we project them. Price fluctuations, often as high as 20 per cent from one year to the next, have negative repercussions, particularly in the short run: They endanger financial stability, they interfere with the continuity of development policies, and they discourage the investments so sorely needed to increase the volume of exports. In addition, they can result in cycles of overproduction and consequent oversupply, which in turn brings down prices.

But the external strangulation of the Latin-American economy is, in the last analysis, a long-term problem, namely, the deterioration of the terms of trade, which limits the capacity to import. The needs for imported equipment, machinery, or raw materials indispensable for maintaining or accelerating the economic development process can be properly satisfied only if the volume of export earnings can be increased. Otherwise it becomes necessary to contract additional debts, as Latin America has been doing in recent years.

Actually, suppliers' credits and short-term financing have increased substantially since 1958 and debt payments have also increased, not only in absolute terms but also in relation to the value of exports. In 1955, according to figures compiled by the Development Assistance Committee (DAC), 7.4 per cent of all exports from the European countries to Latin America were financed on short terms and through suppliers' credits. In 1962 the figure increased to 14.5 per cent. Moreover, the outstanding foreign public debt on long-terms increased in 1961 to some $8 billion. The two principal debtors were Brazil ($2,250 million) and Argentina ($1,500 million). According to information from the International Monetary Fund, the service on those debts, at the end of 1961, was equivalent to 28.8 per cent of the value of all exports of goods and services in the case of Brazil and to 20.3 per cent for Argentina.

Since the debt-servicing capacity of many countries in the region has dropped to dangerously low levels that seriously impair their capacity to import, there appears to be no reasonable alternative, if the growth rate is to be maintained or accelerated, but to diversify the external sector in order to make it more dynamic and less vulnerable. In addition to the "spontaneous" factors leading to a growing deterioration of the terms of trade, to the detriment of raw-material exporting countries, the industrial countries have adopted a number of measures restricting or blocking the access of Latin America's products to their national markets.

It would be impossible, in this limited space, to analyze all the internal factors retarding the development of Latin America. Consequently, only two factors will be mentioned and these are intimately related to the problems being discussed: the narrow limitations of individual national markets and the pattern of production, which in the 1956–1960 period showed a total of $31.6 billion for the primary and secondary sectors combined, of which $17.0 billion was accounted for by raw materials.

POSSIBLE SOLUTIONS

Notwithstanding the usefulness of programs designed to compensate short-term fluctuations and thereby alleviate the problems inherent in development, full economic progress can be attained only through a basic transformation of the pattern of Latin-American production. The experience of the United States in this regard is highly illustrative. In the same way that the English colonies rebelled against their status as mere raw material suppliers for the mother country and began to produce and export manufactured goods, the Latin-American countries must also undertake the task of industrialization, for the position of mere exporters of raw materials and importers of manufactured goods is incompatible with the needs of an accelerated economic and social development.

It is obvious that industrialization requires a radical change in the pattern of their foreign trade. With regard to exports, they must offer a greater variety of products, including a growing proportion of manufactured or semimanufactured goods, in order to increase the value of their exportable natural resources. As far as imports are concerned, Latin-American industry must supply a larger proportion of each country's consumer goods requirements and must expand and diversify the production of capital goods.

Such a trend is already evident in the increasing local production of beverages, canned goods, cement, textiles, and similar products in Latin America.

In mentioning the restrictive measures imposed by the countries of western Europe, we have stated that the European Common Market has created serious problems for Latin-American trade by establishing a common tariff for imports from other parts of the world and by extending preferential treatment to the former European colonies. The common tariff for some Latin-American export items was established initially at a very high level: 80 per cent for sugar, 16 per cent for coffee, and 20 per cent for bananas, to mention only a few examples. The principle governing the import of agricultural products (that is, the imposition of variable duties that automatically placed the price of the imported products at a slightly higher level than that for the corresponding domestic products) has created concern in Latin America because of its possible adverse effect on Latin-American exports. A noteworthy departure from this rule was the reduction of the coffee tariff from 16 to 9.6 per cent.

Many responsible European circles are discussing the possibility of attenuating the negative effects of the Common Market on Latin America. The two specific alternatives now being discussed are the elimination or reduction of taxes on the consumption of certain Latin-American products and the reduction of the import tariff. In this connection, multilateral negotiations might be of mutual benefit to exporters and importers. It might also favor the consuming public in Europe, which now finds it necessary to consume a much smaller amount of the products most seriously effected by taxes or duties, including, particularly, processed goods, which are subject to a higher rate of customs duty than the raw materials used in their manufacture. Expanded opportunities for selling Latin-American products on the European markets would correspondingly increase Latin America's import capacity, and the benefits would therefore be mutual.

While conducting negotiations to soften restrictions on trade, it is also essential to alter the composition and destination of exports. In changing its geographic trade pattern so as to counteract to some extent the adverse effect of the deterioration of certain traditional markets, Latin America must intensify its efforts to establish commercial relations with those regions that have shown a relatively high growth rate, such as the socialist countries. But it would not be reasonable for the Latin-American countries to attempt to gain possible markets in the farthest reaches of the world while at the same time to continue to overlook its own regional market. In so doing, it would be turning its back on its own interests, for its own market, consisting of more than 200 million inhabitants, could be a valuable instrument of economic development.

Actually, as the Latin-American countries find it necessary to combat the external causes of their development gap by proceeding from the production of consumers goods through successive stages of intermediate and capital goods production, they inevitably discover that the limited size of their domestic markets is a sharply restrictive factor. While differing on other items, private entrepreneurs and economic development planners in Latin America unanimously agree that unless the limited national markets can be consolidated, it will not be feasible to encourage key sectors, such as the production of machine tools, construction equipment, chemicals and petrochemicals, locomotives, ships, turbines, and many other capital goods. The relative breadth of the market in Brazil, Mexico, and Argentina was surely a decisive factor in the more rapid industrialization of those countries.

Unfortunately, the countries with small populations have not even been able to advance to the stage of producing substitutes for traditional imports of consumer goods. In most of them, the limited size of the domestic market is accompanied by a static social structure and an inadequate distribution of income, which further diminishes the effective market because a large part of the population has no influence at all on demand. Intraregional trade would not only strengthen the economies of the region, but would also lead to important modifications in the sluggish social structures. It may thus be said that the only possible way of coping with the problem of saturated national markets is to broaden the frontiers of trade, thus expanding the possibilities of investment and industrial production by establishing free trade among the Latin-American countries. In this way, they could also begin to seek in their own environment a solution to two of the problems most seriously hampering the development of the area: (1) modification of the pattern of production by processing their own raw materials; and (2) gaining new markets through the establishment, over a period of years, of a Latin-American common market.

In the past ten or more years, efforts have been under way to establish such a market. In 1960, as an initial step, the Central American Common Market and the Latin-American Free Trade Association were created. *The Central American Common Market* includes Costa Rica, El Salvador, Guatemala, Honduras, and Nicaragua, with a combined population of 11 million and a combined gross national product of $2.2 billion. The member countries are making definite progress toward economic unification. Free trade is already applicable to 90 per cent of all articles, and a common customs tariff for outside imports, now being developed, will be put into effect around 1966. The considerable increase in intra-Central American trade has brought a substantial improvement in highways and roads. A regional highway plan is being considered, and the improvement of existing roads has continued.

Central American integration has political as well as economic implications. There are historical and geographic reasons for this, since the five Central American countries were once integral parts of a single political unit. The final objective of integration is the reunification of the five countries in one great Central American community. This background, as well as the fact that integration has been under way since 1951, explains why the process is proceeding more rapidly in Central America than in the rest of Latin America. It should also be noted that industrialization, while not uniform in all Central American countries, is in the preliminary stages throughout the region, which permits greater flexibility because regional industries can be planned without affecting established facilities.

Intraregional trade has grown at a considerable rate and over a sufficiently long period to demonstrate clearly the impact of closer collaboration and customs tariff reductions. The value of intra-Central American trade increased from $8.3 million in 1950 to $37.4 million in 1961 and is estimated at $47 million for 1962. The share of intraregional trade in the total commerce of the Central American countries has also increased. In 1950, trade between the member countries accounted for 3.6 per cent of all imports and for 2.9 per cent of all exports. In 1961, the percentages rose to 7.6 per cent and 8.3 per cent, respectively. The volume of intra-Central American trade has also increased substantially, from 75,000 tons in 1956 to 158,000 tons in 1960. These figures relate to overland traffic by truck, which accounts for a very high proportion of all trade between the Central American countries.

The integration of Central America is being carried out within a legal and financial framework that is truly impressive, including the Organization of Central American States, the Permanent General Secretariat for Integration, the Central American Bank for Economic Integration, and the Central American Clearing House. Regional cooperation has now been extended to the academic level, embracing such aspects as higher education, training in the fields of agriculture and animal husbandry, sanitation and plague control, and scientific and technological research, to mention only a few fields of activity.

At the meeting of the late President Kennedy with the Presidents of the Central American countries and Panama, in San Jose, Costa Rica, additional measures to further the unification of the Isthmus were announced. The most important measures for immediate implementation were: (1) acceleration of the program of integration; (2) establishment of a customs union within the present decade; (3) establishment of a payments union by 1970; (4) commencement of negotiations with Panama for its entry as an associate member; and (5) acceptance of regional planning. The nine signatory countries of the Treaty of Montevideo, which established the *Latin-American Free Trade Association* (LAFTA), have 82 per cent of Latin America's population and more than 80 per cent of its gross national product.

LAFTA includes Argentina, Brazil, Chile, Colombia, Ecuador, Mexico, Paraguay, Peru, and Uruguay, and will welcome the membership of any other Latin-American country that will accept the conditions set forth in the Treaty of Montevideo. Venezuela has expressed a desire for membership, and both its government and the private sector in that country are considering the relative advantages of such a step, as well as the conditions of membership.

The members of LAFTA have agreed to establish a system of free trade among themselves within a period of twelve years, after which they will consider the possibility of creating a Latin-American common market. The tariff reductions are determined in yearly multilateral negotiations, each of which should result in a reduction of not less than 8 per cent. Two such conferences have already taken place, one in Montevideo (1961) and the other in Mexico City (1962); they have approved tariff concessions covering some 7,000 articles with a total tariff reduction of more than 30 per cent. These reductions became effective in January 1962, and their results since then indicate a trend that should pick up speed as trade relationships are established and national and foreign businessmen take advantage of the opportunities provided by the tariff reductions.

According to preliminary estimates, intraregional trade in 1962 showed an increase of 20 per cent over 1961. What is more, there has been a considerable diversification of trade, particularly in manufactured articles. Argentina's exports to the other LAFTA countries increased 39 per cent. Mexico's exports (of which 70 per cent were manufactured goods) increased 112 per cent and its imports from LAFTA by 48 per cent; Peru's exports rose 60 per cent and its imports by 53 per cent. The volume of trade between Mexico and Brazil rose so spectacularly, from 3,000 tons in 1961 to 54,000 tons in 1962, that it permitted the establishment of a steamship line to provide regular service between those two countries.

Although trade between the members of LAFTA is relatively small in absolute terms and represents less than 10 per cent of their total trade, the results of the first year of free trade exceeded the most optimistic expectations and showed beyond any doubt that it is perfectly possible to increase and diversify regional trade. The private sector quickly awakened to the growing possibilities offered by integration. Latin-American industrialists, bankers, and businessmen in general who are associated with international trade are seeking new formulas for mutual cooperation and the exchange of views. A Latin-American manufacturers' association was recently established by representatives of the nine member countries of LAFTA. Regional organizations have been set up by specific industrial or financial sectors, such as drug, beer and glassware manufacturers, steel industrialists, and insurance companies. Closer cooperation now exists between the steamship companies, commercial airlines, and private banks.

Both the United States and the Latin-American countries have recognized the absolute need for combined efforts to establish the Latin-American common market, realizing that vast expansion of the hitherto splintered markets will help to promote the investments necessary to further the industrial development of the region. This common purpose was reaffirmed in the following passage from the Charter of Punta del Este:

In the application of resources under the Alliance for Progress, special attention should be given not only to investments for multinational projects that will contribute to strengthening the integration process in all its aspects, but also to the necessary financing of industrial production, and to the growing expansion of trade in industrial products within Latin America. . . .

In working toward economic integration and complementary economies, efforts should be made to achieve an appropriate coordination of national plans, or to engage in joint planning for various economies through the existing regional integration organizations. Efforts should also be made to promote an investment policy directed to the progressive elimination of unequal growth rates in the different geographic areas, particularly in the case of countries which are relatively less developed. . . .

When groups of Latin American countries have their own institutions for financing economic integration, the financing should preferably be channeled through these institutions. With respect to regional financing designed to further purposes of existing regional integration instruments, the cooperation of the Inter-American Development Bank should be sought in channeling extra-regional contributions which may be granted for these purposes.

How will Latin-American economic integration affect United States trade with the region? As Latin-American economic integration proceeds, a number of phenomena will become evident. In the first place, there will be a substantial increase in the volume and variety of intraregional trade, strengthening the tendency already observable in Central America and in the LAFTA countries. In other words, there will be a substitution of imports as Latin America produces articles to replace its previous imports from the rest of the world. At the same time, change will take place in the composition of trade between Latin America and other parts of the world. With respect to imports, smaller quantities of consumer goods will be bought abroad, while larger quantities of capital goods and specialized equipment will be required for the completion of social capital projects essential for development and for the establishment and expansion of regional industries. With regard to exports, there is every indication that the supply will be more diversified, with a higher percentage of manufactured or semimanufactured products and a smaller percentage of raw materials.

At first glance, it would seem that the effects of integration (fewer imports and greater competition in other export markets) would be detrimental to the interests of the United States. But this is not the case. The replacement of imports is inherent in development and would inevitably occur whether or not integration took place. Very few underdeveloped countries can afford the luxury of indefinitely importing certain consumer goods, such as textiles, clothing, carbonated beverages, and beer. These are obviously products of popular consumption, and the local businessmen will not be long in learning to manufacture them. Actually, the industrialized nations should encourage this trend, since it offers them an opportunity to sell the machinery and equipment necessary for the production of consumer goods. Even though consumer goods may come to represent a smaller percentage of the total exports to Latin America, the loss would be amply offset by increased exportation of capital goods. The need for capital goods increases as the countries become industrialized and as foreign trade increases in volume and variety. United States exports to the Central American Common Market were 15 per cent higher in 1962 than in 1961, partly as a result of the sale of industrial equipment, ranging from food-processing machinery to equipment for the manufacture of copper wires and cables. Factories are being built to produce such articles as shirts, soap, pencils, and mattresses, thereby creating a demand for machinery.

Increased intraregional trade cannot fail to benefit United States firms operating in Latin America, since their markets will be expanded. The two enterprises that have been classified as Central American integration industries are associated with United States firms. Similarly, the complementation agreements entered into by the LAFTA members for the production of office machinery and equipment will be reflected in greater sales for IBM. Westinghouse Electric International has offered to establish a number of plants to manufacture household appliances within the Central American Common Market, in association with local businessmen. The Latin-American Free Trade Association offers even greater opportunities for United States entrepreneurial talent and for broader application of financial and technological resources for the development of the entire region. Vast opportunities for investment will appear, and a new economic frontier will be added to the limited horizons of the present world. An integrated market of over 200 million will undoubtedly offer new opportunities for growth and trade. This will require increased private foreign investment, which cannot fail to be attracted by the new opportunities, particularly in the manufacturing field, where mixed capital firms are already thriving.

Economic integration will be the leitmotiv of Latin America during this decade. Both domestic and foreign factors will strengthen this tendency, which will in all likelihood continue to gain momentum and speed. Although these events present a challenge to the United States exporter, they also mean an exceptional opportunity to achieve a more intensive and diversified trade as well as investment in a rapidly growing market.

ROLE OF THE INTER-AMERICAN
DEVELOPMENT BANK

The Inter-American Development Bank is a living example of the collective effort of the Latin-American countries. With the cooperation of the United States, this effort has established a financial institution engaged exclusively in promoting and accelerating economic and social development in the region. The development of these countries and the process of regional integration are increasingly dependent on cooperation from external sources. The Inter-American Development Bank, a hemisphere institution composed of the United States and nineteen Latin American countries, was established to channel resources from the United States and from other capital-exporting countries into development of the region.

Although the Bank began its operations only on October 1, 1960, by October 11, 1963, it had already approved 167 loans totaling $778.2 million; thus, during this brief lapse of time, it has become one of the principal sources of capital for financing Latin-American development. Of the 167 loans granted, 102 (totaling $420.3 million) were granted from the Bank's own resources and 65 (aggregating $357.9 million) came from the Social Progress Trust Fund, administered by the Bank by arrangement with the U.S. government. The projects financed by these credits include high-priority operations in the social and economic fields. Among these were 55 loans, totaling $206.2 million, for financing private enterprise, either directly or through national development institutions; 31 loans, totaling $163.9 million, for water supply and sewerage services, so urgently needed in the region; and, finally, 20 loans, aggregating $166.7 million, for the construction of housing for low-income groups.

The funds supplied by the Bank are matched by approximately equivalent contributions in national currencies, so that the cost of the projects to which the Bank has given financial assistance amounts to over $1,900 million. The Bank's own resources amount to approximately $1 billion, of which $850 million make up the ordinary capital resources and $150 million the Fund for Special Operations. In addition, pursuant to a contract entered into with the U.S. government in mid-1961, the Bank administers the Social Progress Trust Fund, whose resources total $394 million. Out of the ordinary capital resources, $400 million represent paid-in capital, and $450 million is callable capital to support the sale of Bank bonds on the private money markets. The pace of the Bank's operations has already made it necessary to consider increasing its original capital resources.

The Bank's board of governors has approved proposals for substantial increases in its resources, which are now being processed in accordance with the laws of each country. The proposals provide for a $1 billion increase in the callable capital of the Bank, which will make it possible to expand the sale of bonds in the private capital markets, and a $75 million increase in the contributions of the member countries to the Fund for Special Operations. In this connection, it is extremely gratifying to the Bank that the U.S. government is at present planning to increase the Social Progress Trust Fund by $200 million.

The Bank's clearly stated policy has been the encouragement and resolute support of the member countries' efforts to establish closer bonds with one another. Consequently, very high priority has been attached to integration, within the technical assistance programs, and this policy is intended to expedite industrial projects with one or more multinational aspects, including ownership, sources of supply, expansion of markets, and similar prospects. At the request of the Colombian and Venezuelan governments, a technical assistance mission from the Bank is now studying the possibilities of integrated development of the border areas of both countries. This first joint effort may furnish profitable experience applicable to economic and social development programs for the border regions of other member countries of the Bank.

The Bank has extended technical assistance to the Central American Bank for Economic Integration during its initial phases. It has maintained close contact with that institution since the beginning of its operations and has granted it a loan of $6 million to be used in financing integration projects. Furthermore, it is now participating, together with the Economic Commission for Latin America (ECLA) and the Latin-American Iron and Steel Institute (ILAFA), in a technical and financial study of the iron and steel industries in Latin America. This study will undoubtedly establish important guidelines for integration of a key industrial sector. A program of technical assistance to encourage and promote integration projects in certain strategic sectors, such as industry, agriculture, transportation, and communications, is another step toward the preparation and evaluation of integration projects. Surveys of the legal and institutional aspects will also be started in order to determine the barriers and obstacles hindering integration, a first step toward removing them.

In October, 1963, IDB took a particularly important step toward economic integration by adopting a program for financing capital-goods exports among its Latin American member countries. By implementing this multilateral system of export financing—the first one established up to the present time—the Bank will not only stimulate economic integration, but at the same time, will encourage the production of capital goods and improve the competitive position of Latin-American exports.

CHAPTER 8

Africa[1]

David B. Bolen

The African independence revolution of the sixties has set in motion a crisis of rising expectations for a better life that cannot be safely ignored by the free world. A little more than a decade ago, there were only four independent states on that continent: Egypt, Ethiopia, Liberia, and South Africa. Today there are more than thirty-five independent African states, of which the vast majority are less than five years old, Virtually all are under great pressure to raise standards of living, and have adopted programs to develop their human and natural resources. Everywhere, efforts are being made to diversify economic structures. African leaders are resolutely determined to strengthen the foundation of their independence through economic development.

Many leaders in Africa recognize that their newly won political freedom is only the means to an end. As they stand with freedom amidst poverty, they are asking themselves where and how their forefathers went wrong. As they look at those yet unfree, they wonder why subservience and domination persist in this age of enlightenment. In the forums of the world Africans generate a crescendo for a rectification of what they see as old wrongs.

1 In the past, writers have sought to deal with Africa in separate compartments, arising from its partitioning in the nineteenth century. With the present drive toward African unity, one must begin to think about Africa as one entity; this chapter adopts this new point of view.

The coordinated decolonization efforts of the Organization for African Unity are a manifestation of these feelings. These efforts may be termed as radical by some, or even irresponsible by others, but these interpretations make them no less serious. Some western European powers have moved with the tide of political change with commendable speed. Much more remains to be done economically. Mankind still faces the challenge of ensuring dignity, human freedom, and equality for all in Africa.

It is not the purpose of this chapter to produce a tidy theory or analysis of the policies and problems of Africa. It is simply to illuminate some of the major politico-economic problems and relationships that have a bearing on the future course of economic and social developments in Africa. For this reason, reference is made to the slave trade and the colonial era. Only in this way can the attitudes, institutions, and prevailing economic structure of independent Africa be clearly understood.

RESOURCE BASE

Africa is well endowed with natural resources and has a great economic potential. The land area of the continent totals almost 12 million square miles. From north to south, the continent exceeds 5,000 miles; from east to west, it approximates 4,700 miles. This is far in excess of the distance of 2,600 miles between New York and San Francisco. About 9 million square miles, or 75 per cent, of Africa's land area lies in the tropics.

Vast areas in Africa have too little or too much rainfall, but the continent still has more arable land per capita than either the United States or the Soviet Union, even discounting the Sahara. Africa has twice as much forest land as the United States. It has nearly as much as the Soviet Union. In some places, however, productivity of agriculture is restricted by heavy tropical rainfall, which causes soil leaching and erosion. But the problem of drought and the problem of soil erosion arising from heavy rainfall need not constitute insurmountable development problems, with continued improvements in technology. Even the Sahara can be made more productive in the context of existing technology.

No other continent must cope with problems of the same magnitude with respect to tropical agriculture. Africans must face up to the implications of this fact. It points up the need for research to develop new techniques to facilitate the adaptation of existing technology to natural endowments. Even under present conditions, Africa produces 80 per cent of the world's palm kernels and palm oil, 70 per cent of its cocoa, 35 per cent of its peanuts, 29 per cent of its sesame seed, and 20 per cent of its coffee.

The vast land mass of Africa is richly endowed with many mineral resources that are of vital importance to Africa's own industrial development. The continent produces in substantial quantities as many as fifty-three of the most important minerals in industrial use today, with the exception of magnesium, mercury, molybdenum, and sulfur. Even these are found in significant quantities. Some of Africa's mineral reserves are of strategic importance in the production process of industrialized societies. Africa has 98 per cent of the world's reserve of diamonds, 80 per cent of the world's reserve of chromite, 70 per cent of its cobalt, 50 per cent of its bauxite, 50 per cent of its gold, 50 per cent of its phosphate rock, 45 per cent of its iron ore, 40 per cent of its uranium, 40 per cent of its tantalite, 25 per cent of its copper, 20 per cent of its manganese ore, and 16 per cent of its tin.[2]

The significance of some of these rich resources becomes more impressive when measured against the resource endowment of such major powers as the United States, the Soviet Union, and Japan. For example, Africa's iron ore reserves are twice as much as those of the United States and two-thirds those of the Soviet Union. It has been estimated that coal reserves in Africa would be enough to last for some 300 years even if Africa's consumption were at the U.S. rate.

There is considerable dispersion of mineral deposits throughout the continent of Africa. Some 90 per cent of the free world's gold and antimony and 55 per cent of the chrome ore are produced in South Africa, while 50 per cent of the diamonds, 90 per cent of the tungsten, and 70 per cent of the cobalt come from the

[2] Bureau of Mines, U.S. Department of Interior, *World Iron Ore Resources and Their Utilization,* United Nations, 1950.

Congo. Guinea accounts for 85 per cent of the bauxite; Morocco, 70 per cent of the phosphate rock; and Northern Rhodesia, 60 per cent of the copper. Algeria produces 60 per cent of Africa's crude petroleum at present.[3] Output of the Algerian fields represents one-third of the Iranian production. Production of the Libyan fields is expected to increase to 600,000 tons in a few years.

Perhaps Africa's most important reserve is its hydroelectric potentiality. The hydroelectric potentiality of Africa exceeds that for any continent. It may well be that Africa has one-third of the hydroelectric potentiality of the entire world.[4] Since Africa has 40 per cent of the world's uranium, it is possible that atomic energy may also be developed as a major source of power.

Africa's resources, however, have not been thoroughly surveyed. But even on the basis of existing information, one may conclude that there is a sufficient natural resource base for substantial industrial expansion and sustained economic growth in some countries. The riches of Africa were an underlying reason for much rivalry and international tension among European countries, particularly in the late nineteenth century.

COLONIAL DEVELOPMENT

Africa is a typically undeveloped continent in spite of its rich resource base. A full understanding of the attitude and urgency with which many African states approach the problem of developing their resources must be viewed against a background of the sweep of human history. Some Africans tend to blame colonial exploitation for their lag behind the modernization of the twentieth century. On the other hand, critics seem to forget that the continent was isolated for centuries before colonization. Then, during the colonization period, communication and exchange of ideas on the basis of equality were minimal. Initially, only the

[3] U.S. Department of Commerce, *A Special Report on Africa—Sales Frontier for U.S. Business,* U.S. Government Printing Office, Washington, D.C., 1963, p. 96.
[4] L. D. Stamp, *Africa: A Study in Tropical Development,* John Wiley & Sons, Inc., N.Y., 1957, p. 523.

exotic aspects of African coastal people were emphasized by European colonizers and travelers. Africans were depicted as savages and barbarians without a capacity to govern.

It was not until after the fifteenth century that European powers definitely began to surge ahead of Africa in terms of material progress. There were several factors in European developments that accounted for this. The more important factors, from an economic point of view, would appear to be a propensity for scientific exploration in Europe, application of science and technology to the production process, the growing power and security of the merchant entrepreneurs and their disposition to innovate. As the Middle Ages ended, merchants in Europe were deploring ostentatious consumption. They were strongly advocating hard and conscientious work, and the doctrine of the survival of the fittest. They held material progress in high esteem. No other society at that time was characterized by these factors, at least not in the same degree.

The Portuguese were the first Europeans to make contact with Africans in 1415, resulting in more than 500 years of varying degrees of African association with the European civilization. One may logically raise the question therefore as to why the advanced technology of Europe was not transferred and absorbed by Africans to create a process of self-generating growth.

The plain fact is that the slave trade was the dominating activity of Europeans in Africa for some 400 years, whereas genuine European interest in the economic development of Africa as a matter of government policy covers a period of only 40 years.[5] The initial activities of missionaries were aimed at converting "heathens." The concept of "just wars" and the imposition of Christian-humanitarian values on so-called primitive peoples were part of the conventional wisdom of the eighteenth century. With growing industrialization and the need for labor, the the-

[5] The first African slaves were taken to Portugal in 1441, and the first transatlantic slave trade began in 1502. Slave trade was made illegal by the British parliament in 1807. A number of nations then followed Britain in the abolition of slavery.

ory of biological racial inferiority was increasingly used as a rationalization for slavery.

The economic impact of the slave trade cannot be calculated with precision. Slaves undoubtedly contributed substantially to the economic development of the West by holding wage costs low, thereby increasing profits and capital formation. It is estimated that, "900,000 Negro slaves had landed in the Americas by the 16th century: the 17th century figure is thought to be at least 2,750,000; the figures for the 18th and 19th centuries cannot have been less than 7 million and 4 million respectively."[6] Africans of previous generations bore some of the responsibility for this traffic in human bondage. The institution of slavery was a major factor that fixed psychological attitudes of Europeans toward Africans, and these tended to influence subsequent developments.

The slave trade was harmful to Africa, if for no other reason than it discouraged other forms of commerce and therefore contributed to stagnation. With the abolition of slavery in the colonies the nature of contacts with Africa changed. There was greater interest by private companies in the export and import trade in primary commodities. Under the theory of eighteenth and nineteenth century classical economists, such as Adam Smith and David Ricardo, all international trading partners were to receive mutual benefits from trade, given certain assumptions. These benefits included larger markets, which permitted economies of scale, increased labor specialization, higher rates of capital accumulation, and external economies. However, African producers and consumers had to contend with the monopsonistic and monopolistic practices of large trading companies. In the absence of free competitive markets and comparable African bargaining power, the real gains from trade were unequal.

The type of trade and investment activity undertaken by private European businessmen was in part consistent with the Ricardian comparative cost doctrine. Under this theory, maximum gains to world economy could be effected if trading part-

6 Roland Oliver and J. S. Fage, *A Short History of Africa*, Penguin Books, Inc., Baltimore, Maryland, 1962, p. 120.

ners specialized in those commodities in which they had a comparative advantage. Accordingly, resources in Africa and other poor countries were allocated to the production of agricultural products, mineral, and other raw materials. Economic development, therefore, had an export bias. It gave rise to cyclical, if not a secular, deterioration in terms of trade. Various imperfections prevented the expansion of exports from having a multiplier-accelerator effect. Growth was unbalanced. The colonial trading system did not operate to transmit skills. It created a phcnomenon that has been described as technological and sociological dualism. Modern sectors in the society existed side by side with the traditional.

J. S. Mill (1848) recognized the importance of the colonial trading system in providing cheap food and raw materials for European countries and in raising rates of profit on investment capital. At the same time, he expressed the belief that "the planting of colonies should be conducted, not with an exclusive view to the private interests of the first founders, but with a deliberate regard to the permanent welfare of the nations afterwards to arise from these beginnings; such regard can only be secured by placing the enterprise, from its commencements, under regulations constructed with the foresight and enlarged views of philosophical legislators."[7]

It appeared that European governments as such had no great interest in extending their sovereignty over African territories prior to the nineteenth century. Consequently, there was no interest in development. Conflicting claims, rivalry, national pride and prestige, and recognition of territories in Africa as a strategic reserve led to heightened interest in Africa and the balkanization of the continent in the nineteenth century. Following the Berlin Conference of 1885, which virtually completed the partitioning of Africa, the interest of European powers tended to decrease. Initially, the territories were ruled by only a few officials. Imposition of low tax rates and prohibition of tribal war were the principal innovations. The dominant government attitude was

[7] J. S. Mill, *Principle of Political Economy,* edited by W. I. Ashley, Longmans Green and Co., London 1940, p. 970.

one of making the colonies self-supporting with respect to fiscal operations and minimizing grant-in-aid from the metropole. Political instability inevitably led to an increase in grant-in-aid to strengthen the military establishment in order to maintain internal security. Essentially, the initial functions of government were therefore to maintain law and order. The missionaries played the major role in the development of education and health. The expansion of productive facilities was a function of private European investors and traders.[8]

It was not until the 1920s that colonial officials began to show some recognition of the views expressed 75 years earlier by J. S. Mill on the responsibility of the colonial power toward the colonies. Britain's greatest African administrator, Lord Lagard, and the French colonial minister, Albert Sarraut, both recognized "that the colonial powers had an obligation, not merely to govern justly, but also to carry the colonial peoples decisively forward both politically and economically."[9] The Ormsby-Gore reports of 1924 and 1926 held that, "economic development throughout tropical Africa must be centered on the indigenous peoples, and that it must start with the development of medical services, educational services and agricultural services."[10] In 1925 the British launched an educational program to subsidize missionary educational facilities. For the next ten to fifteen years, two to four years of schooling was provided for one-fourth of the colonial youth and twelve years of schooling for a select few.[11]

It was not until 1940, with the enactment of the Colonial Development and Welfare Act by Britain, that colonial governments began to provide financial assistance to stimulate economic development. Much has been accomplished. More remains to be done. One of the pressing problems of this generation is to forge viable relationships for a continuation of these enlightened endeavors to complete a job begun years ago.

[8] Roland Oliver and J. D. Fage, *A Short History of Africa,* Penquin Books, Inc., Baltimore, Maryland, 1962, pp. 196–208.
[9] *Ibid.,* pp. 210–211.
[10] *Ibid.*
[11] *Ibid.,* p. 212.

ATTITUDES AND INSTITUTIONS

Attitudes and institutions in any society must be conducive to economic growth in order for it to take place. Attitudes, as embodied in institutions, must place a high value on hard and conscientious work, social and geographic mobility, thrift, disposition to innovate, risk-taking, and respect for the sanctity of private contract. There must be a willingness to conduct economic relations on an impersonal basis so that an individual is rewarded more for merit than for his social status in the community. To the extent that newly independent African states do not adopt measures to develop social characteristics favorable to economic development, their nation building endeavors will be retarded.

The promotion of self-sustaining economic growth in Africa must necessarily be a process of political, psychological, and social as well as economic change. The determinants of growth have not been institutionalized, as they have been in the United States. It is not possible to predict savings of individuals and businesses. There does not exist a set of attitudes and habits that would ensure a rate of savings consistent with the growth objectives of African governments. Unlike advanced societies, one cannot predict a steady flow of technological improvements that will serve as an offset to diminishing returns or that will increase the profitability of investments. These improvements are a function of education and research, which are inadequate in Africa when measured against existing needs. In advanced societies there is more recognition of the importance of organizational, administrative, and managerial efficiency in the production process. Unlike many African countries, there is a greater degree of vertical and horizontal mobility in advanced societies, where social adjustment to technical change is much easier than in Africa.

Intensified contacts of colonial powers with Africans in the nineteenth and twentieth centuries did set in motion the beginnings of a process of social change that was more favorable to economic growth. These contacts tended to disintegrate traditional behavior patterns and initiated a process toward modernity as we know it today. There was necessarily a lag between these disruptive forces and new attitudes and institutions to replace the old. As is obvious, colonial powers did not initiate a process of self-sustained growth or effect a complete social transformation. There were patches of modernization. A small African élite began to appear and acquire social and psychological attitudes conducive to growth. Without fear, prejudice, and segregation, more could have been accomplished.

Perhaps the most important contribution of colonial powers to social change in Africa was the Western notion that all men are equal before the law, that there should be equality of opportunity, and that government policies and political leadership should be determined on the basis of "one man, one vote." It was this revolutionary idea that moved most African territories to independence, with freedom to use local resources to meet their aspiration for a better life. Independence, however, is only a means to an end.

In Africa today the universal objective of rapid economic growth is still restricted by prevailing attitudes and institutions. In this connection, the following passage from an article[12] by D. K. Chisiza of Malawi is significant:

There is a tendency in the West, whether the Westerners themselves know it or not, for people to assume that man lives to work. We believe that man works to live. This view of life gives rise to our high preference for leisure. With us, life has always meant the pursuit of happiness by rejecting isolationism, individualism, negative emotions and tensions on the one hand; and by laying emphasis on a communal way of life, by encouraging positive emotions and relaxation, and by restraining our desires, on the other. We live our lives in the present.

This statement has considerable merit from other points of view, but the attitudes suggested here would not be conducive to rapid economic growth. This type of attitude reflects the extent to which individuals will make an effort to seek out economic opportunities for productive investment. Entrepreneurial drive is

[12] D. K. Chisiza, "The Contemporary Outlook," *The Journal of Modern African Studies*, Vol. 1, No. 1, March 1963, p. 32.

related to the demand for material goods. If the desire for material goods is limited, then it is reasonable to expect that efforts to obtain them will be restrained. Limited communication facilities, mass illiteracy, lack of vertical and horizontal mobility, and related factors restrict the horizon of Africans in the bush. As these types of impediments are removed, the desire for material goods will increase as well as the amount of effort Africans are willing to make to obtain them.

The extended family system in Africa in many ways is an impediment to economic development. In effect, this institution is a built-in social security system. However, it adversely affects private initiative and thrift. Sometimes the individual financial obligations of a large family are expected to be met by the educated, salaried members. Loans extended by government entities to individuals for agricultural and industrial investment have been known to be used to meet obligations under the extended family system.

Some Africans have been affected by the slave-owner mentality toward common labor and toward certain occupations. Among them, there is little respect for manual labor or for the dignity of labor. Some landowners, lawyers, teachers, politicians, and government officials do not wish to perform menial tasks. There has been a distaste for business. In most of Africa, the import, export, and distribution trade is dominated by Europeans, Syrians, Lebanese, Indians, and other aliens. By custom, women in West Africa do handle a significant portion of the retail trade. The entrepreneurial drive exhibited by these so-called mammy traders is deserving of emulation. There is a basic prejudice against agriculture and technical fields. Students in universities prefer in many instances to major in the liberal arts, law, and philosophy rather than business, economics, agriculture, and similar subjects urgently needed for economic development.

The willingness of a people to adopt new ideas and techniques is partly associated with anticipated gains or losses. Village farmers who live at the subsistence level, where crop failures may mean a long period of famine, are understandably reluctant to adopt new techniques to increase agricultural productivity. They do not yet fully understand that the physical universe can be manipulated to serve the interest of mankind. In any event, the diffusion of new ideas and technological improvements are restricted by lack of adequate educational facilities. The factors are crucial in the development process.

In addition to technological improvements, capital formation is a critical dimension in promoting economic growth. Yet there are many purely sociological factors in Africa that limit capital accumulation. The most obvious is the tendency toward ostentatious consumption on the part of individuals as well as governments. This phenomenon may be associated with the colonial era, including outward manifestations of racial superiority by colonial officials and suppressed emotions by Africans. Some governments are already taking forceful action to increase capital formation by curbing ostentatious consumption on the part of higher income groups. They are seeking more efficient allocation of resources and reducing wasteful expenditures on monuments, palaces, and other symbols of affluence.

Because of the revolution of rising expectations, political freedom, and the impact of economic development, traditional attitudes and institutions in Africa will change more rapidly than has been the case in the past. They will become more consistent with well-known ingredients favorable to development. "Imitation effects," "demonstration effects," and other such effects are already operating to place a higher premium on savings, risk-taking, and individual effort. These and related factors are powerful stimuli to economic development. Today, the desire for a bicycle, a house, sumptuous clothing, radio transistors, education, and similar possessions may not be only a status symbol because they also serve as production stimuli. People are increasing their efforts to get them.

The process of rapid social change taking place in Africa is likely to be characterized by considerable stress and strain, giving rise to some political instability. Development will have a differential impact on various groups in the society. As values, attitudes, and institutions change, the old will not automatically be respected. The locus of political power is subject to change as the population shifts from rural to urban areas.

Much has been said about the one-party state in Africa and the role of government in the development process. There is no doubt that governments in Africa are playing a much larger role in molding the pattern of development than was the case in the early stages of economic development in western Europe and the United States. This phenomenon may be associated, among other things, with the lack of private entrepreneurship, with prevailing behavorial patterns, and with institutional structures that tend to restrict development. It is associated with an antipathy toward private enterprise, owing to the fact that business and commerce have been dominated by foreigners who had little regard for the social and economic welfare of indigenous people. Virtually all African governments are committed to a policy of evolving some form of African socialism. In no case does this mean complete state ownership of the means of production, but rather some form of a mixed enterprise system.

It may well be too soon to draw any definitive conclusions as to the optimum role of government and private enterprise in the process of economic development in Africa. Experiences of the United States seem to suggest that a mixed enterprise system is compatible with both maximization of production to satisfy consumer wants and attainment of political aspirations. It would be difficult for African governments to develop without tapping the spring of private initiative. Many clearly recognize the necessary role of private enterprise and encourage business in many ways.

ECONOMIC GROWTH AND
INCOME DISTRIBUTION

European intrusion on the continents of Africa and the Americas began in the fifteenth century, but the disparities in growth rates between these two continents have been tremendous. Africa was locked in a state of static equilibrium for centuries. This was due in part to isolation, unfavorable climatic conditions, and 400 years of slave trade. Colonial trade of the nineteenth century transferred few technological improvements to black Africans. Few Europeans were prepared to emigrate to such places as West Africa, or the "white man's grave." On the other hand, European colonizers in the Americas brought with them managerial skills and technical know-how. More important, they brought with them what Reinhold Niebuhr called the expectation of a "new beginning." Some were motivated by the ideals of Thomas Jefferson: that the ultimate values of society are, "Life, Liberty and the Pursuit of Happiness." Others were motivated by Alexander Hamilton's vision of wealth and power. The contrast between growth in the United States and Africa suggests that resources are important only within the context of contemporary technology and that economic growth depends on human behavior, particularly freedom to use resources in the best interest of the general welfare.

Today, national income of all Africa is only 5 per cent of that of the United States. Gross national product for the continent of Africa amounted to only $29 billion in 1961, compared with $519 billion for the United States. Per capita GNP in Africa amounted to only $120 compared with $2,800 for the United States.[13]

The rate of growth in Africa over a significant period of time cannot be determined with any degree of accuracy. Historically, statistical services have not included the compilation of national income data except for a very few countries. Based on available data for capital formation, it does not appear that growth rates have been very high. Growth has tended to fluctuate with the volume of agricultural output and with export prices. In some African countries, there is some serious doubt as to whether any expansion in per capita income is taking place, in view of high population growth, low rates of capital formation, and low productivity.

It must be remembered that the per capita GNP figure of $120 for Africa does not fully reflect the dismal poverty of the vast majority of Africans. It does not reflect the crippling burden of debilitating disease or the stifling influence of mass illiteracy.

[13] *Selected Economic Data for the Less Developed Countries,* Statistics and Reports Division, Agency for International Development, May 1963, pp. 4 and 8. *International Financial Statistics,* International Monetary Fund, Vol. XV, No. 11, November 1962, p. 272.

There are wide disparities in incomes within national borders and between different nations. This is one of the principal reasons underlying a growing preoccupation with "African socialism" and its promise of ensuring greater economic welfare and social justice.

In the multiracial societies of Angola, Kenya, Mozambique, the Rhodesias, and South Africa, these income disparities are enormous. Even in West Africa, because of the relatively inelastic supply of high-level manpower, there is a substantial gap in incomes between the merchants, civil servants, industrialists, and the unskilled laborers and subsistence farmers comprising the majority of the population. With the attainment of independence the nonindigenous high-income groups may conceivably serve as an exogenous stimulus to efforts to initiate a cumulative growth process. In the past, these high-income groups did induce beneficial investments in social facilities such as housing, schools, health facilities, and utilities. At the same time, they increased the import demand for luxuries and consumer goods. They remitted significant savings abroad. Hence they reduced the size of the market for domestic products and diverted financial resources that could have been available for investment in expanding internal productive capacity.

Africans have an understandable urge to accelerate economic growth, to close the gap between incomes in Africa and those in more advanced societies. These aspirations pose a formidable challenge to the productive capacity, organizing ability, and leadership of the free world. Unless this challenge is met by economic and educational opportunities, African leadership may feel forced to choose the growth models and technique of communist totalitarianism.

POPULATION: ITS DIMENSIONS AND CHARACTERISTICS

Africa's population is approaching 300 million and is increasing at the rate of 2.2 per cent per year.[14] Population growth rates

[14] *Selected Economic Data for the Less Developed Countries,* Statistics and Reports Division, Agency for International Development, May 1963, p. 4.

range from 1 per cent or less in Angola, Cameroon, Gabon, Gambia, Somalia, and Zanzibar to 3 per cent or more in Ghana, Guinea, Kenya, Mauritania, Mauritius, Morocco, Rwanda, Swaziland, and Togo. Thus, for Africa as a whole, a saving rate of at least 8 per cent is required to keep pace with population growth, assuming a capital output ratio of 4.1. For those countries with rates of growth of 3 per cent, an investment rate of 12 per cent is required. Many African states do not have savings of this magnitude. There is a danger therefore that the per capita level of living will remain constant or even decline in some areas, in the absence of external assistance.

In general, the population data for African countries tend to suggest that the initial impact of development will be reflected in increased population. This is already apparent in some of the more advanced countries, such as Algeria, Ghana, Morocco, the Rhodesias, and the Republic of South Africa. Investments in improving health facilities, housing, food, work conditions, and medical research cause a significant drop in mortality rates, resulting in increased population. Eventually one can expect a fall in birth rates as the population reacts more rapidly to social changes, such as a shift of the population from rural to urban areas. This might reduce the rate of population growth. The real significance of these factors is seen in the fact that the initial upsurge in population growth may not be accompanied by a rise in the level of living. The total income may expand, but per capita income may fall, thereby increasing the gap in income between lower and upper income groups and giving rise to political stresses and strains. In any event, this population upsurge would put a strain on available investment capital and productive capacity, at least in the short run. In the long run, population growth could help expand productive capacity.

The land-population ratio in Africa is potentially favorable to economic growth. Population density for the continent as a whole is estimated at only twenty persons per square mile. Considering the African Continent as a whole, the pressure of human resources on the land is not serious when measured against the problems in South Asia and the Far East, where there are 290 and 210 persons per square mile, respectively. In Africa there are

8 acres of agricultural land per capita compared with one-half acre per capita in the Far East.

There is considerable variation in the population size and density among African countries and territories. There are seven independent countries and five territories with a population of 1 million or less. Areas with five or less persons per square mile include Bechuanaland, Central African Republic, Chad, Congo (Brazzaville), Gabon, Libya, Mauritania, and Niger.[15] Countries and territories with fifty or more persons per square mile include Basutoland, Gambia, Ghana, Mauritius, Morocco, Nigeria, Malawi, Togo, Tunisia, and Uganda.

The percentage of Africans living in rural areas is very high, reflecting the undeveloped state of the economies of the African Continent. Africa has fewer people living in towns of more than 20,000 than any other region of the world.[16]

In fact only 6 per cent of Africa's population south of the Sahara lives in towns of 20,000 or more, compared with 34 per cent for the rest of the world. Most of Africa's urban population lives in one or two cities within each country. Hence, Africa faces an enormous problem of effecting an orderly shift of its rural population to urban areas as development proceeds. Such shifts are painful and revolutionary, affecting as they do the basic fabric of society.

The ratio of the labor force to total population in African states is not very favorable for economic development. About 40 per cent of the total population is less than fifteen years of age. In most African countries, for every ten persons of working age (fifteen to fifty-nine), there are seven to nine of nonworking age (under fifteen and over sixty). These factors affect the size of the labor force. Therefore, they have a bearing on economic growth.

Apart from factors restricting the size of the labor force in Africa, the quality of the labor needs to be improved. Productivity as reflected in output per man hour is very low. The output of the African farmer is believed to be only about 4 per cent of the

[15] See *Economic Bulletin for Africa*, Vol. II, No. 2, Economic Commission for Africa, June 1962, pp. 59–81.
[16] *Ibid.*, p. 62.

output of his American counterpart. This is due in part to inadequate nutrition, disease, and primitive farming practices. There is only one physician for every 17,000 people—twenty-five times less than the ratio for the United States. That, only one year after independence, there was only one Congolese doctor in the Congo is indicative of the enormity of health problems in Africa that affect labor productivity. Infant mortality in Africa is ten times higher than in the United States. The literacy rate in Africa as a whole is estimated at only 15 per cent. There is, in particular, an acute shortage of high-level and middle-level manpower. For example, in 1959 there was not a single Congolese lawyer, engineer, or commissioned officer in the Congo. A substantial expansion in health and education is needed to improve the quality of Africa's labor force.

EDUCATION, RESEARCH, AND TECHNOLOGY

Education is an important ingredient of economic expansion in any country. In Africa it is a critical dimension because of the acute shortage of manpower with technical know-how or managerial skills. During the colonial era, education was left to missionaries. It was not until the latter part of the nineteenth century that metropolitan governments began to take action to expand educational facilities in Africa. Even with these efforts, the illiteracy rate in Africa today is still 85 per cent. This situation is serious because, in the absence of adequate education and research facilities, it is difficult to see how any significant growth in technology and labor productivity can be effected. Some economists hold that most of the growth in such advanced countries as the United States is accounted for by improvements in the factors of production and in technology, which in turn can be attributed to education. This, incidentally, leads to the important conclusion that African countries should be interested in the quality and suitability of the technology embodied in their capital stock rather than in an increase in capital per se.[17] Rus-

[17] See Robert Solow, "Technical Change and the Aggregate Production," *Function Review of Economics and Statistics,* August 1957; Moses Abromovitz,

sian snow plows in Guinea may represent a substantial capital investment, but it does not snow in Guinea. Such capital input cannot be adapted to Guinea's factor endowments and therefore contributes nothing to the expansion of production.

The amount of education received by the typical worker in Africa is substantially less than that for his counterpart in industrial societies. There must be a revision of curricula to suit African needs, as well as a substantial expansion of enrollment in primary, secondary, and higher educational institutions in Africa, if the requisite skills so vitally needed for economic development are to be obtained. Equally important is a need for vocational and technical training. Data on educational development in Europe and the United States point up the importance of education in the development process. In the United States, the percentage of total population enrolled in school in the age bracket from five to seventeen rose from 78.3 per cent in 1900 to around 97 per cent in 1963. Enrollment in primary schools in Africa seems to range up to 78 per cent in the Cameroons. Enrollment in secondary schools in Africa in the age bracket from fourteen to seventeen years tends to be below the level prevailing in the United States even in 1900. At that time, secondary school enrollment in the United States in the age bracket of fourteen to seventeen was 11.4 per cent. It rose to around 85 per cent in 1963. In Africa, the percentage of population enrolled in secondary schools does not exceed 25 per cent in any country. In Ghana it is 23 per cent. In most other countries, secondary school enrollment is below 10 per cent.

It is clear that the present thrust of educational development must be in the direction of extending facilities to reduce the present illiteracy rate of 85 per cent and to increase substantially secondary school enrollment and technical education. Secondary school enrollment should not be regarded as merely preparation

Resource and Output Trends in the United States Since 1870, National Bureau of Economic Research, Occasional Paper 52, 1956, p. 11; Solomon Fabricant, *Basic Facts on Productivity Change,* National Bureau of Economic Research, Occasional Paper 63, p. 23; F. Mussel, *Capital Formation and Technological Change,* Cowles Foundation Discussion, Paper 58.

for higher studies. It should be regarded as an end in itself. With respect to higher education, the traditional fields of law and art have been overemphasized. More emphasis must be on science, agriculture, engineering, and technical fields, all important to existing and potential development objectives.

Africans place an extremely high value on education, as reflected in the relatively large expenditures in some countries. The ratio of educational outlays to total development expenditures ranges between 9 and 21 per cent in Ghana, Guinea, Ivory Coast, Kenya, Nigeria, Tanganyika, and the Sudan. The ratio of educational expenditures to total development expenditures is very low in Ethiopia (5 per cent) and in Southern Rhodesia (2 per cent).[18]

In addition to education, investment in research is a key factor in economic development. Research is important to facilitate the adaptation of modern technology to factor endowments. It is important for the efficient organization of production processes and for the improvement of management, marketing, and other such techniques. Some of the African states have recognized the vital importance of research in the development process.

AGRICULTURE

Agriculture is the mainstay of the economies of most African states. Active population engaged in agriculture ranges from about 65 per cent for Tunisia and Morocco to about 90 per cent for such countries as Ethiopia, Guinea, the Ivory Coast, and the Cameroons. Agricultural production as a per cent of gross domestic product (GDP) is very high, particularly in countries with a low per capita income. Agricultural production as a per cent of GDP ranges between 11 per cent and 34 per cent in such countries as South Africa, Tunisia, and Morocco, whereas in such countries as Ethiopia, Nigeria, Uganda, and Ghana, the percentage ranges up to 65 per cent. A large product derived from agriculture, however, does not necessarily mean a low per capita

18 *Economic Bulletin for Africa,* Economic Commission for Africa, Vol. II, No. 2 (June 1962), p. 22.

income. For example, agricultural production as a per cent of GDP in Ghana is estimated at 60 or 65 per cent, but Ghana is among the more advanced countries in Africa in terms of per capita income.[19]

As a general rule, the structural changes that have occurred among various countries in Africa and those observed in the more advanced countries during the process of development suggest that an expansion in agricultural productivity is a prerequisite for industrialization. In the United States, one farm worker produced enough for only four people in 1800. Today, he produces enough for twenty-six people. The percentage of labor force employed in agriculture dropped from 75 per cent in 1800 to 10 per cent today. In Africa, attitudes and institutions must change, to facilitate the adoption of technological improvements in agriculture and to ensure a high degree of labor and occupational mobility. Such mobility will permit shifts of the work force to sectors where the average level of productivity is higher.

The agricultural sector of the economies of most African states at present is characterized by a phenomenon that may be described as agricultural dualism. First, there is a large number of subsistence farmers that is not included in the monetized part of the economy. Secondly, there is the monetized part of the agricultural sector that is based on one or two cash crops. This is a division of labor that was more or less common to the colonial era. It is, in part, consistent with the nineteenth century Ricardian comparative-cost doctrine under which nations would specialize in producing those commodities in which they had a comparative advantage. Thus, today, Africa produces 80 per cent of the world's palm kernels, 79 per cent of its palm oil, and 70 per cent of its cocoa. Agricultural commodities as a per cent of total export income are extremely high in most countries.

The prevailing level of agricultural productivity in Africa is inadequate to keep pace with population growth and to meet the requirements for improved nutritional standards. In fact, per capita food production for 1960–1961 was below the average

[19] *Ibid.*, p. 10.

level prevailing in 1952–1954 for thirteen countries in Africa.[20] For most other countries it would appear that the per capita increase in food production has been less than 3 per cent per annum. As a consequence, commodity import patterns are characterized by a relatively high level of food imports. In 1959 African countries imported food and beverages valued at $1 billion. No country can become fully self-sufficient in food production. However, since most of these African countries are faced with a shortage of foreign exchange for capital investment, the prevailing magnitude of food imports is a serious matter. For example, food imports by Ghana in 1961 amounted to $70 million. At the present rate of increase, food imports would amount to $200 million by 1970. If the ratio of food imports to total imports for 1961 remains fixed, it would be necessary to expand exports from $315 million in 1961 to $1 billion by 1970 in order to effect a trade equilibrium. Given the relatively inelastic supply of cocoa beans, Ghana's principal export commodity, and the prevailing price and income elasticities of demand abroad for cocoa beans, this is virtually impossible.

The essential problem, therefore, for many countries is to effect a reallocation of resources to ensure a greater degree of diversification and particularly to expand food production. This would help ease the pressure on scarce foreign exchange for investment, broaden the tax base, and release labor from agriculture for industrial development. Many African states have an enormous problem arising from the increasing flow of primary school leavers from rural to urban areas. The basic solution to this potentially explosive problem must be found in (1) increased farm incentives, (2) expanded vocational and technical training, and (3) increased industrial investment. Apart from food production, African states have the problem of expanding agricultural output in order to provide a sound raw material base for industrialization. There is also considerable scope in

[20] U.S. Department of Commerce, *A Special Report—African-Sales Frontier for U.S. Business,* U.S. Government Printing Office, Washington, D.C., 1963, p. 97.

some countries for increasing foreign exchange through increased production of primary commodities.

MANUFACTURING

Manufacturing in the vast majority of African states is still in its infancy. The ratio of factory output to gross domestic product in most countries ranges between 2 and 20 per cent, with higher ratios for Egypt, Morocco, and the Rhodesias. Factory output consists for the most part of food, beverages, tobacco, cotton textiles, and furniture. However, metals are fairly important in the Rhodesias, Kenya, Congo (Leopoldville), the Cameroons, Tanganyika, and Guinea. The limited size of markets for most individual African countries, as well as the lack of effective regional economic integration, prevents the optimum utilization of up-to-date industrial technology and therefore damps the pace of growth in manufacturing.

The growth of manufacturing and agricultural production also tends to be restricted by inadequate transport facilities. There are only 40 miles of improved roads per 1,000 square miles.[21] Lack of adequate transport inhibits the mobility of goods and adversely affects desired social change and labor specialization. Because of low population density, a given mileage of transport is much less effective than in heavily populated areas. As a result, transport costs in particular tend to be relatively high in relation to other manufacturing costs.

INTERNATIONAL TRADE

African states are heavily dependent on foreign trade to meet their daily needs for finished goods. This reflects specialization developed during the colonial period, partly in accordance with the Ricardian theory of comparative cost. The ratio of total exports and imports to gross national product is very high. As a result of the heavy dependence on foreign trade for primary

21 *Selected Economic Data for the Less Developed Countries,* Statistics and Reports Division, Agency for International Development, May 1963, p. 5.

commodities, most African states are exposed to fluctuations in demand and prices in industrialized countries.

In many countries, foreign trade is handled by large foreign firms. Financing of such trade is done by European banks. Foreign trading concerns and banks employ few Africans in managerial and other positions of responsibility. As a rule, these institutions have not provided capital to Africans to help establish manufacturing facilities as a source of supply. The degree of control of foreign trade by foreign firms is a constant source of resentment. It is a visible reminder of the colonial era. The existence of these concerns has given rise to the establishment of state trading firms in some countries. It has induced a deliberate effort to diversify markets and sources of supply, if for no other reason than to demonstrate independence and freedom of choice. Some countries assert that their political independence will not be complete until they gain a greater degree of control over their economic structure. It is quite likely, however, that any drastic change in the handling of foreign trade by independent states would disrupt their economies.

Africa's share in total world export and import trade is running around 5 per cent. Exports in 1961 amounted to $5.6 billion, while total world export trade amounted to $118.7 billion. Of total imports valued at $124.6 billion in 1961, Africa accounted for $6.8 billion.[22]

TABLE 1. Trade Balance of Africa 1955–1961

(*Billions of Dollars*)

	Deficit
1955	1.3
1956	1.2
1957	1.8
1958	2.0
1959	1.4
1960	1.6
1961	1.3

Source: United Nations, *Current Economic Indicators*, Vol. 3, No. 3, 1962, p. 6.

[22] *International Financial Statistics,* International Monetary Fund, Vol. XV, No. 11, November 1962, pp. 40–41.

Africa's trade and payments deficits on current account have been financed by foreign grants, loans, credits, and by drawing down gold and foreign exchange holdings. These holdings dropped from $2.7 billion in 1955 to $2.1 billion in 1961, or by 22 per cent.[23]

The commodity pattern of Africa's foreign trade, developed during the colonial era, has shown no major change. The bulk of export income in most countries is accounted for by one or two primary commodities. The pattern is much the same, be it the former or present British, French, or Portuguese Africa territories. Even South Africa is dependent on gold for 38 per cent of its export income. This pattern does not represent a deliberate effort to exploit, but represents an international division of labor that is more or less consistent with factor endowments and comparative cost. It is intended to maximize world trade.

The volume of Africa's exports has shown a steady increase. By

TABLE 2. LEADING EXPORTS OF SELECTED AFRICAN COUNTRIES (1958–1960)

Country	Item	Per Cent
Algeria	Petroleum	45
Morocco	Phosphate rock	22
Tunisia	Diversified	
Central African Republic	Cotton and coffee	71
Chad	Cotton	81
Congo (Brazzaville)	Wood	61
Dahomey	Palm kernels	54
Ivory Coast	Coffee and cocoa	67
Niger	Peanuts	75
Senegal	Peanuts	83
Ghana	Cocoa	58
Kenya	Coffee	19
Nigeria	Palm products	19
Rhodesias-Nyasaland	Copper	52
Sierra Leone	Diamonds	55
South Africa	Gold	38

SOURCE: *Selected Economic Data for Less Developed Countries,* Statistics and Reports Division, Agency for International Development, Washington, D.C., May 1963, p. 5.

[23] *Current Economic Indicators,* United Nations, Vol. 3, No. 3, 1962, p. 9.

1961 these exports had grown by 40 per cent over the 1955 level. Preferential trade arrangements with former metropolitan powers tended to induce investments for expanding the output of primary commodities. It appears that at least part of these investments for expanding productivity in the export industry has been transferred abroad in the form of lower prices, since the unit value of exports has declined as volume increased, particularly where demand in industrial countries has been relatively inelastic. The unit value of exports in Africa has in fact declined by 12 per cent since 1955.

TABLE 3. INDEX OF VOLUME AND UNIT VALUE OF EXPORTS OF AFRICA
(1958 = 100)

Year	Volume	Unit Value
1955	93	103
1956	97	104
1957	100	102
1958	100	100
1959	111	94
1960	120	94
1961	128	90

SOURCE: United Nations, *Current Economic Indicators,* Vol. 3, No. 3, 1962, pp. 2–3.

The pattern of commodity imports into Africa reflects the undeveloped state of the economy. In spite of an abundance of agricultural land, a high level of imports of food and beverages obtains. The lack of industrialization is seen in the relatively high level of imports of consumer goods and industrial raw materials. The need for better allocation of resources is reflected in the moderately low level of imports of capital equipment for the expansion of productive capacity. The relatively high level of imports of building material is indicative of the need for an expanded infrastructure to ensure external economies for industry and agriculture. As development proceeds, this commodity import pattern will change, with increasing importance of machinery and industrial materials and decreasing importance of processed food and other nondurable consumer goods.

Generally in developing countries, import demand tends to increase at a faster rate than export earnings from primary commodities. This does not appear to be the case in Africa, at least for the period from 1955–61. This may reflect the impact of preferential trade arrangements with metropolitan powers for tropical products, which had the affect of expanding export volume. This unusual phenomenon may also reflect certain other bottlenecks in moving forward with the implementation of development programs to diversify economic structures. The volume of total imports by African states increased by only 20 per cent, compared with 40 per cent for exports from 1955–1961. The unit value of imports showed no significant change.

TABLE 4.   INDEX OF VOLUME AND UNIT VALUE OF IMPORTS OF AFRICA
(1958 = 100)

Year	Volume	Unit Value
1955	90	97
1956	90	100
1957	97	103
1958	100	100
1959	100	96
1960	109	97
1961	107	

SOURCE: United Nations, *Current Economic Indicators,* Vol. 3, No. 3, 1962, pp. 4–5.

The tendency for the terms of trade to deteriorate is one of the fundamental problems facing Africa today. The terms of trade, or purchasing power of a given unit of exports in terms of imports, have been reduced by almost 10 per cent since 1955. This situation with respect to individual commodities is quite serious when one considers that export income is one of the principal sources of foreign exchange for development purposes. As indicated in Table 5, the fall in export prices between 1955–1961 ranged between 4 per cent and 40 per cent. In other words, in most African countries, purchasing power has been reduced substantially below what it would have been had export prices remained at a high level, particularly since import prices remained more or less stable.

TABLE 5. EXPORT PRICE INDEX OF SELECTED COMMODITIES
(1958 = 100)

Commodity	1955	1956	1957	1958	1959	1960	1961
Cocoa	83	60	70	100	81	63	50
Coffee	113	119	114	100	79	76	72
Groundnuts	116	122	120	100	101	107	107
Cotton	127	121	113	100	89	95	95
Rubber	140	123	115	100	134	141	107
Petroleum	93	93	98	100	92	90	88
Copper	166	166	112	100	119	124	116
Tin	100	106	102	100	107	108	121
Other Minerals	94	95	100	100	93	91	90

SOURCE: United Nations, *Current Economic Indicators*, Vol. 3, No. 3, 1962, pp. 22 and 23.

The deterioration in terms of trade is not the only problem arising from price movements in the monoeconomies of Africa. Proceeds from exports are an important factor in setting up forces of expansion or contraction. For example, a sharp rise in export prices in the absence of controls would cause a corresponding rise of producer incomes. Wages would tend to rise. Government revenues and expenditures would increase. Rising domestic expenditures and an inelastic local supply of consumer goods would tend to push prices upward. Because of inferior quality and rigidities of domestic supply, import demand would increase. If the export boom were multiplied, it is possible that imports would rise above the initial increase in export income. This would put considerable pressure on the balance of payments. In the absence of adequate reserves to increase imports that would absorb some of the purchasing power, inflation could develop. Social and political disturbances might be associated with such a development.

Movements in the opposite direction tend to develop with rapidly falling export prices. Civil strife might arise from depressed wages and tight economic conditions, particularly if governments undertook to institute austerity measures designed to mobilize savings and direct them into development-program channels so that the economy would move forward.

DIRECTION OF TRADE AND RELATIONS WITH
EUROPEAN COMMON MARKET

One of the essential purposes of the colonial trading system
was to develop sources of raw materials and expand markets of
the colonizing power. Ports, roads, railways, communication, and
marketing facilities were established to foster this trade. The indigenous population became accustomed to the products of the
metropole. Strong language and cultural ties were developed,
particularly with the indigenous élite. In some cases these links
have been reinforced by bilateral agreements of various kinds,
exchange and import controls, and by membership in a common
monetary area.

The strength of these external links varies, depending on the
policies followed by the metropolitan power. Everywhere the pattern is practically the same. The metropolitan powers still play a
predominant but decreasing role in the external trade of their
dependencies or former dependencies. Because of custom, tradition, or fiat, some African countries are still not fully free to
buy in the cheapest market or to sell in the dearest. Where this is
so, development must necessarily be retarded.

TABLE 6. TRADE OF SELECTED FORMER BRITISH AFRICAN COLONIES WITH
THE UNITED KINGDOM[a]

Country	Exports, Per Cent of Total	Imports, Per Cent of Total
Ghana	40	40
Kenya	35	35
Nigeria	50	40
Rhodesias and Nyasaland	45	35
Tanganyika	30	35

SOURCE: U.S. Department of Commerce, *A Special Report on Africa*, U.S. Government Printing Office, March 1963, pp. 99–100.
a Based on 1960 trade data.

The United Kingdom accounts for 30 to 50 per cent of the
export trade of some of the major ex-British colonies in Africa.
Imports by these countries from the United Kingdom represent
35 to 40 per cent of the total. Traditionally, these countries have

run large deficits in trade with the United Kingdom. In the past, they have made an effort to maximize their exports to the dollar area, particularly during the period of the so-called dollar shortage. These net dollar earnings formed part of the dollar pool of the sterling area and were used to offset the United Kingdom's dollar deficit with the United States.

France's trading relations with many of its former dependencies is an outgrowth of the French doctrine of economic and political assimilation. Colonies were supposed to be an extension of the mother country. France's economic relation with its colonies has been described as a closed circuit. Exports were sold to France at support prices. Imports came from France at prices sometimes above world prices. Sheltered markets existed for French commodities, owing to various devices for channeling trade, such as import licensing, exchange controls, preferential tariff treatment, ownership and control of banks and importing firms, and restrictions of entry of non-French firms. All these arrangements were reinforced by technical assistance, budget support, and other programs. French influence, therefore, has been all-pervasive.

TABLE 7. TRADE OF SELECTED FORMER FRENCH AFRICAN COLONIES
WITH FRANCE[a]

Area	Export, Per cent of Total	Imports, Per Cent of Total
Equatorial Africa[b]	52	40
French West Africa[c]	57	60
Algeria	80	90
Morocco	40	50

SOURCE: U.S. Department of Commerce, *A Special Report on Africa*, U.S. Government Printing Office, March 1963, pp. 99–100.
a Based on 1960 trade data.
b Includes Central African Republic, Chad, Congo, and Gabon.
c Includes Dahomey, Guinea, Ivory Coast, Niger, Senegal, Upper Volta.

Today, France's ex-colonies, other than Morocco and Tunisia, are major recipients of grants and loans under the 1958–1962 and 1963–1967 European Economic Community Conventions of Association (EEC). Under these conventions, the following African states are associated overseas members (AOC) of the European

Common Market (EEC): Burundi, Cameroon, Central African Republic, Chad, Congo (Brazzaville), Congo (Leopoldville), Ivory Coast, Dahomey, Gabon, Upper Volta, Madagascar, Malagasy Republic, Mali, Mauritania, Niger, Rwanda, Senegal, Somalia, and Togo. Under the EEC, $581 million was allocated to eighteen independent African countries, dependent French and Dutch areas, and Algeria for the period 1958–1962 in the form of economic development grants. Under the 1963–1967 Convention, $730 million in grants and loans will be available to African countries. The new Convention provides for the progressive dismantling of the French price-support system. It permits the AOC to benefit from EEC common external tariffs on important agricultural exports, and establishes an institutional base for EEC and AOC relations.

British Africa's attitude toward the AOC-EEC arrangement is conditioned by the British and French colonial trading system and drive of African leaders everywhere to promote African unity. Some leaders in former British African colonies argue that the existence of the AOC-EEC arrangement operates against African unity. Because of the balkanization of Africa and the limited size of domestic markets, a large number of countries may not be able to reach a scale of production that would permit the use of the most up-to-date technology. Some French Africans are opposed to British Africa's entry into the AOC-EEC league. At the same time, natural regional groupings between British and French Africa become virtually impossible. The AOC-EEC arrangement is seen as neocolonialism by some leaders in British Africa. From an economic point of view, the trade-diverting effect of the AOC-EEC accord has been injurious to third countries, not only in Africa but also in Latin America and some other undeveloped countries. It may well be that some of the more objectionable features of the AOC-EEC arrangement will be removed under the new Convention.

CAPITAL FORMATION

Economic development is more than a process of improving the size and quality of the labor force through expanded technology, education, research, health, and institutional and attitudinal changes. Capital is needed to combine a skilled labor force into some kind of productive effort. Capital may be looked upon as an instrument for the introduction of new technology. It is a necessary but not a sufficient condition for economic growth. The behavioral pattern of people and their technical and managerial know-how are critical factors.

Capital available for investment essentially represents the difference between consumption and income. In most African countries, the principal determinant of income is the proceeds from exports. The principal determinant of indigenous capital formation is therefore export income from the production of the one or two primary commodities resulting from the type of labor specialization developed in the colonial era.

Exports have an all-pervasive influence on African economies and tend to have the same multiplier effect as capital investments in industrialized societies. Exports affect government revenues from direct and indirect taxation, the level of business profits, personal savings of individuals, and the purchase of government securities by nonbanking institutions. Exports provide the bulk of foreign exchange earnings for the import of capital equipment. It is apparent, therefore, that the level of demand and prices among the European powers that account for the bulk of Africa's trade, plus their bilateral and multilateral economic aid, have a rather decisive influence on the rate of capital formation in Africa. As a consequence, economic growth in Africa is still dependent to a large extent on the level of economic activity of European colonial or former colonial powers and aid from other industrial countries, including the United States.

The mobilization of savings in Africa is extremely difficult because the vast majority of the people live at the subsistence level. However, a significant amount of capital formation does take place among the subsistence farmers, which has not been incorporated in the monetized part of the economy. Self-help projects undertaken at the village level add to productive capacity. These activities include the building of roads with uncompensated communal labor, the forging of an ax by the village blacksmith, or the construction of a hut or grain storage facilities. Community development projects of this nature do add to capital stock. Such projects can contribute to cultural stock and facilitate the introduction of new technology at the village level. The exact magnitude of nonmonetary capital formation is not known. It is doubtful, however, if this type of capital formation can be effective outside the village concerned. For example, it is unlikely that labor in village X would have an incentive to build a road in village Y for the sole benefit of Y.

With respect to the monetized part of the economy, a reduction in current expenditures is an obvious source where savings could be effected. The extended family system operates to retain far too many nonproductive administrative employees. There is considerable scope for a reduction of expenditures for the administration of oppressive legislation, building of jails, maintenance of prisoners, expansion of the police force, and maintenance of the defense establishment. This is particularly true in the remaining colonial areas as well as in countries and territories where government is not based on the universal consent of the governed. The propensity for ostentatious consumption also operates to reduce the availability of funds for capital investment.

The overwhelming dependence of African countries on indirect taxation as a source of funds reflects the structural imbalance and undeveloped state of these countries. Indirect taxes, mainly from import and export duties, account for as much as 75 per cent of total current revenue in some countries. These taxes are relatively easy to collect, but impinge on the vast majority of people who are living at or near the subsistence level. Efforts are made in many countries to frame indirect taxes in such a way as to penalize consumption and to encourage investments in productive enterprises. This is being accomplished by placing high import duties, particularly on luxury goods, and by exempting or imposing low duties on machinery and industrial raw materials.

Government revenues from income and other direct taxes are important in white settler areas where there are substantial foreign investments in the mining industry. In the Rhodesias, for example, direct taxes account for about 55 per cent of total revenue. Direct taxes are very difficult to collect in most countries. It would not be beneficial to increase these rates because it would adversely affect incentives for private investment, both foreign and domestic.

The floating of government securities is an important source of funds for capital investment in non-French areas. This type of borrowing, however, does not shift private savings because returns are more on alternative investment such as real estate. Usually, the banking system subscribes to a substantial portion of securities floated by local governments. Whether this type of borrowing is inflationary depends among other things on the elasticity of domestic supply, monetary requirements for the economy, degree of hoarding, and the level of foreign exchange reserves for the importation of consumer goods to absorb excess purchasing power. Some governments impose compulsory bond schemes or deliberately generate inflation as a device to reduce consumption of some income groups.

Market boards in some countries have been used not only to insulate producers from fluctuations in world commodity prices, but also to act as a countercyclical instrument and a device for the mobilization of savings for investment. By operating through a variable export-tax marketing board mechanism, it is relatively easy for one-commodity economies to influence total effective demand and maintain a reasonable balance between savings and investment. This may be illustrated by a simple equation[24]: $G + I + X = T + S + Bp + M$. If the commodity price increases and exports rise, the economy would not be in balance because total investments would exceed savings. This would tend to generate inflationary pressures. The marketing board may step in and reduce producer prices so that profits equal the rise in income generated from export expansion. On the other hand, if the rise in total government expenditures exceeds revenues, the inflationary tendency of this budget deficit could be offset by raising the export tax on the commodity by an amount sufficient to cover the budget deficit. This illustration is based on the assump-

[24] Let G be total government expenditures; I, private domestic investment; X, exports; T, government tax revenue; S, private savings; Bp, marketing board profits; and M, imports.

tion of rising prices and expanding export income. Even if export prices are stable or declining, it is possible, if politically feasible, to reduce producer prices so as to increase funds for capital investment. Such action might tend to reduce imports for consumption and therefore reduce revenue from import duties. It might also reduce incentives in the export industry for further expansion of productivity or cause a shift of resources to alternative employment opportunities.

The bulk of funds for capital investment in Africa must be found from Africa's own resources; but like the United States and other countries in the early stages of development, African states must also rely to a considerable extent on foreign capital. In fact, no continent is more heavily dependent on foreign capital to finance economic development than is Africa. The degree of dependence varies among countries. Former French African states in particular are heavily dependent on external assistance to finance the foreign exchange component of total development expenditures. The Economic Commission for Africa notes that, "in 1960–1961 the average contribution of foreign funds to total foreign exchange receipts of Africa amounted to 24 per cent, or 28 per cent if the exports and capital transactions of South Africa are excluded." The ratio for all less-developed countries amounts to 19 per cent.[25]

In ex-French colonies south of the Sahara the ratio of total foreign long-term capital to total foreign exchange receipts amounted to more than 50 per cent.[26]

The ratio of inflow of long-term capital to total domestic capital formation is also very high. In Ghana and Morocco, it is nearly 35 per cent. In the former French colonies, it is much higher. It is clear, therefore, that even if domestic capital were adequate to sustain a high level of growth, this capital could not be put to use effectively because the lack of foreign exchange resources would serve as a serious bottleneck. As a result, the

[25] Economic Commission for Africa, *International Economic Assistance to Africa, 1961,* U. N. Economic and Social Council, E/CN.14/209, Feb. 19, 1963, p. 10.
[26] *Ibid.*

total development effort is influenced considerably by the magnitude of foreign capital available to finance the import of plant, machinery, and technical know-how.

Loans and grant obligations by foreign governments and multilateral institutions plus the flow of private capital to Africa have been recently running around $2 billion annually. This assistance was mainly provided by western Europe and the United States. Increases in government bilateral aid have been partly offset by a reduction in the net flow of foreign private capital. For example, the net flow of private capital dropped from roughly $555 million in 1960 to $425 million in 1961.

If the ratio of total foreign capital to domestic capital formation averaged 30 per cent, the total capital formation for Africa would amount to about $8 billion dollars. This would yield a gross product of $2 billion dollars, assuming a capital output ratio of 4.1. Therefore, GNP would increase by about 6 per cent at current prices. Owing to price increases and population growth, the real growth in GNP per capita would probably be less than 2 per cent. A substantial expansion in foreign assistance is therefore needed if the growth rate is to be increased.

The absolute contributions by the metropolitan power have in fact shown a continuous increase. At the same time, the need has increased as African states have expanded government functions from the maintenance of law and order and the building of infrastructure to promoting programs to increase productive capacity. In the wake of attaining independence by a large number of African states in 1960–1961, their relative dependence on the former colonial powers has declined.

The flow of government funds from France accounted for 78 per cent[27] of total bilateral and multilateral assistance to Africa for the period 1953–1954 to 1955–1956. Its share dropped to 70 per cent in 1958–1959 and by 1961 was down to 49 per cent. The magnitude of French funds to Africa, both government and private, amounted to $1 billion in 1960 and 1961.

The relatively low percentage of British assistance to Africa presumably reflects the policy of making the colonial areas "self-

[27] Excluding South Africa and the United Arab Republic.

TABLE 8. Net International Flow of Offical Capital and Donations to Undeveloped Countries, by Source*a* (1953–1954 to 1961)
(Percentage)

Sources	1953–1954 to 1955–1956 Total	Africa	1958–1959 Total	Africa	1960 Total	Africa	1961 Total	Africa
Bilateral	92	96	89	93	94	91	96	93
United States	48	6	51	11	55	20	57	21
France	31	78	22	70	18	50	16	49
United Kingdom	8	10	6	7	7	8	8	14
Germany (Federal Republic)	—	—	2	—	4	—	5	1
Other countries*b*	5	3	8	5	9	13	10	8
Multilateral agencies	8	4	11	7	6	9	4	7
Total	100	100	100	100	100	100	100	100

Source: Economic Commission for Africa, *International Economic Assistance to Africa, 1961*, U.N. Economic and Social Council, E/CN:14/209, Feb. 19, 1963, p. 6.
a Excluding aid from centrally planned economies; for 1960 and 1961, excluding transactions with South Africa and the United Arab Republic.
b Other contributing countries in western Europe, Canada, and Japan.

supporting." The flow of British funds to Africa accounted for 10 per cent of the total in the mid-1950s, dropped to 8 per cent by 1960, and then rose to 14 per cent of total bilateral aid to Africa in 1961. The total flow of British funds to Africa amounted to $317 million in 1961 compared with $188 million in 1960. This growth reflected a rise of $55 million in the flow of private capital and a $74 million increase in government funds, mainly to finance programs in East Africa, including the East African Common Services Organization.

It is evident, therefore, that ties with France and Britain are strong in spite of the relative decline in assistance to Africa in recent years. These countries still account for 63 per cent of total government aid to Africa ,compared with 98 per cent in the mid-1950s. In view of the prosperity of the Federal Republic of Germany, it is of some significance to note that its share in the flow of funds to Africa amounted to only $16 million in 1961.

The ratio of bilateral U.S. assistance to total bilateral aid has shown a steady increase, rising from 11 per cent in 1958–1959 to

21 per cent in 1961. The flow of private and official funds to Africa amounted to $442 million in 1960 and increased to $484 million in 1961. Government's share in this aid increased from $267 million in 1960 to $323 million in 1961. By 1962, U.S. government aid to Africa had reached $500 million. Assuming that the net flow of private capital was maintained at the 1961 level, the total outflow of U.S. loans, grants, and private capital to Africa amounted to $661 million in 1962. The estimate of $161 million for the flow of U.S. private investment to Africa in 1961 compares with estimates of $276 million for France, $101 million for the United Kingdom, and $114 million for Belgium-Luxembourg.

The attainment of independence by African states saw the beginning of a massive effort by the Soviet Union and Communist China to soften these countries for a takeover by a communist government, which remains the ultimate objective of communist countries. The immediate Soviet objectives in Africa have been to get them to take a neutral stand in East-West disputes, to get them to side with the Communist Bloc in such disputes whenever possible, and to aggravate their differences with the West. The policy instruments for the attainment of these objectives include economic aid, trade agreements buttressed by student scholarships, exchange of official visits, and propaganda. The determination of the Communist Bloc to attain these objectives is reflected in total credits and grants amounting to $678 million to eight countries in Africa during the period 1959–1962. Free world commitments for the same period are estimated at $5.8 billion.

SOME CURRENT CRITICAL PROBLEMS

The problems in Southern Africa are of such nature that they could have serious consequences for Africa and the world. In the southern third of Africa, there are 35 million blacks and 3.5 million whites. It has been described as a zone of "white privilege" and "black grievance," where justice demands "one man, one vote" and "political self-determination." All of black Africa is

TABLE 9. COMMUNIST BLOC CREDITS AND GRANTS TO AFRICA, 1959–1962
(Millions of Dollars)

Country	Total	Credits	Grants
Ethiopia	114	112	2
Ghana	200	200	0
Guinea	125	119	6
Mali	100	100	0
Morocco	5	5	0
Somali Republic	63	57	6
Sudan	25	25	0
Tunisia	46	46	0
Total	678	664	14

SOURCE: Bureau of Intelligence and Research, Department of State, *The Sino-Soviet Economic Offensive*, Agency for International Development, Washington, D.C., 1962, p. 9.

emotionally involved in this problem. The 3.5 million whites in this zone of privilege do have skills and capital that are important to growth and the general welfare. African leaders recently made it clear at Addis Ababa that there can be no compromise, no toleration of positions of neutrality, where questions of human dignity and freedom are concerned. They seem to be saying that man does not live by bread alone. They seem prepared to use part of their meager financial resources and limited skilled manpower to help eliminate remaining islands of oppression in Africa. The relative short-run prospects for development in all of Africa will therefore depend in some measure on a peaceful settlement of these pressing problems.

The second big issue in Africa is the question of the development of freedom. The West must not forget that, for countries locked in vicious circles of poverty, communist blandishments are not without appeal. Austerity measures by African states to overcome the handicaps of low income, low capital formation, and low growth sometimes produce political stresses and strains. Receptivity to communist aid and propaganda increases. The Soviets point to their growth since 1917, but always fail to mention the suppression of human freedoms that accompanied this growth. Perhaps more important, they give full support to Africa's present decolonization drive.

The West introduced Judeo-Christian values in Africa, which are the motivating factor behind the prevailing "winds of change" on that continent. It incited a revolution of rising expectations for a better life. Having done this, the West cannot permit Africa to remain a complacent, abandoned ship. It must be realized that the opportunities for communist penetration in Africa vary inversely with the efforts of the West to fulfill its responsibilities toward that continent.

A third major problem in Africa stems from colonialism and the efforts of African states to promote African unity. Some leaders in British Africa contend that the arrangement between the African countries associated with the European Common Market operates against African unity and is simply a device for perpetuating colonial privileges in Africa. It is asserted that the case of "Daniel and the lions may occasionally turn out all right, but it is not a safe basis for economic planning." Yet, it is recognized that many of these states are heavily dependent on trade with and aid from the former colonial power. Economically, the arrangement is a step in the direction of freer trade. At the same time, the Common Market has been particularly injurious to third parties because of its trade-diverting effects. Solutions are seen in promoting the establishment of a regional economic union in Africa that would negotiate with the EEC on the basis of equality. Duty-free treatment should be provided to all tropical products, and compensatory arrangements should be worked out for those states already receiving subsidies and subventions. In view of the suspicion surrounding the Euro-Africa concept, there is some merit in the argument that it is not a viable relation over time. Africa's fear of continued European domination is understandable. In the process of providing assistance, efforts must be made somehow to instill a greater degree of mutual confidence.

With respect to nation building endeavors, there are a whole range of problems associated with known ingredients favorable to economic and social growth. In the first place, a more systematic effort must be made to induce attitudes and institutions favorable to economic growth. Labor productivity, as reflected in output per man-hour, must be expanded. This means improvements in education, research, and health. The lack of trained manpower in Africa is critical. Great progress has been made in this area. More attention needs to be given to secondary vocational and technical education because labor bottlenecks arise not only from the lack of high-level manpower but also from middle-level manpower.

The mobilization of an adequate level of capital is a problem in itself, but the proper allocation of this capital is of greater importance. The economy of Africa is characterized by great structural imbalance, with bias toward exports. It appears that some countries have allocated substantial resources to improve ports, roads, rail, and other forms of transport on the assumption that productive capacity would automatically increase. Domestic supply has been rather inelastic in spite of these facilities, owing to the lack of private entrepeneurs with technical skills and know-how. Furthermore, there has been no great rush of foreign investors to take advantage of these external economies. In those countries with ample infrastructure, there needs to be more investment for the expansion of productive capacity. First priority should be given to agriculture so as to expand foreign exchange earnings, effect foreign exchange savings, and expand the tax base. As productivity in agriculture expands, more investments could be made in industry.

A final problem that needs to be given serious attention arises from the terms of loans extended to African countries. The interest rates are too high. More important, a grace period should be provided before amortization begins so that opportunity to implement development will allow a return on the investment. It should be noted that the local cost component of projects financed by foreign loans is at least 70 per cent in many countries. It is apparent that loans could place a strain on fiscal operations and even aggravate the foreign exchange situation if the domestic cost component must be financed by deficit borrowing from the banking system before expansion from production occurs.

CHAPTER 9

The Middle East[1]

Charles Malik

For the purposes of this chapter, the name "Middle East" covers the countries falling between and including Turkey in the north, Yemen and the Sudan in the south, Iran in the east, and Cyprus in the west. With the possible exclusion of Iran and Iraq in the east and Yeman and the Sudan in the south, this area used to be referred to, for the most part, and is still sometimes referred to, as the "Near East." "Near" relates the region to that to which it is near, namely, in this case, to Europe; "Middle" places it between

[1] The writer is fundamentally interested in philosophical and spiritual matters and in world affairs, and what particularly concerns him in these latter is the performance of Western civilization in the modern world, namely, the many sided challenges which face it and how it is meeting them. He accepted the assignment to write this chapter partly because it contained, besides economic matters, reference to general political and social conditions, and partly because he was assured by competent colleagues of his on the Faculty of the American University of Beirut that they would provide him with the basic economic data. On the side of data and facts, this inquiry would have been impossible without the invaluable assistance of Professor Elias Saba, Chairman of the Department of Economics at the American University of Beirut, and Professor Khalil Salem, Assistant Professor in the same Department.

The following abbreviations have been used for references in this chapter:

R & C: W. Stanley Rycroft and Myrtle M. Clemmer, *A Factual Study of the Middle East,* Office for Research, Commission on Ecumenical Mission and Relations, The United Presbyterian Church in the U.S.A., 475 Riverside Drive, New York, 1962.

1962 UNSY: United Nations *Statistical Yearbook,* 1962.

MEED: "Economic Developments in the Middle East, 1959–1961," Supplement to *World Economic Survey, 1961,* United Nations, New York, 1962.

1961 ITSY: United Nations *Yearbook of International Trade Statistics, 1961.*

two things to which it is near, namely, the West and the East proper. The fact that "Middle" has predominated in recent usage over "Near" measures the rise of the East in world-economic and world-political affairs. This region can no longer be related only to one of the two terms to which it is geographically properly related. But although its relatedness to the East is recognized by the use of the word "Middle," the continued use of the word "East" indicates that its relatedness to the West still predominates. From the point of view of India or regions farther east, this area is rather "Near West" or "Middle West." It is a fact, however, that the interaction (political, social, economic, cultural, religious) of this region with Europe and the West in general throughout history, as is clearly recognized by speaking of this area as "the cradle of Western civilization" (it is never, for instance, referred to as "the cradle of Indian or Eastern civilization"), has been far more critical and creative than its interaction with areas and cultures east. We are thinking in effect of Turkey, Cyprus, Israel, Iran, and the Arabic-speaking countries east of and including Egypt and the Sudan.

GENERAL CHARACTER OF THE MIDDLE EAST

Seven features determine between themselves the entire destiny of the Middle East:

1. Taken as a whole, the most important single physical feature of the area is the dominance of the desert. Man, since the beginning of time, has been desperately fighting aridity practically everywhere in the Middle East, and therefore water is by far the most important single commodity. This circumstance has more than anything else determined the history, economics, and culture of the whole area. He who has not meditated long and deeply on, and who has not profoundly taken in, the Middle East, does not understand the total meaning of the desert in human life.

2. Rooted in the fact of the desert is the second reason for the enormous human heterogeneity of the area. Unlike the sea, the desert divides; it divides even more than, or at least as much as, mountains; and oases of human settlements separated by vast expanses of sand never join into a single, firm, homogeneous whole. Vast differences span the Middle East from one point to another:

differences in forms of government, in economic attainments and economic possibilities, in cultural level, in social structure, in religion, language, and race. Even the Arabic-speaking Near East is marked by sharp contrasts; for example, between Yemen and the Sudan on the one hand, and Lebanon and Syria on the other. Very few substantive propositions are unequivocally true of all the peoples of the Middle East. Thus, to generalize in this area is to tread on the most treacherous of grounds. The area taken as a whole is a unity only geographically.

3. The Middle East as here defined joins three continents: Asia, Africa, and Europe. No area in the world is more strategically important than this one. Despite recent developments in the art of war, every great power continues to lend the Middle East a significant share of its strategic calculation. The destiny of the Middle East is fundamentally determined by its unique location at the heart of the Eastern Hemisphere where the three old continents meet.

The Middle East is the birthplace of the three great Semitic monotheistic religions: Judaism, Christianity, and Islam. The holy places of these three world religions exist in the Middle East. People outside the Middle East, therefore, are personally interested in its conditions and development, and this fact enters into the determination of its destiny.

5. The Christians in the Middle East are about 6 per cent, and the Jews, including those in the State of Israel are a little less than 2 per cent of the total population of the region. Thus the overwhelming majority of the peoples of the Middle East confess Islam in one or another of its many persuasions. Islam, therefore, both as to its fundamental nature and as to how it is going to develop, is a basic determinant of the destiny of the Middle East.

6. The Middle East has a larger and richer history than that of any other part of the world, although this history (again due ultimately in the first instance to the desert) is quite checkered and disconnected. In fact, one can show, in a sense to be determined independently, that the whole notion of history and development began in the Middle East; therefore it is correct to claim that *history itself is one of the inventions of the Middle East.* The vast living deposit of history that characterizes Middle

Eastern existence—physically, mentally, and culturally—is one of the fundamental determinants of its destiny.

7. And finally there is oil. By one of the fortuitous quirks of organic-geological formation, it appears that there is more oil under the sands of the Middle East than in all the rest of the world. It follows that no major event can take place or threaten to take place in the Middle East without the chancelleries of a score of all the powers, as well as of other nations and the managements of hundreds of corporations all over the world, immediately taking notice and moving to do something about it.

These seven features—the desert, human heterogeneity, strategic location, religion, Islam, history, and oil—set the Middle East apart, characterize its existence, and determine its destiny.

ECONOMIC PROBLEMS AND POLICIES

We are here studying the economic problems and policies of the Middle East and therefore we touch on other matters only insofar as they affect these. The respective tables reflect the principal relevant data. Each table lists the countries for which these data have been accumulated, and each pertains to a particular economic, geographic, or vital statistic factor.

TABLE 1.   RELEVANT DATA: AREA[a] (Square Miles)

Aden Area	117,130
Cyprus	3,572
Iran	628,060
Iraq	172,000
Israel	7,993
Jordan	37,500
Kuwait	5,800
Lebanon	4,000
Muscat and Oman	82,000
Persian Gulf Principalities	
(Bahrain, Qatar, and the	
Trucial States)	40,550
Saudi Arabia	870,000
Sudan	967,500
Syria	72,234
Turkey	296,500
U.A.R. (Egypt)	386,198
Yemen	75,000
Total	3,766,037

a SOURCE: R & C, p. 24.

TABLE 2. RELEVANT DATA: RAINFALL (Millimeters)

Aden Area[a]	. . .
Cyprus	305–1143
Iran	127–1524
Iraq	106–560
Israel[b]	. . .
Jordan	190–450
Kuwait	51–102
Lebanon	700–900
Muscat and Oman[c]	. . .
Persian Gulf Principalities (Bahrain, Qatar, and the Trucial States)	51–102
Saudi Arabia	102–510
Sudan	0–1524
Syria	215–675
Turkey	309–2489
U.A.R. (Egypt)	5–180
Yemen	406–813

SOURCE: *Worldmark Encyclopedia of the Nations* and *Foreign Trade.* (New York: Harper & Row, 1963).

a Averages about 3 inches annually.

b Fluctuates between 42.5 inches in Upper Galilee and 0.8 inches in Eilat.

c Varies from 2 to 12 inches, but averages about 4 inches annually.

TABLE 3. RELEVANT DATA: NATURAL RESOURCES

Aden Area	. . .
Cyprus	Cuprous pyrite, iron pyrite, asbestos, chrome, iron ore, gypsum, and terra umbra.
Iran	Oil, copper, iron, lead, zinc and coal
Iraq	Oil, sulfur
Israel	Potassium chloride, sodium chloride, calcium chloride, magnesium chloride, and magnesium bromide
Jordan	Phosphate, manganese, copper, marble, and potash
Kuwait	Oil
Lebanon	Water, climate, geographical position
Muscat and Oman	. . .
Persian Gulf Principalities (Bahrain, Qatar and the Trucial States)	Oil
Saudi Arabia	Oil
Sudan	Water, iron ore, and copper
Syria	Manganese and oil
Turkey	Copper, iron ore, chrome ore, sulfur, coal, lignite, manganese
U.A.R. (Egypt)	Oil, water phosphates, iron, manganese, lead, and zinc
Yemen	Iron and coal

SOURCE: *Worldmark Encyclopedia of the Nations.*

TABLE 4. RELEVANT DATA: POPULATION

Aden Area	913,000
Cyprus	581,000
Iran	20,678,000
Iraq	7,085,000
Israel	2,232,000
Jordan	1,757,000
Kuwait	219,000*
Lebanon	1,646,000
Muscat and Oman	550,000
Persian Gulf Principalities	
(Bahrain, Qatar and the Trucial States)	288,000
Saudi Arabia	6,036,000
Sudan	12,289,000
Syria	4,839,000
Turkey	27,829,000
U.A.R. (Egypt)	26,059,000
Yemen	5,000,000
Total	118,001,000

SOURCE: R & C, p. 24; based on United Nations statistics, data available as of April 1, 1962. There are later figures that can be computed country by country from the 1962 *Statistical Yearbook* of the United Nations.

a The official census of the government of Kuwait puts the figure for 1961 at 320,000.

TABLE 5. RELEVANT DATA: POPULATION GROWTH

	Percentage Increase Between 1950–1960
Aden Area	..
Cyprus	16
Iran	24
Iraq	34
Israel	68
Jordan	34
Kuwait	29
Lebanon	31
Muscat and Oman	..
Persian Gulf Principalities	
(Bahrain, Qatar, and the Trucial States)	32
Saudi Arabia	..
Sudan	..
Syria	42
Turkey	33
U.A.R. (Egypt)	27
Yemen	..
Percentage income (1950–1960) for countries with figures above.	34

SOURCE: R & C, p. 26; based on United Nations sources.

	Total Area	Arable Land and Land Under Tree Crops	Percentage of Total	Irrigated Land	Percentage of Arable Land and Land Under Tree Crops	Number of People per One Hectare of Arable Land and Land Under Tree Crops[a]
Aden Area						
Cyprus (1958)	925	434	46.9	80	18.4	1.3
Iran (1950)	163,000	16,760	10.3	1,600	9.5	1.2
Iraq (1955)	44,444	5,457	12.3	2,912	53.4	1.3
Israel (1959)	2,070	401	19.4	126	31.2	5.6
Jordan (1954)	9,661	893	9.2	32	3.6	2.0
Kuwait						
Lebanon (1959)	1,040	...[b]	...	71	...	...
Muscat and Oman						
Persian Gulf Principalities (Bahrain, Qatar, and the Trucial States)						
Saudi Arabia (1952)	160,000	210	0.1	...	...	28.7
Sudan						
Syria (1959)	18,448	5,491	29.8	476	8.7	1.0
Turkey (1959)	77,698	24,972	32.1	1,988	8.0	1.1
U.A.R. (Egypt) (1957)	100,000	2,610	2.6	2,610	100.0	10.0
Yemen						

SOURCE: MEED, p. 99, taken from "Food and Agriculture Organization of the United Nations," *Production Yearbook, 1960* (Rome).

a These figures are obtained by dividing the population figures of Table 4 by the figures in the column here under "Arable Land and Land Under Tree Crops."

b It is strange that data on arable land and land under tree crops in Lebanon were not available or were not separately reported.

TABLE 7. RELEVANT DATA: LIFE SPAN

Aden Area	..
Cyprus	66
Iran	Under 50
Iraq	Under 50
Israel	70
Jordan	Under 50
Kuwait	..
Lebanon	Under 50
Muscat and Oman	
Persian Gulf Principalities (Bahrain, Qatar, and the Trucial States)	
Saudi Arabia	40
Sudan	Under 50
Syria	Under 50
Turkey	60
U.A.R. (Egypt)	42
Yemen	35

SOURCE: R & C, p. 25. These figures are altogether unreliable. It is impossible that Cyprus has a life span of 66 and Lebanon has one under 50. Also, if Iran, Iraq, Jordan, and the Sudan have a life span described as "under 50," then certainly Lebanon's life span cannot be described as such. Finally, Lebanon's life span is certainly higher than Turkey's. This table on the life span of the countries of the Middle East is a perfect illustration of the primitive, sometimes incorrect, and often misleading, state of statistical information about the peoples of the Middle East.

TABLE 8. RELEVANT DATA: ILLITERACY
(1960 Percentage)

Aden Area	..
Cyprus	35
Iran	75–85
Iraq	85
Israel	5
Jordan	70
Kuwait	..
Lebanon	25
Muscat and Oman	..
Persian Gulf Principalities (Bahrain, Qatar, and the Trucial States)	
Saudi Arabia	85 or more
Sudan	93
Syria	40 or more
Turkey	60
U.A.R. (Egypt)	70
Yemen	95

SOURCE: R & C, p. 100. Other sources give different figures. Illiteracy in Lebanon is almost certainly less than 25 per cent.

TABLE 9. RELEVANT DATA: INDICATOR 9, EDUCATION SITUATION[a]

	Number of Students Studying in Home Country[b]		Number of Students at Institutions of Higher Learning Abroad (1958–1959)[f]	
	Technical Education[c]	Higher Education[d]	Western Europe	United States
Aden Area(1958)	300	...	...	...
Cyprus (1958)	397	...	169	53
Iran (1959)	8,997	18,085	3,395	2,104
Iraq (1958)	7,382	12,115	645	732
Israel (1959)	15,206	11,500	643	723
Jordan (1959)	1,292	...	392	591
Kuwait (1959)	1,242	...	13	35
Lebanon (1956)	e	3,999	595	544
Muscat and Oman ...				
Persian Gulf Principalities (Bahrain, Qatar, and the Trucial States) (1959)	441			
Saudi Arabia (1959)	1,081	206	15	66
Sudan (1959)	2,041	2,704	131	53
Syria (1959)	5,567	9,899	1,015	312
Turkey (1959)	74,205	52,060	1,515	779
U.A.R. (Egypt) (1959)	98,080	95,864	2,078	453
Yemen (1958)	61	...	6	12

a From the figures given here, one can make no valid comparison between these countries, either as to their cultural level or as to the academic standards of the technical or higher education fostered by them, or as to the type and quality of education pursued and realized by their students abroad.

b R & C, pp. 85–89; taken from United Nations *Statistical Yearbook 1961.* For more detailed information about all sorts of educational aspects, see R & C.

c This term includes postprimary vocational education that aims to prepare the pupils directly for a certain profession or trade.

d This term includes universities and postsecondary professional schools.

e One does not understand why this item is left blank in the original source, as Lebanon has many technical schools, in the sense here defined, with hundreds and perhaps thousands of students preparing for some vocation or trade.

f R & C, p. 97; taken from Francis Boardman, *Institutions of Higher Learning in the Middle East,* Middle East Institute, Washington, 1961, p. 7. It is well known that there are hundreds, perhaps thousands, of Middle Eastern students studying in communist countries; the figures given here refer only to students studying in western Europe or the United States.

TABLE 10. RELEVANT DATA: MAJOR ECONOMIC SECTORS*a*

Aden Area	Trade
Cyprus (1961)	Agriculture (24), industry (11), trade (10)
Iran	Oil, agriculture
Iraq	Oil (38), agriculture (18)
Israel (1960)	Industry (23), trade (20), agriculture (12)
Jordan (1959)	Trade (21), agriculture (14), transportation (13)
Kuwait	Oil, trade
Lebanon (1958)	Trade (27), agriculture (17), industry (14)
Muscat and Oman	
Persian Gulf Principalities (Bahrain, Qatar, and the Trucial States)	Oil
Saudi Arabia	Oil
Sudan (1960)	Agriculture (57), transportation and trade (14), construction (7)
Syria (1959)	Agriculture (37), industry (15), trade (14)
Turkey (1960)	Agriculture (41), industry (14), trade (8)
U.A.R. (Egypt) (1956)	Agriculture (33), industry (13), trade (10)*b*
Yemen	. . .

a The figures between parentheses express the adjoining sector's percentage of the gross domestic product for the indicated year. 1962 UNSY, pp. 498–504.
b This figure is for 1954.

TABLE 11. RELEVANT DATA: ECONOMIC SYSTEM*a*

Aden Area	A
Cyprus	A
Iran	A
Iraq	A
Israel	B
Jordan	A
Kuwait	A
Lebanon	A
Muscat and Oman	..
Persian Gulf Principalities (Bahrain, Qatar, and the Trucial States)	
Saudi Arabia	A
Sudan	A
Syria	C
Turkey	B
U.A.R. (Egypt)	C
Yemen	..

a In the notation we are using, A stands for an economic system nearest to a free enterprise system; B stands for an economic system intermediate between A and C; and C stands for an economic system nearest to a socialist system.

TABLE 12. Relevant Data: Middle Class^a

Aden Area	B
Cyprus	A
Iran	B
Iraq	B
Israel	A
Jordan	B
Kuwait	B
Lebanon	A
Muscat and Oman	D
Persian Gulf Principalities (Bahrain, Qatar, and the Trucial States)	D
Saudi Arabia	D
Sudan	D
Syria	B
Turkey	A
U.A.R. (Egypt)	C
Yemen	D

a By a middle class existing in a given country we mean that that country has a substantial class (in terms of economic activity) of doctors, lawyers, engineers, technicians, intellectuals, journalists, businessmen, merchants, petit bourgeoisie, and small landowners, who own their means of production and carry on their economic activity independently of the government, in the sense that, although the government may indeed do business with them, they are not government employees nor does the government control their economic activity. In the notation we use above, A stands for where a middle class, as here defined, exists and is likely to continue to exist; B stands for where a middle class exists but its fate is uncertain; C stands for where a middle class exists but is on the way out; and D stands for where it least exists.

TABLE 13. Relevant Data: Per Capita Income

	Per Capita Income in Local Currency		U.S. Dollar Equivalent
Aden area			
Cyprus (1961)	128.3	Cyprus pounds	
Iran			
Iraq (1956)	47.7	Iraqi dinars	133
Israel (1961)	1870	Israeli pounds	623
Jordan (1960)	56	Jordanian dinars	157
Kuwait			
Lebanon (1961)	1118	Lebanese pounds	372
Muscat and Oman			
Persian Gulf Principalities (Bahrain, Qatar, and the Trucial States)			
Saudi Arabia			
Sudan (1960)	32	Sudanese pounds	92
Syria (1961)	478	Syrian pounds	123
Turkey (1961)	1624	Turkish pounds	214
U.A.R. (Egypt) (1958)	48	Egyptian pounds	110
Yemen			

Source: Computed from figures obtained from 1962 UNSY.

TABLE 14. Relevant Data: Growth in Per Capita Income[a]

	Average Percentage Rate of Growth of Per Capita Income	Same Rate Deflated by the Cost of Living Index
Aden area		
Cyprus		
Iran		
Iraq (1954–1960)	5.4	2.4
Israel (1956–1960)	10.2	6.2
Jordan (1955–1959)	6.0	3.5
Kuwait		
Lebanon (1953–1957)	3.0	3.0
Muscat and Oman		
Persian Gulf Principalities (Bahrain, Qatar, and the Trucial States)		
Saudi Arabia		
Sudan (1957–1960)	1.3	Not available
Syria (1954–1960)	—1.5	Not available
Turkey		
U.A.R. (Egypt (1954–1960)	4.4	1.4
Yemen		

a This table is computed as follows:

1. Tabulate national income data as given in Issam Ashur's *Income Statistics in Arab Countries* of *the Arab Economic Report* (in Arabic), June, 1962, of the General Federation of the Chambers of Commerce, Industry and Agriculture of Arab Countries (pp. 91–118).
2. Tabulate national income data for Israel for the indicated period as given in IFS.
3. Tabulate population data for each year of the indicated period from (a) UAR, Egyptian Region, Statistical Department, *Statistical Pocket Yearbook, 1959;* United Nations, Department of Economic Affairs, *Demographic Yearbook, 1961;* United Nations, *Statistical Yearbook,* 1955–1961; Jordan, official *Statistical Yearbook,* 1952–1960; and Syria, official *Statistical Abstract,* 1956 and 1960.
4. Divide national income data as given in 1 and 2 by the population for the respective years, as given in 3, to obtain the per capita income for each year.
5. Compute the percentage rate of growth of the per capita income for each year over the year preceding.
6. Average these rates of growth for the given period of years. This gives column 1.
7. Deflate these average rates of growth by the cost of living index of the respective countries. This gives column 2.

TABLE 15. RELEVANT DATA: PROVEN OIL RESERVE
(In Millions of Barrels)

	Estimates of Proven Reserves as of January 1, 1962	Percentage of World Total
Aden Area	...	...
Cyprus	...	...
Iran	35,000	11.3
Iraq	26,500	8.6
Israel	34	...
Jordan	...	...
Kuwait	62,000	20.0
Lebanon	...	...
Muscat and Oman	...	...
Persian Gulf Principalities (Bahrain, Qatar, and the Trucial States)	12,495	4.0
Saudi Arabia	52,000	16.8
Sudan	...	...
Syria	100	...
Turkey	75	...
U.A.R. (Egypt)	710	0.2
Total	188,914	60.9
World Total	309,975	100.0

SOURCE: *Oil and Gas Journal* (Tulsa, Oklahoma) January 29, 1962. Quoted in R & C, p. 49.

TABLE 16. RELEVANT DATA: MIDDLE EAST CRUDE OIL PRODUCTION
(Thousands of Barrels per Day)

	1950	1955	1959
Aden Area	...	...	...
Cyprus	...	...	...
Iran	665	328	923
Iraq	128	691	848
Israel	...	...	...
Jordan	...	...	...
Kuwait	344	1,092	1,383
Lebanon	...	...	...
Muscat and Oman	...	...	...
Persian Gulf Principalities (Bahrain, Qatar, and the Trucial States)	63	169	330
Saudi Arabia	547	965	1,059
Sudan	...	...	...
Syria	...	...	...
Turkey	...	...	...
U.A.R. (Egypt)	...	...	...
Yemen	...	...	...
Total	1,747	3,245	4,543

SOURCE: R & C, p. 48; from *Aramco Handbook*, 1960. For the place of the Middle East with respect to the total world population of crude petroleum, see Table 19.

TABLE 17. RELEVANT DATA: FOREIGN TRADE

	Total Imports in Local Currency or in U.S. Dollars[a]	Total Exports in Local Currency or in U.S. Dollars[a]
Aden Area		
Cyprus (1961)[b]	40 million pounds	16 million pounds
Iran (1960)[b]	50 billion rials	62 billion rials
Iraq (1961)[b]	146 million dinars	231 million dinars
Israel (1961)[b]	586 million dollars[k]	245 million dollars[k]
Jordan (1961)[b]	42 million dinars	43 million dinars
Kuwait (1957)[c]	162 million dollars[k]	875 million dollars[k]
Lebanon (1961)[d]	1,061 million pounds	397 million pounds
Muscat and Oman		
Persian Gulf Principalities (Bahrain, Qatar, and the Trucial States)	[g]	
Saudi Arabia (1960–61)[e]	1.1 billion rials	3.9 billion rials
Sudan (1961)[b]	83 million pounds	59 million pounds
Syria (1961)[b]	644 million pounds[i]	350 million pounds[i]
Turkey (1961)[b]	4.6 million liras	3.1 billion liras
U.A.R. (Egypt) (1961)[f]	244 million pounds	169 million pounds[j]
Yemen	[h]	

a For the breakdown of these total figures into their respective components for each country, see the references below from which they are drawn. With the exception of the oil-producing countries (Iran, Iraq, Kuwait, the Persian Gulf Principalities, and Saudi Arabia) and Jordan, the value of the total imports of every country in the Middle East exceeds that of its total exports. Imports include foodstuffs, textiles, iron and steel, construction materials, machinery (including motor vehicles and their accessories), petroleum products, pharmaceuticals, books and other consumers goods, and a few investment goods. Exports include agricultural products (cotton, wool, tobacco, dates, cereals, vegetables, citrus fruits, etc.), raw materials (crude oil, various kinds of ores, fertilizers, etc.), and manufactured goods (textiles, finished pearls, motor and aviation fuel, etc.).

b 1961 ITSY.

c *Worldmark Encyclopedia of the Nations*, p. 789.

d Lebanon's official *Statistical Bulletin* (in Arabic), 1960–1961.

e Saudi Arabia's official *Statistics for Foreign Trade* (in Arabic), 1960–1961.

f International Monetary Fund, International Financial Statistics, Vol. XVI, No. 7, (July 1963) p. 263.

g The Government of Bahrain's Annual Report for 1961 shows that Bahrain's imports for 1961 amounted to $48.5 million (U.S.); its exports, other than oil (716 million metric tons in 1961) were actually negligible. According to the *Worldmark Encyclopedia of the Nations*, p. 789, Qatar's exports in 1958 were valued at $50 million, consisting almost entirely of crude oil.

h There are no reliable statistics on Yemen's foreign trade, but its principal export is coffee; it also exports hides, herbs, and agates. Its imports include foodstuffs, petroleum, iron and steel, and other consumers goods.

i Trade with Egypt being excluded.

j Cotton alone accounted for 105 million pounds of this figure. As an indication of Egypt's industrial development, its exports of finished and semifinished products amounted in 1961 to 27 million pounds; that is, 16 per cent of its total exports.

k The figures for imports and exports are all given in local currencies except those for Israel and Kuwait, which are given in U.S. dollars.

TABLE 18. RELEVANT DATA: COMPANIES TO GOVERNMENTS;
DIRECT PAYMENTS BY PETROLEUM COMPANIES TO GOVERNMENTS
(Millions of Dollars)

	1950	1956	1960
Aden Area	...	...	...
Cyprus	...	...	...
Iran	91	153	285
Iraq	19	194	267
Israel	...	...	...
Jordan	...	...	...
Kuwait	12	293	409
Lebanon	...	...	...
Muscat and Oman	...	...	...
Persian Gulf Principalities (Bahrain, Qatar, and the Trucial States)	3	46	67
Saudi Arabia	113	283	332
Sudan	...	...	...
Syria	...	...	...
Turkey	...	...	...
U.A.R. (Egypt)	...	...	...
Yemen	...	...	...
Total	238	969	1,360

SOURCE: MEED, p. 146.

TABLE 19. WORLD PRODUCTION OF CRUDE PETROLEUM, BY REGION
(Thousands of Tons, Percentage)

Region	1958	1959	1960	1961a	1961 Per Cent of World Total	Per Cent Change, 1961 over 1958
Middle East	215,002	231,574	265,112	282,296	25.2	31.3
North America	353,320	372,900	373,963	384,200	34.3	8.7
Latin America	176,227	188,662	197,672	202,055	18.1	14.7
Eastern Europeb	126,750	143,592	162,653	181,650	16.2	43.3
Far Eastc	25,502	29,319	32,293	33,425	3.0	31.1
Western Europe	12,112	12,931	14,108	15,065	1.3	24.4
Africa	1,358	2,809	10,668	19,720	1.8	1,352.1
World total	910,300	981,800	1,056,800	1,118,900	100.0	22.9

SOURCE: MEED, p. 135.
a Estimates.
b Including the Soviet Union and Yugoslavia.
c Including China (mainland).

The rest of this chapter is in effect a series of reflections on, or deductions from the preceding tables of relevant data. The reader is therefore invited to ponder the significance of these figures and draw his own conclusions from them. I shall here add a few general observations.

1. It is only lately (for the most part since World War II and in particular during the past decade) that the science of statistics has been applied in the Middle East. Not only are there still many lacunae to be filled, but the available data themselves are often unreliable. One does the best one can to obtain as precise an idea as possible, and when better data are compiled and become available, of course one turns to them. It must also be kept in mind that "due to variations in national methods of compiling data, information for the various countries is not always strictly comparable." (MEED, p.iii) It is enough for the present purposes to ascribe responsibility for the data used to the sources from which they are drawn. Where sources are not explicitly indicated, the writer alone is responsible for the opinions offered.

2. The desert, oil, and poverty—these three stand out at practically every point.

3. Table 6 on arable and irrigated land and on people per hectare is most significant. To appreciate the full meaning of these matters, the reader should go back to the complete tabulation of the Food and Agriculture Organization (MEED, p. 99). The density of people per hectare of arable land and land under tree crops is virtually the same throughout (a little more than one person per hectare on the average) except for Saudi Arabia, Egypt, and Israel, where it is 28.7, 10.0, and 5.6 persons per hectare, respectively. But if account is taken not only of what is designated "arable land and land under tree crops," but of the other economically productive areas described as "permanent meadows and pastures," "forested land," and land "unused but potentially productive," we obtain the figures of population density as given in Table 20.

The economic value of a hectare under the four descriptions,

TABLE 20.   POPULATION DENSITY PER HECTARE OF ECONOMICALLY
PRODUCING OR PRODUCTIVE LAND

	Area in Thousands of Hectares That Is Either Already Economically Producing or Potentially Economically Productive	Population	Persons per Hectare of Area in First Column
Aden Area	...	...	...
Cyprus	729	581,000	0.8
Iran	78,760	20,678,000	0.3
Iraq	20,202	7,085,000	0.4
Israel	1,272	2,232,000	1.8
Jordan	2,558	1,757,000	0.7
Kuwait	...	...	...
Lebanon	734	1,646,000	2.2
Muscat and Oman	...	...	...
Persian Gulf Principalities	...	...	...
Saudi Arabia	93,370	1,036,000	0.06
Sudan	...	...	...
Syria	14,366	4,839,000	0.3
Turkey	64,556	27,829,000	0.4
U.A.R. (Egypt)	3,127	26,059,000	8.3
Yemen	...	...	...

"arable land and land under tree crops," permanent meadows and pastures," "forested land," and land "unused but potentially productive," is clearly not the same, and some sort of a "production coefficient" ought to be devised (a difficult requirement but theoretically quite possible of achievement) to render economically additive the figures given by the Food and Agriculture Organization under these diverse headings. When such a "production coefficient" is scientifically worked out, we shall have a different series of figures for the first column of Table 20, based on one and the same "production unit." The figures then will be more strictly comparable and the population density per hectare, which will then be different from the figures set forth under the third column in Table 20, will be more meaningful. Despite all these qualifications, the density figures given in Table 20 are most significant. So far as what we have been calling the meaning of the desert is concerned, namely, so far as land that is actually producing or that is potentially productive is concerned (and without taking into account the standard of living and the "production coefficient" we referred to above), Egypt is effectively 21 times more densely populated than Turkey or Iraq, 27 times more densely populated than Syria or Iran, 140 times (further reservations must be made here) more densely populated than Saudi Arabia, 4 times more densely populated than Lebanon, 12 times more densely populated than Jordan, 5 times more densely populated than Israel, and 10 times more densely populated than Cyprus.[2] Put in general qualitative terms (which happen in this instance to be more precise), the possibilities for further exploitation of available land are, as revealed by the figures of the Food and Agriculture Organization, much smaller for Egypt (the High Dam here not taken into account) than for any other country in the Middle East. The implications of this fact, both politically and with respect to economic policies and problems of the Middle East, are obvious. It is also obvious that everything that can be done to help Egypt to solve its economic problems should be done, not only because the solution of these problems is important for Egypt (that in itself would be enough to justify such action), but also because their solution is vital for peace and contentment in the Middle East.

4. The figures on illiteracy (Table 8) are not very accurate, but they give a general indication of the state of affairs obtaining. Furthermore, as far as mobilizing the masses for political or other purposes is concerned, what is important today is not whether the masses can read and write, but whether they can hear. A small transistor radio (and they are getting smaller and smaller every day) in the hand or in the pocket of the most illiterate man can put him in touch with sources of information and instruction almost anywhere in the world.

2 In his article on *Two Centers of Arab Power* (*Foreign Affairs,* July, 1959) and in the book of which he is co-author with Ibrahim Abdelkader Ibrahim, entitled *Human Resources for Egyptian Enterprise* (McGraw-Hill Book Co., Inc., New York, 1958), Frederick Harbison makes interesting observations on the comparative Egyptian demographic situation.

GENERAL MATERIAL–ECONOMIC SITUATION

There are four broadly distinguishable zones in the Middle East:

1. A plateau extending through Asia Minor and Iran in the north.
2. A vast desert in the south.
3. Several disconnected ranges of mountains and hills in southern and northeastern Turkey, in northern Iran and Iraq, in Lebanon and Western Syria, and in the Yemen.
4. A zone intermediate between desert on the one hand and plateau and mountain on the other, consisting of Cyprus, Israel, parts of Lebanon and Syria, Jordan, Iraq, and the Persian Gulf area.

Climatic conditions are therefore most varied: intense heat and practically no rainfall in the desert domain, heavy rain and low winter temperatures in Turkey and Iran, and a relatively mild climate with a marked Mediterranean rhythm of winter rain and summer drought in the intermediate zone. Under these conditions, agriculture has developed a threefold pattern: irrigation, for the most part in the great valleys of the Nile and the Tigris and Euphrates in Egypt and Iraq; dry farming in the intermediate zone; and nomadic pastoralism in the endless stretches of the desert. But the cultivated land is limited to less than 8 per cent of the total area, and where it depends on rainfall, it is vulnerable to seasonal precipitational vagaries.

Although generalization is hazardous, one may say that economic and social existence in the general area of the Middle East is characterized by the facts that:

1. It is predominantly agrarian, the rural population accounting for 60 to 85 per cent of the total population.
2. On the whole, Middle East farming is not commercialized, being largely for local subsistence with emphasis mostly on cereals.
3. Share tenants and wage farmers constitute the mass of the

rural population, earning a low share of the value of their product, exercising practically no political power, and standing in marked contrast to the rich and powerful landowners and urban merchants or to the politicians and army officers who have seized power.

4. The small rural industries that exist employ for the most outdated techniques and suffer comparatively from low productivity.
5. The middle class, although growing in some countries, is still insufficient to bridge the chasm between the few wealthy and the many poor.
6. A relative dearth of arable land and a general insufficiency of water supply present serious obstacles to economic growth and development programs.

This generalization must be qualified by observing that:

1. The lower Nile Valley, a good proportion of Lebanon's, Syria's and Israel's cultivated land, certain parts of the Sudan, and a rather small district in southern Iraq, have developed commercialized farming.
2. A serious attempt at industrialization is being made in Egypt.
3. Socializing tendencies and policies have been responsible for the distribution of considerable land among the peasants, notably in Egypt, Syria, Iraq, Iran, and Turkey.
4. Where "socialism" has struck as a government policy, the middle class is being liquidated and only state capitalism is left, namely, the government with its vast bureaucracy controlling the output of the toiling masses, both peasants and industrial workers.
5. Cyprus, Israel, and Lebanon are an exception in that they have a relatively large middle class.
6. There is plenty of arable land still unused in Cyprus, Iran, Iraq, Israel, Jordan, Syria, and Turkey.

Industry, although following an appreciable expansionary trend for a decade, is generally still in its infancy and constitutes, apart from oil production, a secondary source of income. The urge at industrialization is widespread, but its fulfillment is limited by the relative absence of mineral resources and technological culture. Since World War II, there has been some development in light industries, particularly textiles (cotton, wool, and silk), the processing of agricultural products (sugar, tobacco, and fruits), and the manufacture of cement and cement products. There are some assembly plants for motor vehicles and electrical and other machinery in Egypt, Israel, and Turkey. But the share of industry in the national income is still relatively small.

There has been thus a generally heavy dependence on primary products for exports. Agricultural products, though falling in relative importance, accounted in 1960 for 63 per cent of the total value of exports, exclusive of oil exports. Moreover, as far as the agricultural sector is concerned, most countries depend on one commodity or a limited group of commodities: Egypt on cotton, wheat, and barley; Iran on cotton, almonds, nuts, and raisins; Iraq on dates and barley; Israel on citrus fruits; Lebanon on fruits and vegetables; Syria on wheat, barley, and cotton; and Turkey on tobacco, cotton, wheat, fruits, and nuts.

The Middle East trade, including petroleum, totaled in 1960 about $5.1 billion for exports and $4.4 billion for imports, showing thus a surplus in the balance of trade of $700 million. Petroleum exports amounted in 1960 to $3.6 billion, or approximately 71 per cent of the total exports; without these exports, the region's trade balance would show a deficit of $2.9 billion. Taken as a whole, the Middle East depends for the financing of its imports primarily on its oil exports. An examination of the trends of exports and imports indicates a continuous increase of this dependence on oil. The value of both imports and exports has been rising at almost the same rate: imports rose by 18.9 per cent and exports by 18.6 per cent over the period of 1957–1960. Commodity exports other than oil increased at a moderate rate.

Manufactured products constitute the bulk of the imports of the Middle East. They vary for 1960 between 34 per cent of the total imports of Cyprus, as the lowest, and 62 per cent of the total imports of Iran, as the highest.

One may note two important consequences of this broad composition of foreign trade: (1) Earnings from exports are vulnerable to forces operating in foreign markets over which the governments of the Middle East have no significant control. (2) As far as nonpetroleum exports are concerned, the countries of the region have had the worst of two worlds—falling prices of the bulk of these exports, and rising prices of the larger part of their imports—in a word, a general deterioration in their terms of trade. As the Middle East depends greatly on foreign trade (the ratio of the value of foreign trade to gross domestic product averaging about 40 per cent for the whole region), its economies are particularly susceptible to business fluctuations abroad, and its ability to ensure a stable inflow of foreign goods or of funds for development is limited. The political implications of this general situation, both internal and external to the Middle East, are obvious.

To sum up this preliminary survey of the general economic situation: The Middle East is overwhelmingly arid; agriculture is mostly primitive, though steadily improving in some countries; except for oil, the Middle East is very poor in natural resources; its imports are financed primarily by its petroleum exports; scientific and technological know-how is very rudimentary; industry is at its earliest stages and will always be limited by the paucity of known mineral resources; and, while depending to a large extent on foreign trade, the Middle East can exert no appreciable control over the factors and forces that determine this trade.

The demographic situation is compounding the economic problems. It is estimated that in the decade 1950–1960, the population of the Middle East has increased roughly 34 per cent; Iran increasing 24 per cent; Iraq, 34 per cent; Israel, 68 per cent; Syria, 42 per cent; Turkey, 33 per cent, and the United Arab Republic (Egypt), 27 per cent. It is thus estimated that at this rate of population growth, in 1975 Iran will number 34.3 million; Iraq, 9.2 million; Israel, 3.8 million; Jordan, 2.3 million; Lebanon, 2.3 million; Saudi Arabia, 9.5 million; the Sudan, 12.2 million; Syria, 7.2 million; Turkey, 40 million; and the United Arab Republic (Egypt), 38.3 million; with the total population of the Middle East rising then to 165 million. The question arises whether the economic development of the Middle East is keeping pace with its population growth. Nor is it enough that the two phenomena only "keep pace" with each other, for there is a third phenomenon that is also decisive, and that is the rising expectations of the people for a better life as a result of increased literacy, of the general enlightenment consequent upon the use of the radio and television, and of the unrealistic promises that leaders sometimes make to the masses for political purposes. Thus, since the standard of living is already very low, and since the peoples are increasingly demanding from their leaders higher and higher levels of material existence, economic development must move much faster than population growth. Unless these three phenomena—economic development, population growth, and psychological expectations—are properly adjusted to one another, the Middle East faces a long period of instability and turmoil, extending perhaps for decades and generations if not, in the absence of an international revolution or a fundamental scientific-technological revolution, indefinitely. Because of its central world location, a chronically unstable and disaffected Middle East carries grave implications for world peace.

One method of bringing about this adjustment is the development of strong authoritarian regimes that will keep the lid down. This cannot last indefinitely because these days the people know what is happening elsewhere in the world, and if they do not, others will see to it that they do. So, to aid the strong authoritarian hand, which will always be necessary, resort has been had to imparting some consoling ideology, some "ism" (and with the modern techniques of scientific conditioning, this is not difficult to implement), which will cause people to forget about their lot and live in substitute dreams, hopes, and abstract ideas. In this way, certain modern ideologies become real opiates of the people. But again it is doubtful that strong rule, even if supported and supplemented by the most ingeniously devised and the best technologically implemented ideology, can these days take people's minds off their condition for long. Sooner or later the day of reckoning will come when the people, having waited long enough and becoming absolutely fed up, will demand that the real goods be delivered.

Another method of adjusting economic development, population growth, and rising expectations to one another is birth control. President Nasser of the United Arab Republic announced in 1963 that he was seriously considering the use of scientific methods of birth control in Egypt, and other responsible leaders in Asia and Africa have shown similar interest in this matter; and there is some experimentation going on in some countries on it. Whether birth control is practicable, namely, whether governments can really press it upon people, remains to be seen. But even if population growth is completely eliminated through a most successful campaign for birth control, so that the populations of the countries of the Middle East are all kept at their present level, or even if these populations slightly decrease, and in some cases even if they are halved, the standard of living of some of these countries is so low even at their present population level, and will be so low even if they are halved, and their natural possibilities for economic expansion are so limited, that inner tension due to rising expectations for a better life will not be appreciably affected by birth control. It is obvious we are dealing here with a radical situation as it is, and only drastic international measures in the interest of peace can really help.

ECONOMIC RESOURCES

Oil is by far the most important mineral resource of the Middle East. There is phosphate and potash in Jordan; the former dominates the exports of the country while the latter is still to be extensively developed. About one-half of Cyprus's exports are metalliferous ores and concentrates, chiefly cuprous pyrites, iron pyrites, asbestos, and chromite. Turkey is one of the world's largest producers of chrome, and has in addition important deposits of iron and coal and moderate deposits of bauxite, boracite, lead, zinc, sulfur, salt, and magnesite. In recent decades the government has encouraged the exploitation of this wealth, especially of coal in which large public funds have been invested.

But by far the most important single economic resource in the Middle East is oil. The region maintains the position of the second largest crude oil-producing area in the world, supplying in 1961 25.2 per cent of the world production of crude petroleum, North America leading with 34.3 per cent of the total world production. The chief oil-producing countries of the region are, by order of importance, Kuwait, Saudi Arabia, Iran, and Iraq, supplying together approximately 92 per cent of the total oil production of the region. The rate of growth in crude oil production varies substantially from country to country; nevertheless, the relative share of these four countries in the area's total production and the order of their importance have been maintained for the past decade.

Proven oil reserves in the Middle East amount to 188,914 millions of barrels today, or about 61 per cent, of the world's total proven reserves. Kuwait alone has 20 per cent of the world's total reserves; Saudi Arabia, 16.8 per cent; and Iran, 11.3 per cent. Experts confide privately that they would not be surprised if ten or fifteen years from now the figure of 188,914 million barrels of proven oil reserves in the Middle East were revised to double or triple that amount.

Oil-producing countries of the Middle East derive a considerable income from oil in the form of direct payments by the petroleum companies to the respective governments. These direct payments rose from $1,196 million in 1958 to $1,375 million in 1960. Kuwait, Saudi Arabia, Iran, and Iraq receive together about 95 per cent of this revenue, each earning, respectively, 30 per cent, 26 per cent, 20.5 per cent, and 19 per cent. In addition, the oil companies' tremendous capital and operating expenditures supply a substantial contribution to the income of these countries, amounting for 1958–1959 to approximately $385 million.

Other countries of the Middle East through which pipelines pass, namely, Jordan, Lebanon, and Syria, receive revenues from oil in the form of transit fees. These fees are determined by the terms of transit payment agreements between the pipeline companies and the countries concerned, amounting today to about

$4 million for Jordan, $9 million for Lebanon, and $25 million for Syria annually. The United Arab Republic (Egypt) also earns transit fees in the form of revenue from the transport of oil through the Suez Canal, which amounted in 1960 to $101 million.

The current great expansion of the Middle East oil industry parallels a correspondingly growing world dependence on this region's oil. If its expansion so far has been spectacular, its future development is likely to be even more so. In 1956 total Middle East oil production was approximately 172 million tons and satisfied over 20 per cent of the energy requirements of the world market outside the Soviet bloc. In 1960 it rose to 265.1 million tons, and in 1961 to 282.3 million tons, or 30 per cent of total world production, again outside the Soviet bloc, or 25.2 per cent of world production, including this zone. In 1965 the world will depend on Middle East oil to satisfy some 35 per cent of the 1200 million tons of its expected oil requirements, and in 1975 Middle East oil is expected to supply 50 per cent of the total world oil requirements, which will then rise to 1600 million tons a year. These figures alone demonstrate the decisive importance of the future of this industry.[3] The ownership of the Middle East oil companies is given in Table 21.[4]

EFFECTS OF EUROPEAN COMMON MARKET

The European Common Market arrangements are not likely to result in the short run in significant direct effects on Middle East economies and trade. Long-run direct effects are dependent on

The impact of the Market upon the volume and proceeds of Middle East exports, other than oil, to the countries of the Market will depend, fundamental political-international considerations apart, on (1) the height of the future unified tariff of the several unknowns and cannot be foretold now.

[3] On oil production and world needs for petroleum products, see Royal Institute of International Affairs, *The Middle East, A Political and Economic Survey*, 3d ed., Oxford University Press, New York, 1958, pp. 57–63.
[4] *Middle East Petroleum Data*, Arabian American Oil Company, Dhahran, Saudi Arabia, September 1962.

TABLE 21. MIDDLE EAST OIL COMPANIES

	Per Cent Ownership
1. Bahrain:	
The Bahrain Petroleum Company, Ltd.	
Standard Oil Co. of California	50
Texaco, Inc.	50
2. Iran:	
Iranian Oil Participants, Ltd.	
British Petroleum Company, Ltd.	40
Royal Dutch/Shell Group	14
Compagnie Francaise des Petroles	6
Standard Oil Company (New Jersey)	7
Standard Oil Company of California	7
Texaco, Inc.	7
Gulf Oil Corporation	7
Socony Mobil Oil Company	7
Iricon Agency, Ltd.	5
"SIRIP" Societe Irano-Italeinne Des Petroles	
NIOC	50
AGIP Mineraria	50
3. Iraq:	
Iraq Petroleum Company, Ltd.	
British Petroleum Company, Ltd.	23.75
Royal Dutch/Shell Group	23.75
Compagnie Francaise des Petroles	23.75
Near East Development Corp.	23.75
(Standard Oil Co. [N.J.], [50%])	
(Socony Mobil Oil Co., [50%])	
Participation & Exp. Corp.	5.00
(C. S. Gulbenkian Estate)	
Basrah Petroleum Company, Ltd.	
(Same ownership as IPC, Ltd.)	
Mosul Petroleum Company, Ltd.	
(Same ownership as IPC, Ltd.)	
Petroleum Administration Board	
(Khanaqin)	
Iraq Government	100
4. Kuwait:	
Kuwait Oil Company, Ltd.	
BP (Kuwait), Ltd.	50
Gulf Kuwait Company	50
(Gulf Oil Corporation)	
5. Qatar:	
Qatar Petroleum Company, Ltd.	
(Same ownership as IPC, Ltd.)	

TABLE 21. MIDDLE EAST OIL COMPANIES *(Cont.)*

	Per Cent Ownership
6. Saudia Arabia—Kuwait Neutral Zone:	
American Independent Oil Company (Onshore)	
(Holding an undivided one-half interest)	
Getty Oil Company (Onshore)	
(Holding an undivided one-half interest)	
Arabian Oil Company (Offshore)	
Saudi Arabian Government	10.0
Kuwait Government	10.0
Kansai Power Company (Japan)	7.3
Tokoyo Power Company (Japan)	6.9
Yawata Steel Company (Japan)	6.9
Fuji Steel Company (Japan)	6.9
Nippon Kokan (Japan)	6.9
Fifty-seven other companies (Japan) and individuals	45.1
7. Saudi Arabia:	
Arabian American Oil Company	
Standard Oil Company of California	30
Texaco, Inc.	30
Standard Oil Co. (N.J.)	30
Socony Mobil Oil Company	10
8. Abu Dhabi:	
Abu Dhabi Marine Areas, Ltd.	
British Petroleum Co., Ltd.	66⅔
Cie Francaise des Petroles	33⅓

Market, (2) the supply conditions of the associated territories for goods that compete or will compete with Middle East exports, and (3) the rise in the demand for imports to be expected from the formation of the Market.

The unified tariff will raise the duty on imports from the Middle East into some countries of the Market and will lower it on imports into some other member countries. It is difficult to say now whether on balance the effect will be adverse or favorable to the region's export trade to the countries of the Market. Judging, however, from the nature of Middle East exports, other than oil, to the Common Market countries and from their relative importance in the total export trade of the region, the significance of such effect would be limited. The main commodities, other than oil, exported by the Middle East to members of the Common Market are, in order of importance: raw cotton, wheat, ground nuts, cakes of oleaginous seeds, onions, Arabic gum, sesame, raw skin and hides, and barley. All of these products are classified as raw materials for industry or as foodstuffs, and therefore the unified tariff thereon will not be high.

Despite the fact that the unified tariff rates on these products will be low, the Common Market will probably discriminate against Middle East exports in favor of the associated territories insofar as these can supply competitive products. But whether or not such discrimination will be effective will depend on the cost conditions in these territories and ultimately on the future competitiveness of their supply conditions. Further, the relative importance of these materials in the export trade of the Middle East countries is very limited. Only raw cotton exports to the Market countries occupy a position of some importance: 15.5 per cent of the total exports of Syria, 14 per cent of the total exports of the Sudan, and 9.1 per cent of the total exports of Egypt. Among other exports to the Market countries, wheat and barley account for 8.4 per cent and dates for 1.5 per cent of the total exports of Iraq; ground nuts account for 5.4 per cent of the total exports of the Sudan; and none of the other products accounts for as much as 1 per cent of the total trade of the country concerned.

The formation of the European Common Market is expected to accelerate the rate of growth of the economies of member countries. The resultant rise in income will lead to increased expenditures for goods and services and will probably mean greater imports. There is no reason to believe that the Middle East will not share in the benefits of such a development. But considering the nature of Middle East exports to Europe, one cannot assume a high income elasticity of demand for them, with the possible exception of services, and therefore one should not exaggerate the importance of this effect of the formation of the Market.

The above argument is limited, first, by excluding oil from its purview; secondly, by relating only to the direct effects of the Common Market upon the nonoil exports; and thirdly, by not touching upon the possible effect of the Common Market upon the pattern of imports into the Middle East. These three limitations must now be corrected.

As we showed above in the section on oil, the expansion of the Middle East oil industry, even taking into account oil developments in Libya, Algeria, and other parts of Africa, will cause the economies of Europe and the Middle East to be intimately interlocked. Until nuclear energy replaces petroleum energy for industrial purposes, the Middle East will continue to count on world industrial markets, principally Europe (the Soviet bloc is more than self-sufficient in this regard), for the sale of its oil, and with the growth of the Common Market there will be an increased demand for and dependence upon Middle East oil. The two economies being thus somewhat complementary, European industry running mostly on the oil of the Middle East, and this latter having its principal outlet in Europe, there will be increasing interdependence between them.

Again, the creation of a huge integrated European economy, competing vigorously in world markets with the two existing unitary economies of the United States and the Soviet bloc, is likely to exert a significant effect upon the imports pattern of the Middle East. Because of its past experience in these areas, Europe knows more about the needs of these developing peoples than America, and since its products, both by reason of lower costs of production and the other advantages accruing from a unified European economy, will probably be quite competitive in relation to American goods, European industry could in time capture and hold most of the markets of the Middle East.

This conclusion is supported by the trend discernible in the following figures (Table 22) on imports into the Middle East from Europe and America during the last quarter of a century. European imports into the Middle East were 30 per cent of the total imports into the region just before World War II; they dropped to 11.2 per cent in 1948 and have been steadily rising since then (with a slight disturbance about the time of Suez), until they amounted in 1961 to 25.0 per cent of the total. On the other hand, American exports to the region were 4.4 per cent of

TABLE 22. AMERICAN AND EUROPEAN EXPORTS TO THE MIDDLE EAST
(1938–1961)

	1938	1948	1952	1953	1954	1955	1956	1957	1958	1959	1960	1961
Total imports into the Middle East (million dollars)	720	2,230	2,680	2,520	2,650	3,090	3,290	3,620	3,860	4,010	4,390	4,600
U.S. exports into the Middle East (million dollars)	32	295	375	335	325	425	515	470	505	595	680	730
EEC exports to the Middle East (million dollars)	215	250	480	520	605	710	740	815	950	950	1,160	1,130
U.S. percentage of total	4.4	13.2	14.0	13.3	12.3	13.8	15.7	13.0	13.1	14.8	15.5	15.6
EEC percentage of total	30.0	11.2	17.9	20.1	22.8	23.0	22.5	22.5	24.6	23.7	26.4	25.0

SOURCE: United Nations *Statistical Yearbook, 1962.*

the total in 1938 and rose to 13.2 per cent ten years later; since then they kept more or less the same level, rising to a maximum of 15.7 per cent in 1956, falling below this level the three years following, and picking up again to 15.5 per cent and 15.6 per cent in 1960 and 1961, respectively. The trend is very clear as to the better relative performance of European trade in the Middle Eastern market, and there is no reason to suppose that a strong Common Market will not enhance even this trend.

Further, Europe could at some point in the future attract for investment in its own flourishing economies a substantial part of the accumulated oil money in the Middle East. Some of this money is now drawn to Japan and other non-European investment areas, but a strong European Common Market could offer more attractive terms.

Finally, whatever the direct effect of the Common Market upon the economies of the Middle East, its possible indirect effect is likely to be quite important. The voice of Europe in the affairs of the Middle East has been muffled since World War II, and especially since Suez, by the voices of Russia and America. If the Common Market should help in re-establishing the relative world position of Europe, then Europe could exert a more decisive influence on the course of events in the Middle East. Since international economics is not independent of international politics, this restored European weight in world councils could have important consequences, even upon the economic development of this region. It must never be forgotten that America is not as critically related to the Middle East as Europe and Russia, and therefore these two between them could in time dominate the affairs of the Middle East to the exclusion of America.

DEVELOPMENT AND CAPITAL RESOURCE

Almost all the governments of the Middle East have by now accepted and espoused the principle of economic planning for development. Most of them have already formulated their plans and put them into application; a few are still considering them.

The wave of direct governmental responsibility for the material welfare of the people, known in our times by various names, including the term *socialism*, has thus reached the Middle East. Economic planning differs widely from country to country, being carried out for the most part by the government in some cases and including, where free economic enterprise is still allowed, the private sector as well in others.

Table 23 shows planned public expenditures in most Middle Eastern countries. They are based on a 1961 United Nations report. Since then, many changes have been introduced in the planning of the governments of the Middle East. This is a fluid situation reviewed and revised year by year, and any picture presented reveals only the state of affairs at the moment the picture was taken.

It will be seen from these figures that, subject to footnotes *o* and *p*, public development expenditures on agriculture have ranged from a meagre 3.9 per cent of the government's total in Saudi Arabia to a substantial 50.9 per cent of the government's total in Syria; industry's share ranged between 1.6 per cent in Jordan and 36.8 per cent in the United Arab Republic (Egypt) (for which, however, see footnote *r*); and transportation expenditures varied between 16.0 per cent of the total in the United Arab Republic (Egypt) and 37.1 per cent in Saudi Arabia.

Unlike the popular model of an underdeveloped economy, the Middle East, taken as a whole, does not suffer from lack of capital funds. This does not mean, however, that there are no countries in the area the development programs of which are hindered by the unavailability of capital, and which therefore require foreign capital to help them in the execution of these programs. Examples of precisely such countries are Egypt, Turkey, and Israel. But if all the capital available for investment in the area is taken into consideration—whether it has originated in authentic domestic savings (including oil revenues) or has come in the form of foreign aid and investment—then it would be difficult to say that the Middle East has an absorptive capacity that exceeds this amount of capital. The truth could be that the

TABLE 23. PLANNING[a] PUBLIC[b] DEVELOPMENT

Country	Period Planned	Total in National Currency Planned for Period	Percentage of Total for[c]			Dollar Equivalent of Currency Unit as of Summer 1963[d]
			Agriculture	Industry	Transportation and Communication	
Cyprus	1962–1966	61.9[e] million pounds	30.5	20.2	28.1	75.75
Iran	1962–1963 to 1967–1968	190.2 billion rials	19.2	28.2	25.3	0.35
Iraq	1961–1965	556.4 million dinars	20.3	30.0	24.5	3.0
Israel	1960–1961 to 1960–1963	1,427.5[f] million pounds	29.4[g]	17.4[h]	16.1[i]	0.35
Jordan	1962–1967	66.9 million dinars	43.0	1.6	23.9	3.14
Lebanon	1962–1967	450.0 million pounds	16.2[j]	16.0[k]	27.6	4.50
Saudi Arabia	1960[l]	200.3 million pounds	3.9	[m]	37.1[n]	3.82
Syria	1960–1961 to 1964–1965	1,720 million pounds	50.9	14.0	22.5	9.0
Turkey	1959–1962	16.34 billion[o] liras				
U.A.R. (Egypt)	1960–1961 to 1964–1965	1,696.9 million pounds[p]	20.3[q]	36.8[r]	16.0[s]	0.43

a MEED, pp. 171–180.

b The United Nations source a gives for some countries (for example, Jordan, Syria, and Turkey) figures for their private development planning; because such figures are not given for all countries, and because all countries have public development figures, in the present table only figures for public development are included.

c In the table here we are showing only three sectors of the national economy where public development plans have been adopted, namely, agriculture, industry, and transport and communications. These are in general the most important sectors. There have been also important plans affecting, for Cyprus, water supplies; for Iran, social affairs; for Iraq, buildings and housing; for Israel, mines and quarries, housing, and tourism; for Jordan, social development; for Lebanon, drinking water, antiquities, and reconstruction; for Saudi Arabia, construction, and education; for Syria, social development; and for the United Arab Republic (Egypt), dwellings and services.

d Figures for all countries are in current prices except those of Turkey at 1961 prices and those of Egypt at 1959–1960 prices. The dollar equivalence of the national currency unit (pound, rial, dinar, etc.) is given to enable the reader to convert the diverse currencies to a single currency for purposes of rough comparison.

e For greater precision and detail concerning all these figures, including the sources of income on which some of these countries (for example, Iran, Iraq, Jordan, and Syria) count for defraying these expenditures, see the United Nations source material under *a* above.

f This figure is subject to correction according to the interpretation of the last item entitled "miscellaneous items and adjustments" in the United Nations table on Israel.

g This percentage covers expenditures for the three years for the two items marked "agriculture" and "Jordan water project."

h This percentage covers expenditures for the three years for the three items marked "industry and crafts," "electricity," and "oil pipelines and wells."

i This percentage covers expenditures for the three years for the two items marked "transport" and "road construction and maintenance."

j This percentage covers expenditures for the two items marked "irrigation" and "river beds."

k This percentage covers the item marked "electricity."

l The United Nations source gives figures only for 1960. It is estimated that Saudi Arabia's total development allocations rose by 50 per cent in 1961 and 100 per cent in 1962. For a short discussion of the budget of Saudi Arabia, see "Current Saudi Budget Stresses New Development Projects," *Middle East Express* (Beirut), April 2, 1962, p. 5.

m The United Nations source does not include figures for public development in industry in Saudi Arabia.

n This percentage covers expenditures for the two items marked "roads" and "communication."

o Turkey's figures are tabulated differently, and from the way they are tabulated, one cannot compute how much is allocated for agriculture, how much for industry, and how much for transport and communications. For the four years 1959–1962, there are figures for three items under "public investments"; these three items are designated "general and annexed budgets," "local authorities," and "state economic enterprises." Public and private average annual investments (the public being slightly greater for the four years) together amount to about 14.5 per cent of the average annual national expenditure for the four years.

p The United Nations tabulation for the United Arab Republic (Egypt) is headed "total investment." It is here assumed that this means total public investments.

q This percentage covers expenditures for the two items marked "agriculture" and "irrigation and drainage."

r This percentage covers expenditures for the three items marked "high dam," "industry," and "electricity."

s This percentage covers expenditures for the two items marked "transport, communications and storage" and "Suez Canal."

Middle East would even then still be in a position to export some capital for investment abroad.

But if the *total amount* of available capital in the Middle East does not constitute an obstacle to development, the *distribution* of this capital among the countries of the region leaves a lot to be desired. A glance at Table 15, the proven oil reserves in the Middle East, reveals at once how unevenly distributed this enormous natural resource is among the sixteen or more countries of the area. This whole wealth has by a freak of biological-geological happenings fallen exclusively to the lot of the five countries bordering the Persian Gulf: Iran, Iraq, Kuwait, the Persian Gulf Principalities (Bahrain, Qatar, the Trucial States), and Saudi Arabia. As a result, it is quite correct to conceive of the Middle East as being more or less distinctly divided into the "haves" and the "have nots," the "fortunate" that hug the Persian Gulf and the "unfortunate" that lie beyond. A beginning has been made in the matter of redistribution of capital within the area by the establishment, in 1962, of the Kuwait Fund for Arab Economic Development. A wider, multilateral approach is likely to be more effective. But this whole question raises issues of the most far-reaching character, belonging to half a dozen orders—political, economic, cultural, regional, international, and intercultural—issues that, considered concretely and realistically, will make short shrift of any sentimental, abstract, idealistic approach to this matter.

Another bottleneck in the development in the Middle East is the relative lack of skilled manpower. It is true that technology can be imported, but unless the imported technology takes roots in its new home, and unless it becomes an integral part of the culture of the people, the economy of that people will continue to labor under serious handicaps. Great scientific cultures did not develop overnight; they are organically rooted in a special outlook on nature, man, matter and truth, an outlook that goes back to the ancient Greeks; and when the Arabs and Moslems in the Middle Ages fell under Greek influence, they made great and lasting contributions in virtually every branch of science. It takes several generations before the scientific habit of mind, with its absolute detachment and dedication to truth beyond and above all politics and all personal interests, matures to the point of creativity in a culture not yet used to it, and because the Middle East has already in its background a brilliant scientific medieval past, and because its modern scientific Western inoculation has not been negligible during the past one hundred years, this period of gestation can perhaps in its case be considerably shortened. But so long as science has not reached the point of creativity, and in the Middle East it has not, economic development can move only slowly. In the Middle East today, the lack of high-talented manpower is perhaps the narrowest bottleneck along the path of economic development. It is thus highly disheartening to see that official development policies have given but scant attention to vocational, technical, and scientific training, as well as to other attempts at widening this bottleneck. For some time to come (how long, one cannot tell) the Middle East cannot develop itself by itself; it is compelled, if it is to be developed fast enough, to remain for some time dependent upon the great storehouses of science, technology, and theory flourishing elsewhere in the world.

One cannot discuss the question of economic development in the Middle East without mentioning the fact that vast sums of money are diverted to armaments, either because of the direct involvement of some countries of the region in the cold war or because of the Arab-Israeli conflict; sums that could be invested instead in more productive schemes of development if people felt secure or if they did not feel that they suffered some wrong which they should somehow endeavor to right.

Finally, perhaps it goes without saying that the political instability of the area is extremely detrimental to economic development, both private and public. For instability and unpredictability are inimical to planning and investment, where the future is a most decisive factor. The whole philosophy of planning rests on being able to count on an open and dependable future. Instability in the area does not stem from factors inherent in the area alone, and therefore cannot be done away with by the single efforts of the Middle Eastern peoples themselves. Middle

Eastern development is a function of the conflicting convergence of the whole world upon this central region.[4] This, along with the fact that the countries of the Middle East are not, through their own actions, helping much the cause of stability in the region, is sufficient cause for the continuance of instability, and therefore for the retardation of development, in the area for some time to come.

POLITICAL IMPLICATIONS

Economic activity is a function of the total life of a people. It cannot be understood apart from raising more fundamental issues. What now, we ask, are the fundamental problems of the Middle East? What sort of challenge does it pose to high statesmanship everywhere?

There are problems outstanding for each country and problems appertaining to the region as a whole.

Kemal Ataturk's revolution was a great event in the modern history of the Middle East. There is room for a further and deeper development of this revolution. Bold Western vision and wise and farsighted Western action can help considerably in this regard. Turkey has been relatively isolated from the affairs of the Middle East; this is not natural, for Asia Minor, all throughout history, in Homeric, Alexandrian, Byzantine, and Ottoman days, always had a decisive say in the determination of events in this region. It is therefore altogether artificial to conceive of Turkey as lying, or to wish that it lay, for long outside the inner stream of history of the Middle East. If Turkey continues to be looked upon as only the sentinel of the Straits, as only the northern gateway to the Middle East, it could sooner or later find it ex-

---

[4] See in this connection some of the published work of F. H. Harbison, especially his article in the July 1959 number of *Foreign Affairs* entitled, "Two Centers of Arab Power." Some of Harbison's political judgments are debatable, but the following passage from this article agrees with our view: "Neither Egypt nor Iraq, however, has control over her own economic destiny. The economic and political development of both has been and will continue to be in the future strongly influenced by the interests and policies of foreign powers."

pedient to come to some agreement with its giant neighbor to the north and turn neutralist. Thus the problem for statesmanship is to go beyond the conception of Turkey as a military instrument only, to devote thinking and planning to its political, social, economic, intellectual, and spiritual development, and on the basis of this development, to promote greater interest by Turkey in the affairs of the Middle East.

Whether the enlightened reforms of the Shah of Iran will succeed in the face of the present determined opposition remains to be seen. Iran, too, could find it natural and expedient to make a deal with its neighbor to the north if its destiny is interpreted only in political, economic, and military terms. Here, too, much greater thought must be given to social, educational, intellectual, and spiritual development, especially as Iran in its history was most creative artistically, philosophically, and spiritually. I doubt whether a revolution from below in Iran will unfold itself in such a manner as to be advantageous to the fundamental interests of the West. It appears, therefore, that the best alternative is to support the Shah, but with much greater emphasis on the social and intellectual development of the people.

The fundamental problem of Cyprus is how the two components of the population, the Greeks and the Turks, could, with the help of Greece and Turkey themselves, live harmoniously together with single-minded loyalty to their joint commonwealth.

Although Israel has developed economically and socially and has made progress in its relations with many countries in Asia and Africa, its paramount problem remains its place in and its relations to its immediate environment, the Arab world. This is the most baffling of problems. The issues raised here are simply political and economic; no fundamental issue in human life, from the highest concerning God to the simplest concerning ordinary human relations, is not raised by the advent of Israel in the Middle East.

The fundamental problems of the Arab Near East are five:

1. How the Arab states are going to embody their already existing general vague sense of unity—linguistic, cultural, politi-

cal—in some stable and internationally recognized political entity.

2. How they may develop themselves and raise their standard of living, and in particular, how they may effect a better redistribution of the natural wealth of the region among themselves.

3. How the Arab-Israeli conflict is going to be resolved.

4. How they will develop their relations both to the other states in the Middle East and to the great powers of the West and the East.

5. What type of intellectual and spiritual development is going to take place in their realm, namely, what sort of Arab man, Arab mind, and Arab fundamental outlook is going to emerge, ten years hence, fifty years hence, from the many seething factors bearing upon their development and destiny.

The fundamental problems of the Middle East as a whole are seven. (Both at the beginning of this chapter and here at the end we have taken a general fundamental look at the Middle East as a whole. At both places we came out with seven points; the coincidence of this number is accidental, and although some of these points are interrelated, we are here viewing the Middle East from a different perspective.)

1. How Islam, as a religion, as a political and social system, as a legal doctrine, and as a distinctive outlook on man and the world, is going to evolve.

2. What modality the eternal Eastern question is going to assume in the future, namely, how the great powers—United States, Europe, Russia, and now China and India—are going to express their strategic, political, and economic interests in this central region on which world interests necessarily converge.

3. How deep and revolutionary will be the impact of science, technology, and industry upon the thinking and life of the Middle East.

4. The Middle East occupies an outstanding geographical position in the world. Consequently, the human-spiritual influences

that radiate from it are of the utmost importance. Everybody is interested in ascertaining what kind of civilization and what sort of outlook on life and existence are going to mature in these parts. The destiny of the Middle East is determined by whether the forces let loose in it are going to make of it a source of light and freedom and vision and helpfulness, or whether these same forces will cause it to mean, for itself and for the world, darkness, narrowness, bigotry, negativity, hatred, violence, and self-withdrawal.

5. People feel their problems deeply in the Middle East. It is their nature, but it is also the nature of the problems themselves. In itself, depth of feeling is good, but the problem then becomes how to lead this feeling into constructive and creative channels. This is the proper task of high statesmanship. There are many nationalities and religions, many different roots, backgrounds, and traditions; there are diverse ideologies sweeping upon the minds of men. The future of the Middle East depends on whether this caldron of diversity, difference, and conflict can boil without boiling over, whether a positive order of justice and understanding can be established.

6. Behind every problem and every possibility in the Arab Middle East stands the problem of the relation of Egyptian demography to Egyptian natural resources. Talk as much as you want, plan as much as your ingenuity allows, about any issue whatsoever; in the end you will inevitably come up against the stark fact of 30 million people, who will be double this number at the present rate of increase by the end of this century, hemmed in by a land whose natural resources alone, even if exploited most intensively and most efficiently, cannot possibly support them on a presently acceptable level of existence. This problem can be solved only through science, the right spirit, and the highest statesmanship, all working together in the interest of truth, freedom, and the deepest humanitarian instinct in man.

7. A most fundamental transformation awaits the Middle East, greater than any it has witnessed in its long and checkered past, when nuclear energy is effectively married to the desalination of sea water on a vast scale. The entire desert area will then bloom

into two or three crops a year, and the Middle East will support hundreds of millions of new people with a much higher standard of living than is now possible with its present economic resources. The oil reserves will be exhausted one day (in 100, in 200 years), and the desert will once again reassert its perennial sway; and even if this mineral wealth lasted a 1000 years, the possibilities of investing it in the region, while the desert preponderated, would be exceedingly limited. But the energy of the sun, the energy of the atom (they are fundamentally one and the same), belong to a different order of existence altogether; they last as long as man and matter last. The problem of the Middle East is how to lick the desert and all that the desert means. This has never happened before; always it was the desert that finally won, never man. This challenge is so formidable that nothing short of so great and so elemental a power as nuclear energy can meet it. In that eventuality, what is of the utmost importance is the type of civilization that the Middle East will promote and support—I mean the kind of society, the type of human person, the outlook on life, the spirit that will then emerge. Because of the unique central location of this region, when atom, sea, sun and soil, harnessed to one another, sustain a population of a billion people, the rest of the world cannot be indifferent to the type of civilization arising in the Middle East. The Middle East, then, must first look after its mind and its spirit if it is to meet the challenges of its material existence. The ultimate problems of the Middle East, as indeed of every region in the world, are all human and spiritual.

CHAPTER 10

Israel

David Horowitz

Israel is a small country and its relative weight in the economic life of the world is insignificant. However, its experience in development under difficult conditions and against tremendous odds allows for some universal conclusions that may be pertinent to the discussion of methods and approaches to the development of new states.

Thus, in this contribution to the clarification of Israel's problems and policies, interest is mainly focused on the more universal aspects of Israel's experience.

RESOURCES AND DEMOGRAPHY

Hemmed in between four states—Egypt, Jordan, Syria, and Lebanon—and extending over an area of 8,000 square miles, more than half of them desert and only about one third cultivable, Israel possesses few natural resources. Its actual and potential water resources are estimated at 1,800 million cubic meters per annum, of which 1,200 million cubic meters are already utilized. (The main potential source is the diversion of the Jordan waters completed in 1964 at a cost of some $120 million.) In an arid country this scarcity of water puts a rigid limit to the expansion of agriculture.

Sources of energy in the country are negligible. There is no coal or hydroelectric power, and oil output is only 7 to 8 per cent of fuel requirements. Thus the only source of energy is thermo-generated electricity based on imported fuel.

Mineral wealth is confined to rich deposits of potash, bromides, and magnesium in the Dead Sea, extensive phosphate deposits in the Negev, and to some 17 million tons of copper ores of poor content (1.5 per cent). All these minerals, with the exception of magnesium, are already being commercially exploited.

The country is not endowed with timber or any other valuable resources.

The geographical location of the country as a link between three continents is most favorable. However, Israel is deprived of these advantages by its geopolitical position, as a result of which its trade is boycotted, the Suez Canal is blockaded to its shipping, and land communications with all the neighboring states are cut off.

On this narrow basis of scarce natural resources, an expanding economic entity is being constructed, which is to support a rapidly growing population.

Demography is the decisive and crucial factor determining the economic and social development of Israel. The growth of its population, by far exceeding even the rapid pace usual in under-developed countries, expanded the scope and revolutionized the pattern of its society and economy. The population has increased from 810,000 on May 15, 1948, to 2,288,000 at the beginning of 1963, or by 182 per cent, almost threefold. The main source of this growth was immigration, which accounted for one million, or 66 per cent, while natural increase was responsible for half a million, or 34 per cent of the increase. The number of new immigrants during the past fifteen years since the establishment of the State of Israel, exceeded the number during the entire preceding eighty-year period of Jewish settlement in Palestine.

Comparison with countries where the population increase has been most rapid is illuminating: India, 1.9 per cent per year; Egypt, 2.4 per cent; Latin America, 2.2 per cent; in Israel the increase has averaged over 6 per cent per annum during the past fifteen years. Israel has thus probably had one of the highest rates of demographic increase in the world during this period.

Moreover, immigration proceeds in a series of waves, each new wave of immigration starting on a broader basis. Inevitably, the fluctuations in the growth of the population and the concomitant broad swings of the economic pendulum have been uneven, and this process caused difficulties and frictions of readjustment. These fluctuations have also reinforced the impact of population growth on economic conditions. The driving force in this wave-like motion is not an economic one. Immigration to Israel is not subject only to the interplay of economic forces and conditions; it is also determined by racial, political, and national conditions in certain countries of the world and by the impact of the Jewish movement of national renascence.

Population movements caused by noneconomic factors are no new departure in history. They do not conform to the ordinary pattern of migratory movements, which are generally determined by the conditions prevailing in the countries of immigration rather than those obtaining in the countries of emigration. Immigration into Israel is not a process of readjustment by moving from areas of greater to areas of lesser pressure on economic resources; it is impelled by political and extra-economic forces. The most frequently quoted analysis of immigration into Palestine is that of the British mandatory government's commissioner of migration in his report of 1935:

Jewish immigration into Palestine differs from other migration in that it is not solely the response to economic attractions of the country of immigration. No doubt a proportion of Jewish immigration into Palestine does correspond with ordinary migration in this sense; but a proportion of Jewish immigrants comprises those who have no special interest in Palestine but are repelled from the countries from which they have emigrated. Natural migration is, in effect, the result of the work of the country of immigration conceived as a suction-pump; immigration into Palestine is the result of the combined action of Palestine as a suction-pump and the country of emigration as a force-pump. And it is this fact which gives sufficient reason for any difference there may be between the characters and attributes of the Jewish immigrant population in Palestine and those immigrant populations elsewhere; and for supposing that a theory of migration accounting for the phenomenon of immigration generally may not account for the phenomenon of migration into Palestine.

This analysis under the mandatory regime is even more valid with regard to immigration into Israel since 1948. In short, in immigration to Israel, the "push" is stronger than the "pull," and the repellent forces are predominant. The social, political, and psychological background of the D.P. camps in Germany and the economic and social conditions of Jews in eastern Europe and the Arab countries of Asia and North Africa led to entire communities being transplanted to Isreal. The occupational structure of this mass of immigrants was not adapted to the needs of the country. An occupational reshuffle of most of the incoming population became imperative.

A statistical analysis of a sample of the occupational distribution of the immigrants during the period of large-scale immigration (1950–1952) reflected a rather lopsided structure: liberal professions, 8.4 per cent; management and office workers, 15.0 per cent; traders, merchants, and agents, 18.6 per cent; agricultural workers and farmers, 4.4 per cent; artisans and production workers, 34.3 per cent; laborers, 9.0 per cent; transportation workers, 2.6 per cent; building workers, 2.4 per cent; services workers, 3.2 per cent; and unclassified, 0.6 per cent. On the other hand, the occupational distribution in Israel in 1961 was: liberal professions, 12.8 per cent; management and office workers, 18.1 per cent; traders, merchants, and agents, 8.4 per cent; farmers, 14.3 per cent; transportation workers, 4.7 per cent; building workers, 7.8 per cent; artisans and other workers, 22.6 per cent; services workers, 11.3 per cent.

The contrast is striking. Hundreds of thousands of new immigrants who were merchants, peddlers, and clerks in their country of origin had to be absorbed in agriculture, industry, the army, shipping, and so forth. Within a short period of time, they had to be taught to till the ground, turn a lathe, guard the frontiers, or sail the seas. This transformation was not confined to the occupational sphere. The newcomers had to be imbued with the civic spirit and tradition, the social, economic, and political values, already created and crystallized in the new nation. Geographical transplantation is a one-time act, but social and economic integration is a protracted process. While the former is a logistic task, involving transportation and housing, the latter represents the core of Israel's economic and social reconstruction. Furthermore, some of the immigrants were accustomed to a European standard of living, which had to be maintained within the framework of a poor, underdeveloped economy. Of course it would have been unthinkable—for economic, social, and national reasons—to maintain a dual standard of living, one for those from the West and one for those from the East, and everything had to be done to equalize standards, that is, to carry out a leveling-up process. Last but not least, people coming from over a hundred countries, with nearly as many languages, sometimes centuries apart in their cultural level, had to be welded into a single ethnic and national entity.

The pressure of a rapidly growing population on limited resources might have been expected to lead to a decline in standards of living and consumption, with all the concomitant phenomena of malnutrition, shortened expectation of life, and retarded cultural and educational progress. However, all statistical data indicate rapidly rising standards of living and increasing consumption.

STANDARD OF LIVING AND INCOME DISTRIBUTION

The most revealing of indicators of income are those reflecting personal consumption per head in real terms, which have increased since 1950 at an average rate of 5.5 per cent per annum. The ownership of durable consumer goods corroborates this general indication. In 1962 there were in Israel for every ten families (family = four persons), five families with electric refrigerators, nine families with radio sets, seven families with gas ranges, etc.

Government expenditure for social services, health, and education have increased since 1955 in real terms at a rate of 9.5 per cent per annum, substantially more rapidly than the population. Infant mortality, at a rate of 12.6 per thousand, compares favorably with that of the most progressive states, such as: New Zealand, 14.0; Sweden, 13.7; Switzerland, 12.0; U.S.A., 12.7; Britain, 20.2. Life expectation at birth is 70.5 years for men and 73.6 years for women, as compared with: 68 and 73 years, respectively, in New Zealand; 72 and 75 in Sweden; 66 and 71 in Switzerland; 67 and 74 in the U.S.A.; and 68 and 74 in Great Britain.

However, the most comprehensive of all indicators is the national income per head at constant prices and, even more important, the dynamic trend of this figure over the years. Statistics are available only for the years 1950–1962, and here the trend is unmistakable. Taking 1950 as the base year, the national income index at 1950 prices was, during the years 1950–1954, 136.4 on the average, and 222.4 on the average for 1955–1959; it was 311.3 during 1960–1962. The corresponding figures for per capita national income for the same periods are 111.4; 147.0; 160.0, respectively. Whatever the average level of income per head, this could conceal a maldistribution of income and thus poverty and destitution among some groups of the population. However, the distribution of national income in Israel is on the whole more egalitarian than in more progressive countries of the West. The standard of living is also determined by the very comprehensive social services—education, health, housing, provided by the State —and an egalitarian wage structure. Progressive taxation effectively redistributes the national income. The government aims at the establishment of a welfare state and maintenance of full employment on a comprehensive scale, and all its policies are shaped accordingly.

It is true that the impact of technological change, which was conducive to a steeper differentiation in wages and salaries, the bouts of inflation caused by unorthodox financing of large-scale immigration and other needs, and the rise in land values have led to the accumulation of wealth by some sections, and the traditional spirit of egalitarianism has been weakened to some extent in the past decade. The influx of immigrant groups with a lower level of education and with few skills added momentum to this trend. In the newly established "development" towns, populated mainly by immigrants, the standards of living are lower than those in the old-established settlements. However, as the immigrants acquire new skills and become integrated into the economic structure of the country, these differences are narrowing. Government policy aims at leveling-up and rapidly amalgamating the various communities, and at integrating the immigrant with the established population.

To sum up: The distribution of national income is characterized by remarkably narrow differentials, thanks to the government's welfare-state policies, a highly organized labor movement, progressive taxation, full employment, and the rapid integration of new immigrants in the economy. It is more differentiated, however, than in the past, when an extremely egalitarian trend prevailed and led to a far-reaching elimination of significant and substantial income differentials. Immigration led to a dual expansion: a horizontal broadening of the quantitative population basis, and a vertical rise in consumption standards as elaborated later.

The very substantial import of capital serves mainly to expand investment, but part of it stimulates consumption by expanding purchasing power, and thus raises the standard of life. Rapid economic growth assures full employment, and thus generates larger incomes. Full employment is also conducive to an increase of real wages per employee at a rate of 3.4 per cent per annum, which reinforces this trend.

Thus, the percolation of a part of the imported capital into channels of consumption, rapid economic growth, and full employment have counteracted the economic effects of the pressure of a rapidly growing population on limited natural resources.

ECONOMIC GROWTH

Israel's sustained economic growth is reflected in the annual average increase of the gross national product by 9.5 per cent in real terms, over the past fifteen years, in comparison with an annual average of 5.5 per cent in the European Economic Community, 3 per cent in the European Free Trade area, and 3.3 per cent in the United States.

Increased agricultural output, one of the most important components of economic growth, provided the rapidly growing population with an ample supply of foodstuffs. In 1949, locally produced foodstuffs supplied up to 50 per cent of the needs of a population of approximately one million; in 1962, local agriculture provided over 75 per cent of the food for a population of $2\frac{1}{4}$ million, at a much higher standard of nutrition. The objectives of agricultural policy, aimed at providing an adequate supply of locally produced foodstuffs and increasing agricultural exports, could be achieved only through a shift from less valuable to more valuable crops.

The available area of cultivable land limited the production of energy-producing foodstuffs such as cereals, and made it imperative to concentrate mainly on protective foodstuffs such as dairy produce, fruit, and vegetables, and industrial crops such as cotton and ground nuts. Extensive agriculture as the main basis of expansion was ruled out in Israel by natural conditions, and thus the emphasis was on intensive farming based on irrigation. In an arid country irrigation is likely to determine the pace and scope of agricultural development. In Israel, an irrigated acre can produce crops four or five times more valuable than an acre of unirrigated land. In fifteen years the area of irrigated land has increased in Israel by 360 per cent.

The shift to production of protective foodstuffs, which raised the value of total agricultural production, was made possible by:

1. A general rise in the standard of living, which always results in a shift from consumption of energy-producing to protective foodstuffs.
2. Expansion of irrigation and increased investment per agricultural earner.
3. General trends in nutritional habits.

This analysis applies mainly to production for the domestic market.

A simultaneous expansion took place in agricultural exports, from $6.5 million (after a decline during World War II), in 1949 to $68.4 million in 1962. These consist mainly of citrus fruit: oranges, grapefruit, etc. The economic significance of the expansion of citrus plantations lies in the high capital investment per earner and the tendency to substitute capital for space, which is of great importance for a small country with a high density of population.

Agricultural exports other than citrus also increased, although on a small scale. They consist mainly of off-season vegetables and fruit, through the utilization of climatic and soil differences between Israel and Europe, the latter being the almost exclusive market for these products. With the improvement of transport facilities, this is a promising line of development, considering the steady rise in consumption of these products, caused by the remarkable increase of the national income in Europe.

Increasing productivity emancipates the volume of agricultural production from a too close dependence on the area of cultivable land. To mention a few examples: The yield of wheat increased in Israel from about 75 kilograms per dunam in the 1940s to 125 kilograms in the 1960s. The yield of milk in the Netherlands is 4,150 kilograms per cow; in Germany, 3,300; in France, 2,255; in Britain, 2,830; in Greece, 800; and in Israel, 4,380 kilograms per cow. The same trend of rising productivity is evident in most of Israel's agriculture.

In most of the comparisons of agricultural productivity, the extremes of low and high yields and more or less valuable crops per farmer or per unit of production cannot be explained by natural conditions. The interchangeability of artificial and natural conditions seems to play an important role in these developments. The change in the pattern of consumption is one of these factors. The decrease in the consumption of carbohydrates per head of the population and the increase in the intake of proteins, correlated with the increase of national income per head, are cases in point.

The development of this highly intensive agriculture on irrigated land, with selected seeds and improved rotation of crops, makes it very dependent on high capital investment and a large input from outside the farming sectors, such as fertilizers, machinery and spare parts, certain feeding stuffs for cattle and poultry, etc. However, expanding agriculture is an objective of economic policy in Israel for many reasons beyond purely economic considerations. These are: the dispersal of the population, the establishment of a base of farming population for the state, and the diversification of the economy. There is some internal contradiction in this development. Modern intensive farming depends on a large urban market. Natural conditions and the maintenance of the farmers' standard of living indicate this form of intensive farming, but on the other hand, this development in itself reduces the share of the agricultural population in the total.

Lord Boyd-Orr commented as follows on the rise of productivity in agriculture in Palestine before World War II:

In the Jewish settlement in Palestine, agriculture has been raised to such a high level of efficiency that although the settlement only occupies 7 per cent of the total land, it is claimed that it produces about 50 per cent of the total agricultural output. To enable it to reach this high level of efficiency, however, there are three workers in other industries for one in agriculture.

This trend to urbanization was furthered by the rapid expansion of industry. A good indication of the growth of industry is the number of workers employed, who totaled 200,000 in 1962 as against 100,000 in 1950. Production increased at a more rapid rate than the number of workers because of a rise in productivity and increasing mechanization and use of labor-saving devices.

As most of Israel's industry is producing for the domestic market, it is orientated toward a growing population and an expanding home market. Industrialization is thus made possible by the very process of transplantation, linked with the import of capital for investment in industry, the immigration of experts and skilled labor, and expanding markets resulting from immigration. The general world tendency of industry toward decentralization, and its far-reaching emancipation from dependence on local raw materials and other natural conditions, are conducive to this development in a country with scanty resources like Israel.

Israel lacks most of the raw materials for its growing industry, but local natural resources are becoming increasingly interchangeable with capital, skill, knowledge, and with deliberate policies of industrialization.

Industry is being increasingly attracted to marketing facilities, which are becoming a decisive factor in determining its location. Thus, the most potent consideration for the expansion of industry is an economy of growing population. Israel's industry takes advantage of this trend. The economy of a growing population is interrelated with industrial development first by providing increasing market facilities. Simultaneously, expanding markets and subsequently larger-scale production reduce costs and increase productivity. An expanding population, by establishing technical and economic minima of production, makes it possible to produce an increasing variety of industrial goods.

In the course of time, the structure of industry was subjected to change and became more export-orientated. Industrial exports increased from $23 million in 1949 to $203.8 million in 1962, and the share of exports in industrial production rose from less than 10 per cent in 1949 to 24 per cent in 1962. The location of many industries is to an increasing extent determined by such factors as an industrial milieu, which comprises more than the availability of skilled labor and depends on science and know-how, research laboratories and training schools, tradition, managerial ability, techniques, etc.

Immigration movements have more than once in history been the precursors of industrial growth. Huguenot refugees from France in the days of the Reformation and the Puritans arriving in America transplanted their industries to the countries of their adoption. The wool industry was developed in England by Flemish refugees, and the clothing industry in the United States by the Russian Jewish immigrants of the 1890s. It is natural for artisans and workers to attempt to pursue their old occupations under the new conditions, and this tendency is a powerful factor in reproducing in the young country the industries of the more developed countries from which the immigrants hail.

Industrial development in Israel, which utilized an access of skill thanks to immigration, predominantly in the interwar period, proceeded mainly in two directions:

1. Industries based on local raw materials, such as the manufacture of fertilizers, deriving its raw materials from the rich resources of the Dead Sea; potash and bromides and phosphate deposits in the Negev; copper mining on a limited scale near Eilat, on the Red Sea coast; the manufacture of food products by processing agricultural produce such as citrus, other fruit, and vegetables; the building materials industry, producing cement, etc.; textile spinning and weaving, using locally grown cotton, etc.

2. Industries processing imported raw materials, in which skill and know-how are the only relative advantages because the raw materials involved are either very light, such as diamonds, so that the freight differential is negligible, or form a relatively small part of the value of the final product, as with some kinds of machinery.

Thanks mainly to immigration in the interwar period, Israel has the advantages of relatively plentiful skilled labor and entrepreneurial initiative, of a high scientific potential, a relatively low level of wages for highly skilled labor and managerial skill, and a plentiful supply of professional and technical knowledge.

The fact that immigration into Palestine was, to a great extent, the result of extra-economic factors, increased the proportion of skilled and trained experts and workers to the total number of immigrants. Thus, the industrialization of Israel is the result of the combination of capital import and population growth by immigration, that is, of transplantation in its three aspects:

1. Markets. An expanding population provided a large enough domestic market and opened up possibilities for diversified industry by establishing technical and economic minima and reducing the cost of production.
2. Skilled labor, initiative, and expert knowledge imported into the country in this stage of industrial development.

3. Capital imports linked with immigration, that is, in a process
    of co-migration.

Branches of the economy other than agriculture and industry
followed suit. The particularly heavy investment in building,
aggregating $1,000 million in the last eight years (figures are
available only as from 1955), was due to the large immigration,
which made it necessary to build on a grand scale to provide
housing for the increasing population and also stimulated industrial development. The share of building workers in the total
labor force reached the high level of almost 10 per cent.

With the development of a modern economy, the tertiary stage
of production, including state services, increased both absolutely
and relatively, with a corresponding increase in national income.
Owing to the rise of output per worker at a rate of 4 to 5 per
cent per annum in the total economy, the increase in all main
lines of production exceeded the increase of population. Advantages of larger-scale production, higher capital investment, with a
concurrent improvement and augmentation of capital equipment, and vocational training contributed to the increase of
productivity as a component of economic growth.

ELEMENTS OF GROWTH

If some universal conclusions are to be drawn from the case
study of Israel as to the possibilities and pattern of economic
growth, the process of growth itself must be analyzed and its
component elements subjected to closer scrutiny.

The development of an underdeveloped country is impossible
without large amounts of capital. Modern technology and capital-
intensive industries increase the importance of capital supply for
the development of young, underdeveloped countries. Natural
resources represent only the potentiality of a country, and their
utilization depends to a great extent upon the availability of capital equipment.

The problem is aggravated by the rapid growth of population.
The relation between the increment of population, the access of

new capital, and the average unit of capital per capita is most relevant to the rise or deterioration of the standard of living. In an underdeveloped country with a rapidly increasing population, capital accumulation cannot be quick enough to lead to adequate expansion of production capacity. This capacity should keep pace with a rapid growth of population, if no external resources of loans or invested capital are available, because the ability of a country to absorb an increased population depends to a large extent upon its capital equipment and the level of education, skill, know-how, and technical ability of its producers.

However, the flow of capital intended for new development and for the mitigation of the stresses and strains on the economy in underdeveloped countries, for raising the standards of living and encouraging international trade, and above all, for expanding the capacity of production, can be derived only from two sources: capital formation through saving and accumulation, and import of capital.

The first industrial revolution was based on a very high rate of savings and private accumulation of capital. The distribution of the national income in those times was instrumental in accelerating the formation of capital by assuring a high rate of profit and maintaining wage rates at levels just sufficient for the maintenance and reproduction of the labor force. Such wage levels were possible because of the existence of an unemployed reserve army of labor. Such conditions prevailed within the framework of a society in which democracy was in its infancy and the broad masses of the population were either inarticulate or deprived of political influence. The totalitarian regimes repeated this performance. Rapid industrialization and an occupational reshuffle, heavy industries, and large-scale urbanization were made possible only by the rapid formation of capital through forced savings. The totalitarian regime was strong, stern, and severe enough to enforce this solution of its problem of primary accumulation of capital. Such an economic policy, however, can be enforced only in a predemocratic or totalitarian regime by the most ruthless methods of repression.

An attempt to execute such a policy within the framework of a democratic society would inevitably lead to the conclusion that if capital formation is to be achieved by coercion, a totalitarian regime would be preferable because it is much more efficient in this kind of operation. It certainly would be tougher in its method of squeezing out every ounce of resources from a very narrow margin over and above the subsistence level.

Thus, rapid economic growth in nontotalitarian democratic countries can be effected only by supplementing the rather modest capital formation based on savings by outside assistance. A striking instance of what can be achieved by capital import, which at least partly served as a substitute for the primary formation of capital, is provided by Israel's achievements in settlement and development. Of course the fact that very rapid economic development was achieved under a democratic and stable regime is the result of several factors, of which the import of capital is only one, although a significant one. The particular political conditions, the spiritual background, the quality of the human material, the tension under which the effort was carried out, the security conditions, all created a unique set of circumstances. Import of capital did not, of course, eliminate entirely the need for policies that must be unpopular: For some time a regime of austerity had to be maintained, heavy taxation imposed, and resources diverted from consumption to investment. However, evidently the financing by internal capital formation of development on the scale carried out in Israel would have resulted, if at all possible, in stresses and strains on the social and political structure of the country, which have no precedent in history and were well-nigh impossible.

The import of capital into Israel during a period of fifteen years bears witness to the truth of this contention. Over $4 billion imported into Israel made the investment of some $2,750 million possible. This investment was distributed over the various branches of the economy as follows: about a quarter went to industry, mining, and electricity; about 20 per cent to agriculture and irrigation; 12 per cent were invested in transportation and communications; 35 per cent were invested in housing and building, and the remainder was invested in services. This capital was derived from a variety of sources, but the overwhelming proportion came from public and semipublic funds. This fact, more than any preconceived views, motivated the planning of development and the establishment of a scale of priorities in investment. The import of capital made it possible to dispense with rapid formation of capital and the drastic reduction of living standards by the diversion of resources from consumption to investment. Moreover, a substantial part of this capital did not necessitate any capital charges on account of principal and interest. This applies particularly to reparations and restitution funds from Germany, gift funds raised by Jewish communities all over the world, and U.S. government assistance. Payment of interest on loans and dividends to private investors abroad on a small scale are an exception. At any rate, the theoretical assumption that economic growth is to a great extent predicated among other factors on the scope of investment has been borne out by the experience of Israel.

Another aspect of the problem is the effect of the transition to a capital-intensive economy on the occupational distribution of the population. The accretion of capital equipment subjected the economic structure of Israel to a radical change. It superimposed on the economy an industrialized system of production, increased the share of "tertiary" income (owing to a greater division of labor), and created new employment facilities. There are, of course, definite qualifications to this statement. If substantial results in economic growth are to be achieved, the import of capital must be rapid and on a large scale; it must be invested in productive assets and not hoarded; and its utilization must be based on sound economic analysis of investment opportunities and a proper order of priorities. If all these conditions are present, a breakthrough to self-perpetuating, sustained economic growth can be achieved, bearing out the functional connection between capital investment and the pace of economic growth.

Israel's experience proves that sustained economic growth at an accelerated pace can be achieved under a regime of democracy, provided substantial imports of capital, allowing for a slower pace of internal capital formation, are available for a sufficiently long period of time. Even if the imponderables, which play such an important role in Israel, are taken into account, it seems reasonable to draw some universal conclusions from its developments.

HUMAN AND NATURAL RESOURCES CONTRIBUTING TO GROWTH

The labor force in Israel increased within the past fifteen years from 427,000 in 1950 to 808,000 in 1962 (that is, by 90 per cent), mainly by immigration. This expansion was essential for economic growth, as otherwise the large-scale capital investment would have caused bottlenecks due to shortage of labor. Such a situation actually prevailed in 1962, despite the fact that the labor force increased in that year by some 4.5 per cent.

It is worthy of mention that this rapid rise did not result in increased unemployment, except in the first period of the establishment of the state. On the contrary, the employment curve rose steadily, following increased immigration and in sympathy with the expansion of productive forces, and unemployment was generally in inverse proportion to immigration. With some slight deviations caused by time lag, the peaks of immigration coincided with troughs of unemployment, and vice versa.

This fact is a practical corroboration of the theoretical case against the "lump of labor" theory. Professor R. F. Harrod comments as follows on the theoretical aspect of the problem:

The notion that the existence of unemployment is a good reason for discouraging immigration appears wholly fallacious. Each extra resident is a consumer as well as a producer. The notion that a bare reduction of the number of residents would serve to reduce the number of unemployed, and an increase to increase unemployment, has always been regarded as crude in the extreme by those who have given any thought to the problem involved.

The Israel experiment corroborates, as far as it goes, by the test of practical and empirical experience, the conclusions arrived at by analytical methods. The transformation of the economy by co-migration (of capital and labor), the extensive building movement, the creation of marketing possibilities, and the resulting expansion of production show how immigration creates its own conditions of absorption, how economic conditions may become a function of the migration process. It seems that it is not the volume of labor, but the proportion of labor to various economic factors, that determines the degree of employment or unemployment.

The distribution of the labor force in the main branches of the economy—primary production (agriculture and mining), secondary production (manufacturing, industry), and tertiary production (services, commerce, etc.)—in 1962 was as follows: 15.5 per cent in agriculture; 25 per cent in industry; 9.7 per cent in building; 2 per cent in electricity and public works; 12.3 per cent in trade and finance; 6.1 per cent in transportation; 21.7 per cent in public services; and 7.6 per cent in personal services. However, the contribution of the labor force to economic growth was not confined to its quantitative growth. The output per worker has increased at an average rate of 4 to 5 per cent per annum, reflecting the broader capital equipment basis as well as progress in managerial skill and labor productivity.

Here the quality of the immigrant population is of great importance. The bulk of the immigrant population had to undergo a process of occupational reshuffle. However, this process and the resultant economic growth were facilitated by the availability of a nucleus of highly skilled labor—technicians, experts, scientists, manufacturers with experience gained abroad, designers, engineers, agronomists, diamond cutters and polishers, horticulturists, irrigation engineers, and the like—which established the essential precondition of rising productivity. The knowledge of industrial and agricultural techniques accelerated economic growth. The establishment and rapid growth of seats of higher learning, laboratories, libraries, etc., sponsored by the government and various groups from abroad, the spread of scientific knowledge, all combined to increase Israel's know-how potentiality. The immigrant population in Israel was thus endowed with a sufficient proportion of skilled and trained manpower to provide the qualitative background for the process of transplantation. The enterprising qualities of the population also seem to have been adequate to the task. Rapid economic growth in Israel was thus facilitated by the process of co-migration, that is, immigration with a concurrent increase of labor force, combined with the necessary investment of capital and rise of productivity.

No less important for economic growth were the imponderables involved in the historical, national, and social background of economic activity. These factors and the enthusiastic dedication to the cause, resulting from aspirations deeply rooted in the soul of the nation, are of vital importance, although they do not lend themselves to a quantitative evaluation. The threat of physical destruction, the people's singleness of purpose, the sense of bitter necessity and historical mission, the psychology of siege and "backs-to-the-sea," all these were instrumental in giving a tremendous impetus to the work of reconstruction.

The process of transplantation of population is determined to a considerable extent by the economic absorptive capacity of the receiving country. But this is an undefined and hardly definable concept; it is very doubtful if it can ever be gauged in fixed arithmetical terms. It is the function of a large number of variables, which depend in turn on the particular experience of each individual country. The equilibrium of the various components of an economy in their dynamic interaction as well as technical culture and social relations, such as distribution of wealth and income, affect the capacity of a country to support its population at a reasonable standard of life.

The utilization of resources is at least as important as their availability. Increase of productivity per man-day of labor would be the direct result of more intensive utilization of productive resources. In all periods, population density has been determined in part by historical and economic factors, and natural conditions have never provided a complete explanation of the difference between various areas. This tendency toward the emancipation of population potentialities from close dependence on natural resources has been reinforced with the development of modern technology. The basic fact of present economic development is that there is a shift in the importance of the factors conditioning a country's absorptive capacity. The almost physiocratic idea of absorptive capacity, which links it extremely closely with available space and natural resources, does not conform to new economic conditions prevailing at the present time.

Since agriculture has ceased to be the central occupation in progressive communities, the importance of natural resources in limiting absorptive capacity has diminished. A large number of new factors, physical and economic, each having a direct bearing on absorptive capacity, and the possibility of consciously shaping conditions by means of economic policy, have nowadays to be taken into account. Historical, economic, and social criteria must be applied to the process of economic absorption. The fact that space is receding in importance in comparison with the other factors does not prove that the greater the density, the closer the approach to an optimum population. It only corroborates the thesis that absorptive capacity is a relative concept.

Interchangeability of capital, space, and other resources is of decisive importance, particularly in view of the correlation between capital investment and productivity. The interchangeability of capital, skill, space, and natural resources is thus one of the more important explanations of economic growth in Israel.

ECONOMICS OF TRANSPLANTATION

Sudden expansion of demand, influx of capital, diffusion of capital through building activities, stimuli to establish an apparatus of production on the basis of new marketing facilities, and the resulting dynamic expansion of the economy followed large-scale immigration to Israel. Here, the thesis that immigration is a function of the economic conditions of the country is reversed: economic conditions become a function of immigration. Building and public works in Israel were a natural outcome of the co-migration of capital and men. They acted as an ignition spark, setting in motion a general process of expansion, tiding the immigrants over the transition period, and serving as a lever to all other forms of enterprise. Building is an excellent "diffuser" of imported capital. The additional purchasing power and the new demand thus created necessitated the development of secondary and tertiary stages of production. The interaction of these factors is closely connected with the problem of purchasing power. The fact that effective demand financed by capital import has not lagged behind production goes a long way toward explaining the rapid development of Israel. An effective market is helpful in attracting new industries to what would hitherto have been considered the most unlikely areas. The capital imported into the country and available here was ready to seize any opportunity for investment, if only a market could be found. The flow of immigration with increased real income provided the market, and capital was immediately invested in production necessary to meet the expanded demand. This expansion is, of course, always dependent on the country's natural limitations, but as modern production develops, these have less influence. Another essential condition is an adequate supply of capital.

It is true that, in most underdeveloped countries, the rapid increase of population is a factor retarding economic growth and is certainly detrimental to the rise of standards of living. Thus the growth of population as stimulating economic growth is predicated on a unique breakthrough by a massive influx of capital, availability of skills, and institutional and entrepreneurial initiative and ability. This definition qualifies the statement referring to the positive effect of a rapidly increasing population on economic growth.

The preponderance of building and citrus investment in the Israel economy in the initial period helped to bridge the gap between purchasing power and production, and stimulated the development of the productive capacity. Citriculture was dependent on the world market, but this, however, was expanding, owing to the rise of national income in Europe and new nutritional habits. Thus, the home market could rely on a considerable number of producers of an export commodity endowed with an adequate purchasing power. The building industry relied on a cumulative demand reinforced by steady immigration. Thus, initial expansion was based on branches that did not encounter marketing difficulties and which later made the shift to production for the home market possible.

The import of capital itself could not have caused an investment boom of the kind that took place in Israel. The spark of economic initiative could pass only between the two poles: accumulated capital on the one hand and reinforced demand connected with new immigration on the other. It could be sustained only on the basis of the peculiar composition of investment in Israel, which concentrated during the initial period on exports and building, and later chiefly on expansion of production for the home market established in the first period. Of course this process of repeated reinforcement of demand by new immigration, construction, and import of capital has its limits. However, in a period of initial structural development, "full employment" can be achieved and continued for a considerable length of time.

The central feature of the development of Israel is that whole communities have been transplanted to, and established in, the country, with all the prerequisites of capital, manpower, and skill as well as purchasing power for the creation of an internal market, which are necessary for such resettlement. The various elements of economic growth, as enumerated, derived from different parts of the world; the dynamic reaction of the economic structure of the immigration country to the process of migration released new economic forces. The settlement of Israel was therefore not a colonization venture following the traditional pattern of production of primary commodities for the world market. It was a transplantation of population, a transfer in sudden, large, wavelike motions of an immigrant population possessing the prerequisites of skill and capital and automatically providing its own internal market. This rapid movement of people within a short period of time constituted an artificial noneconomic driving power.

The explanation of the success of transplantation, in the present economic situation, lies in the conditions of economic equilibrium that it created and the effective demand that it generated. If transplantation is large and rapid enough and does not peter out into a slow and gradual infiltration, it creates a dynamic equilibrium in which disturbances are overcome by the process of growth. During transplantation, the dynamic equilibrium creates new possibilities of absorption and becomes more important than either space or natural resources.

However, expansion, rise, or decline in an economic process of this type are mainly due to changes in its component factors and their quantitative relations. They depend upon approximations to an equilibrium of factors making for growth and not on approximations to an optimum population. This concept is subject to certain qualifications:

1. Co-migration, that is, the simultaneous influx of immigrants and capital, is a precondition of such development.
2. The process is possible only if transplantation is on a large scale and condensed within a short period of time.
3. Certain shifts in occupational distribution, qualities of human material, and a strong extra-economic power as a driving force are indispensable.

Problems and Policies

The problems and difficulties that Israel encounters in its economic growth are as formidable as its achievements. The gravest and most stubborn of Israel's economic problems is endemic and persistent inflation. It was rampant in the first period of independence as a result of monetary expansion and budgetary deficits. It is prevalent now, although in a mitigated form, as a kind of imported inflation.

The fifteen years of the state's existence were a period of accelerated and hectic development, of rapid expansion, which impaired the stability of the economy. By 1962 the gross national product had increased, in real terms, by 260 per cent and the supply of money (annual average) by 795 per cent. Prices increased by nearly 300 per cent.

In the first period after the establishment of the state, inflation was caused by budgetary deficits, which totaled during the first three years, up to the first monetary reform in 1952, the substantial sum of IL.150 million. During this period, prices increased by 114 per cent and the means of payment by 217 per cent. Under the pressure of unprecedented demographic expansion, which doubled the population within less than four years, heavy defense expenditure, and hectic economic development, monetary expansion proceeded at a rapid pace as the normal instruments for financing the large influx of population and its integration in the country's economy proved inadequate. It was a kind of war economy, in which unorthodox financial methods inevitably led to a runaway inflation, depletion of foreign currency reserves, and physical shortages. Moreover, the geopolitical and military background are permanently adverse factors, involving a heavy expenditure for arms and consequently a drain on economic resources.

After the relative success of monetary reform in 1952 and the introduction of a monetary policy aimed at an equilibrium, and following the decline in the rate of immigration, a period of creeping inflation began, in which the rise of prices was less pronounced. In this period, means of payment continued to increase at a rate of 17.3 per cent and prices at an average rate of 6.5 per cent per annum. The sources of monetary expansion, although much more moderate and on a smaller scale, were the same: deficit financing of state budgets and expansion of credit. The absorption of the unintegrated backlog of immigration, the cost of defense, and the continuation of economic development combined to increase expenditure; in addition, bank credit expanded at an average rate of 15.8 per cent per annum.

Inflationary pressures as reflected in the consumer price index increased again in the year 1961, after three years of mild price increases averaging 2 per cent per annum. Prices in 1961 increased by 7 per cent. These substantial increases reflected inflationary pressures mitigated by the rapid growth of the gross national product by 9.1 per cent per annum and by the excess of imports over exports, which aggregated $334 million in 1960, $402 million in 1961, and $434 million in 1962. However, this was no longer a government-induced inflation, since the budgets in the last three years were balanced, and even a small cash surplus appeared.

The new wave of imported inflation started in 1960 and continued through 1962. It was mainly caused by a large surplus in the balance of payments. In the three years 1960, 1961, and 1962, the state's reserves in gold and foreign currency increased by $325 million. The money supply increased by 73 per cent, totaling IL.530 million. This very large import of capital generated inflationary pressures because the influx of new capital exceeded the deficit in the trade balance, and consequently, reserves of foreign currency increased. This process was intensified in 1962 by a new devaluation, which was made imperative by the preceding developments that had made the existing rate of exchange unrealistic.

During the whole period of fifteen years, the most striking feature of development in Israel was the complete absence of the usual business cycle. At no time could the economic condition of the country be defined as one of recession. It was a one-way traffic; dynamic growth and inflationary pressure with its harmful effects were never absent. Inflationary developments in the initial period were mainly the result of governmental budgetary deficits, caused by an attempt to appropriate additional resources for development through what is defined as "inflationary saving." In this case, when there were hardly any dormant factors of production available that could be galvanized by monetary expansion and deficit financing, a point was very soon reached at which bottlenecks prevented expansion of production beyond the average annual rate of 9.5 per cent, which was in any case high enough. Monetary expansion beyond that point led to rising prices and a deterioration in the balance of payments.

The rapid economic growth, linked with full employment, resulted in a condition of overheated economic activity, a superboom. The economy suffered from four excesses: overliquidity, overconsumption, overinvestment, and overemployment, resulting in shortage of labor. The large development budget and private investment injected more projects and money into the economy than could be handled by the physical factors of production available. The rise in incomes following boom conditions and full employment generated additional inflationary pressures. The import of capital, even though desirable, led under conditions of already overheated economic activity to further monetary expansion and imported inflation.

What were the forces countervailing such powerful stimuli and incentives? The policy adopted by the Government of Israel is based on a two-pronged approach to the control of inflation from both the cost and demand sides. It consists of the comprehensive application of fiscal, monetary, and income policies. From the cost side, prices are being restrained by all means, short of physical controls. Competition is fostered through the liberalization of trade and the elimination of administrative restrictions. Wage and income restraint is enforced to a high degree and measures are being taken against cartels. The budget achieves substantial surpluses, and in the field of monetary policy, open-market operations and credit restrictions are widely used as instruments for mopping up purchasing power. By all these means, the monetary expansion caused by imported inflation is being partly compensated. This is admittedly a hard road, and such a policy encounters great opposition in view of the rigidity of the public's desires and aspirations. It has to overcome the expansionist tradition deeply rooted in this country, according to which any pace of activity and development is desirable and should be encouraged and stimulated under any circumstances. An additional psychological difficulty is that the new policy is to be carried into effect under conditions not of physical shortage but of plenty. On the other hand, the very rapid rise in standards of living and consumption, which is demonstrated by all indications of consumption of food, durable consumer goods, and services in the past few years, has provided the necessary conditions for such a policy.

The problem of inflation is closely connected with that of the balance of payments. Israel has, as already mentioned, a surplus balance of payments and a very adverse trade balance. The excess of imports over exports in the past five years has been as follows: $333 million in 1958, $316 million in 1959, $334 million in 1960, $402 million in 1961, and $434 million in 1962. If the progress toward economic emancipation and independence from foreign assistance is to be measured by the balance of payments, the adverse balance of trade has to be rectified after a period of hectic development necessitating large capital import. This does not mean physical self-sufficiency, which is impossible in the modern world in general, and in a small country like Israel in particular. It does mean an exchange of goods with other nations, always provided the *value* of goods and services produced in the country is sufficient to provide for all the needs of the population, for current consumption, and for investment.

Moreover, the situation must be seen in the context of the outlook for the balance of payments. The expectation is that within the next quinquennium, the present trend of increasing surpluses in the balance of payments will disappear, and an actual shortage of foreign currency may arise. This would create a difficult situation because a shortage of foreign currency could not only curtail imports of consumer goods but also could affect production by a shortage of raw materials, fuel, etc. In such a case, unemployment and physical shortages would be unavoidable.

The answer to this problem is to telescope into a decade an economic development that should normally take half a century, and thus win the race against time. The problem of the time lag between investment and the fruition of the investment must be taken into account in this context. As the sources of foreign assistance, which promote the economic growth of the country, are likely to dwindle into insignificance within a quinquennium, their place must be filled by an increase in the gross national product, and this is the connotation of winning the race against time.

Some progress has been made in this direction. First, while the total excess of imports over exports increased from $282 million in 1950 to $434 million in 1962, the deficit in the trade balance per head of population decreased in the same period from $222 to $190. In 1950, exports provided the equivalent of 14 per cent of imports, the remainder being financed by imports of capital, while in 1962 the share of export cover was 53 per cent. Moreover, although the absolute excess of imports over exports increased, it should be remembered that while in 1954 capital import provided 18 per cent of the total resources devoted to consumption and investment, in Israel today it provides only 10 per cent. This is the result of the fruition of investments and economic growth.

In this context, another problem is encountered: that of integration with world markets. Evidently, further improvement in the balance of trade could be achieved only by the expansion of exports. These, it is true, increased from $46 million in 1950 to $480 million in 1962, but imports increased concurrently. The problem is one of competitive capacity. In the course of rapid physical expansion, the achievement and maintenance of competitive capacity were to some extent neglected, and inflation had, of course, a detrimental effect on the ability to compete on world markets. Moreover, the world is advancing on the road to economic integration. One of the milestones on this road is regional integration, such as is most strikingly demonstrated in the Common Market.

Israel shares with most of the world's small countries the need to allocate a substantial proportion of its resources to exports. Small countries naturally tend toward greater dependence on foreign trade than do powers rich in natural resources, though even the largest countries are not completely self-sufficient and have had to abandon any inclination toward economic self-sufficiency. Territories with small populations and limited resources require a correspondingly greater quantity and variety of imported materials for their own production. In order to earn the foreign currency needed for these purchases, they must accordingly increase their exports so as to ensure full employment and the self-sustained growth of the economy. The internal market is limited, production inevitably reaches the point of saturation on domestic markets, and the sale of surplus commodities on the world market is the only outlet. Exports are thus related to the objective of maintaining production and employment because they finance the means of acquiring the import component, without which the economy will run down and unemployment will spread. This raises acutely the question of Israel's competitive capacity.

It is likely that the main further increase in Israel's exports will be to the developed countries, which today absorb about 85 per cent of them. Israel's agricultural products, grown in a sub-tropical climate, are evidently not marketable in countries of similar climate and natural conditions, but sell well in the temperate zones. European countries buy Israeli fruit, especially citrus, and off-season vegetables. Israel's relationship with Europe can be compared, to some extent, to that between the Imperial Valley and the industrialized East Coast of the United States.

As for industrial products, Israel has few local raw materials with the exception of minerals from the Dead Sea. Consequently, her industry must mainly concentrate on processing functions, that is, on utilizing raw materials bought from abroad and re-exporting the finished products. Israel's contribution is skill, labor, and capital (as in the cases of Switzerland and Holland). Such circumstances favor the manufacture and processing of diamonds, chemicals, fine metal instruments, electrical and electronic appliances, etc. Customers for such industries are found in countries with high incomes and developed industries. Moreover, production on a small scale for a population of two or even three million cannot be economical. An artificial growth under a protective tariff would create a discord with world economic trends and distort the pattern of production. Israel's economy has expanded at a rapid pace, and it has to make the decisive steps toward maturity and integration with world markets. This is the reason why Israel is vitally interested in an association with the Common Market, which now absorbs some 26 per cent of its exports.

Israel's is a pattern of an economy subject to many dynamic, powerful, and contradictory trends and tendencies. Its problems are formidable, sometimes overwhelming. The attempt to achieve balanced growth, to maintain the dynamic character of development, and to confine it within a framework of stability and equilibrium make unpopular policies imperative. The excessive rise in consumption per head and standards of living must be restrained if a balance in the external payments account is to be achieved, and the low rate of internal saving must be increased if investment is to become gradually independent of unilateral transfers of capital. To achieve this, a surplus budget, a wages and incomes policy aimed at restraint, and severe limitation of credits are indispensable. The Israel government's income and fiscal and monetary policies have all these objectives in view. They run counter to popular pressures and desires, and generate unavoidable clashes and conflicts within the economy of a country under geopolitical conditions of siege and isolation. The maintenance of rapid economic growth under a democratic regime in spite of difficult geopolitical conditions in an environment of dictatorships and autocracies is the most important objective in the purpose and performance of Israel's economic policies.

The large import of capital into the country is derived mainly from public and semipublic sources, and passes through the channels of the government or public organizations like the Jewish Agency. These circumstances are responsible for the creation of a very large sector of public and semipublic economic enterprises in agriculture, industry, transport, building, and almost every branch of the economy. Investment by the state through the development budget and public institutions is practically impossible without planning and priorities established by these public investors. The policy of the government and the exigencies of the situation, as well as the need to build a bridge to world markets, all converge to reinforce a general tendency toward liberalization of the economy. This policy of a liberalized economy, based on a large sector of public and semipublic enterprises and therefore committed to planning and priorities, is fraught with difficulties and contradictions.

Finally, the socio-economic structure of the economy is one of unusual diversity. The governmental, private, and cooperative labor sectors coexist in a kind of symbiosis, in an economy subordinated to the overriding broad political objectives of the state. The very fact of the investment of immense amounts of public capital provides the precondition for the development of a kind of mixed economy. It is too early to pronounce a final judgment as to the success of this experiment. On the face of it, the philosophy behind this maze of crosscurrents is a pragmatic one, arising out of the conditions of the economy and society. Its core is the acquiescence in a coexistence and the organic growth of a polymorphous society. Thus in Israel a new socio-economic morphology comes into existence, with a diversity of socio-economic entities and flexibility of their mutual adaptation.

This experiment in rapid economic growth and control of inflation, development in the framework of stability, economic expansion under democracy, control and liberalization, and a polymorphia of socio-economic forms is being implemented in a small country and within a relatively short period of time. It has considerable achievements against great odds to its credit and formidable difficulties ahead of it. The people and the State of Israel are confronted with many and difficult problems of controlling inflation, of a take-off to self-sustaining economic growth, of the balance of payments, of geopolitical isolation, and of the diversity of the country's socio-economic structure.

The outcome of their endeavors will determine the more universal conclusions that may be drawn from events and developments within this diminutive national unit.

CHAPTER 11

India

Gaganvihari Mehta

India is a federated economy, with fifteen constituent states organized on a linguistic basis. She has a written constitution that embodies a declaration of rights, defines the powers of the government and the states in relation to each other and the people, and provides for an independent judiciary. India has a parliamentary system of government, both for the central and for the constituent states. Her population is about 455 million, and her per capita income is $70 annually.

India has adopted a system of planning to quicken the pace of economic development. The five-year plans lay down the investment envisaged in all spheres of economic activity (agriculture and irrigation, industry and mining, power, transport and communications, and social welfare), the sources from which the investment is to be financed, and the detailed capacity and production targets for different industries.

A license is necessary to set up or expand any large-scale manufacturing unit, and this is generally given with reference to the targets set under the plans. Government permission is also necessary for raising funds on the market, for collaboration arrangements, and for import of equipment and materials. Industrial policy is governed by the Industrial Policy Resolution of 1956. This demarcates the spheres of activity of the government and the private sectors. Basic industries like iron and steel are in the government sector, and though constituted as limited companies, are financed entirely by the government.

Of the total investment in industry envisaged under the Third Plan (1961–1966), 60 per cent is to be made in the government sector and 40 per cent in the private sector. There are various financing agencies, sponsored (Industrial Finance Corporation of India) or assisted (The Industrial Credit and Investment Corporation of India Ltd.) by the government, which provide funds to industry in the private sector.

The government's policy toward foreign capital is laid down in a statement of the prime minister made in 1949. This guarantees nondiscrimination and, subject to the balance of payments position, repatriation of profits and capital. A majority of the ownership in Indian hands, though favored, is not insisted upon.

DEFINING THE PROBLEM

When India became free in 1947, she had as a legacy, besides administrative machinery developed under a hundred years of British rule and unified political control, the immediate problems also of partition and integration of princely states and a more long-term problem of poverty. Thanks to the administrative acumen of Sardar Vallabhbhai Patel (deputy prime minister at the time), the integration of the princely states was brought about with more ease than was anticipated. Partition problems, except those that normally arise between two sovereign states, have also been gradually solved. Poverty, on the other hand, has proved to be a more enduring problem. India is a large land mass and a greater population mass. In many ways, India's problem of poverty is woven around its population problem. At the last census in 1961, India had a population of 439 million and a total area of 1.18 million square miles. This, moreover, represented a rise of 78 million over the previous census, a total growth of 21 per cent in a decade. On this basis, the prospects are that India will have a population of 555 million in 1971 and 625 million in 1976.

This large population mass, increasing at an annual rate of more than 2 per cent, accentuates the problem of economic development. For one thing, a rising population involves a draft on resources for providing noneconomic overhead such as schools, public health amenities, and housing, to mention a few. At present, the percentage of literacy in India is 24, and a part of the resources that could otherwise go to improve the extent and *quality* of education must be devoted to providing literacy to the increasing number of children who come for primary education. That is true also of health measures.

What is still more important, with an increasing population, an increase in national income is necessary just to keep up the same level of per capita income. To put it in concrete terms, given a capital-output ratio of 3:1 and a population growth rate of 2 per cent (which assumptions are applicable to India), a country needs to invest from its current income at the rate of 6 per cent just to maintain per capita incomes. In fact, though accurate figures are not available, this was about the position in India in the 1930s and the 1940s. The population rise, therefore, neutralizes a part of the current investment effort.

Economic Growth Until 1950–1951

India's economic growth rate before World War II was just sufficient to keep pace with the population growth rate. This was so despite the fact that India had sufficient resources of many basic materials (for example, iron and manganese ore, bauxite, and coal deposits, though of an inferior quality and concentrated in the eastern and northeastern parts of India) and that there existed in India adequate entrepreneurial resources. For example, by 1939, India was self-sufficient, at the levels of demand then existing, in iron and steel, cement, cotton textiles, jute, coal, and tea. Moreover, the first three of these industries were set up by Indian enterprise. The first large-scale steel plant was conceived nearly sixty years ago, and Indian enterprise entered even as competitive a line as shipping more than forty years ago.

If development was not more rapid then, it was partly because of lack of confidence and partly because of lack of capital. Protection given to infant industry was halting, and imports were not controlled. Markets for many products were too small to allow the undertaking of their production. And the private investor preferred investing in an established industry and an established unit rather than in new industries or new units. Further, when an entrepreneur set up a new unit in a basic industry like iron and steel, he often had to promote or finance industries to use the basic unit's products; this is how the iron and steel complex at Jamshedpur came to grow.

THE THREE FIVE-YEAR PLANS[1]

In many ways, therefore, when India embarked upon its experiment in planning in 1950–1951, the situation was mixed.

[1] The basic documents on the Indian economy are the five-year plans—*The First Five-Year Plan, The Second Five-Year Plan,* and *The Third Five-Year Plan*—brought out by the Planning Commission, Government of India. Besides laying down the targets, these documents also contain basic data about the Indian economy and an enunciation of the philosophy and the policies underlying the planning decisions. Many commentaries, in the form of both books and articles, have appeared on India's experiment at planning. One of the more recent ones is, *Prospects for Indian Development,* by Wilfred Malenbaum.

Data on industrial production is published in the *Monthly Statistics of the Production of Selected Industries of India,* and on foreign trade in the *Monthly Statistics of the Foreign Trade of India.* The first is brought out by the Department of Commercial Intelligence and Statistics, Government of India, and the second by the Central Statistical Organization, Government of India. Data on national income is published yearly in a special paper entitled *Estimates of National Income,* brought out by the Central Statistical Organization, Government of India.

The Reserve Bank publishes data and original research work on the Indian economy, particularly on money and banking, in the *Reserve Bank of India Bulletin* (a monthly publication), *Report on Currency and Finance* (issued yearly), and *Report of the Central Board of Directors* (made annually). An article on *Savings in the Indian Economy* appeared in the August 1961 issue of the *Reserve Bank of India Bulletin.* The article on *Distribution of Income 1953–1954/1956–1957* appeared in the September 1962 issue of the Bulletin. The Reserve Bank of India also brings out special monographs, one of the recent ones being *India's Balance of Payments 1948–1949 to 1961–1962.*

The Indian Investment Centre was set up in 1961. Its publications to date include: *Objects and Functions, Exchange Control, Taxation, Basic Facts of the Indian Economy,* and the "Investing in India" series.

The basis for industrial expansion—an impartial administrative framework, an efficient system of law, a reasonably established infrastructure (including railways, road system, ports, and power), industrial resources and entrepreneurial ability—all these existed within the economy. A tradition of industrial growth had been built up (particularly in the preceding quarter of a century, though the scale was not sufficient) in relation particularly to population growth. What needed to be done was to bring about a setting under which the rate of growth could be increased (at least sufficiently to involve a break from the past) and the higher growth rate so achieved could be maintained.

This was the stage at which planning was introduced in India. The first plan was primarily a systematic organization of schemes, many of which had been started or at least conceived in the pre-planning period. Under it, the rate of investment was to increase from about 5 per cent of national income in 1950–1951 to 7.3 per cent in 1955–1956.

It was under the second plan that a planned strategy was formulated to accelerate the rate of progress. It was proposed at once to increase the rate of investment from 7.3 per cent in 1955–1956 to about 11 per cent in 1960–1961, and to devote a larger proportion of such investment to the setting up of heavy industries (particularly, iron and steel capacity). Since these heavy industries are placed in the public sector, the plan strategy involved a shift in industrial investment in favor of the public sector.

The third plan (which, as framed, was about 50 per cent larger than the second) tried to continue the strategy laid down under the second plan. The rate of investment was to increase from about 11 per cent of national income in 1960–1961 to about 14 per cent in 1965–1966. The concentration toward heavy industries and the public sector remained, although within the heavy industry sector the investment was planned to be more diversified.

Tables 1 and 2 show the distribution of plan outlays under the first three plans, and their financing.

TABLE 1. PLAN OUTLAYS BY GOVERNMENT
(*In Millions of Dollars*)

	First Plan[a] 1951–1952 to 1955–1956		Second Plan[a] 1956–1957 to 1960–1961		Third Plan[b] 1961–1962 to 1965–1966	
Agriculture	611	(15)	1,113	(12)	2,243	(14)
Irrigation	651	(16)	882	(9)	1,365	(9)
Power	546	(13)	934	(10)	2,125	(13)
Industry and Mining	246	(6)	2,258	(23)	3,746	(24)
Transport and Communications	1,098	(27)	2,730	(28)	3,121	(20)
Others	964	(23)	1,743	(18)	3,150	(20)
Total	4,116	(100)	9,660	(100)	15,750	(100)

NOTE: Figures in parentheses are percentages of the total. Plan outlays include expenditures of a current nature and therefore exceed investment envisaged under the plans. Investment in the government sector was $3,275 million during the first plan, $7,665 million during the second plan, and $13,230 million during the third plan.
a Actual.
b Planned.

TABLE 2. FINANCING OF THE PLAN OUTLAYS
(*In Millions of Dollars*)

	First Plan 1951–1952 to 1955–1956	Second Plan 1956–1957 to 1960–1961	Third Plan 1961–1962 to 1965–1966
Internal Resources	3,721a	7,371b	11,130c
Government revenues including new taxation		2,150	5,103
Contribution from railways, public enterprises, and steel equalization fund		395	1,376
Loans including small savings and provident fund contributions		2,835	3,496
Deficit financing		1,991	1,155
External assistance	395	2,289b	4,620c

a A detailed break-up of the first plan sources of finance is not available.
b Figures for 1960–1961. Total: $9,660 million.
c Figures for 1965–1966. Total: $15,750 million.

EXPERIENCE UNDER PLANNING: PUBLIC SECTOR

Planning may be defined as a system of deliberately and systematically allocating resources over investment sectors and over time. As mentioned above, the first plan was only an agglomeration of various investment schemes, most of which had already been started. India had then little experience in planning to guide it. The major problem at that time was to keep investment within the limits of available resources and to determine a broad order of priorities.

As a result, the investment rate implied under the first plan was about 6.7 per cent of national income; moreover, the distribution of outlays was concentrated in agriculture and irrigation (31 per cent) and only 6 per cent of the outlay was devoted to industry.

The results of the first plan exceeded the planners' expectations. This was proved by:

1. As against an expected rise of 12 per cent in national income during the plan period, the actual rise achieved was 18 per cent.

2. The dependence on foreign assistance was kept low, the actual drawing down of foreign currency reserves being $256 million as against a planned estimate of $609 million.

3. Over the plan period, the price level (as reflected by the index number of wholesale prices) actually declined, indicating that there was no undue strain on resources.

Partly owing to the success of the first plan and partly because the planning machinery had become more fully established, the second plan was formulated on a more ambitious scale. Not only did it involve a doubling of the rate of investment; it also sought to rearrange priorities so as to lay a greater emphasis on industry (and, within industry, on heavy industry) and to relegate agriculture to a lower place.

This reallocation was not accidental, but was a deliberate strategy in planning. As income growth is related to investment, it was assumed that the higher rate of investment would lead to faster income growth, and the annual rate of income growth planned was 5 per cent[2] under the second plan (as against 2.4 per

2 The annual rates of income growth referred to throughout this chapter are calculated as simple averages of five-year growth rates.

cent planned and 3.6 per cent achieved during the first plan). Moreover, as investment rate growth was assumed to be related to the output of basic industries, it was expected that, with the greater emphasis on heavy industry, the investment rate would rise automatically in the future.

Such was the philosophy underlying the second plan; the actual results, however, were different. Within two years of the commencement of the second plan, the substantial foreign currency reserves that India had were drawn down by $1,000 million, leaving as a balance the bare minimum required to be maintained by her currency law. The second plan itself had to be appraised and reappraised, and massive aid had to be obtained from the World Bank and various countries.

If the first plan succeeded beyond expectations, the second plan led to results which, to put it mildly, were below expectations. As measured against the three indices cited earlier, (1) the actual rise in national income during the second plan was only 21.7 per cent, against the planned rise of 25 per cent; (2) the foreign currency reserves were reduced to their minimum level, and almost all new economic development became dependent on foreign aid forthcoming; and (3) the price level rose by 35 per cent over the plan period.

The Third Plan was framed under the shadow of the difficulties that had arisen in the execution of the second plan. In some respects, it was more realistically framed: the total investment under the third plan was to rise by 50 per cent over that planned under the second plan; moreover, a larger proportion (23 per cent) of the total outlay was to be devoted to agriculture and irrigation; and, the outlay for industry was to be more diversified among types of industries, only about 40 per cent being allocated for setting up steel capacity (against 80 per cent of the industrial outlay under the second plan).

It is not easy to judge the results of the third plan, partly because only two years have elapsed since its commencement and partly because of the change in the character of the problem caused by Chinese aggression on Indian territory. A drastic budget was introduced in early 1963 to provide for increased defense expenditures without cutting back on development expenditures. However, the development tempo has seemed to lag under these pressures. Judging the experience so far by the three indices that were used for the first plan, (1) the rise in national income in the two years is at an annual rate of about 2.5 per cent, against a planned rate of 6 per cent, which is barely sufficient to keep pace with population growth; (2) foreign currency reserves remain at a minimum; and (3) the price level has risen by about 3 per cent in two years, and has shown a tendency to rise at an accelerated rate.

EXPERIENCE UNDER PLANNING: PRIVATE SECTOR

The pace of investment in the private sector also quickened under planning, as shown by Table 3.

TABLE 3.   INVESTMENT IN THE PRIVATE SECTOR
(In Millions of Dollars)

	First Plan 1951–1952 to 1955–1956	Second Plan 1956–1957 to 1960–1961	Third Plan 1961–1962 to 1965–1966
Organized Industry and Mining	489	1,418[b]	2,205[c]
Other Sectors	3,291[a]	5,092[b]	6,405[c]
Agriculture and Irrigation		1,313	1,680
Power		84	105
Village and Small Industries		367	578
Transport and Communications		283	525
Others		3,045	3,517

a A detailed break-up of private sector investment in other sectors is not available.
b Figures for 1960–1961. Total: $6,510 million.
c Figures for 1965–1966. Total: $8,610 million.

Along with total investment, investment in industry also increased. While some hesitation was noticeable in the initial stages of planning both among Indian and foreign investors, there has, particularly since the foreign exchange crisis of 1957–1958, been a considerable upsurge of private investment. This upsurge has been due to many factors.

While the government has not overtly revised its industrial policy as enunciated in 1956, it has had a pragmatic approach in interpreting it and a flexible policy in implementing it. For instance, the government agreed to permit the setting up of nitrogenous fertilizer factories in the private sector, although under the Industrial Policy Resolution, further development of this industry is to be brought about by the government. So, also in relation to foreign private enterprise, the government has not always insisted on majority Indian participation, but where justified by the nature of the industry or other advantages, the government has agreed to foreigners having a majority holding, including 100 per cent foreign holding in the case of some companies. Foreign private investment is now taking place at the rate of about $100 million per year.

A second factor was the opportunity provided by the foreign exchange crisis of 1957–1958. With the sudden curb on imports, it became profitable to manufacture internally many goods that used to be imported. Entrepreneurs were aided in their attempt to start industries by the fact that the government adopted a more liberal policy in granting licenses to set up factories and that the investing public responded vigorously to capital issues by companies, old and new.

At the same time, attempts were also being made to interest foreign private enterprise in India's industrial development. The Indian Investment Centre was set up in 1961 to provide guidance to Indian and foreign entrepreneurs regarding investment possibilities ad collaboration arrangements in India. The Centre has done valuable work in interesting foreign entrepreneurs in investing in India: by publishing brochures on various aspects of economic policy, by personal contacts with potential foreign investors, by overcoming various misgivings and clarifying procedural problems, and by acting as liaison between foreign investors on the one hand and the government and the Indian investors on the other. A noticeable feature in foreign collaboration arrangements is the increasing interest shown by non-British, particularly American and German, enterprises in investing in India.

Table 4 gives data on various aspects of private investment in India in the past seven years. The upsurge in private investment was brought to a halt as a result of the renewed foreign exchange

TABLE 4. PRIVATE INVESTMENT IN INDIA

	1956	1957	1958	1959	1960	1961	1962
New capital issues:							
Number	47	48	48	69	104	160	159
Amount in							
millions of dollars	95	52	54	91	128	138	217
Foreign collaboration:							
Number of agreements							
approved	17	24	109	172	390	402	298

crisis in early 1962 and the Chinese aggression toward the end of 1962. As India has cut her imports drastically to a level even below that required for the maintenance requirements of the factories already established, a restriction on imports directly affects adversely the profitability of existing enterprises. Moreover, as foreign exchange for the import of capital goods itself is restricted and committed to agreed projects, industry has less scope to meet its requirements by resort to import substitution. Added to this is the factor that the Chinese aggression has led to increased taxation, the transfer of scarce resources toward defense efforts, and the creation of uncertainty about the future. The pace of investment has consequently slowed down, and this may continue until the economic and political conditions become more normal.

ACHIEVEMENTS UNDER PLANNING

A balance sheet of twelve years of planning presents a mixed picture. On the credit side may be placed the substantial rises in output achieved during the past twelve years and the intangible yet nonetheless valuable achievement of bringing about development consciousness and the feeling that stagnation and poverty are not inevitable. The growth in national income, achieved since planning began, is shown in Table 5.

TABLE 5. NATIONAL INCOME
(In Millions of Dollars)

Source	At Current Prices			At Constant Prices		
	1950–1951	1955–1956	1960–1961	1950–1951	1955–1956	1960–1961
Agriculture	10,269	9,492	14,490	9,114	10,542	12,411
Mining, manufacturing, and small enterprises	3,213	3,885	5,460	3,108	3,696	4,431
Commerce, transport, and communications	3,549	3,948	4,914	3,486	4,137	5,166
Others	9,982	3,633	4,872	2,877	3,633	4,767
			736	18,585	22,008	26,775

first two plans by about 45 has risen from 55 million n 1960–1961. The acreage 52 million in 1950–1951 cultivated area on single Consumption of fertilizers 0–1951 to 200,000 tons in from 7,000 tons to 70,000 At the same time, India, gaged in agriculture, still

en more rapid strides, al- to 1960–1961 decade. Ex- of textile manufactures nicals and chemical prod- tal products 280, of ma- and of electrical machin- ies, 420. The machinery nd India now fabricates nical plants, textile ma- . Figures of production of important industrial products are shown in Table 6.

TABLE 6.   PRODUCTION IN SELECTED INDUSTRIES

Item	Unit	1950– 1951	1955– 1956	1962– 1963	1965– 1966a
Steel ingots	Million tons	1.4	1.7	3.3	9.2
Aluminum	Thousand tons	3.7	7.3	18.2	80.0
Machine tools (organized sector)	Value in $ million	0.71	1.64	15.2	63
Electric cables (ACSR conductors)	Thousand tons	1.7	8.7	23.6	44
Ball and roller bearings	Million units	0.1	0.9	3.2	15
Automobiles	Thousand units	16.5	25.3	52.1	100
Tractors	Thousand units	...	...	...	10
Bicycles (organized sector)	Thousand units	101	513	1,060	2,000
Diesel engines (stationary)	Thousand units	5.5	10.0	43.2	66
Sewing machines (organized sector)	Thousand units	33	111	297	700
Nitrogenous fertilizers	Thousand tons of N	9	79	97	800
Phosphatic fertilizers	Thousand tons of P_2O_5	9	12	53	400
Sulfuric acid	Thousand tons	99	164	354	1,500
Caustic soda	Thousand tons	11	35	97	340
Petroleum products	Million tons	...	3.6	5.7	9.9
Cement	Million tons	2.7	4.6	7.8	13
Paper and paper board	Thousand tons	114	187	343	700
Cotton textiles (mill made)	Million yards	3,718	5,101	5,048	5,800
Rayon filament	Million pounds	0.4	16	47	140
Sugar	Million tons	1.12	1.86	3.0	3.5

a Figures for 1965–1966 are targets.

The output of coal increased from 32.3 million tons in 1950–1951 to 54.6 million tons in 1960–1961. The capacity for generating power increased from 2.3 million kilowatt-hours in 1950–1951 to 5.7 million kilowatt-hours in 1960–1961. Yet the industrial development has been so rapid that shortages of coal and power have been felt by industry in most places.

The progress in the social field is equally significant. Primary education has expanded, and the percentage of literacy rose from 17 in the 1951 census to 24 in the 1961 census. The percentage of school-going children in the primary stage (age group 6 to 11 years) increased from 42.6 in 1950–1951 to 61.1 in 1960–1961, and in the middle stage (age group 11 to 14 years) from 12.7 in 1950–1951 to 22.8 in 1960–1961. Higher education, particularly in science, technology, and medicine, has also been correspondingly expanded; students in colleges of engineering and technology and in agricultural colleges increased more than three times during the same period.

Similarly, public health facilities have been expanded. The infant mortality rate declined from 182 per thousand births in 1941–1951 to 135 in 1956–1961, and the over-all mortality rate from 27.4 to 21.6 per thousand population. Family planning is part of government policy, and the allocation for family-planning programs was raised from $6 million under the second plan to $57 million under the third plan.

DISTRIBUTION OF INCOME AND WEALTH

The impact of planning on distribution of income and wealth is difficult to gauge. The need for promoting greater economic equality has been stated in the Indian Constitution as a long-term objective and in the five-year plans as a short-term objective. Measures of equality are still not agreed upon; moreover, in a country like India, with a very low per capita income, equality may be in terms of poverty. In this context, actual measurement of trends in distribution of income and wealth becomes difficult. A predominant part of the population lives at substandard levels, and no reliable data are available about it; income-tax statistics do not cover even a quarter of 1 per cent of the country's population. The policy issue itself, therefore, is not one of *redistributing* income, as in advanced countries, but one of *increasing per capita* income in aggregate and particularly for the low-income groups.

As regards household incomes, a study[3] by the Reserve Bank research staff estimated that "during this period [1953–1954 to 1956–1957], 95 per cent of total households were in the low in-

[3] Distribution of Income 1953–1954 to 1956–1957; *Reserve Bank of India Bulletin*, September 1962.

come (yearly income up to $630) group and derived 80 per cent of total personal income, while 5 per cent of the total households were in the high-income group (yearly income above $630), obtaining 20 per cent of total income." Two major conclusions are drawn in the study: "The degree of inequality in the income distribution appears to have increased somewhat" over the period; and "direct taxes did not affect the pattern of changes in personal income to any significant extent."

A committee was also appointed to inquire into the distribution of wealth in India. The committee has not yet issued its report. However, some press reports on its findings appear to suggest that it has found a growing concentration of wealth in certain sectors, particularly the corporate sector. This the committee is reported to attribute partly to the government's policy of indiscriminate protection to industry through measures of import and foreign exchange control.

It is not possible to give definitive conclusions about the trends in the distribution of income or wealth in India. However, some qualitative assessment may be possible by considering the various factors influencing income and wealth and their distribution:

1. Over the period of planning, per capita income has increased by about 20 per cent.

2. As Table 5 shows, the fastest-growing sources of income are industry and the tertiary sector. There has been capital appreciation in the corporate sector (partly as a consequence of a highly protected market). However, wealth held in money or money-equivalent form (provident fund contributions, life insurance savings) would have been eroded as a result of rising prices, uncompensated by an adequate return on it, owing to the government's cheap money policy.

3. Land reform legislation has made for wider distribution of land; however, there has been no expropriation of land.

4. Income-tax rates, particularly in the higher ranges, were revised downward during the 1950s from their high war and immediate postwar levels; wealth tax was introduced in the late 1950s. Indirect taxation has been increased, mainly to raise re-

sources for the government's requirements; within this, discriminatory taxation is levied on what are called luxury or semiluxury goods (cars, refrigerators, air conditioners, radios).

5. A large part of the social legislation concerning factory workers tends to give them fringe benefits (housing, medical facilities), which help to increase their real income as a privileged class.

Recently, as a result of heavy taxation measures to meet the needs of an increased defense budget, the strain on available resources has increased. This has made imperative the maintaining of the social content of planning. Planners themselves have been concerned at the failure of the plans to make a noticeable dent in poverty, and it is likely that in future plans, greater attempts will be made to raise minimum levels of living.

EXTERNAL TRADE RELATIONS

India's trade with other countries has also undergone remarkable changes in amount, composition, and sources during the plan era. Although exports have shown a tendency to rise only marginally in value, imports have tended to rise much faster, as shown in Table 7.

TABLE 7. RISE OF IMPORTS
(*In Millions of Dollars*)

	1950–1951	1955–1956	1960–1961	1962–1963
Imports	1,366	1,624	2,315	2,262
Exports	1,358	1,345	1,324	1,457

If imports have not increased faster, it is mainly due to rigid control on imports, owing to the paucity of foreign exchange. These imports cuts have been more severe with respect to consumer goods than to raw materials and intermediate goods. Table 8 shows the composition of India's imports. Most of the capital goods financing is done through direct aid given by vari-

TABLE 8. COMPOSITION OF IMPORTS
(In Millions of Dollars)

	1950–1951	1955–1956	1960–1961
Consumer goods*a*	95	126	103
Raw materials and metals	533	605	686
Capital goods*b*	243	462	629

a Excluding food grains.

b Machinery of all kinds and transport equipment (excluding locomotives).

ous countries, and the amount available is governed not only by India's requirements but also by the aid-giving countries' budgetary and balance of payments position.

Exports have not changed in character. About 60 per cent of exports are accounted for by traditional items (cotton and cotton textiles, jute yarn and manufactures, tea and hides, and skins). Cotton textile export targets have not been achieved, and other traditional exports have been subject to fluctuations in prices common to agricultural commodities. The increase in exports of nontraditional items (engineering and other manufactured goods) remains marginal.

A third factor to note is the direction of India's foreign trade, as shown by Table 9. The table brings out two major points: the

TABLE 9. DISTRIBUTION OF EXPORTS AND IMPORTS
(In Millions of Dollars)

		1950–1951	1955–1956	1956–1957	1960–1961	1962–1963
United Kingdom	Imports	412	544	713	552	374
	Exports	303	366	402	363	344
United States	Imports	253	268	421	777	662
	Exports	313	206	203	200	246
EEC countries*a*	Imports	111	250	454	325	322
	Exports	95	116	116	101	103
East European countries*b*	Imports	9	23	85	124	223
	Exports	4	11	42	98	196

a Comprising Belgium and Luxemburg, France, West Germany, Italy, and the Netherlands. Figures for 1950–1951 and 1955–1956 are obtained by addition, and are not strictly comparable with the figures for later years.

b Comprising Bulgaria, Czechoslovakia, East Germany, Hungary, Poland, Rumania, U.S.S.R., and Yugoslavia. Figures for 1950–1951 and 1955–1956 are obtained by addition and are not strictly comparable with the figures for later years.

growing trade relations with the eastern European countries and the large deficit with the Common Market of the European Economic Community.

India's trading relations are increasingly governed more and more by her balance-of-payments position. Her sources of imports are, therefore, determined by the direction of her exports and by the sources of aid. One of the principal factors making for trade between India and the eastern European countries is the existence of bilateral trading arrangements under which eastern European countries take payment in the local currency (rupees), which can be used for local purchases only. On the other hand, India's purchases from the United States have been maintained only by the generous assistance made available by that country.

India's trade with the United Kingdom is more balanced than with the EEC countries. To some extent (for example, for tea and jute), the United Kingdom acts as the extrepot, exaggerating thereby her own balance and accentuating the EEC countries' surplus with India. However, even allowing for indirect imports of Indian goods by the EEC countries, India's balance with them remains highly unfavorable. India is therefore directly concerned over the external tariff policy of the EEC countries. Her ability to buy from these countries is directly related to their imports from India, supplemented by such aid (credits and grants) as they may make available. While India has not favored a discriminatory policy with regard to her imports, it would need to be recognized by these countries that a liberal attitude on their part with regard to imports and aid would help India to maintain and expand her trading relations with them.

SHORTCOMINGS OF PLANNING

The economic achievements mentioned earlier are considerable, although not all should be attributed to planning. In a country like India, with a stagnant agriculture and an undiversified economy, with an abnormally low purchasing power, with abysmal poverty and illiteracy, there is no doubt that planning of some kind is essential. However, Indian planning has shown up some shortcomings, which should be mentioned.

As stated earlier, what may be called the strategy of planning evolved at the beginning of the second plan, that is, much after planning itself came to be accepted. This strategy was to concentrate investment in heavy basic industries (and, as a corollary, to meet the increased demand for consumer goods by the promotion of cottage industries).

This, of course, is not the only or always the best means for rapid development. There are other methods such as development of import-substituting industries or development of agriculture or of consumer goods industries. Moreover, in adopting any strategy for development, it is necessary to take into account its impact on the investment rate and also the fact that India does not have a wholly closed economy. An open economy—an economy that has normal economic relations with other countries—has greater flexibility in arranging its investment priorities and also greater risks in failing to take into account comparative cost factors. In setting a strategy for development, it would have been appropriate to adopt policies that had a broader impact on the economy and to undertake projects justified by cost considerations. It appears that the strategy actually adopted tended to ignore these considerations. For instance, expressing this theme in concrete terms, for the cost of a million-ton steel project, it would be possible to set up seven to eight large (80,000 ton) nitrogenous fertilizer plants. Before deciding between these two alternatives, it would be worth while to measure the relative impact of each project on the Indian economy, including its role in fostering further development. Evidently, no such comparative analysis was undertaken to support decisions on alternative industrial priorities, the adoption of the "strategy" being deemed to be an adequate reason for favoring steel plants. Nor did the government have an integrated system of planning under which the development of one industry was allowed or used to generate the growth of other industries. To give a few examples: Although rayon spinning was set up more than a decade ago, no steps were taken until recently to develop a rayon-grade pulp industry; so, also, the development of styrene monomer was undertaken long after polystyrene started to be manufactured.

Another result of such planning has been the setting up of many industries that (because of scale, location, or other factors) have high costs and are therefore unable to compete in external markets.[4]

Another serious defect of planning in India is its failure to have a savings policy. While investment rose from 5 per cent of national income in 1950–1951 to 11 per cent of national income in 1960–1961, savings rose during the same period from 5 per cent[5] to 8.5 per cent.

Much of the increase in investment during the planning period has thus been financed out of an increase in domestic savings rather than by resort to foreign aid. For example, of the additional investment of $4,389 million in the public sector during the second plan, $1,894 million (or 43 per cent) was obtained through foreign aid; also, of the additional investment of $5,565 million during the third plan, $2,331 million (or 42 per cent) was to be found from further foreign aid; and even this, as has been shown by the experience of the past two years, appears to be an underestimate by at least 25 or 30 per cent. In other words, while foreign aid (both grants and loans) formed 10 per cent of the financing required under the first plan, it formed 24 per cent under the second plan, and has been "fixed" at 29 per cent for the third plan. The element of foreign aid, as we now find, is more important than it was in the initial period of planning.

One of the factors in the growing importance of foreign aid is the failure of India's export effort (assuming that the import bill is governed by the plan requirements). India's exports in 1950–1951 formed 6.5 per cent of her national income; the percentage of exports in 1960–1961 to her national income was 4.5. Thus, of the increased output during the decade, a smaller percentage is

---

[4] The impact of this on foreign trade was dealt with earlier; its impact on plan financing will be discussed subsequently. It also affects adversely the consumer: Many manufactured consumer goods, the imports of which had to be stopped or curtailed after the 1957–1958 rundown of foreign currency reserves, now cost the consumers two to three times the international prices.

[5] The Reserve Bank data place savings in 1950–1951 at a higher rate.

being exported than originally.[6] Or, to give another index of
the foreign trade position, the third plan visualized that India's
total exports during the third plan would not be sufficient to
cover even the *maintenance imports* required during the period,
and the whole of the capital import bill for the period would
have to be met from foreign aid. The development strategy thus
has failed to generate the foreign exchange resources required to
carry it out.

PROBLEMS FACING THE INDIAN ECONOMY

India's economy faces the strains and stresses of development.
While the size of the country is of advantage with respect to
natural resources and the potential market, it also creates several
problems of adjustment between various states and territories.
The Indian Constitution is federal in character and the union
(or federal) government, which has residual powers, exercises
considerable authority and influence through financial control.
But the process of development itself creates an imbalance in the
economy, and regional interests have to be weighed against the
strict demands of efficiency. Every country has political pressures
and regional influences and these are accentuated in a developing economy where needs outstrip resources and time is a vital
factor.

India has had the advantage of a stable political regime, the
rule of law, and a well-knit and fairly efficient administrative
machinery. All this has enabled gradual political, social, and
economic evolution. The Indian political tradition values continuity, not violent upheavals; constituted authority, not revolutionary *diktat*. The pattern of future society as visualized by
informed and enlightened Indians assigns a positive and constructive role to the state in ensuring favorable conditions for
economic development, in mobilizing and augmenting financial

[6] The reasons for this have been given earlier: Investment has taken place
in high-cost noncompetitive lines; it is also due to the failure to pursue
vigorously a policy of import substitution (particularly in chemicals and in
automobile industries).

and technical resources so as to improve standards of living, and in securing an equitable distribution of national wealth.

An economy that is controlled and regulated by the state offers opportunities for private enterprise to expand as well as to make gains, not all of which are legitimate. Private enterprise has played an increasingly important part in the industrial development of India during the period of planned development and can continue to do so in the future, provided it is efficient and maintains standards of integrity.

The economic picture today, however, is such as to cause concern. After a steady growth during the first-plan period and the upsurge of the second-plan period, the economy has shown signs of faltering during the past two years, which are the first two years of the third plan. The Chinese aggression and the orientation that it demands toward defense has aggravated the problem. The rate of economic expansion has slowed down, and with fluctuations in the quantum of foreign aid, uncertain factors have become predominant in the process of planning. This is illustrated in the recent controversy over the project of a steel plant at Bokaro. Planning has had to be adapted to implement schemes suited to the kind of foreign aid available rather than to answer economic needs. What is required is not haphazard solution or improvisation but basic reconsideration of the whole ideology and strategy of planning as well as a discipline in carrying out decisions. Such rethinking needs to take into account some basic problems facing the Indian economy. These are in many ways interrelated and will have to be tackled with a sense of realism and determination.

A high priority needs to be given to the population problem. India's is one of the few governments that has officially recognized the need to promote family planning. Nevertheless, the resources, efforts, and measures devoted to this task have been wholly incommensurate with the imperative requirements of the problem. Resources devoted to control of population would help to increase the general welfare in no less a measure than those utilized for giant schemes and for what Professor Galbraith has called "symbolic modernization."

India's imports of agricultural commodities, such as food grains and cotton are, no doubt, marginal at the present level of consumption. But India is a predominantly agricultural country with low levels of productivity; with two-thirds of the population going without adequate food and the normal intake of calories at about two-thirds of the bare minimum, there is immense scope for increasing the levels of consumption. That large quantities of food grains have to be imported year after year and valuable foreign exchange spent on their purchase and transport is a measure of the national failure to solve a fundamental economic problem. It hardly needs any emphasis that food is basic in a backward economy and that the high cost of inadequacy or uncertainty of the supply of essential articles of daily consumption causes social discontent. Fertilizers should have, for instance, a priority over heavy machinery, or the development of efficient agriculture should receive much greater attention, not merely from the point of view of financial resources but also of administration.

Another problem that deserves immediate consideration is the full utilization of industrial capacity available in the country. It seems incomprehensible that Indian planners seem intent on putting up factories even when it is not possible to have the wherewithal to work them with raw materials, power, and ancillary services. It is time for a stock-taking of industrial capacity and for adoption of measures to run the industrial apparatus at its maximum. A poor country like India can hardly afford to keep its industrial capacity idle.

One of the factors that hampers full utilization of industrial capacity is the lack of imported raw materials. An estimate made by Sir Donald MacDougall, in 1961, suggested that additional imports of $210 million might lead to an additional output fifteen to twenty times that amount from the capacity then existing. Since then, no improvement is evident; if anything, conditions have worsened. Given the problems of aid and the difficulties of countries providing the aid, such imports can be made only by increasing exports. The objective should be to encourage efficient industry that can compete under normal incentives in world markets. Efficient industry alone can be the basis of a sound policy of development.

These are some of the problems that the government and people of India will have to tackle if the country is to have healthy as well as rapid industrial development and build sound foundations for economic progress. Development is a long-term process, which in a democratic setup can proceed on the basis of trial and error. Fortunately, India has a fairly wide area of agreement about the methods of development as well as about its broad objectives. The government wants to effect change and reform by consent, not by coercion. National progress depends, in the ultimate analysis, on enterprising and imaginative leadership, a diffused sense of responsibility, and a national discipline. It is general policy to achieve economic development while maintaining individual freedom and promoting social justice. This is the great challenge faced by India, but it is also a noble adventure.

CHAPTER 12

Two Economic Worlds: The Free and the Communist Nations

Reinhard Kamitz

In analyzing the international economic relations between the West and the East, there must be drawn up a definite dividing line, highlighted by existing differences in the political structures and economic activities. In fact, the distinction should be made between the free nations in contrast to the high communist countries, since in the free world, communism is a synonym for a system that is not free.

In the West, freedom means, to put it simply, the right to lead one's own life as one wants to, to lay down rules within the community, and to bring about any desired changes. Freely elected representatives have to abide by the rules or laws that citizens establish for themselves and for the community. The approach is based on equality for all members of the community and on respect for the opinions of others, even if these opinions differ.

These principles apply to the economic as well as to the political life, for freedom is indivisible. It cannot be hemmed in at one point without negatively affecting other fields of endeavors. An essential part of this freedom is the opportunity to accumulate and to utilize private wealth, within the limits of the law.

Ownership by the entrepreneur of the means of production is a basis for free economic activity, and the existence of many entrepreneurs allow the worker a freedom of choice of his place of work.

In such an economic system, man's needs become the objective, profit is the stimulus, competition is the instrumentality, and price is the criterion. Through the mechanism of supply and demand, the market determines the nature and volume of production. In this context, money's special function is that of a yardstick; it also serves as a medium of exchange and of accumulating capital.

ECONOMIC DIFFERENCES

Lenin himself illustrated the pivotal role of money in the capitalistic economic system. In one passage of his writings, he said that in order to destroy the bourgeois society, one must first destroy its monetary system. That quotation we should always bear in mind when making economic decisions, notably those affecting monetary policy. We tend to expect too much of it, especially in cases where self-restraint is not practiced. Monetary policy cannot do the job when those in charge are seeking the easy way out or lack the determination to live in accordance with the principles of freedom.

Day in and day out, the countries of the free world witness a multitude of sins that are committed against the ideal of freedom, chiefly in the economic sphere. This weakness, while lamentable, is part and parcel of the pattern that grants us the freedom either to live up to our obligations or to relinquish them. In contrasting the free world concept with the communist system, the ideological antagonism is patent. Under communism there is but a single political party. Its decisions are deemed infallible and assume dogmatic character. Deviations are not tolerated. In the case of communists in other communist countries, bitter political conflict results from charges of "deviationism."

Everyone has to conform to the ideology of communism. Business and industry, to which that political tenet applies with special force, are in consequence subjected to a peculiar orientation. It is not admissible to form an individual opinion about the economic efficiency, of a measure, its value, or its impracticability. Businessmen or industrialists receive orders that derive from an all-encompassing plan and must be obeyed. So dictatorial a system cannot be implemented fully as long as private ownership of the means of production still exists. For that reason, the nationalization of private property becomes a necessity. The state must concentrate in its own hand all the means required for shaping the economy, whether these already exist or are yet to be created, and it utilizes them to achieve the objectives of the ultimate "plan."

The immediate aims of communist policy are rapid economic growth, industrialization, economic independence from other countries, and curtailment of the time span normally required for certain operations. These objectives reflect the determination of communists to obtain structural changes in the economy, to bring about the kind of transformation attainable only over a considerable period of time. Therefore, the policy is predicated on long-range prognostications that take the form of so-called Perspective Plans extending over fifteen to twenty years. The various stages thereof are marked by five-year, six-year, or seven-year plans. They, in their turn, are broken down into one-year plans. What is the procedure in elaborating these plans? The government, being the executive organ for carrying out the decisions of the Communist Party, establishes the objectives and the basic tasks. Next, directives are worked out for drafting the plans. Through the trade organizations of the ministries involved, or through regional commissions, the production quotas imposed on the different branches of the economy are allocated to the enterprises. According to Eastern sources, discussions and corrections are possible in this phase. Then the suppliers and the customers among the enterprises coordinate their plans for production and sale. That technical process is followed by the coordination of the resulting draft plans. This key function is carried out by the Supreme State Planning Bureau, an agency which, subject to the government's directives, prepares the countrywide plans and controls their observance after the government has approved them.

In the communist countries, the state planning bureaus consist of ministers or special commissioners for certain branches of economic activity. The chairmen, generally members of the Party Secretariat or Central Committee, are high-ranking government leaders. Through their centralized direction, which is chiefly concentrated on production, the agencies ensure that production does not lack the requisite supply of raw materials, semimanufactured goods, and manpower. Distribution within the manufacturing apparatus is another responsibility of these Bureaus. In addition, these central bodies reach out into other economic spheres like agriculture, foreign trade, and finance. Since the focus is on industrial production, consumer requirements are merely a subsidiary factor, which is taken into account when adjusting prices and wages. The individual consumer obtains only the share of the national product that remains after state and industry requirements have been satisfied. He cannot object to the priority that the law accords to other sectors of the economy. The output of consumer goods can be increased in one way only, namely, by exceeding the production goals in a given sector of the plan. However, there is little leeway for the achievement of such feats. The reserves allowed for by the plan are sparse indeed, and the straitjacket of bureaucratic planning procedures leaves very little opportunity for individual initiative, for any supplemental production requires increased output and additional materials as well as more manpower, and these extra requirements somewhere along the line of the manufacturing process place the rigid framework of the "plan" in jeopardy. Bonuses and other measures to spur production do exist, but they are set up to benefit solely those areas of the economy whose development is consonant with political objectives. In places where a sizable contribution could be made to the raising of living standards, individual enterprise lacks scope and financial incentive because creative forces are hobbled and initiative is stifled.

The citizens of the communist world are told that, although their living standard may not be so high as that of other countries, they can count on smooth economic development free of crisis and depression, a state of affairs upon which they cannot, it is claimed, rely in the free world. In reality, and leaving aside the question whether economic developments laid down in the plans are sound, one might well say that the planned economy of the communist countries is in a permanent state of crisis, as shown by the chronic shortages in food supply and consumer goods, whereas in countries whose economy is based on capitalist principles, the citizens are supplied better, and with goods of more satisfactory quality. No great crises have marred the postwar era in the countries where capitalism prevails.

ECONOMIC INTERRELATIONS

What about economic relations between communist countries and the free world? An assessment of the possibilities should be predicated on familiarity with needs, production, prices, and wages. Available statistical data of the East, open to doubt as these may be, indicate that the demand for almost all articles, notably foodstuffs and consumer goods, is heavy indeed. Free access to the communist market is not possible, however. The potential is there, but the opportunities for sales are contingent upon the provisions of the economic plan currently in force, especially the foreign-trade plan.

A foreign-trade plan consists of the merchandise plan, which comprises import requirements and goods available for export, and of the foreign-exchange plan, which deals with payments, prices, terms, trade conditions, and the payments balance of various countries or currency areas. As in the all-encompassing economic plan, the foreign-trade plan is established on a long-term (five to seven years) basis. Within its framework, short-term one-year plans are then established. They, in turn, are broken down into quarterly plans.

In each country, the ministry of commerce is responsible for the conduct of foreign trade. It coordinates the plan drafted by the state trade organizations in various fields, determines trade policy, and concludes international trade agreements. Since foreign markets are unpredictable and cannot be compelled to accommodate themselves to the rigid and inflexible pattern that is the hallmark of the plans in other respects, the regime permits a degree of adaptability in the sphere of foreign trade.

In almost all communist countries, the handling of foreign trade is in the hands of special government agencies that have a monopoly on the import or export, or both, of certain goods. They are equipped with specialized knowledge of the entire market, both at home and abroad. Legally, their status is that of independent corporations, and they abide by customary international standards in carrying out foreign-trade transactions. Although they are wholly owned by the state, the government does not assume liability for the business deals they engage in.

Under the communist flag, an outstanding characteristic of foreign trade is bilateralism. It signifies that certain countries will supply certain goods, a stipulation that restricts the chances of would-be exporters elsewhere. This is especially true of the kind of import policy that, designed to meet immediate and urgent needs, was prevalent until long after World War II.

For the past several years, political considerations have led to greater imports from underdeveloped countries. Such imports satisfy a domestic demand, which, not being essential, would not have been considered before political priority began to be accorded to Asia and Africa. The chief objective is to link the supplying countries to the communist economic bloc, to make them dependent upon the simultaneous shipment of consumer and capital goods from the communist realm. The goods, which the East bloc imports with these aspects in view, are at times sold to third countries, either to realize a profit or in response to political speculations involving the terms of the deal and the country of final destination.

The economic structure of the communist countries is anything but homogeneous. Highly industrialized states like the U.S.S.R., Czechoslovakia, and East Germany are within the communist ranks, but so are such underdeveloped European and Asiatic countries as Albania, North Korea, and North Vietnam. All these countries, nonetheless, have some features in common with regard to their trade methods. The two main principles governing the importing countries' foreign-trade policy are rapid industrialization and the attainment of independence from other countries. Alternately, one or the other of these two principles comes to the fore.

Communist countries make abundant use of the international division of labor, though this is a feature of capitalism, and on occasion they utilize comparative cost analysis for the purpose. They adhere to the postulate that the maximum price is to be achieved for exports while the minimum price is paid for imports, and that practice is supplemented by consideration of the best ways of benefiting the national economy. Hence, priority is given to goods with relatively low domestic production cost when exports are at stake, while preference is accorded to imports with the relatively highest domestic expenditure. To that end, the industrialized countries of the East bloc have computed a system of efficiency coefficients, with savings in foreign-currency outlay being the decisive factor. A survey of the more important merchandise categories imported from Western countries by the East bloc lists the following groups: basic industrial equipment (plant installations, machinery, electronic and other apparatus, tools and utensils, precision instruments, pipes, ball bearings, machine tools, turbines, transformers); ships plus marine equipment and port installations; vehicles; steel, rolled steel and nonferrous semifinished products; chemicals, fertilizer, synthetic fibers, and cellulose; lubricants; textiles; breeding cattle, fish, and fish products; finally, tropical fruit, groceries, and consumer goods.

Exports are not selected merely in order to balance imports, but to serve certain economic, political, and propaganda goals as well; for example, the disposal of excess goods, the exploitation of economic difficulties encountered by other countries, and the effort to render the purchasing country dependent. At one time, the communist states endeavored to export raw materials to the largest possible extent. The existence of standardized and internationally comparable prices, the facility with which the market position can be surveyed, and the fact that technical servicing is not required were among the advantages of concentrating on the export of raw materials. When it was realized that the export of capital goods to the developing countries offered a better opportunity for economic penetration of the receiving countries, the situation changed. Today the more important export categories are: petroleum and petroleum products; anthracite coal and coke; ore and ore concentrates; steel and nonferrous metals; industrial equipment, especially for mining and petroleum production; machinery and tools; vehicles and chemicals; agricultural and wood products; skins, furs, and consumer goods.

With respect to volume, interesting development trends can be discerned in the foreign-trade pattern of the communist countries. The latter were able to keep pace with the growth of world trade over the past few years, accounting for a constant 12 per cent thereof. This proportion becomes more significant when trade within the East bloc itself is regarded separately. It mounted steadily during the first postwar years, but then slowed down, beginning in the mid-1950s. Altogether, the share of intra-bloc trade has declined from three-quarters to two-thirds of the bloc's foreign trade. The volume of trade with noncommunist countries rose correspondingly, from one-quarter to one-third of the total with regard to both imports and exports, which constitutes a sizable factor in the economies of the communist countries. For the free world, over-all trade with the East bloc is of less importance. Even though the volume has increased, trade with the East bloc remained below an average of 5 per cent of total foreign trade (at least up to 1961).

Within the free world, and also within the East bloc, there is wide divergence between the individual countries with respect to the extent of their trade with the other bloc. Among the noncommunist countries, geographical location chiefly determines the role of trade with the East. The greater the distance from the communist part of the world, the fewer are the commercial exchanges, which in many cases remain below the insignificant amount of 1 per cent of the over-all foreign-trade volume. A common frontier with a communist state, on the other hand, often makes the free-world country amenable to strong economic and political pressure, so that the proportion of East bloc trade rises to more than 20 per cent in some cases. Among the communist states, trade with the West accounts for a ratio ranging from 20 to 40 per cent.

The system of planned economy, which prevails in the communist world and encompasses imports and exports as well, forces trade relations with the free world into unnatural patterns. Moreover, the necessity of deferring to the "plan" imposes a peculiar posture upon both sides. When communist trade negotiators appear in the free world, whether as buyers or sellers, they encounter a market mechanism alien to their thinking, and the same holds true when Western trade negotiators journey to the capitals of the East bloc. In the free world, essentially supply and demand, with the aid of the price mechanism, govern the market. This does not imply that the entry of imports into the various national markets is free of restrictions. The multitude of countries, their dissimilar economic structures, and the diverse stages of their economic development cannot but influence the degree to which freedom of trade is granted.

Yet it is easy to perceive that, although restraints on the exchange of goods were introduced in the wake of World War II, they have since been systematically lifted. Today, the important trade centers of the West retain very few of those commercial restrictions. Quantitative limitations hampering the expansion of trade have been almost completely eliminated from the European scene by the gradual stepping up of liberalization measures—thanks to the effort, undertaken on a regional basis, of the OEEC and later of the OECD. Lowering and removing the quantitative restrictions that are still applied to countries outside that Community, together with nondiscriminatory tariff policies and a reduction of customs duties in general, are the aims of GATT. Repeatedly, GATT has initiated measures designed to implement these aims.

GATT was successful in extending the applicability of concessions like the most-favored-nation clause, thus channeling much of world trade into the mainstream of economic concepts that are in line with free enterprise. These policies of GATT were rendered possible by the member nations' readiness to cooperate, to abide by the voluntarily adopted rules of the game, and even to sacrifice self-interests whenever that proved indispensable in order to achieve an expansion of trade.

Most of the free countries have ratified the GATT treaties and are full members. Czechoslovakia and Cuba are the only full members among the communist states, while a somewhat looser affiliation is maintained by Poland and by Yugoslavia. Under the circumstances, the communist bloc has benefited only partially from the relaxation of trade and tariff restrictions achieved by GATT, but it should be borne in mind that all who engage in free-world economic activity have much the same start basically.

Anyone can make use of ample statistics and publications to gather information about the economy of a given country, to cite an example, no matter what his nationality. Anyone can conduct market research or go in for advertising and publicity. Anyone can bid for a contract or avail himself of banks, of existing commercial and distribution organizations. Forms of capital investment are rarely restricted, whether the foreign investor wishes to establish a plant or business, whether he wishes to form a partnership or to purchase an interest in some firm. Where restrictions remain on the books, they are not a serious obstacle in practice because financial transactions are protected by anonymity. Hence, the communist governmental agencies in charge of foreign trade encounter conditions in the free world that place them on the same level as other foreign competitors. They are not discriminated against, even if they are not put on a par with domestic businessmen and industrialists. Limitations resulting from the bilateralism of trade dealings with the communist countries are part and parcel of the system of bilateralism, which the communist trade partners insist on, and are not directed against the communist country as such.

This emerges most clearly in connection with the quantitative limitations regarding the exchange of goods, conditions that are contained in the trade agreements concluded between states of the communist and of the noncommunist world. In countries with a free economy, these conditions are considered an assurance that demand probably exists for the stipulated volume of goods and that the goods will be admitted if there are customers. Such quantitative limitations in a trade agreement do not constitute a guarantee that the goods can in fact be sold. No business could be expected to purchase merchandise for which sales prospects are lacking. It is the ultimate consumer who decides what he does and what he does not want to buy. He makes the decision as he sees fit. This is the crux of the matter insofar as competition in the market place is concerned: The consumer's taste, inclinations, and quality requirements are his own, and it is only up to a point that his decision is influenced by the price.

MARKET MANIPULATIONS

While consumers and purchasers in the free world do take price into account, it is not their sole criterion in making a choice. Their dissatisfaction is often due to deficient quality and unattractive styling or to other considerations that are only in part susceptible to rational explanation. Foreign-trade officials in the communist states tend to be perplexed by such negative reactions. Not being sufficiently familiar with Western ways to understand the reasons, they endeavor to surmount sales resistance by offering price concessions.

In lowering their prices to a level likely to overcome some of these objections raised in the West, communist foreign-trade officials come close to the practice that is frowned on as *dumping*. In other cases, particularly where development countries are the trade partners, communist trade negotiators seek to win contracts by granting long-term credits at low interest rates and by making other concessions. Either way, the approach is based on a characteristic feature of the communist economic system, namely, deliberate manipulation of prices. To ascertain whether dumping is being committed, it is customary in the West to compare the asked prices with production costs or the sales prices in the country of origin. Another possibility is a comparison with prices charged for the same goods in third countries to which they have been exported. In state planning headquarters, a precise cost analysis is no doubt performed, but the findings of such communist cost accountants are never publicized. Neither are prices revealed.

It is open to question whether plant managers themselves are aware of the competitive standing of their products with respect to prices. As a rule, they have no knowledge regarding price or profitability of their own products which are sold abroad. Profit-and-loss statements are not prepared by each exporting plant individually, but are compiled in the aggregate by the Central Bank or Foreign Trade Bank that is charged with the financing of exports. In general, the effort to arrive at comparisons between prices charged in the free world and those prevailing in the Soviet bloc becomes an almost unmanageable task. Raw materials, parts, and semimanufactured goods pass from state enterprise to state enterprise in the course of the manufacturing process. As the items move, each enterprise is debited and credited with an accounting price that bears no discernible relationship to prices charged abroad at the equivalent stage of the manufacturing process. The domestic consumer, moreover, often is charged a price that diverges widely from the production cost. Finally, it should not be forgotten that many communist countries use multiple rates of exchange in their dealings with other countries. Taking all these circumstances into account, it is not astonishing that outside observers are not in a position to arrive at an even approximately correct assessment of the price-cost ratio. One of the functions of the communist price system is control of domestic consumption, and the secretiveness referred to here is another of its functions.

As for the credit terms granted to foreign customers, no standards are enforced. There is a state credit monopoly, and one of its activities is the financing of exports. Because profits are not a primary objective, and since no allowance needs to be made for bad credit risks, the rate of interest becomes a token gesture. The excessively long-term repayment period that is granted in certain cases therefore reflects nothing but the conscious subordination of commercial and balance-of-payments considerations.

The facts described above are of key significance for businessmen of the West who wish to compete in the market places of the communist East. It seems illogical that customs tariffs should be maintained there, since imports are strictly controlled and part of the plan. But they provide better tactical negotiation positions as an instrumentality of foreign trade, and therefore they are retained.

The liberalization moves undertaken within the framework of GATT and of regional agreements such as the Common Market have led to a substantial easing of restrictions on international trade and to a considerable reduction of customs duties. The communist countries have benefited from such liberalization to the extent that they are members of GATT, but they have taken no action to lower their own commercial barriers. Therefore, no benefits have had to be passed on to Western countries on the basis of the most-favored-nation clause contained in the bilateral trade agreements they have concluded with the West. Even though the communist countries have thus contributed nothing to the reduction of trade restrictions, they endeavor to share in the benefits, notably in the field of customs tariffs, which the Western countries have accorded each other in the course of regional economic integration. They do not consider that exceptions in the case of customs union and free-trade zones apply to regional markets. Because they claim that the most-favored-nation clause has been violated, they therefore threaten to charge the maximum rates provided for in the autonomous tariff rather than the lower tariffs that are customary.

By proceeding in this way, the countries in which all foreign trade is state trade seek to create the impression that customs duties have the effect of raising the domestic price of the merchandise. In reality, however, customs duties have no effect on domestic prices. Nor is there a connection between the price paid to the foreign supplier by the state trade organization and the price charged by the domestic state distribution organization. Since the consumer price is set quite apart from the amount of customs duty paid and from the price listed in the invoice of the foreign exporter, foreign suppliers cannot engage in price competition on communist markets. Under the circumstances, the lack of opportunity for the kind of client cultivation customary in the free world merely illustrates the inequality in competitive standing between West and East. The value of market research and advertising in communist countries might be dubious even if these activities were possible, but the very fact that they are never authorized, for a variety of ostensible reasons, constitutes discrimination. So does the limitation to domestic enterprises of authorization to act as agent or representative for the foreign product and to service it. The countries of the free world are expected to put up with this discrimination and to accept it as being inevitable. The communist states, by contrast, react with pronounced irritability to obstacles that the West places in the path of their own economic activity, even when there are good grounds to apply such restraints for security reasons.

At regular intervals, representatives of countries in the communist bloc point to the necessity of expanding international trade, and bring forward proposals to that effect (the holding of World Trade Conferences, for example). As long as the countries adhering to communist state capitalism do nothing to lift trade restrictions, these proposals are empty rhetoric. If they took action to lower the barriers, that would be their own down-to-earth contribution to the expansion of international trade.

Restrictions on Trade Relations

East-West trade has shown a greater increase than world trade, as was set forth above in both actual and relative terms. If this growth trend is to gather greater momentum, the two parties are called upon to seek new ways.

In the free countries, too, there are restrictions on trade relations with the communist states. Were these special regulations to be rescinded, the volume of merchandise exchanged between the two parts of the world might well rise. As for imports from the East, restrictions take the form of customs duties, quotas, and embargoes. Imports are rarely embargoed in order to protect the domestic market. More generally, such measures are a result of political conflicts that have spread to the trade arena. Hence, their elimination is not a question of trade policy alone, but must be preceded by a change in the political atmosphere. Quotas, while more directly an issue of economic policy, are influenced by basic political attitudes as well. There can be more flexibility, however, in seeking to resolve the difficulties that quotas do conjure up. The long-term trade agreements favored by the communist states could provide a means to overcome the quota barriers, especially if the preservation of rigid bilateralism were not insisted upon by the communist side.

Rigid bilateralism is the fundamental evil that inhibits the intensification of East-West trade, curtails the potential for growth that exists, and provokes countermeasures. Bilateralism forces trade relations to retain the accustomed pattern, precludes both sides from taking advantage of the possibilities offered by the international division of labor, and finally, runs counter to the free-enterprise principle of untrammeled choice in selecting one's trade partner. Nor are the anomalies deriving from bilateralism limited to the exchange of goods as such. The exigencies of existing trade channels lead to distortions in the structure of production, prices, and costs, as well as in monetary matters. The junction of bilateralism in the exchange of goods with bilateralism in the exchange of foreign currencies (that is, in international payments) impairs the freedom of decisions on foreign exchange holdings because bilateral clearings have in actual experience shown an inherent tendency to develop imbalances, which in turn must be offset by technical credits. Bilateral balances are not readily usable. Efforts to overcome this limitation through technical devices (for example, multilateral compensation within the EEC) have been none too successful. These difficulties accentuate the unsuitability of bilateralism.

Most European countries that have forsaken bilateralism have suffered no ill effects in their balance of trade and of payments. On the contrary, foreign trade has picked up when bilateralism was abandoned. In case an expansion of trade with the communist states should be aimed at, these European countries would have to make greater use of the multilateral arrangements, a use some of them have already embarked on in guarded fashion. Were this to happen, it could be the start for an expansion of trade relations.

The communist states claim that fluctuations in the rate of freely convertible currencies are one of the reasons for their aversion to settling transactions that way. They themselves employ the major Western currencies as a medium of exchange in international trade, but manifest their distrust of the currencies' stability and support their scepticism with references to the periodic international speculation campaigns against the dollar and the pound sterling. The fact is that no safeguards, other than the gold standard, are possible against exchange losses due to changes in parity even in bilateral clearing arrangements, since dollars or pounds sterling are generally utilized in the text of trade and payments agreements. The right way to diminish the risk of exchange losses is certainly not the expectation that the communist bloc's trading partners of the free world will accept an Eastern currency as the proper medium in which to conduct the payments traffic between West and East. For one thing, changes of parity are rather more frequent in the case of Eastern than of Western currencies. To provide more effective safeguards against the risk of currency losses, and to arrive at better judgments about the likelihood of such risks, it is advisable to cooperate more intensively under the aegis of international bodies concerned with monetary matters.

Cooperation within international bodies affords sufficient opportunity to obtain deeper insights into the members' economic and monetary situation, and also to improve contacts in the sphere of banking and insurance. On the part of the West, contacts of this kind are quite meager because, in the communist bloc, state institutions handling these matters are monopolies. Officials in the Soviet orbit, on the other hand, have their own banks and insurance companies in the West, and therefore do not find it difficult to secure information and cultivate contacts.

International cooperation is the best means not only for dispelling difficulties with respect to monetary questions, but also for overcoming them in the area of tariffs. Yet only a few communist countries have recourse to this method. Customs duties are merely an instrumentality of trade-policy control in the communist economic system and therefore play a subordinate role, while tariffs are key factors in gaining access to free-world markets. In view of this, it is hard to understand why communist states, who complain habitually about the customs discrimination allegedly practiced against them, do not take advantage of the possibilities open to them in the proper international organizations and thus seek a satisfactory solution.

In the East bloc, there is no reliance on the political good faith of the capitalistic nations. As long as this distrust exists, and as long as aggressive intent is imputed to the trade partners in the capitalist states and while paradoxically accusing them of weakness when they strive for the peaceful settlement of controversies, a relaxation of Western export restrictions on goods intended for the East bloc is hardly imminent. Those restrictions are chiefly concerned with goods of strategic or parastrategic value. Where import quotas exist, they are not present as ideas of Western trade negotiators, but were incorporated into the bilateral trade agreement because they fitted into the communist pattern of economic control. This all-encompassing control system, based as it is on a predetermined plan, makes no provision for unilateral enlargement of quotas. In certain cases, it even precludes export shipments from the communist orbit to countries of the free world. The goods or commodities in question are deemed of possible military value to the latter.

The withholding of these shipments has the effect of forcing countermeasures on the free countries, who are determined to uphold the common defense. Their goal is the inhibition of any undesirable addition to the military potential of the communist world. The countermeasures they take are carried out pursuant to international agreements, which are implemented by appropriate national regulations. What is considered strategically important is a matter of judgment. The way in which the embargo is interpreted, and the strictness with which it is applied, is frequently a reaction to the attitude of the ideological opponent and to the aggressiveness with which he pursues his political and economic tactics at that particular juncture.

EAST-WEST TRADE EXPANSION

When weighing the pro and con of East-West trade, as it now is, and of the chances for its expansion, it can be taken for granted that the possibility of distinct harm to one's own national economy or political independence will be the primary consideration when setting limits to the trade volume. Depending on the economic and political objectives connected with the cultivation of commercial relations, and upon the likelihood that a transaction may impinge upon a sensitive point of either party, advantages and drawbacks are variable. The free countries, for instance, are interested in increasing their consumer-goods export to the communist areas. This would expose a vulnerable side of the planned-economy system, a fact that is taken into account by the policy-making officials of the communist countries in coming to a decision about the kinds of imports they authorize. Consumer-goods exports to communist areas provide the West with a series of psychological benefits. The merchandise is likely to evoke interest for its country of origin, and it enables the ultimate consumer to draw comparisons as to quality, comparisons that can awaken a continuing demand for that merchandise.

The consequences of such a peaceful penetration of the communist realm should certainly not be underestimated, for in a wide strata of the population, more prejudices can be dispelled thereby than by skillful propaganda. This is especially the case when supply troubles have arisen and vital Western consumer goods, foodstuffs in particular, are distributed to fill the gap. The Western goods, being an impressive demonstration of free-world capabilities in the economic sphere, can upset the picture painted by ideological propaganda regarding deficiencies and shortcomings in the capitalist world. From the strictly business aspect, too, Western deliveries to the communist bloc are in many ways favorable. They open up new markets for the production facilities of the West, enlarge the distribution radius of goods in foreign trade, and make possible a better exploitation of plant capacity. Whenever regular deliveries over the long stretch are envisaged, in line with the planned-economy concept of the other trade partner, the Western plant's production risk is diminished, and it can achieve a better cost structure. This is the case, for example, with machinery and factory equipment if experience shows that orders for supplementary equipment and replacement parts will be forthcoming.

It is dubious, on the other hand, whether trade with the communist East can really, as is sometimes contended, cushion a depression or lift the economy of a Western country. The idea that there are countries in the free world whose national economies, taken as a whole, would receive a substantial boost from a stepping-up of the East-West trade volume has questionable validity, since that volume accounts for a very small percentage of the economy everywhere. The possibility does exist, however, that particular lines of business, in which activity happens to be slack, will receive new stimulus from East-West trade. Such prospects are dependent in large part upon the readiness of the communist planned economy to absorb Western goods. Prices and payment conditions are other determining factors because an economically distressed branch of business cannot obtain relief through sales to the East bloc if long-term credit is demanded or a barter deal proposed that would offer payment in goods for which there is no real demand in the West.

For the countries of the free world, imports from the communist orbit can mean a further broadening of the already wide range of stocks on hand or an enlargement of the supply basis. The industrialized nations of the West are, as a rule, not dependent upon the communist economic area for basic raw materials and equipment, but there is a market in the West for goods meeting elevated requirements. The communist countries, on their part, can secure foreign exchange by supplying these goods. They are in need of hard currency to equalize their balance of payments with the free world, unless they wish to meet the deficit in their balance of trade with gold bullion.

As far as trade relations with underdeveloped countries are concerned, the principal advantage for the communist bloc is the gaining of a foothold in the local market and the infiltration of influence that is hopefully considered to go beyond the purely economic contacts. Developing countries import capital goods at a frantic pace, bypassing the lengthy technological phase that would otherwise be devoted to construction and to the development of new production processes. At the same time, communist planners are provided with the extensive information required to assess the technical potentiality of that particular country. In consequence of better and more rapid plan work, they can concentrate on prestige projects without having to curtail the consumption quota too drastically. The communist trade agencies do not have to negotiate with partners holding an analogous monopoly position. From a large number of competing bids, they can choose the one that best appeals to them from the point of view of price, quality, and contract terms.

There is no need to dwell on the disadvantages experienced by communist states in their foreign-trade relations with the free world, since by and large these are the converse of the advantages that the countries of the free world derive. However, certain aspects of foreign imports are regarded as negative in the communist bloc. One such aspect is the need for the procurement abroad of supplementary deliveries and of spare parts when technologically advanced machinery, equipment, and plants have been purchased; in certain cases, the recruitment of foreign experts is also necessary. Moreover, large imports of technical goods are bound to infringe on the security mentality that is so excessively pronounced in the communist countries. They do not wish to divulge information to their ideological opponent, which might allow him to draw conclusions about weak points in their technological apparatus, about industrial areas where extraordinary efforts are being concentrated, and otherwise acquaint him with knowledge that could be used strategically.

For the countries of the free world, too, trade with the East brings manifold drawbacks. If the share of imports from communist areas increases (for example, imports of raw materials), then a certain dependence is created and the market for trade partners in the free world shrinks correspondingly. The impact can be unfavorable, especially in the case of developing countries searching for markets. The communist states make it a practice to establish corporations and trade agencies or to purchase an interest in existing firms without revealing the fact to the outside world. Freedom of trade and business makes this legitimate, but the penetration often does not stop in the economic field.

In assembling the goods to be offered to purchasers in the communist bloc, Western exporters face a predicament, since large-scale shipments of consumer goods are not what the communist countries desire. The export of capital goods, plant equipment, and specialized technical machinery would be more in line with East bloc wishes, but the producing countries deliberately impose restrictions on certain of these deliveries. Furthermore, the divergent interpretations of the "strategic goods" concept breeds the possibility of conflict in the ranks of the free world, and a mistaken zeal for competition may threaten to disrupt the unity of the free world, which is rooted in spiritual principles.

With the slackening of economic growth in 1962, it seemed that stepped-up cultivation of trade relations with the East was just ahead; this created grounds for potential conflict within the Western camp. More recently, however, an improvement of the economic situation is once again beginning to make itself felt. This, it is hoped, will serve to dispel the doubts that arose in some quarters about the soundness of the free-enterprise economy, doubts that were fostered by the East with the aid of lavish propaganda efforts.

In the communist countries, too, it was recently possible to discern, in the sparse statistics made available by Eastern sources, a slackening in the upward trend of the economy. There has been a noticeable decrease over the past four years in the growth of the investment rate, of national income, and of industrial production and foreign trade volume; all this is in marked contrast to the increments provided for in these categories by the "plan." This weakening of the former momentum shows that the economy, once it has reached a certain degree of maturity, obeys its own laws rather than the directives put out by state planners.

Now that the slower economic pace in the industrialized parts of the free world has been overcome, a major obstruction no longer threatens to exacerbate the tensions that stand in the way of trade relations between industrialized and underdeveloped countries. The free world has ample resources to satisfy needs and requirements in adequate fashion and also to furnish support to development areas, although the basis ought to be shifted from pure aid to active collaboration. In the materialistic sphere, indispensable prerequisites therefore are an increase in trade through an opening of their markets by the industralized countries, and an increase in production together with its adaptation to the demands of the developing countries as well as the domestic market.

In the spiritual sphere, the indispensable prerequisites are of a different order. It must be recognized that, before sweeping changes and new beginnings take effect, a sufficient time span has to be allowed. It should not be abridged arbitrarily. In the West, industrialization has extended over centuries and proceeded in a special intellectual climate. That process cannot be repeated by a leap forward in one or two decades, although the communists like to claim that they are able to accomplish it.

POLITICAL EFFECTS OF COMMUNIST
TRADE EXPANSION

The developing countries, on their part, tend to believe implicitly such promises and assurances about the infallibility of communist methods for creating a modern industrial economy. They do not have the facilities for verifying communist claims and lack experience in systematic economic development, and furthermore the communist illusion of miraculous industrialization is better in tune with their craving for prestige. There is a danger that they may align their ideological as well as economic orientation accordingly and thus imperil the future economic structure of the free world.

Yet the Soviet Union itself has demonstrated that it is not feasible to omit a well-defined phase in the course of economic development without suffering corresponding damage elsewhere.

A tremendous waste of productive forces, the disruption of agriculture, and the imposition of an all-encompassing police state was the heavy price paid by the U.S.S.R. so as to attain its impressive industrialization. The new states should bear that experience in mind.

In the developing countries, the best-managed and most efficient enterprises are the farms and plantations held by the capitalist owners. On contrast, the Soviet Union, in order to supply its people with the bare food requirements after thirty years of communist-planned economy and extensive agricultural mechanization, has found it necessary to plant crops in vast uncultivated regions, the lower yield per acre notwithstanding. In these three decades, during which the population increased by a fifth, Soviet cattle stocks diminished by a tenth. In agriculture, five to seven times as much manpower as in the United States is utilized to produce a given quantity of grain, while in cattle raising the multiple is 16. These data, which were announced by Premier Khrushchev himself, illustrate the nationwide failure of the communist economic system and are one of the causes for the effort of the communist bloc to imitate the West by creating regional cooperation in economic matters.

COMECON provides the framework for this cooperation. It was founded as far back as 1949, but showed few signs of life for almost ten years. The membership is composed of the Soviet Union, Poland, Bulgaria, Romania, Czechoslovakia, East Germany, and Mongolia. Delegates of China, North Korea, North Vietnam, and occasionally Yugoslavia, attend in the capacity of observers. Albania, which joined in the organization's early days, has left it in the meantime. Its statutes define the task of COMECON as planned development of the national economies, acceleration of economic and technical progress, stepping-up of industrialization, increase of work productivity and advancement of living standards through cooperation, coordination of planning and elaboration, as well as implementation of common measures. These measures include common financing of major projects that are of interest to more than one state; having certain countries specialize in certain lines of goods in an international socialist division of labor; and promoting the exchange of goods, services, and technical know-how.

COMECON operates by way of the Secretariat, permanent commissions, meetings of the delegates, and council sessions. The member states are obliged to ensure the carrying out of recommendations by the council and its organs, to which they have given their assent, to lend their support to the council, and to place documentations as well as information at its disposal. In other words, the goals of this communist body devoted to cooperation within the bloc are, to put it in a nutshell, superplanning, superindustrialization, and supercontrol.

This "New Look" of communist economic policy originated in 1959, and it was no accident that it took place a year after the European Economic Community (EEC) entered into force. It would not be correct to attach to COMECON the "integration" label that is used in Europe to designate a new pattern of international cooperation. Parallels between COMECON and EEC do exist, it is true; with regard to monetary questions, for example, COMECON has instituted a Permanent Commission for Foreign Currency and Finance and has founded a Bank of Socialist Countries.

In the EEC—and these are fundamental characteristics—the member nations have equal rights; the community can be said to be one of consumers, one that is based on the competitive principle. Political views in the member nations do vary, but a generally consonant political will and a tendency toward voluntary surrender of sovereignty are beginning to emerge. COMECON, on the other hand, follows the leadership of the Soviet Union and is a community of producing countries, basically uniform in ideology, which claims to be predicated on specialization of the member states that seek to remain as independent as possible.

The EFTA, which has remained on the scene as relic of an attempt at integration that did not reach its far-ranging goal, stands amid those two polarized configurations of European cooperation, EEC and COMECON. Their polarization notwithstanding, a positive assessment of the prospects for further expansion of trade and commercial contacts between East and West appears warranted. Although such a trend remains clouded by guarded deliberations within COMECON about trade contracts with the EEC, the efforts of the EEC to minimize for third countries the drawbacks that arise from the formation of a homogeneous economic area reflect conciliatory moves. Next to the general cooperation for a reduction of trade and tariff restrictions carried on in the framework of GATT, notably with the United States, it is the treaties of association with the African underdeveloped countries that are designed to achieve an expansion of trade.

The nations of the free world should not, however, focus their cooperation solely on improving efficiency and increasing commercial relations. Rather, they should also strive to strengthen the foundations on which the free-enterprise economy rests. Sound competition by a multitude of independent business and industrial firms is more conducive to healthy development of the economy than are efforts to remodel it in the image of economic plans. Reinvigorating the idea of private property by the promotion of capital accumulation is also a better basis for healthy development, as is maintenance of a sound and stable currency and an economic policy attuned to community needs and individual rights.

The danger does exist that elements of the planned-economy concept will infiltrate the West. These elements might contaminate its outlook when new forms of international cooperation are sought, so that the free world would be drawn into the quagmire of the planned-economy mentality. Thus, as a matter of survival, it must avoid any tinge of a hostile ideology. Once the free world avails itself of the resources at its disposal and applies them properly, it will be strong enough to meet the challenge of communist objectives and to find solutions for the problems and difficulties that handicap international economic security.

CHAPTER 13

The Balance of Payments

Paul W. McCracken

In its statement of February 26, 1958, the Federal Reserve reported that the U.S. monetary gold stock had declined exactly $100 million from the preceding week, to a figure of $22,685,000,-000. This news was greeted with something less than a headline response. Indeed, if anyone had possessed the temerity to suggest that this signified the beginning of trouble for the United States in its international financial life, his warning would have been the recipient of bemused treatment. Here, clearly, was some sort of troglodytic Nervous Nellie, so out of touch with contemporary reality as to be unaware that we live in a world of dollar shortages, a world where Uncle Sam was all too strong in the international arena.

The fact is that our timorous friend would in this case have been correct. The $100 million decline in the U.S. monetary gold stock in the week of February 26, 1958, was destined to be the beginning of a shrinkage that has persisted into the sixth year, and has reduced the U.S. gold stock roughly $7 billion. This loss of almost one-third of its gold, with a reduction of its "free gold" (gold in excess of that needed to meet the statutory 25 per cent requirement against Federal Reserve note and deposit liabilities) of perhaps 75 per cent, has been a regrettable enough problem in itself. Fort Knox and its contents have had the leading role in their full share of national jokes. The sophisticated mind may regard this persistent affection for the yellow metal as an atavistic obsession, but gold still need have no psychological scars from any sense of rejection. As long as gold is generally wanted (a phenomenon not exactly of recent origin), the U.S. loss of $7 billion worth could not be considered an inconsequential matter. Moreover, with the gold reserve requirement immobilizing about $12 billion of U.S. gold, the sharp decline in "free gold" to roughly $4 billion has reduced substantially the scope for the easy exercise of monetary and credit policy.

The primary importance of this gold loss, however, has been that it has served as a prod, forcing the United States to face some fundamental problems in its external economic relationships. The loss of gold, it has now become clear, came about for about three reasons—two of lesser importance and one that is fundamental. First, in 1957, the year before the gold drains began, the United States held 60 per cent more gold than all other countries combined (Table 1). It was to be expected that some

TABLE 1.   FREE WORLD GOLD HOLDINGS, 1957–1963
(*In Billions*)

Country	1957	1963	Change
United States	$22.9	$15.6	$—7.3
Belgium	0.9	1.4	0.5
France	0.6	3.2	2.6
Germany	2.5	3.8	1.3
Italy	0.5	2.3	1.8
South Africa	0.2	0.6	0.4
Switzerland	1.7	2.8	1.1
United Kingdom	1.6	2.5	0.9
All other	6.4	8.0	1.6
All countries	$37.3	$40.2	$ 2.9

SOURCE: *International Financial Statistics*, September 1963, p. 18, and June 1964, p. 16. Period is from year-end 1957 to year-end 1963.

redistribution of the world's gold stocks would occur as soon as other countries had regained enough financial strength to do something about the matter. Second, a great deal depended on which countries were accumulating international reserves. Some countries are willing to hold these reserves as foreign exchange, but others, as a matter of policy, tend to convert into gold those reserves not immediately needed.

Finally, the development at the heart of U.S. gold losses was the fact that world holdings of dollars were rising rapidly in the 1950s. At the outset, this was highly desirable. Foreign exchange reserves of other nations were low, and these needed to be replenished as a part of reconstructing the postwar international financial structure. By the latter part of the past decade, however, two things happened. Other major currencies (the pound, mark, franc, etc.) became convertible, thereby augmenting the supply of foreign exchange resources that could be used freely in international financial transactions. And in 1958 the flow of U.S. dollars into foreign holdings accelerated substantially—at a time when the foreign tills were already becoming well restocked. Thus, other nations were increasingly in a position to exchange dollars for gold at the U.S. Treasury, simply because their holdings of dollars and other readily convertible currencies were ample; and beginning in 1958 exchange them into gold they did.

Why were foreign holdings of dollars rising, and rising at an accelerating pace after 1957? This was occurring, of course, because of a deficit in the U.S. balance of payments. In fact, it then came as something of a surprise to all but a few technical experts to learn that, with the lone exception of the small surplus in 1957, the U.S. balance of payments had shown a deficit every year since 1950. From 1950 to 1957 the deficit varied over a wide range, but averaged $1.3 billion per year (Table 2). A deficit of this moderate size, as pointed out earlier, was desirable in these years because it was providing other nations with supplies of a strong currency at a time when these countries needed to build up their international monetary reserves. Unfortunately, in 1958, the deficit enlarged at almost precisely the time the world needs for dollars were diminishing and a reduction in the deficit would have been desirable. Thus, in the past five years, the deficit in the U.S. balance of payments has developed from an obscure problem that most people did not understand, and many had never

TABLE 2. Deficit in U.S. Balance of Payments
(In Millions)

Year	Amount	Year	Amount
1950	$3,580	1957a	$ (520)
1951	305	1958	3,529
1952	1,046	1959	3,743
1953	2,152	1960	3,881
1954	1,550	1961	2,370
1955	1,145	1962	2,203
1956	935	1963	2,644

Source: 1950–1959: *Balance of Payments Statistical Supplement,* rev. ed., pp. 3–4; 1960–1963: *Survey of Current Business,* June 1964, p. 10.
a Surplus.

even heard of, into a central concern of national economic policy.

What Is the "Deficit?"

Before turning to an examination of the various diagnoses of the imbalance in U.S. international payments, it is well to deal with a preliminary matter first. Just what is the deficit in U.S. balance-of-payments account? "The deficit" in this account is so much talked about that we may assume it to be simply the extent to which one side of the account does not add up to as much as the other side. It is a statistically precise and ineluctably invariant "gap." Payments exceed receipts; this is the usual way to describe the deficit.

The problem is not actually that simple. The fact is that this balance-of-payments account is basically a double-entry arraying of data. For each debit there is, in principle, a credit. Except for technical measurement problems, the "two sides" must add to the same total. If there is a deficit, it consists of certain items in the account which we decide to call "the deficit." We see this if we begin with a T-account that simply arrays the items. In Table 3 the two sides have the same total. There is here no item carrying an explicit label of *deficit.* This table simply reflects the fact that each transaction has two sides. If the whole balance of pay-

TABLE 3. U.S. BALANCE OF PAYMENTS, 1963
(In Billions)

Payments		Receipts	
Imports, mdse.	$17.0	Exports, mdse.	$21.9
Military expenditures	2.9	Gold exports	0.5
Other services	6.3	Military sales	0.6
Remittances and pensions	0.8	Income on investments	
Govt. grants and capital		Private	4.0
Long-term	4.5	Government	0.5
Short-term	0.1	Exports, misc. services	4.6
Private capital		Repayments, U.S. govt. loans	
Direct	1.9	Scheduled	0.6
Long-term portfolio	1.6	Nonscheduled	0.3
Short-term	0.7	Foreign capital	
Errors and unrecorded items	0.3	Short-term	2.3
Total Payments	$36.1	Long-term	0.3
		Govt. liabilities	0.4
		Total Receipts	$36.1

SOURCE: Basic data from the U.S. Department of Commerce. Data may not total because of rounding.

ments consisted of an export to France paid for by francs, the table would show exports on one side and an inflow of foreign capital (the francs) on the other. If the transaction consisted of a bank loan to Japan, there would be an outflow of U.S. capital (the dollars Japan acquired) and an inflow of foreign capital into the United States (the bank note held and which constitutes a claim against Japan). Gold sales are, in principle, simply an export, and do not destroy the double-entry nature of the data in the table.

What "the deficit" is in this picture depends, therefore, on the transactions in this table that might be storing up trouble. A country whose currency is not generally acceptable in international transactions may watch changes in its holdings of foreign exchange reserves (dollars, pounds, etc.). The United States has a broader problem. Its own currency (dollars) is widely held internationally. It needs to be careful that its international liabilities (the dollars held by other countries) do not get too large. If these foreign-held dollars come into the possession of central banks or government treasuries abroad (so-called official holders), they become a claim on the gold stock. The deficit, therefore, is considered to be a loss (export, in the sense of changed ownership) of gold, the loss of U.S. holdings of foreign currencies (not quantitatively important), and an increase of foreign short-term claims on the United States (which might become a claim on its gold stock).

From this it is clear that different people may have differing views about what ought to be considered as "the deficit." Large nonrecurring transactions might be omitted in order to measure the more nearly "true" deficit for any period. Or changes in short-term claims (capital) may be omitted, on the assumption that these are highly volatile, but will tend over a longer period to average out close to zero.

Should the deficit include reductions in gold and foreign exchange and the whole increase in foreign short-term claims (inflow of foreign short-term capital), or should it include the increase in foreign short-term claims against the United States less the increase in U.S. short-term claims on other countries? At first glance the net idea looks reasonable enough, for otherwise peculiar results might appear. Suppose, for example, that an American wants a bank balance in London and therefore buys pounds in exchange for dollars. The American now has pounds and someone in the United Kingdom (for example, a British bank) has dollars. British claims on the United States have increased, but U.S. claims on the United Kingdom have increased by the same amount. There has been a movement of U.S. short-term capital abroad, but an equal movement of foreign short-term capital to the United States. Yet this transaction increases the U.S. balance-of-payments deficit as now defined because the increase in foreign claims against the United States is included gross—not netted against changes in U.S. short-term claims against others. There is a reason, however, for this assymetry. These dollars held by the foreign bank may, if nervousness about the dollar develops, be sold to the central bank or treasury. Then it will become a potential claim on the U.S. gold stock. The pounds that the American obtained from this initial transaction belong to him. They are not in the coffers of the U.S. Treasury, available to be used by it if needed. Thus, while in some sort of bookkeeping sense the international "net worth" of the United States is not altered, if a transaction puts dollars in the hands of a Britisher and pounds in the hands of an American, the transaction is not neutral in its impact on the international financial position of the United States.

The question of defining the deficit is one that could be explored ad infinitum, and numerous very real and difficult conceptual problems are involved. This quick discussion may, however, be enough to highlight an important point. The balance of payments is a double-entry, balancing summary of a set of transactions. A decision must therefore be made about which items in the account will be called components of "the deficit." There can thus be different definitions of the deficit for different countries and different measures of the deficit for the same country when different questions arise.

THE STRUCTURAL DIAGNOSIS

Whatever the disagreements about precisely how the deficit ought to be defined, there is general agreement that there is a deficit and that the objective of policy must be to reduce and eventually to eliminate it. We do not get very far trying to solve this problem until various diagnoses array themselves fairly naturally into about three different but not necessarily mutually exclusive groups. First, there is the diagnosis that runs heavily in terms of the peculiar structure of the U.S. international payments pattern. Data for 1963 will serve to illustrate the point. Commercial exports of goods and services (the sum of lines 1, 4, 5, and 6 on the right side of Table 4) in 1963 were $31.0 billion, substantially above payments for imports of goods and services, excluding military expenditures, of $23.3 billion. The balance on "current account" was strong, with a surplus of $7.7 billion. The trouble is that other items in the U.S. balance of payments overwhelmed this large surplus on current account, leaving at the end of the year a deficit of $2.7 billion. The leakage of dollars out of the United States due to military installations was $2.9

TABLE 4.   U.S. BALANCE OF PAYMENTS, 1963
(*In Billions*)

Payments		Receipts	
Imports, mdse.	$17.0	Exports, mdse.	$21.9
Military expenditures	2.9	Military sales	0.6
Other services	6.3	Income on investments	
Remittances and pensions	0.8	Private	4.0
Govt. grants and capital	4.5	Government	0.5
U.S. private capital		Exports, misc. services	4.6
Direct	1.9	Repayments on U.S. govt. loans	
Long-term portfolio	1.6	Scheduled	0.6
Short-term	0.7	Nonscheduled	0.3
Errors and omissions	0.3	Foreign capital, long-term	0.3
Total	$36.0	Govt. liabilities	0.4
		Total	$33.3
		Deficit	2.6
		Total	$36.0

SOURCE: *Survey of Current Business*, June 1964, pp. 10–11. Data may not total because of rounding.

billion; there was an outflow of U.S. capital to the tune of $4.5 billion (including $0.3 billion of unrecorded transactions that were probably an outflow of short-term capital), and U.S. government grants and loans accounted for another gross outflow of $4.5 billion.

If the imbalance in U.S. international payments is thought to be caused by certain large "noncurrent" drains of dollars (for example, foreign aid, or the leakage of dollars because of military installations), the indicated solution is to reduce these specific drains. And much of the U.S. administration's effort has been aimed in this direction. In spite of rising costs, the gross military leakage has not been increasing, having held at about $3 billion annually in recent years. This is itself an accomplishment. In his 1963 message on the balance-of-payments problem, the President indicated that the secretary of defense expected to reduce this figure by $300 million annually before the end of 1964. Moreover, the administration has had some success in persuading Germany to purchase military equipment from the United States up to that part of the $3 billion accruing to that country, and we see the effect of this in the "military sales" item on the right side of the balance-of-payments statement. These "offset purchases" have been rising in recent years, and the Department of Defense is pressing for further expansion. Unfortunately, none of the other nations receiving substantial amounts of dollars incident to these military leakages (Japan, Canada, France, and the United Kingdom) has been willing to offset these receipts by corresponding purchases of military equipment in the United States.

As a result of reductions in the gross leakage and increased "offset" purchases, the U.S. administration hopes to reduce substantially the military drain on the balance of payments. The Department of Defense has set as its objective a net drain of only $1.0 billion in fiscal year 1966, compared with $2.7 billion in 1961 (Table 5).

TABLE 5. U.S. DEFENSE EXPENDITURES AND RECEIPTS ENTERING
INTO THE INTERNATIONAL BALANCE OF PAYMENTS,
FISCAL YEARS 1961–1966
(*In Billions*)

Fiscal Year	Expenditures	Receipts	Contribution to Payments Deficit
1961	$3,059	$ 376	$2,683
1962	2,916	505	2,411
1963	3,015	740	2,275
1966	. . .	. . .	1,000

SOURCE: Department of Commerce. For 1966 estimate see Testimony of Assistant Secretary of Defense Charles J. Hitch before Subcommittee on International Exchange and Payments of the Joint Economic Committee (87th Congress, 2d Session, Dec. 12–14, 1962), p. 56.

It is essential to bear in mind that a dollar reduction in the military leakage may not mean a dollar reduction in the balance-of-payments deficit. If these other nations receive fewer dollars, or agree to make "offset" purchases of military equipment, their regular imports from the United States may be affected adversely. This is particularly likely to be true of countries with episodic balance-of-payments problems of their own. Or the offset buying may to some extent consist of what they would in any case have purchased—not, therefore, representing additional U.S. exports.

A second candidate for scrutiny, on the part of those who emphasize the structural nature of the balance-of-payments problem, is obviously foreign aid. In Table 4 this item is recorded as a $4.5 billion payment, or outflow, for 1963. It is larger than the total deficit. Moreover, this item shows an increase of about 30 per cent during the three years from 1960 to 1963. Here, clearly, seems to be an item that could be pruned substantially in the interests of a stronger dollar internationally.

Whatever our views about the wisdom of a foreign aid program, or whether recipient countries use these resources well, an examination of the data makes it clear that foreign aid did not add $4.5 billion to the deficit in 1963. For one thing, some repayments on aid loans made earlier are now being received, though this shows up on the other side of U.S. accounts. About four-fifths of U.S. aid commitments are now tied to the financing of exports. Thus, for each gross dollar of aid showing in the accounts, 80 cents of exports are automatically on the other side. Moreover, it has been estimated that close to half of the remaining 20 per cent will turn out to have been spent in the United States.[1] The U.S. administration has also pressed those countries who earlier had borrowed from the United States, incident to the postwar reconstruction of their economies, to prepay these obligations. Thus, in 1961 and 1962, about $1.3 billion of receipts were provided by these nonscheduled payments of debts owed to the United States.

As we look over the balance-of-payments table, outside the current accounts transactions, another substantial amount catches our eye. That item is the outflow of U.S. private capital. Recorded capital outflows in 1963 were $4.0 billion, and a considerable part of the "errors and unrecorded transactions" item is also probably an outflow of private capital. The three categories of private capital outflows have in recent years been behaving quite differently. Direct investments abroad by U.S. firms have been quite stable in recent years, at about $1.6–1.8 billion per year. This direct investment would include such things as oil-well drilling and exploration, building manufacturing plants abroad, and the purchase of foreign firms. Long-term portfolio invest-

[1] Walter S. Salant et al., The United States Balance of Payments in 1968 (Brookings Institution, 1963), pp. 170–171.

ment by U.S. residents in foreign securities, the second major component of the private capital outflow, has been rising rapidly in recent years. From 1960 to 1962 this item increased almost 50

TABLE 6. U.S. PRIVATE CAPITAL OUTFLOWS, 1957–1963
(In Millions)

Year	Total	Direct	Long-Term Portfolio	Short-Term
1957	$3,577	$2,422	$ 859	$ 276
1958	2,936	1,181	1,444	311
1959	2,375	1,372	926	77
1960	3,882	1,694	850	1,338
1961	3,953	1,475	1,006	1,472
1962	3,273	1,557	1,209	507
1963	4,082	1,799	1,641	642

SOURCE: Balance of Payments Statistical Supplement, rev. ed. (Commerce, 1963), and Survey of Current Business, March 1964, p. 16.

per cent, and the pace accelerated substantially in the first half of 1963. The most conspicuous feature of short-term capital outflows is their volatility. These have moved over a wide range from a nominal $77 million in 1959 to $1.5 billion in 1961.

To what extent should we direct a skeptical eye at this $4 billion annual outflow of dollars on capital account as we cast about for ways to close the balance-of-payments deficit? The possibility of some solution in this area seems to be a strong one. These outflows are large, and in late 1962 and early 1963 they showed a disturbing tendency to rise. Alarmed by this development, the U.S. administration in mid-1963 proposed a so-called interest equalization tax to retard U.S. purchases of foreign securities.

The role of capital outflows in the payments problem, however, turns out to be a complex problem. While these show up as a large item on the payments side, the fact that large amounts of American capital have been invested abroad is now giving rise to a return flow of earnings that is of impressive size. In fact, earnings from private foreign investments in 1963 were $4.0 billion, about equal to the recorded outflow of private capital in that year. On a net basis, the private capital account in U.S. balance of payments has been showing a surplus. If the pace of investing abroad were curtailed, the return flow of earnings in the future world, the large AID programs, and the substantial outflow of problems down the road more severe. Moreover, programs to expand exports, if they are to have any promise of success, must include extension of credits for financing this trade, and this financing would show up as an outflow of U.S. capital. Clearly, the role of capital movements in the payments deficit is not one to be treated in a heavy-handed manner.

Here, then, is one diagnosis of the U.S. problem. Its balance-of-payments on current account shows a substantial surplus. This surplus, large as it is, is too small to cover the large outflows of dollars arising from the national security activities around the world, the large AID programs, and the substantial outflow of capital. Those who emphasize this structural aspect of the payments problem recognize full well that in any balancing set of data, one cannot technically point to any three of the considerable number of items as the problem. These items could be what they are and we should still have no problem if other items were different. Moreover, it is recognized that U.S. exports could be adversely affected if these three major items (in 1963 representing a gross dollar outflow of over $10 billion) were reduced. Even so, it is reasonable to suppose that a country with this $10 billion gross drain might find balance in its international payments more difficult to achieve and to sustain. Efforts directed specifically toward relieving the pressure on payments of these items is understandable.

THE EXCESS-LIQUIDITY DIAGNOSIS

There is an alternative approach to a diagnosis of the U.S balance-of-payments problem.[2] Those who hold this view insist that the United States is in trouble simply because there is more money than the domestic economy needs. These surplus funds

[2] The comments in this section are drawn largely from another publication. See Paul W. McCracken and Emile Benoit, *The Balance of Payments and Domestic Prosperity,* University of Michigan, 1963, pp. 11–13.

are bound to spill over the border, causing a balance-of-payments deficit. This approach naturally lends itself to figures of speech having to do with bathtubs or lakes, and they are often employed. If the faucet is running water into the tub more rapidly than it can be handled by the drain at the bottom, the tub will eventually run over unless the faucet is adjusted. The water will, of course, run over at the low point along the edge of the tub, but building up the low spots (dealing with specific leakages) will not solve the problem. The water will still run over somewhere as long as too much is being poured into the tub.

These hydrostatic analogies are sufficiently apt that the basic economic point often gets lost amidst the fluids. There is, however, a basic economic point. When the world's major international currencies became readily convertible in early 1959, the basis for an international market for money and capital had been created. In a market, funds tend to be attracted from areas where interest and profit rates are low to places where they are high. If funds become superabundant in the U.S. economy, things begin to happen. These funds start to move to money-market centers where interest rates are higher. Some U.S. corporations may decide to provide from here funds that their foreign subsidiaries would otherwise need to borrow at relatively high interest rates in their own countries. Moreover, low rates in the United States tend to encourage foreign borrowers to acquire needed funds there, whether the need is for short-term credit from banks or for long-term funds to be raised in the U.S. capital market.

That excessively easy credit and a plethora of domestic monetary liquidity might exacerbate the imbalance in international payments is reasonable enough. This dimension of the problem has been reflected in economic policy as the Federal Reserve and the Treasury have endeavored to avoid low interest rates that would increase balance-of-payments pressures.

THE EXCHANGE-RATE DIAGNOSIS

A third diagnosis of this problem runs in terms of exchange rates. The U.S. balance-of-payments problem has been persisting for long enough and is large enough to qualify as a fundamental disequilibrium. If a seminar on international finance were asked to suggest possible explanations of some nameless country's fundamental payments disequilibrium, it would probably have a maladjusted exchange rate on the list of possibilities.

There are, broadly speaking, three points of view on this exchange-rate matter. First, there are those who propose that the United States jettison the present system of fixed exchange rates and allow these rates to float, changing in response to shifting market forces. This has, in principle, some advantages. It would give countries more freedom to pursue domestic economic policies, with less need to worry about payments deficits. International liquidity problems would be less formidable, since exchange rate adjustments rather than international reserves would provide the adjustment to changing forces. Equilibrium exchange rates among currencies may well change over time, and flexible rates would provide an orderly market procedure to effect these adjustments, one of the great weaknesses of the present system.

At the other end of the spectrum are those who strongly support fixed rates of exchange and, specifically, the present exchange rates between the dollar and other major currencies. Uncertainty about exchange rates would impede trade, would relax the desirable tendency for the balance of payments to exert discipline on domestic policies, would be a repudiation of the whole Bretton Woods approach to rebuilding the international financial structure, and would penalize those who have been good citizens of the international club by holding dollars instead of converting into gold. This is obviously the official view, though for equally obvious reasons, officials do not make many speeches about the merits of not devaluing the dollar.[3]

There is an intermediate position held by those who favor fixed exchange rates but who believe that the dollar is over-

---

[3] It is interesting to note in this connection that the studies launched at the 1963 meetings of the International Monetary Fund explicitly exclude any consideration of flexible exchange rates. See the *New York Times*, Oct. 3, 1963, p. 1.

valued and that a way must be found to correct this. Those who hold this view point to several considerations. A country with an overvalued currency can expect a chronic deficit in its external transactions and may have some difficulty in pursuing a sufficiently expansionist economic policy at home to sustain full employment. This is the present situation in the United States. Moreover, some statistical evidence on the parity purchasing power of the dollar vis à vis other currencies suggests that the dollar is overvalued.[4] This results fundamentally from the fact other major currencies were stabilized at too cheap an exchange rate after World War II (something which for a time was camouflaged by limited productive capacity abroad incident to the postwar rehabilitation of these economies). Only if the United States faces up to this, according to this line of argument, will it be able to get out of the impasse of recent years.

This whole matter of the exchange-rate dimension of the problem has, of course, great difficulty in getting dispassionate, candid, frank consideration, but two conclusions do seem warranted. Betting on a devaluation of the dollar relative to other currencies would at this juncture be a poor wager. It is truly not even in the vocabulary (to use a customary phrase) of present U.S. economic policy. Moreover, comparisons of how much a dollar will buy in the United States with how much a dollar's worth of a foreign currency will buy in that country tell surprisingly little about equilibrium exchange rates, since only transactions in the international arena are relevant. Finally, and the most conclusive reason for confidence in the present exchange rate between the dollar and other major currencies, devaluation of the dollar would ipso facto mean appreciation of the pound or Canadian dollar or mark or franc relative to the U.S. currency. And there is not much reason to think that these nations would support a devaluation of the dollar even if the United States were to conclude that it was desirable.

At the same time, the United States does need to face up to a

4 H. S. Houthakker, "Exchange Rate Adjustment" in *Factors Affecting the United States Balance of Payments*, Joint Economic Committee (87th Congress, 2d Session, 1962), pp. 296–298.

problem here. Patterns of demand and production change, countries pursue different policies, and price-cost trends differ among countries. Exchange rates, which once represented equilibrium, may come to be seriously out of equilibrium. There is no reason in principle to think that the dollar is forever immune to these changes. The present system of fixed rates does in practice require virtually a crisis to force an adjustment that might at some indefinite future time be desirable.

PROSPECTS FOR EQUILIBRIUM

It may be appropriate to conclude this chapter with a few comments about prospects for closing the gap in the U.S. balance of payments. These comments must necessarily be exceedingly tentative. Since, the deficit is the difference between two sides of a statement or account, each of which amounts to about $30 billion, a change of only a few percentage points on both sides could convert the deficit into a surplus; or, if the other way, into a widening deficit of ominous dimensions. Even so, the objective of policy is to close this gap, so it is not amiss to inquire about the chances of effecting this.

It is not difficult to think of reasons for continued concern. Recent developments dramatize (perhaps overly so) the fact that U.S. exports may continue to be adversely affected by the emergence of the Common Market in Europe and perhaps common markets elsewhere. American tourist expenditures abroad have been rising recently (with the exception of 1961) at the rate of about 10 per cent per year. A rapid further growth can be expected in the future. Low air fares (as well as, in some cases, low internal prices) make other countries readily and cheaply accessible to people of even moderate income. The sheer size and highly developed nature of the U.S. capital market almost certainly mean a continued substantial volume of foreign borrowing in this country. Reducing sharply the leakages incident to aid and defense confronts the United States with some exceedingly difficult and painful choices and will not be easily accomplished.

At the same time, some things suggest that time may be on the

TABLE 7. INCREASE IN WAGES AND COST OF LIVING, 1962–1963

Country	Wages	Cost of Living
France	9%	5%
Germany	7	3
Italy	10	7
Japan	10	8
United Kingdom	4	3
United States	4	1

SOURCE: *International Financial Statistics*, June 1964.

side of the United States. First, cost-price levels in Europe have been rising more rapidly than in the United States (Table 7). In France, Italy, and in Japan particularly (among the more industrially advanced nations), inflation once again in 1963 became a matter of concern. And in most of these countries, the rise in costs was enough both to push up prices significantly and to reduce profit margins. Clearly, recent movements in costs and prices have improved the international competitive position of the U. S. economy.

Second, measures to reduce the balance-of-payments leakages incident to both aid and military activities are not yet fully reflected in data now available. In the fiscal year 1962, the share of aid expenditures paid to non-United States recipients was 50 per cent. In 1963 the proportion dropped to 35 per cent, and the obligations or commitments made in fiscal year 1963, which are antecedent to expenditures, were at the rate of only 24 per cent scheduled to accrue to non-United States recipients.[5] This change, of course, shows up in the balance-of-payments data as incremental exports on the receipts side rather than as a reduction in the gross aid figure on the payments side. It is the stated objective of the Department of Defense to reduce the military leakage, as pointed out earlier, to $1 billion by fiscal year 1966. This is an ambitious target, but a substantial further reduction in this leakage is a reasonable expectation.

[5] See Frank C. Coffin's testimony before the Subcommittee on International Exchange and Payments, Joint Economic Committee (87th Congress, 2d Session, Dec. 12–14, 1962), p. 63.

Finally, a more rapid pace of domestic economic expansion in the United States should fundamentally work in the direction of improving its balance-of-payments position. A more vigorous domestic economy in the years ahead is now a reasonable expectation. Periods of retarded economic growth have occurred before in U.S. history, but none has lasted for any extended time. A period now of accelerated expansion would be in line with historical experience. The tax reduction in March 1964 will give substantial impetus in that direction, and the technical position of the economy (the age distribution of the population, probable family formation rates, etc.) is also becoming more favorable to rapid expansion.

A more vigorous domestic economy will have a complex influence on the U.S. balance of payments. A higher and more rapidly expanding national income will tend to enlarge imports, and that will aggravate the imbalance in external payments. If the stronger demand for output were to result in more rapidly rising costs and prices, the effect on U.S. balance of payments could be quite adverse, though any attempt artificially to hold the lid on prices in the face of rising costs, which would be interpreted as a drive for a lower-profit economy, could be expected to have even more ominous repercussions. A policy of trying to avoid a rise in interest rates in the face of more active demands for money would also have to be put on the list of things that would exacerbate the external payments problem.

A more vigorous domestic economy could, however, have ultimately some very beneficial effects on the international payments position. The active demand for money and credit would move interest rates to higher levels, and through market-place forces rather than by explicit Federal Reserve action. A more expansive domestic economy would be a more profitable economy, one with enlarged opportunities for the attractive employment of domestic and foreign capital funds in the United States. Clearly, a more prosperous domestic economic situation should improve the balance of payments on capital account.

The effect of the balance on current account is more complex. In the short run, the impact of a more rapidly rising level of business activity at home, as pointed out above, would probably be to increase the payments deficit as imports responded to rising incomes. In the longer run, there are influences that would tend to be in the other direction. A more prosperous economy is a more innovative economy, one with a more vigorous pace of product development. The U.S. position in the world export market depends heavily on its being able to move from Model II to Model III when its competitors abroad are trying to move from Model I to Model II.[6] In fact, a narrowing of this product gap has been a part of the problem in this decade. If the country could have an economy with a more active rate of innovation and product development, U.S. penetration in the world export market ought to improve—or at least certainly would be stronger.

There is some evidence from recent international experience to support this optimistic prognosis about the impact on payments imbalance of a more rapidly growing economy at home. The countries who have increased their share of the world export market since 1957 (the year before the U.S. balance of payments

TABLE 8. SHARE OF WORLD EXPORTS

Country	1957	1963
Canada	5.4%	5.0%
France	5.1	6.0
Germany	8.6	10.8
Italy	2.5	3.7
Japan	2.9	4.0
United Kingdom	9.6	8.7
United States	20.9	17.1

SOURCE: Basic data from *International Financial Statistics.*

began to deteriorate) are nations such as France, Germany, Italy, and Japan, whose domestic economies have also been relatively strong. The U.S. share of world exports, by contrast, declined from 21 per cent in 1957 to 17 per cent in 1963. It is interesting to note that Canada and the United Kingdom, who also have

[6] This figure of speech comes from Ray Eppert, president of the Burroughs Corporation.

been bothered by sluggish domestic economies, also lost penetration in the world export market during this period.

The empirical evidence from the U.S. experience generally in the postwar period also suggests that a stronger U.S. economy need not enlarge its payments deficit and might strengthen it. For the postwar period as a whole, there has been a discernible positive correlation between the surplus in the U.S. balance of payments and the deviation of real GNP from that which in each year would have represented comfortably full employment of labor and other productive resources, and a clear negative correlation between capital outflows and this deviation of output from par.[7] Each $1 billion shortfall of GNP from par was associated in the postwar period with roughly a $40 million deterioration in the U.S. over-all balance of payments, and close to a $50 million enlarged outflow of U.S. private capital. If, in 1963, the shortfall of GNP from par was about $30 billion, this (our postwar experience suggests) might have contributed something like $1 billion to $1½ billion to the deficit. Of course, there may be a timing problem as the domestic economy moves ahead more rapidly. The rise in imports probably would come along promptly, but the favorable effects to be expected on capital account might well require time to make themselves felt. At the same time, experience does suggest that the United States need not cling to a chronically below-par domestic economic performance, fearful about what a little life in the economy at home might do to our payments position.

SUMMARY

No plowing of such a well-worked field as the U.S. balance-of-payments problem is likely to uncover anything very startling or

[7] See Paul W. McCracken and Emile Benoit, *The Balance of Payments and Domestic Prosperity*, University of Michigan, 1963, pp. 30–35. It is true that studies have produced somewhat unclear results about the effect on capital movements of interest rate differentials. See, for example, Benjamin J. Cohen, "A Survey of Capital Movements and Findings Regarding Their Interest Sensitivity," Hearings Before the Joint Economic Committee (88th Congress, 1st Session, July 8–9, 1963), pp. 192–208.

new. It may, however, be worth while to state briefly a few conclusions that seem to emerge from this survey. First, the basic
cause of the payments deficit is tridimensional—partly structural,
arising out of leakages from military expenditures abroad and
from aid programs; partly the fact that an international market
for money and capital has been re-established; and partly a complex response to the arthritic domestic economic performance of
the United States in recent years. Second, the evidence does not
support the view that the exchange rate between the dollar
and other major currencies is too high to achieve payments
equilibrium, but it is also clear that the present international
financial machinery is ill-adapted to deal with a maladjusted exchange rate for the dollar, if that should ever be a problem. Finally, there need not be any fundamental conflict between the
objectives of improving the U.S. external payments position and
the pace of the economy at home. Indeed, the greater danger is
that, misconceiving the dynamics of this relationship between
payments disequilibrium and domestic economic problems, the
United States will either back into something akin to an international competition for deflation or wobble from one ad hoc
exchange control to another. Then, perhaps to its own surprise,
it will have gone a long way toward a battery of controls that will
be a substantial departure from the liberal international trade
and financial policy that has been the U.S. objective since the
war.

CHAPTER 14

The Present World Monetary Mechanism

Karl Blessing

History teaches us that a well-functioning international monetary system is the indispensable prerequisite for a flourishing and expanding world trade. Disorder in international monetary affairs has always led to a decline of the international division of labor and to disintegration. If it is our desire to achieve close integration in the free world, we must therefore do everything to keep the international monetary system in shape and to strengthen it. This task concerns every one of us, for we are all in the same boat. The bigger countries, of course, face a greater responsibility than the smaller ones.

STRENGTHS AND WEAKNESSES

The existing international monetary system has recently come in for a good deal of criticism, and all kinds of reformatory proposals have been advanced. In this chapter an attempt will be made to show up the strong and the weak points of our present international monetary system, and to subject the more important proposals for its reform to closer scrutiny. This will automatically lead to an evaluation of the system and of the services that it can now and in the future render to the free world.

Frequently, a certain lack of stability of the two key currencies of the Western world, the dollar and pound sterling, is invoked as a reason to criticize the international monetary order and to call it inadequate and in need for reform. Some people even predict an impending collapse of this monetary system. In this connection, not infrequently, parallels are drawn between the present situation and conditions immediately preceding the outbreak of the monetary and economic crisis of the 1930s. Such ill prophecies of the critics are, however, considerably toned down by the frequent contradictions in their diagnoses and arguments, which are apt to cancel each other out. Whereas some utter warnings against the deflationary perils of our international monetary system, others look upon it as an inflationary mechanism that should be halted as soon as possible. Things are similar with regard to the reform proposals; whereas some people wish to restore the "classical" gold standard, others clamor for the establishment of a new monetary setup, which exists only on their drawing boards.

Despite these contradictions, the responsible monetary authorities should not make light of the doubts and the concern regarding the stability of the present monetary system. Let us first establish what the conditions are that a well-functioning monetary order must fulfill. These conditions may be summarized as follows: An international monetary system must, on the one hand, be flexible enough to afford the participating countries sound expansion of their economies and their mutual trade relations; on the other hand, it must impose upon the participants such discipline and such consideration for one another as is necessary in order to ensure healthy growth of international trade, with stable and harmonious monetary relations as the basis.

Many critics contend that the present gold exchange standard inadequately answers the demands made on a durable monetary order. Let us therefore take a closer look at the deficiencies of which it is accused.

Frequently it is claimed that the present monetary system does not supply the world with sufficient "international liquidity," that is, available monetary reserves. The Western world, it is said, therefore constantly faces the risk of running into a deflationary crisis caused by lack of liquidity, which would entail competitive devaluations, exchange controls, trade restrictions, and other phenomena known from the past. To support this theory, all kinds of arguments are advanced. The one most frequently heard says that the monetary reserves of the world are not sufficient to finance expanding world trade and rising world production. This particular argument is highly disputable. It goes without saying that an increase in trade—both domestic and foreign—calls for expanded credit facilities in order to guarantee sufficient finance. Contrary to what was the case at the time of the gold standard, when regulations for the gold cover of the note circulation still applied, domestic lending nowadays is largely independent of monetary reserves; it can therefore usually be adjusted to rising turnovers without the monetary reserves having to be stepped up. Foreign trade transactions are financed in the currencies of the principal industrial countries; here, again, there is no direct connection between rising world trade and monetary reserves. The demand for monetary reserves thus does not immediately result from the domestic or foreign turnover. It is a result in fact of the fluctuations in the balances of payments, especially the extent and duration of balance-of-payments deficits. Per Jacobsson was perfectly right when he said: "There can be no question of an inherent parallelism between the expansion of credit and growth of reserves."

This view is supported by experience over the past ten or fifteen years: The rapid and unparalleled expansion of international trade (6 per cent annual average) since 1948 and the simultaneous removal of major restrictions in trade and payments have been practicable even though the official monetary reserves of the Western world during the same time rose much less, actually by no more than about 2 per cent a year on average.

The present supply of international liquidity cannot be said to be insufficient. The course that prices during the past few years have taken internationally does not denote deflationary pressure.

The total monetary reserves of the world amounted in mid-1964 to about $66 billion, of which almost $41 billion are kept in gold and more than $25 billion in foreign currencies. Of the latter, the official dollar balances alone represent more than $12 billion, thus clearly reflecting the overriding importance of the U.S. dollar as a reserve currency. The figures do not include credit facilities at the big international monetary institutions and such facilities as are provided under bilateral support arrangements, all of which basically fulfill the same function as the monetary reserves themselves, since they help to overcome short-term balance-of-payments troubles or in more profound disturbances afford time for the necessary measures of adjustment. Since most of these credit facilities cannot (for good reason) be automatically available, they are normally not included in international liquidity in the statistics. The existence of this "potential liquidity" is, however, an important factor when judging our present monetary system. This is another reason why one must not compare today's supply of monetary reserves with that of any one time in the past for the purpose of drawing conclusions as to the adequacy or inadequacy of international liquidity, quite apart from the difficulty of assigning the attribute "normal" to any specific liquidity supply in the past.

The argument of the critics is that the weaknesses of the international monetary system may not be obvious at the present time because its defects are now veiled by other developments, but that they will certainly come to the surface in the future. It is pointed out that the increase in foreign currency reserves during the past few years was to an overwhelming degree caused by the balance-of-payments deficits of the United States, in other words by the increase in its short-term indebtedness vis-à-vis the rest of the world. The margin left to the reserve currency countries to increase their short-term liabilities, and thus their ability to create international liquidity, is, the critics claim, rather limited, and may be said to have already reached the point where confidence in these currencies will rapidly wane. This, it is said, means that the United States is faced with the necessity to seek a speedy squaring of its balance of payments, with the result that an important source of international liquidity will dry up. The world would then depend on the insufficient increase in monetary reserves from current gold production and Russian gold sales and would fail to meet by a long way the current demand, however this is computed. Should the United States then actually achieve surpluses in its balance of payments, this would be tantamount to a mopping up of international liquidity, since the European countries would then try to finance the deficits in their balances of payments by resorting to their dollar balances, thus creating a situation where these dollar balances would dwindle and the total holdings of official monetary reserves would decline accordingly.

There can be no doubt that if the international balance-of-payments equilibrium is re-established, national monetary reserves will mainly depend on accruals of monetary gold. According to past experience, supplies of gold from current production and Russian sales together amount to approximately $1.5 billion a year, a substantial portion of which, however, goes into private hoarding and industrial consumption. All the same, about $0.7 to $0.8 billion a year might remain available to stock up national monetary reserves, and this would permit the total reserves to rise by 1.1 to 1.2 per cent per annum. This might not meet all liquidity needs in the future, but the danger of an acute shortage of reserves is nevertheless rather remote. Thus a better regional distribution of existing monetary reserves might contribute toward averting a threatening scarcity of international liquidity. Since there is no indication of a complete removal of the balance-of-payments deficit of the United States for the time being, the danger of international liquidity's becoming scarcer is consequently a matter to tackle in the future rather than in the present. Moreover, the demand for liquidity will considerably lessen when the international balances of payments again approach equilibrium.

Conditions before World War I show very clearly what a small amount of reserves is needed in a well-balanced world economy: the Bank of England and the other central banks disposed of gold reserves that were negligible as compared with present amounts. A national isolated liquidity demand, such as keeps arising from time to time on account of disturbances in the balance of payments of some particular country, must be coped with by means of international cooperation and credit facilities. To try to counter it in advance by overabundant liquidity in the whole world, as is occasionally recommended, would be a highly dangerous procedure, and would be highly detrimental to the stability of our monetary system. The establishment of a well-functioning network of bilateral and international credit aids, on the other hand, would be a suitable and presumably expandable method of cushioning temporary scarcities of monetary reserves (such as are quite likely to occur in the presence of major short-term capital movements) and of protecting the currencies involved from critical situations.

Lastly, as regards the possibility of American surpluses and the attendant danger of a reduction of dollar balances and consequently of international liquidity, the quarters responsible for U.S. monetary policy have already announced that in such a case they would be prepared to hold in their monetary reserves convertible currencies of other countries that are not normally reserve currencies. To some extent, the American monetary authorities have already during the present deficit period taken steps to establish an operating fund of other convertible currencies and thus to develop a mechanism that would be able to come into operation immediately in the event of American surpluses. Liquidity would thus not necessarily be automatically reduced in the event of American surpluses; on the contrary—if the countries concerned so desired and deemed necessary—a renewed increase of liquidity might take place, namely, by the accumulation of foreign currency assets, which would be effected by the United States.

Another defect with which the present monetary system is charged is the supposedly privileged role it allots to those countries whose currency is held by other nations as a foreign currency reserve. According to this argument, the United States has an advantage over the other countries because it has easy access to "painless deficits," that is, short-term credits. Whereas the nonreserve countries normally have to settle their balance-of-payments deficits in cash, that is, to the debit of their official gold and currency reserves, the reserve-currency countries are able to finance them by creating international liquidity. Apart from the discriminatory treatment inherent in this procedure (the argument runs), the system is in effect nothing but mutual bill jobbing in that the claims arising against the reserve-currency countries are left there in the form of dollar or sterling balances. In other words: The gold exchange standard is an inflationary machinery because the credit expansion in the surplus countries is not offset by a contraction in the deficit countries if the latter at the same time happen to be reserve-currency countries. An even greater danger, it is claimed, is that the pile of indebtedness, built up from the claims on the reserve-currency countries left there, is likely at any time to teeter or, in fact, to be brought to the point of collapse by a run on these currencies.

Here, again, the question arises whether these theories do not reveal serious weaknesses of our present monetary system. As regards the privileged position of the key-currency countries and their "painless deficits," we should not—if this were really true—now be facing the problem of American gold losses. Since the end of 1949, the gold holdings of the United States have decreased by as much as $8.9 billion, or by about 36 per cent of the level at that time. In 1949 the United States held 74 per cent of the world's gold (outside the Soviet bloc); today the ratio is less than 40 per cent. Moreover, rivals for the reserve currencies would have come forward if the latter's role were really so privileged and attractive. In actual fact, however, we see little inclination on the part of other countries to assume a similar role and a correspondingly great responsibility.

It is no mere chance that some reform plans are commended by the very argument that the reserve-currency countries should be relieved of the burden they have to shoulder, which for a large part, it is claimed, consists in the fact that in protecting their own economic interests, they are too greatly hampered by considerations of the peculiar status of their currencies. It would appear that here again the arguments of the critics cancel out each other, for clearly the role of reserve currency is both a privilege and a burden for the country concerned. Also, the reproach that easy access of the reserve-currency countries to short-term credits tempts them to engage in unsound economic policies is hardly confirmed by the actual course of events. The underemployment prevailing in America, at any rate, does not indicate that the United States has permitted itself, in view of the alleged privilege of the "painless deficits," to slide into demand inflation.

As for the contractive or expansive effects of deficits and surpluses of the balance of payments, whose impact is said to be insufficient under the present gold exchange standard, it cannot be denied that as a rule the adjustment process under the gold standard did work more speedily and effectively. Even then, however, there were periods of sterilization of monetary reserves and of policies not exactly in conformity with balance-of-payments requirements. With regard to today's situation, it can be said that all important industrial countries now, more than before, pursue domestic policies oriented toward meeting balance-of-payments needs. This does not mean that further progress toward achieving a faster and more effective adjustment process should not be one of the main tasks of international monetary cooperation.

Naturally the high short-term indebtedness, with consequent vulnerability of the reserve currencies, presents a serious problem. In fact, the net reserve position, both of the United Kingdom since the war and of the United States for some time past, is negative, which means that the short-term liabilities of either country are higher than its own gross reserves.

This clearly shows that the credit-creating reserve centers also face a liquidity problem. As long as they pursue sound policies and see to it that by their balance-of-payments deficits they do not create more exchange claims against themselves than the other countries are prepared to hold, the requisite climate of confidence is ensured, even when the net positions of the reserve centers are negative. After all, a bank does not betray the confidence placed in it merely because it is unable to satisfy all its creditors at the same time. It is difficult to see why the Western world should not be able to live with the gold exchange standard and its risks, taking into account the present extent of international cooperation and the means at the disposal of the International Monetary Fund.

PROPOSALS FOR CHANGING THE PRESENT SYSTEM

What alternative action do the critics advocate in exchange for the existing and, in their opinion, imperfect monetary system? In this section the more important approaches to a fundamental reform of the international monetary order will be discussed.

Academic circles believe that every monetary system based on fixed parities, however perfectly and ingeniously it may have been conceived, is bound to show serious functional defects under present-day conditions and is incapable of guaranteeing lasting equilibrium in international payments. It is contended that fixed rates of exchange render simultaneous realization of the aims of the "magic triangle" (that is, balance-of-payments equilibrium, full employment, and price stability) still more difficult or even impossible. Stable exchange rates, it is asserted, tend to speed up creeping inflation, which exists in some countries, in that nations with a stable price level are forced to import inflation from other areas through involuntary surpluses in their balance of payments. This danger, it is claimed, can be averted only under a system of flexible exchange rates, which at the same time would solve the problem of an adequate supply of international liquidity because the squaring of the balance of payments automatically effected by the adjustment of exchange rates would render the maintenance of monetary reserves largely unnecessary, or at least less important.

Against this, practical experience gained during the postwar period from the comparatively few cases in which flexible exchange rates have been applied leads one to conclude that a system wherein the rates for *all* important currencies fluctuate freely against each other does not constitute a practicable monetary order. To cover medium- or longer-term exchange risks in the exchange markets does not seem to be possible in sufficient measure under such a system. Flexible exchange rates would impair international money and capital transactions; they would deprive foreign trade of a safe basis for pricing; they would encourage unprincipled conduct in monetary matters; they would promote exchange speculation; and under certain conditions, they might even lead to an abuse of exchange rates as a tool of trade policy.

These objections, which in principle can also be advanced against the general system of fixed parities with exchange-rate margins far in excess of those now ruling, must not be construed as a defense of fixed exchange rates at any cost, nor (far less) as an argument in favor of unrealistic exchange rates. Countries with weak currencies should, as a general principle—this being the practice recommended by the IMF—bring the exchange rates of their currencies, once they have become unrealistic by inflation, back to equilibrium either by the free play of supply and demand in the market or by the expedient of a nonrecurring adjustment.

As a general system, however, freely fluctuating exchange rates, on the other hand, by releasing the countries from the discipline of having to conform to balance-of-payments requirements, might well have disintegrating effects on the economy of the free world and thus be ruled out as a solution for a reorganization of the international monetary system. Within the European Common Market, at any rate, such a system would certainly not be applicable because it would be quite contrary to the realization of an economic union.

One proposal, which recurs fairly regularly in the discussion of monetary problems, is a recommendation to raise the gold price; that is, to effect a uniform reduction in the parities of all currencies in relation to gold. This path is advocated in the first place by those who consider existing international liquidity to be inadequate and seek to increase it by simply stepping up the nominal value of the gold holdings, thus creating an additional incentive for gold production. It is furthermore supported by those who wish to see gold reinstated as the only and exclusive reserve medium and to obviate its relative scarcity by a drastic increase in the gold price.

There are a number of very serious objections to this proposal. The advantages to be gained from raising the gold price would favor countries with important gold holdings and the gold-producing countries (primarily South Africa and the Soviet Union), without the latter being able to ensure that future gold production will be adequate at all times. The countries with weak reserves on the other hand, would profit little, if at all, from a change in the gold price. The problem of the international balance-of-payments disequilibrium and of faulty regional distribution of international liquidity would thus be mitigated only temporarily, and for some countries only, without however being solved. Moreover, such a step would discredit the holding of foreign currency reserves and especially sap confidence in the value of the dollar while at the same time putting a premium on private gold hoarding and encouraging speculation on further increases in the gold price. Expectations of a periodic recurrence of a raising of the gold price, however, would of necessity jeopardize the gold exchange standard and thus achieve exactly the opposite of what some of its advocates hope it will do. Finally, the technical and procedural difficulties of a general increase of the gold price, especially if it was attended by a realignment of the exchange rates, and the almost inevitable grave disturbances of the exchange markets during the preparation of such a step are points that should be mentioned. Nor should proponents of change overlook the danger of inflationary impulses emanating from the book profits made by the monetary authorities and their possible use for additional public expenditure.

The recommendation is frequently heard that the gold standard should be reintroduced in the unrestricted form in which it existed before World War I, and that the foreign-exchange element of the present gold-exchange standard—which, after all, accounts for more than one-third of all existing reserves—should simply be abolished. No matter whether the aim is the general restoration of the old gold bullion standard, or whether the gold standard sought is to apply merely for the settlement of balances among central banks, the prerequisite would be a substantial increase in the gold price. For only thus would the monetary gold holdings of the reserve currency countries be nominally up-valued enough for the liabilities of the reserve centers vis-à-vis the monetary authorities of the rest of the world to be repayable in gold at the new valuation rate. The same arguments advanced against the beforementioned raising of the gold price, also hold good against this proposal. In addition, those advocating a return to the gold standard tend to overlook the fact that the classical gold standard, even in its best years, did not possess all the virtues that are often ascribed to it nowadays; neither was it able completely to prevent the occurrence of balance-of-payments difficulties, nor did it guarantee price stability.

Under present-day conditions of downward inflexibility of prices and wages and the priorities now applying to economic objectives, no proposals embodying the restoration of the old gold standard are realistic. Whether we regret it or not, the fact is that the world wants to be free of the ties of the gold standard and its automatism, not least because it finds the whole system lacking in flexibility and thus sees in it a potential cause of deflation. Indeed, the danger should not be overlooked that a revived gold standard would make international liquidity scarcer because the continued supply of monetary reserves would depend exclusively on current gold production. Great as the merits of the gold standard were around the turn of the century, it would contribute little to the solution of our problems today.

The proposal for creation of a multiple currency standard goes in a direction exactly opposite to the restoration of the gold standard. The existing reserve currencies are not to be deprived of their function; on the contrary, their number is to be increased so as to facilitate the creation of additional international liquidity in the form of foreign-exchange balances and to distribute more widely the burden of the responsibilities so far borne by the two reserve centers, the United States and the United Kingdom. Particularly the Continental European currencies, it is claimed, have meanwhile become so strong that they are capable of assuming the function of a reserve currency. This role would be easy for them to fill, in contrast to the U.S. dollar and sterling, since these countries have hardly any short-term indebtedness and comparatively high monetary reserves, which means that they enjoy considerable international confidence. Also, the international monetary system would thus attain a better "symmetry," meaning that the special status of the reserve centers would be abolished or alleviated.

As regards these proposals, it should be observed that it is now the policy of the U.S. monetary authorities to maintain a certain operating fund in other convertible currencies, which has to some extent already rendered more "multilateral" the holding of foreign currencies within the limits of the existing monetary system. Also, responsible monetary authorities in the United States have voiced their intention to continue this policy on a larger scale in the event of surpluses in the U.S. balance of payments.

However desirable and worthy of encouragement such a development is, one must not lose sight of the limits inherent in the nature of these things. After all, reserve currencies are not "made" by decisions and decrees, but acquire this function gradually in the course of an historic process and, of course, only if they meet specific requirements. Only such currencies are recognized and in demand as reserve media as are commonly used in international trade also for business transactions and are backed by highly developed money and capital markets and efficient industries with a wide range of flexible supply. Thus, in times of crisis, these currencies permit the conversion of foreign-held exchange balances into the goods and services needed by the rest of the world.

Moreover, the fact is all too frequently overlooked that the creation of one or more new reserve currencies would in itself solve neither the problem of international liquidity supply nor that of relief for the existing reserve centers. If the exchange balances held at the existing reserve centers were withdrawn and transferred to other places, international liquidity would remain unaffected, whereas quite sizable balance-of-payments problems might arise for the existing reserve centers. Not until the new reserve centers became capable of assuming balance-of-payments deficits, and were prepared to incur short-term indebtedness, could they relieve the "old" reserve currencies and contribute toward supplying the rest of the world with available monetary reserves. If, on the other hand, they should run a surplus, exactly the contrary would happen, and the consequences for our monetary order might, if anything, be negative.

Other suggestions propose to abolish the existing exchange balances in the reserve currencies and replace them with balances held with an international central bank. Since the time when Lord Keynes presented his well-known plan in 1943 and suggested the creation of an international clearing union with its own international currency unit, which was to be the sole reserve means besides gold, numerous plans have been recommended. Except for a number of more or less marked deviations, all have a common basic concept in that they provide for a supranational institution in which most of the authors wish to see vested the sole right to create international liquidity. An international, super central bank, possibly along the lines of a modified International Monetary Fund, would be substituted for the existing reserve centers and would, according to Professor Triffin (who may be said to be the chief protagonist of this school of thought), have the function of gradually replacing the monetary reserves held in national currencies by IMF credit balances. These credit balances would have a gold-value guarantee and would be freely convertible; and their volume would have to be regulated, by the institution's own credit operations in accordance with objective principles, in such a manner that world liquidity could develop in harmony with the international demand for monetary reserves.

Among the most important prerequisites for the attainment of these objectives would be the introduction of a system of obligatory interest-bearing deposits to replace the existing quota system of the IMF; the creation of "additional" sight deposits by credit and open-market operations on the initiative of the modified IMF; the granting of a gold-value guarantee by the existing reserve-currency countries for their short-term liabilities held by the IMF and gradual repayment of the latter to the IMF (which in practice would be possible only from current balance-of-payments surpluses or the gold holdings of the reserve-currency countries). More or less substantially deviating from this basic scheme, other authors have proposed similar or even more radical solutions. Mr. Stamp, for example, suggests that IMF should issue bonds with a gold-value guarantee for distribution to the governments of the developing countries; these bonds would then have to be accepted by the surplus countries as payment in unlimited amounts and would be included in their monetary reserves.

Without going into greater detail about the manifold technical problems, a few more fundamental consequences of these proposals may be pointed out here: In the present system, where control, contrary to the plan of a super central bank, is decentralized, confidence in its stability depends on convertibility of the foreign-currency balances into gold. This depends in turn on the soundness of the economic and monetary policies of the reserve-currency countries. Obviously, this would not be much different under a centralized system. Confidence in the solvency and liquidity of such an institution, burdened as it would be with a truly enormous responsibility, and in the foreign-currency balances created by it, would not be easy to inspire, and, in the long run, it would be probably even more difficult to retain. At the moment it appears entirely improbable that the various countries will be prepared to turn over to a central body the task of regulating the money supply and thus the ultimate decision on inflation or deflation, all the more so because the conflicting interests of more than one hundred members would hardly permit a consensus. There are good reasons why the "General Arrangements to Borrow" within the framework of the IMF have been so designed that the smaller and more homogeneous circle of the ten lending countries (the so-called Group of Ten, or Paris Club) can wield considerable influence on any utilization of the funds. It is therefore not surprising that the leading countries, at any rate in the foreseeable future, would rather expand and strengthen the existing international monetary order than enter into far-reaching experiments that, under today's circumstances, appear to be very risky.

EVALUATION OF THE EXISTING SYSTEM

A fact that is all too frequently overlooked by the critics and reformers is that our present gold-exchange standard is very different from that of the 1930s. This becomes clear if one analyzes the present monetary system more closely. Originally, gold was the only medium within this system for the international settlement of payments and the accumulation of monetary reserves. Later, its flexibility became greater in that foreign currencies also began to exercise this function. First sterling and later the dollar took on the new role, thanks to their leading position in international trade and thanks to the fact that behind them were the investment and financing facilities of the highly developed markets of London and New York. After World War II, the IMF entered the picture as an important new factor. Thus, the international monetary system received a true center and a new fabric, whereas up to that time it had been based solely on the interdependence of the principal international credit markets and on the attitude of the monetary authorities, which, however, since the monetary crisis of 1931 was by no means uniform.

The IMF does not have the functions and powers of a central bank. It is dependent on instruments other than those a national central bank uses to control its domestic credit system. The IMF therefore has to rely on the voluntary cooperation of the national authorities, which fully share in the responsibility for the existence and smooth functioning of the international monetary system. Experience gained since the war, especially during the past ten years, shows that the concept of decentralized decision and voluntary cooperation chosen in Bretton Woods, and since then variously supplemented and improved, meets present conditions well; moreover, it has the advantage of being flexible enough to be adaptable to future requirements.

The IMF plays a dual part: On the one hand it imposes upon the member countries certain rules of behavior; it makes them adhere to a code of contractual rules for their domestic and foreign monetary policies. On the other hand, the Fund is in a position in the event of balance-of-payments difficulties to afford its members temporary financial assistance to enable them to take the economic and monetary measures necessary for the squaring of their balance of payments. As regards such measures, the Fund addresses recommendations to, and imposes conditions on, the appropriate national authorities.

The resources of the Fund consist of gold and currencies of the member countries. As a rule, each country pays to the Fund in gold an amount equivalent to 25 per cent of its quota, calculated along certain lines, and the remainder of the quota in its own currency, always in the form of a non-interest-bearing note, which, if necessary, can be converted by the Fund into the national currency. In mid-1964 the Fund had available operating resources in the value of about $10 billion, of which about $3 billion were gold and almost $7 billion in currencies of the ten principal industrial countries.

In the first years of its existence, the IMF was not yet able completely to fulfill its function as a central institution of the international monetary system, particularly since during that time the structural dollar problem of Europe was successfully tackled in other ways, such as with the aid of the Marshall Plan. During that period of comparative inactivity in outside relations, which lasted until about 1955, the IMF organized its operating procedure, developed forms of technical assistance to member countries, and obtained agreement on the principles and practice of the use of IMF resources. In its business practice, the Fund has successfully enforced the principle that in cases where balance-of-payments deficits were due to unsound monetary policy of the applying country, the credit aid was made conditional on the execution of stabilization programs agreed upon with the Fund. In the case of stand-by arrangements, "declarations of intent" are always embodied in the contract terms.

It was not until late in 1956 that the IMF was able to engage in financial activity on a larger scale by granting assistance in the amount of $1.3 billion to the United Kingdom in connection with the Suez crisis. Thanks to this prompt action on the part of the Fund, it was possible at the time to strengthen the position of sterling in a crucial moment and to avoid a breakdown of the international exchange-rate structure.

When, after most of the west European countries had proclaimed nonresident convertibility of their currencies in December 1958, unexpected changes in the direction of massive capital movements became the main danger for the monetary system, the IMF changed its attitude on the subject of using Fund resources for capital transactions. It declared itself willing also to make its resources available toward overcoming such payments problems as were primarily due to capital movements and, in particular, to short-term speculative movements of money from one country to another or from a reserve currency into gold.

After most of the European currencies had made the transition to formal convertibility within the meaning of Article VIII of the IMF Articles of Agreement in February 1961, the Fund was able to extend its practice of annual consultations to all member countries. While previously such consultations were limited to countries that still maintained exchange restrictions, these reviews of economic developments and policies, which are very useful for the countries themselves, have since then not only been continued with the European countries, but are now also being held with Canada and the United States.

For several years now the IMF has, step by step, developed the practice, which in 1962 was also formally adopted, of advising members in the selection of currencies suitable for drawings and repayments, thereby exercising an influence on the use of the currencies in accordance with the payments and reserve positions of the member countries concerned and with the requirements of the changing international-payments situation. This practice brought considerable relief for the U.S. dollar.

Whereas up to 1958 the Fund operated almost exclusively on a dollar basis, so that in that year about 90 per cent of the whole drawings, in an equivalent of $3 billion, were made in U.S. dollars, the proportion of dollars in over-all drawings in the following years decreased to 77, 53, and 33 per cent, respectively. In 1962 no more than 19 per cent of all drawings, as against 55 per cent of all repayments, were made in U.S. dollars. As a consequence, the net creditor position of the United States in the Fund, which at the end of 1958 had amounted to about $1.3 billion has largely been replaced by net creditor positions, totaling about $1.1 billion, of other members of the group of the ten principal industrial countries, in particular in favor of EEC countries and Japan, whose currencies have been drawn by other countries.

In its original form, the IMF was not equipped to offer aid in favor of the key currencies as well, but in January 1962 the ten principal industrial countries of the world made a supplementary arrangement, the so-called General Arrangements to Borrow. This enables the IMF to play its part as a shelter in the event of an acute balance-of-payments crisis for the reserve centers as well, in order (as the preamble says) to "forestall or cope with an impairment of the international monetary system." These additional facilities amount to $6 billion, of which the nonreserve countries, if necessary, contribute up to about $3 billion. Switzerland, too, which as a nonmember of IMF could not immediately participate in the General Arrangements to Borrow, has, under a parallel agreement with the IMF under similar circumstances and conditions, assumed the commitment to grant currency assistance up to a maximum of $200 million. Access to these resources is not automatic, but is controlled, and like all major cases of recourse to IMF, availability is tied to recommendations and conditions in the field of economic and monetary policies. Also, the lending countries, as already mentioned, have reserved the right to be consulted.

The latest initiative of IMF resulted in creating a new financing facility, particularly for members relying primarily on exports of raw materials, to help them cope with short-term fluctuations in the value of their exports.

When considering the role of IMF, two facts have to be emphasized: For one thing, the IMF makes it possible for currencies other than the key currencies proper to be likewise drawn upon for the international settlement of payments (although only within the quotas fixed in the IMF). This has the effect of creating a certain multilateralization of the system, and as we can see today, provides a certain relief for the reserve currencies proper. For another, the Articles of Agreement of the IMF stipulate certain rules of conduct that are binding on all member countries; in other words, contrary to the gold-exchange standard of the 1930s, our monetary system has undergone a kind of codification. The IMF can use its substantial financial resources toward making sure that these rules are kept. The rehabilitations of currencies effected during the past fifteen years with the aid of IMF show clearly that the Fund has become an important stabilizer in our monetary system, a stabilizer that was lacking in the former gold-exchange standard.

BUILDING ADDITIONAL LINES OF DEFENSE

Additional lines of defense against short-term speculative attacks on the reserve currencies, such as may happen at any time under a system of convertible currencies, have been built up in recent years. These additional defense measures had their origin in the immediate reaction of the monetary authorities to the disturbances in the exchange markets following the revaluation of the Deutsche mark and the Dutch guilder in March 1961. At that time, the west European central banks, in accordance with an understanding arrived at in Basle, began to intervene in the exchange markets in favor of sterling, and made available to the Bank of England foreign-exchange facilities as a first line of defense. Beginning in August 1961, these short-term credits were quickly repaid out of the aid made available by the IMF as a second line of defense.

Decisive importance for the building of additional lines of defense must be accorded to the reorientation of the American exchange policy initiated under the impact of the erratic movements of short-term capital between the principal financial centers of the world in the spring and summer of 1961. In order to be able to cushion sudden tensions before they induced movements of gold or crises of confidence in the exchange markets, the American monetary authorities began to add foreign currencies to their gold reserve; in addition, with a view to warding off speculative bearish pressures on forward dollars, they had re-course, together with the Deutsche Bundesbank, for the first time since World War II, to interventions in the forward market for U.S. dollars and Deutsche marks, thus preventing a further spreading of money movements between the United States and the Federal Republic of Germany, which were partly speculative and partly induced by interest rate considerations. In the mean-time, the American monetary authorities extended their inter-ventions with foreign currencies, which originated from the acute conditions in 1961, to the spot markets, and in accordance with what other countries had been practicing, included them as an-other weapon of their monetary defense. Their cooperation with the monetary authorities of other countries also covered opera-tions in the London gold market. In the so-called gold pool, set up at the end of 1961, a number of central banks joined forces for concerted action in sales and purchases of gold in the London market through the Bank of England as the common "agent"; they thereby prevented speculative disturbances by uncontrolled fluctuations of the free gold price and distrust in the solvency of the reserve currencies.

Another innovation in the exchange policies of the American monetary authorities was the gradual build-up of a network of reciprocal currency agreements between the Federal Reserve Sys-tem on the one hand and almost all major European central banks, the Bank for International Settlements, and the Bank of Canada, on the other; in the aggregate it amounted to more than $2 billion at the end of 1963. These arrangements for mutual support by the central banks in the form of swaps (that is, without exchange risk for the lending central bank) permit the monetary reserves to be adjusted more flexibly to current requirements without loss of time. These swap facilities have proved parti-cularly useful for the United States, more recently, however, also for some other participants which can thus obtain in good time such convertible foreign currencies as they need for interventions in the exchange markets.

Since the fall of 1962, the American monetary authorities have adopted the practice of selling to various foreign monetary authorities special certificates and notes of the U.S. Treasury, expressed in the currency of the holder and having maturities of up to about twenty-four months. This method represents another line of defense behind the short-term swap credit lines, but in front of the drawings that can be made on the Fund; by this expedient, swap operations between the central banks may be consolidated or somewhat more persistent disequilibria can be bridged.

FURTHER EVOLUTION OF THE SYSTEM

During 1964, twenty years after Bretton Woods, the IMF as well as the ten leading industrial countries participating in the "General Arrangements to Borrow," commonly known as the "Group of Ten," undertook a thorough examination of the outlook for the functioning of the international monetary system and of its probable future needs of liquidity. The results of these two reviews were placed before the general public in the IMF Annual Report for 1963 and in a Ministerial Statement of the Group of Ten, to which there was annexed a comprehensive study by the deputies of the Ministers and Governors.

Both documents reflect a remarkable consensus of opinion. There was general agreement that supplies of gold and reserve currencies are fully adequate for the present and are likely to be so for the immediate future, all the more so as the reserves are supplemented by a broad range of credit facilities. Particular emphasis was laid in the two studies on the close interrelationship between the liquidity needs of the system and the process of adjustment, i.e., the observance of a strict discipline with respect to the external balance. Although international consultation has greatly improved the measures and instruments to avoid imbalances and to correct them if and when they occur, the Group of Ten has initiated a new effort to improve further the adjustment process. In this context it will explore the question whether standards of "good behavior" can be formulated against which the actual policies of countries can be judged. Working Party 3 of OECD, the body for monetary cooperation among the leading industrial countries of the free world, has already embarked upon studies in this field.

In appraising the present system and the lines of its future development, the monetary experts have considered the various techniques for providing countries with credit facilities to supplement reserves. While reciprocal support operations have already in the past been subject to consultation in various bodies, the Group of Ten felt that there was still room for intensifying the cooperation in this field and to give countries more comprehensive and up-to-date information of the financing of deficits and surpluses. To this end, a procedure of "multilateral surveillance" of bilateral financing and liquidity creation has been introduced which consists of a regular exchange of information through the Bank for International Settlements and of a full exchange of views in the monetary watch-dog committee of OECD already mentioned.

The other actions resulting from this general stock-taking of the present system have likewise been on the evolutionary side and not in favour of radical reforms. ". . . Ministers and Governors reaffirmed their conviction that a structure based, as the present is, on fixed exchange rates and the established price of gold, has proved its value as a foundation on which to build for the future." As to the longer term outlook, it has not been denied by the experts that a rising turnover in international payments may entail some increase in the size of fluctuations in the balance of payments and that new gold production may not meet all liquidity needs in the future. It also became apparent in the examinations that, while dollar holdings may in times to come contribute less to the growth in international liquidity, no other currency seems to volunteer as a candidate for the status of a reserve currency. Certainly, multilateral and bilateral credit facilities will continue to contribute as in the past to the needed growth in world liquidity. In the longer run, however, the need for some additional kind of international reserve asset, to be created inside or outside the IMF, may not be excluded. The Group of Ten, being aware that this would raise many complex questions, has established a study group with the explicit mandate to ascertain the implication of such a further evolution of the present system. But as the supplies of gold and reserve currencies are at present fully adequate, there is no immediate need to reach an early decision, and the studies will be pursued without undue haste. This attitude is even more justified as the Governors of the IMF at their Tokyo meeting in September 1964 agreed in principle to a moderate increase in the IMF quotas (and to a relative adjustment of individual quotas which are clearly out of line), in order to strengthen the general position of the Fund in the longer run. The General Arrangements to Borrow, which expire in the fall of 1966, will also have to be reviewed in the course of 1965 with respect to their renewal or modification. All these reviews and actions demonstrate quite clearly—if further proof were needed—that the international monetary system is not left to itself but is under constant scrutiny by the responsible policy-makers.

Conclusions

A monetary order meeting all perfectionist demands is not likely ever to come into being. The gold standard, too, contrary to the opinion of some textbooks, was not perfect. Even in its heyday it was unable to guarantee price stability. Our present monetary system is certainly not perfect either, but it is much better than its reputation. How else can one explain the fact that on the many occasions when its strength was put to the test in the postwar period, it has proved to be amazingly robust and flexible? Never before in the history of currencies has there been such a rapid expansion of world production and of world trade, and there can be no doubt that the international monetary system has contributed a great deal to this state of affairs. During the early postwar years it has enabled the international monetary reserves to be rebuilt; otherwise, neither the liberalization of world trade nor the return of the European currencies to free convertibility could have been achieved. It has been able to cope with fundamental structural changes, with the burdens resulting from the Korean crisis and the Suez crisis, as well as with the effects of misdirected national monetary policies in some countries, without any significant impairment of the international exchange of goods. This robustness is in a large measure due to the fact that the gold-exchange standard was constantly developed on the basis of experience gained, and is still in a process of continuous development today. In the IMF and its binding rules of conduct, the gold-exchange standard has been given a new form of organization, which may possibly be improved and supplemented still further. The Achilles heel of this monetary system, the vulnerability of the key currencies, has been afforded better protection by the "General Arrangements to Borrow" agreement and the various forms of cooperation among the central banks. At longer term, of course, only the key currency countries themselves can ensure the necessary confidence by sound domestic economic policies. In particular, the United States as the leading country of the world economy and the center of gravity of the gold-exchange standard in its present form is burdened with great responsibility.

The most important achievements of the present monetary system, however, are the smoothly functioning international monetary cooperation in its various forms and the feeling of common responsibility which it encourages. Today, this cooperation is so firmly rooted that it guarantees constant contact between the monetary authorities of all principal countries and ensures that all problems and critical situations will be promptly discussed in bodies composed of competent monetary experts who can instantly cope with any potential dangers. The more important points of contact in this monetary cooperation are the Board of Executive Directors of the IMF, the Board of Directors of the Bank for International Settlements, the Monetary Committees of OECD and EEC, and the Board of Management of the European Monetary Agreement. There are close cross-connections between these various bodies. All these institutions provide a guarantee against a repetition of the events of 1931, all the more so because close cooperation has engendered the feeling of common responsibility for our monetary system, a feeling that was lacking in the crisis at that time. Recent trends and in particular the development of new techniques in international monetary management, like those indicated in the studies of the IMF and the Group of Ten, demonstrate that the world payments system is in a constant state of evolution and adaptation to the needs of a changing world economy.

The danger of a world-wide deflationary crisis hardly exists in the foreseeable future, at least not in connection with the supply of international liquidity. Therefore, there is no urgent call for radical reforms. Nor can the reserve currencies in the near future be dispensed with in our monetary order; in fact, the proposals of some authors who wish to do away with them are dubious. All proposals and suggestions, on the other hand, aiming at a better distribution of burdens and risks, command our attention. Extension of the coordination of monetary policies to embrace a reasonable relationship between gold and foreign-currency reserves is therefore desirable.

Improvements in the international monetary system cannot be expected only on the institutional level. Several reform proposals suffer from the failing of seeking technical perfection. Even the most perfectly constructed institutions are of little use if monetary disorder reigns in important countries, and no monetary system, whatever its design, can replace sound economic, monetary, and financial policies. What is more desirable than institutions is the readiness on the part of all parties concerned to abide by the rules of the game and to exercise the discipline demanded by a sound monetary order. This applies not only to the central banks, but also to governments and parliaments, and last but not least, it applies to employers and employees.

APPENDIX I

Background of the Common Market

Baron Pierre Bonvoisin

At this point, halfway along the so-called transition period of the Common Market, it is well worth looking back at concepts that gave birth to this ambitious venture.

FORCES STIMULATING EUROPEAN UNITY

At the end of World War II, Europe emerged replenished politically and economically. The conditions prevailing were:

1. *Politically.* On the world scene, the United States and Russia had virtually taken over the responsibilities the European nations had discharged. The subdivisions of the Continent constituted a dangerous factor of political disequilibrium. Communist pressure was serious.

2. *Economically.* The economic picture was equally disquieting. Partitioned markets, customs controls, exchange restrictions, and incapacitated or obsolescent industrial installations overburdened the weakened economy. The danger was twofold: the stifling between the two political powers and the imbalance of payments generating a serious shortage of dollars. Moreover, among other postwar conditions, there was a general trend in most European countries toward the establishment of social security schemes. The unions and labor at large were increasing and pressing demands.

But Europe was conscious of its economic weakness. With a view to helping in the resumption of sound commercial and financial practices within an orderly expanding world economy, the United States granted loans to several European countries, and the first stage of recovery, 1947–1949, began.

In 1947, Belgium, the Netherlands, and Luxemburg were the first countries to join in an economic union, through the setting up of BENELUX, which had been decided upon as early as 1944, in London. On the one hand, the achievements of the Belgium-Luxemburg Economic Union, created in 1921, and the fact that they were aware of the narrow limits of their markets, on the other hand, prompted the three countries to devise a customs agreement that would eventually develop into an economic union. The way to integration was thus paved. The pooling of all efforts was the condition for the help granted in terms of goods or capital offered by the Marshall Plan to all European countries. Only sixteen countries—among them the Benelux countries, France, Great Britain, Italy, and Switzerland—responded to these proposals. On April 16, 1948, the Organization for European Economic Co-operation (OEEC) was created. This intergovernmental organization was to divide the American credits and to promote the establishment of a free trade area. In 1950, within the OEEC, the European Payments Union (EPU) was created as a technical organization aimed at facilitating the carrying-out of payments whose final purpose was the re-establishment of currency convertibility

In 1948, Great Britain, France, and the Benelux countries signed a Treaty of *military* alliance: the Western European Union (WEU), and in 1949, the first *political* European institution was formed, namely, the Council of Europe, which consists of an intergovernmental committee and an interparliamentary consultative assembly.

Following these developments, the financial rehabilitation entered a second stage, 1950–1954. Beginning with the Marshall Plan, the construction of Europe definitely entered a second phase, since it proposed "to place the whole of the Franco-German steel and coal production under the control of a common High Authority in an organization open to other European countries." These proposals met with the favorable reaction of the governments of Bonn, Brussels, The Hague, Luxemburg, and Rome. On April 18, 1951, the Treaty of Paris, which afterward was ratified by large majorities in the parliaments of the six countries, established the European Coal and Steel Community (ECSC), which came into being on July 15, 1952. The ECSC established a common market, applying to an important economic sector, that was open to other European countries wishing to join or to associate themselves with the Community. It recommended a customs union, common rules of competition, and productive investments. Its supranational character lay mainly in its institutional organs, inasmuch as it was placed under the control of:

1. A High Authority, that is, a permanent autonomous executive body.
2. A special council of ministers, vested with power of decision.

The steel and coal trade grew rapidly within the ECSC and several countries, among which were the United States and the United Kingdom, sent ambassadors to the High Authority. Although these moves toward European integration seemed to meet with some success in the economic field, the recovery experienced a disappointing setback in 1956 when the treaty establishing a European Defense Community (EDC) and a European Political Community (EPC) failed.

After the failure of both political and military integrations, the political and economic advantages of large markets and the results actually attained by the ECSC naturally led to a reconsideration of the idea of an economic union. At the request of the Benelux countries, the six member countries of the ECSC convened in Messina, on June 1, 1955, to resume talks on the European idea in its economic perspective. They also considered the pooling of all efforts in order to prepare the community to meet the atomic challenge. Representatives of Great Britain took part in the preliminary talks, on the basis of a report prepared by an intergovernmental committee, but soon made clear that they could not follow the "six" toward further integration. After long and difficult negotiations, the six governments agreed, in February 1957, upon the objectives and the provisional ways of implementation, and these decisions became the fundamental principles of the Treaty of Rome.

On March 25, 1957, the six countries signed the Treaty of Rome, establishing a European Economic Community (EEC), generally called the "Common Market," and a European Atomic Energy Community, designated as EURATOM. The treaty was ratified by the national parliaments by strong majorities, and the two new communities entered into being in January 1948.

STRUCTURE OF THE COMMON MARKET
ORGANIZATION

To attain its object, that is, to create a vast area governed by a common economic policy, the EEC must carry out the integration of the markets. The treaty assigned far-reaching objectives, that is, the promotion of:

1. A smooth development of the various economic activities.
2. A steady and balanced expansion.
3. An increased stability.
4. An accelerated improvement of the standards of living.
5. Closer relations between member states.

The Treaty of Rome was essentially of an economic nature, as it was aimed simultaneously at a customs union and an economic union. The signatories set a transition period of twelve to fifteen years for the progressive realization of this double union. Although the treaty was not a political alliance, it called for certain transfers of national sovereignty to a supranational body. This, incidentally, was one of Great Britain's main objections. Full membership would be open not only to the original signatories but also to any other country prepared to agree to the rules of the organization.

Furthermore, a more flexible formula provided for "associated members" without voting rights, the first associated countries being overseas countries and territories (1957) and Greece (1962). On the other hand, the "six" were members of larger organizations such as the OECD and GATT. There would be no discriminations on grounds of nationality. Article 240 provided for an unlimited duration.

The treaty comprised a charter which, while fixing the objectives and setting a frame for the supranational authority's intervention, also would allow the latter to retain a large discretionary power. The Customs Union, which implied the free movement of goods and of production media, represented the very foundation of the community. To encourage free trade, all goods were to be subjected to a progressive lowering of customs tariffs. This implied the complete elimination of any customs duties of any quotas, as well as the setting up of common external tariffs. A more flexible regime would apply to agricultural produce.

The Treaty provided for the progressive suppression of all restrictions to the free movement of services; it however, merely outlined the principles and the objectives, which would be subsequently defined, by the council. Special provisions governed transportation matters.

The right of establishment and the free movement of persons were laid down as a principle, but specific recommendations were not made because these matters related to rather delicate problems of a social or political nature. Similarly, allowance was made for free movement of capital. The member states were progressively to abolish the restrictions to the free movement of capital between them, during the transition period, and to the extent that might be required for smooth operation of the Common Market (Article 67). The establishment of a complete and totally integrated Common Market would rest on solid foundations only if this were accomplished following a common economic policy. It is, however, quite impossible to disregard national economic policies, and the common policy cannot be adopted until conflicting interests have been resolved by a common denominator.

Free competition, which is necessary to the smooth operation of the Common Market, was to be governed by common regulations. These would guard against any sort of commercial and juridical interferences that might impair the effects of the liberty of movement. Competition would also be aided by harmonizing legislation. The signatories undertook to harmonize their fiscal, financial, commercial, and social laws so as to bring them in line with one another and thus avoid disparities at the national leve

Europe is concerned with the peaceful use of atomic energy to the highest degree, since it has to import increasing quantities of fuel, to cope with a consumption of energy that doubles every ten years. On March 25, 1957, the "six" signed a second treaty, establishing a European Atomic Energy Community (EURATOM), and on January 1, 1959, created a particular Common Market. According to forecasts made in 1957, EURATOM's output of nuclear electricity should be equivalent, by 1980, to the present production derived from conventional sources. To reach this aim, EURATOM should simultaneously carry out four essential tasks:

1. Develop nuclear research and train the future top engineers.
2. Provide for the construction of nuclear power stations and for the necessary investment.
3. Arrange for the regular supply of nuclear raw materials and processed ores.
4. Provide for safety control installations and health protection.

The special fission materials would be the community's own property. Arrangements provided for the exchange of information and know-how (not only with the members of the community but also with the United States, Great Britain, and Canada) and participation in international research. Membership in EURATOM would be open to all.

In order to operate and develop the Common Market, the EEC, a legal entity, acts through an assembly, a council of ministers, a commission, a court of justice, and a set of consultative and executive bodies. Salient features are:

1. The EEC institutions, while derived from those of the ECSC, have a less marked supranational character.
2. To strike a balance between the legitimate interests of the member states and those of the Community, the treaty provided for a twin-headed executive authority, namely, the council of ministers and the commission.
3. All partners contribute to the budget of the Community.
4. The seat is established in Brussels.

The assembly (called European Parliamentary Assembly),[1] is the organ exercising the political control of the institutions of the community. Pending the election of the "Peoples' delegates," through general direct elections that will be organized following a uniform procedure, the assembly consists of 142 delegates from national parliaments: Germany, France, and Italy each have thirty-six delegates; Belgium and the Netherlands, fourteen; and Luxemburg, six. In principle, the assembly rules according to the simple majority of the votes cast. The assembly has power to deliberate and to control the executive bodies of the three Communities. Its only effective power, however, is its right to defeat the commission by passing censure motions, to be supported by two-thirds of the votes cast and the majority of its members.

The Council of National Ministers, a political organ, is the supreme authority of the EEC. Its principal decisions are taken by a simple majority of the members of the council. In cases specially stated, the treaty requires either unanimity (mainly in the first stages of the Common Market) or a qualified majority of twelve out of seventeen votes. In the latter case, the members' voting powers are computed as follows: Germany, France, and Italy have four votes each; Belgium and the Netherlands have two votes each; and Luxemburg has one vote.

Being simultaneously an executive and a legislative body, the council ensures the coordination of the general economic policies of the "six" and holds a binding power of decision. However, the council acts only upon proposals of the commission and is entitled to amend such proposals only by the unanimity of its members.

[1] Not to be mistaken for the Consultative Assembly of the Council of Europe.

The European Commission is responsible only to the assembly and accepts no instructions from any government or any other body. It consists of nine members appointed for four years, by common consent of the governments. It does not include more than two members having the same nationality. Its members are not entitled to carry out any other professional activity, whether remunerated or not.

The council and the commission engage in mutual consultation and devise in common the modalities of their future cooperation. The commission supervises the carrying out of the provisions of the treaty and is endowed with a power of decision, a power of recommendation, and a power of advice; as a permanent institution, it represents the community. Thanks to its "right of recommendation," the commission takes an active part in the council's power of decision.

The Court of Justice is an institution common to all three communities; it is composed of seven judges, who in turn are assisted by two attorneys-general. The court verifies the lawfulness of the actions taken by the executive organs. The court also rules on the interpretation to be given to the treaty, on the carrying out of the obligations imposed upon the member-states, and on any dispute among the latter. The court's judgments have full force of law. In principle, appeals have no suspensive effects.

In addition to the four basic institutions described above, three consultative bodies function as follows:

1. The Economic and Social Committee is common to the EEC and to EURATOM. It is composed of 101 members, who are chosen on a personal basis and as representatives of both economic and social life in the Community. The committee acts as a consultative body to the executive organs; in some instances, this consultation is compulsory.

2. The member states and the commission each designate two members of the Monetary Committee. As a consultative body, the committee is entrusted with: (1) the survey of the monetary and financial situation within each of the six countries and the community as a whole, as well as the general payments arrangements, and (2) the furnishing of advice for the benefit of the executive organs.

3. The Transport Committee comprises several experts, chosen by their respective governments, to advise the commission whenever the latter deems it appropriate. However, competence in this field is shared with the transport section of the Economic and Social Committee.

The basic institutions and consultative bodies are complemented by operating bodies. These include:

1. The European Investment Bank (EIB) is endowed with a legal personality entirely distinct from that of the Community; it was constituted with a capital of 1 billion EMA accounts units[2] (one EMA unit = U.S. $1). Its task is to assist in a balanced development of the Common Market by means of its own resources and by resorting to the capital markets. It is a nonprofit organization that grants loans and gives its guarantee to help in financing projects aimed at the development of economically underdeveloped areas, the modernization or re-equipment of existing enterprises or the creation of new ones, as well as projects of common interest to several member countries and which cannot be wholly financed by means available within any individual country.

2. The European Social Fund Committee is composed of one member of the commission, of representatives of the various governments, of the trade unions, and of employers' associations. It is designed to improve employment possibilities within the Community and thus contribute to raising the standard of living.

3. The European Development Fund for Overseas Territories obtains its resources from contributions made by the "six" and is designed to promote the economic and social development of those overseas territories which at one time were colonies of certain member countries.

POLICIES AND AIMS OF THE COMMON MARKET

The means placed at the disposal of the various institutions provided for the progressive realization of:

1. A *customs union* through free movement of goods, persons, services, and capital.
2. An *economic union* through harmonization and coordination of economic, fiscal, monetary, and social policies, the ultimate goal being a general economic policy common to all member countries.

The customs union coheres intercommunity relations by eliminating customs duties and taxes having an equivalent effect. Moreover, the "six" abstain from introducing new customs duties or taxes with equivalent effect on goods moving within the community. According to the treaty provisions, existing customs duties were to be progressively abolished during the transitional period. The latter would be divided into three stages of four years each, the individual duration of which could

[2] The European Monetary Agreement, which succeeded the European Payments Union.

be extended by one or two years, although the total duration of the period was not to exceed fifteen years.

For each product, the basic duty on which successive cuts was to be effected[3] was the duty in force on January 1, 1957. The timetable of these cuts is given in Table 1.

TABLE 1.   TIMETABLE OF CUSTOMS DUTIES REDUCTIONS

	Period of Time	Percentage Rate of Cuts	
		On Total Duties	Minimum Per Product[a]
First Stage			
Phase 1	12 months	10	10
Phase 2	18 months	10	5
Phase 3	18 months	10	5
Total	4 years	30	25
Second Stage			
Phase 1	18 months	10	5
Phase 2	18 months	10	5
Phase 3	18 months	10	5
Total	4 years	30	25
Third Stage[b]			
Total	4 years	40	50
Transition period	12 years	100	100

a At the end of the first and second stages, a minimum of 25 per cent per product must be attained.

b Phases and percentages to be decided upon by the council, acting by a qualified majority.

In addition, export customs duties and taxes having an equivalent effect were to be suppressed by the end of the first stage. Customs duties of a fiscal nature were to be cut down at a rate similar to that applied to ordinary customs duties, but with a minimum of 10 per cent per phase.

With respect to relations with the rest of the world, a common external tariff was defined in the treaty. The member countries would contribute to the development of international trade and the reduction of the obstacles to international trade by entering into reciprocal agreements aimed at cutting down customs duties to a point below the general level. In principle, the common external tariff duty to be applied

3 In fact, on January 1, 1962, customs duties on industrial products had been lowered by 40 per cent.

would be the average of the duties applied within the four customs territories on January 1, 1957. However, in the case of various groups of products, enumerated in seven distinct lists, the level of duties would be limited to a given percentage. Furthermore, the council would have the right to grant gradually decreasing tariff quotas, which would enable interested countries to import certain goods while paying reduced customs duties or no duties at all.

A progressive enforcement schedule was set up. On items where the difference between the customs duties applied on January 1, 1957, and the common tariff duties *did not* exceed 15 per cent, the latter would be applied at the end of the first stage.[4] In other cases, the treaty provided for a 30 per cent cut of the difference by the end of the first stage, another 30 per cent cut by the end of the second stage, and full enforcement of the common external tariff not later than the end of the transitional period.

Certain quantitative restrictions applied to three areas:

1. Imports. In addition to banning new quantitative restrictions and measures leading to equivalent results, the treaty decided upon a progressive extension of existing quotas, tending to their final abolition by the end of the transitional period.[5] Bilateral quotas, that is, those negotiated separately between certain partners, were, as of January 1, 1959 converted into common quotas applicable to all other member countries without discrimination. The treaty provided for a different rate of increase for the whole of the common quotas and for each separate product. However, the commission would decide upon the procedure to be applied for the removal between member countries of existing measures having an effect equivalent to that of the quotas.

2. Exports. Quantitative export restrictions in force when the treaty came into effect were to be removed not later than by the end of the first stage.

3. State Monopolies. National monopolies of a commercial nature, either "de jure" or "de facto," would be amended so as to preclude any discrimination between citizens of member countries by the end of the transitional period.

A major area of concern was agricultural policy. As it is practically impossible to liberate agricultural products at the rate set down for

---

[4] In fact, they came into force one year ahead of schedule.
[5] Except for agricultural products, this abolition was achieved on January 1, 1962.

industrial goods and as it would be unthinkable to exclude an economic sector of such importance, the treaty chose to adopt the following attitude: While the ultimate goal remains the realization of a common agricultural policy, a number of transitional measures must be provided for. Except for the special provisions mentioned below, agricultural products were to be subject to the general regulations laid down for the establishment of the Common Market.

1. Common Agricultural Policy. The object of this common policy would be gradually applied in such a way as to be fully in force at the end of the transitional period. Its essential aims would be to increase productivity, to provide the farming population with a decent standard of living, to stabilize markets, to ensure supplies, and to ascertain reasonable prices on the consumer market. Depending upon the products, the common organization for agricultural markets would take one of several aspects. These included common regulations in matters of competition, certain reserves being made with regard to subsidies authorized by the council; compulsory coordination of the various national market organizations; and a European market organization. Having compared the various agricultural policies on the basis of the balance of resources and needs, the council would be in a position to make the appropriate decisions.[6]

2. Transitional Measures. Each member state was authorized to apply, in the case of certain products, a minimum price system free from all discrimination, according to which imports can be temporarily suspended or reduced However, this safeguard clause should, under no circumstances, entail a reduction of intercommunity exchanges reaching below the general level attained on January 1, 1958. On the coming into effect of the treaty, objective criteria for the establishment of this system would be decided upon by the council by a unanimous vote. At the end of the transitional period, the council would lay down the regulations to be applied to minimum prices still subsisting within the framework of the common agricultural policy.

The quantities involved in these agreements would be superior to those comprised in existing contracts because the basis taken would be the average volume of trade between the member countries during the three years preceding the coming into effect of the treaty. These agreements would entail a rise of prices, which would have to ascend gradually to the level of the prices paid to national producers on the buying country's internal market. Under reserve of the various exceptions sanc-

6 The minority is at liberty to appeal to the Court of Justice.

tioned by the treaty, this harmonization must be fully realized, at the very latest, by the end of the transitional period.

Transportation provisions complete the jurisdiction of the customs union as set forth in the treaty. The ever-growing importance of transportation together with the application of discriminating tariffs impeding the free circulation of goods made it impossible not to include transportation in the common market. On the other hand, the free circulation of services in matters of transportation could be regulated only through appropriate provisions. Up to the present time, the treaty is applicable only to railroads, waterways, and highways.

In order to devise a common transportation policy, the council, acting on the unanimity of votes up to the end of the second phase (and thereafter on a qualified majority), was to decide upon two facets of the policy: (1) common rules to be applied to international transportation leaving or arriving within one of the member countries or whose itinerary crosses one or several of these countries; and (2) conditions regulating the admission of nonresident transportation enterprises in a member country.

Provisions to be enforced immediately included:

1. Until a common policy had been laid down, no member country would be entitled to make use of the various regulations in force prior to January 1958 in a manner such as to discriminate against transportation enterprises belonging to another member country.
2. As far as internal traffic was concerned, all freight price discriminations based on the origin or destination of transported goods were to be abolished not later than at the end of the second stage.
3. Beginning with the second stage, it would be forbidden to member states to impose on internal transportation, those prices and conditions tending to assist or protect the interests of one or several private enterprises except when such prices were designed to safeguard free competition.
4. Charges collected by a transportation enterprise at the crossing of borders were not to exceed a reasonable level; they would be gradually reduced.
5. A consulting committee, composed of experts, was set up to assist the commission.

The second objective of the Common Market, namely, economic union, required careful delineation of policy. Because of the various implications involved, implementation of the economic union was to be effected over a more or less extended period of time. Therefore, the only regulations laid down by the Treaty of Rome in that connection were those considered indispensable to ensure the satisfactory progress of the Common Market. To avoid certain inconveniences resulting from the freeing of trade and also to prepare the way to a general economic policy, the treaty favored the harmonization or coordination of national economic policies. Common rules were formulated as safeguards as follows:

1. Free competition is the best guarantee offered by the Common Market. Therefore, agreements and monopolies were subject to strict control. Any agreements between enterprises, any decisions aiming at the association of enterprises, and any concerted practices likely to affect trade between the "six" or impede, restrict, or distort the full play of free competition within the Common Market would be incompatible with the idea of the community. However, the treaty made provisions for a certain number of constructive agreements. With respect to monopolies, abusive use of a prominent position within the Common Market, or a substantial part of it, would also be incompatible with the ideal of the community, and was therefore prohibited insofar as such practice would be likely to affect the free competition between member states.

If advised of the use of dumping practices within the Common Market, the commission would make the necessary recommendations to the parties concerned in order to have them put an end to such practices. However, should these recommendations remain unheeded, it would be the commission's right to allow the affected party to take the necessary protective measures.

Government assistance and subsidies were prohibited. Except for certain cases, specifically described, any assistance granted by a state or obtained through the state's resources in any way whatsoever, would be prohibited insofar as such assistance might have a distorting or damaging effect on competitive conditions. An appeal could be introduced with the Court of Justice against the commission's decisions tending to abolish or alter such form of assistance.

2. Fiscal regulations were designed to do away, by the beginning of the second stage, with the fiscal discriminations resulting from taxes on imported goods and refunds on exported products.

3. With respect to legislation, the Treaty provided for bringing into line national legislation on the matter of taxes on the turnover figure, excise duties, and other forms of indirect taxation.

The coordination of economic policies was planned in three areas:

1. Cyclical Policy. The six member countries would engage in mutual consultations to decide upon the steps to be taken under given economic circumstances. The council, acting on a unanimity of votes, would be equipped to make appropriate decisions.

2. Monetary Policy. Each member country would endeavor to achieve a satisfactory balance of payments, to preserve confidence in its currency, to maintain a high rate of employment and stable prices. This would be effected, first, by a free circulation of capital. The monetary policy of each member must allow free circulation of capital. Although no definite program of liberation was established, the treaty provided for certain rules concerning the prohibition of new restrictions, the alleviation of exchange regulations, and the gradual freeing of current payments.

Second, a coordinated monetary policy was outlined. The six member countries would provide for cooperation between their administrations, as well as between their central banks, to achieve the all round coordination of their economic policies. Each government would handle its foreign exchange policy in the light of the member-countries' common interest. In the event of one member country being faced with balance-of-payments difficulties, the commission would examine the situation immediately as well as the course to be adopted under the circumstances. To do so, the commission would draw on every means placed at its disposal. Should these prove inadequate, the council would be prepared, on a qualified majority of votes, to introduce what is called "mutual help," which might range from a concerted action with other international organizations to the granting of limited credits. In this connection, the Monetary Committee and the European Investment Bank[7] could also be called upon.

3. The commercial policy with third countries extended the premise that the six member countries wished to contribute to the well-balanced development of world trade, to the gradual abolishment of restrictions impeding the latter, and to the cutting down of customs barriers. Within the allotted transitional period, several important steps have been considered, among which are: coordination of commercial relations with the rest of the world; adjustment of existing tariff agreements and negotiations with third countries on the terms of the common external tariff; bringing into line of liberalization lists agreed

[7] See the discussion about institutions in the preceding section.

upon between member countries and other countries; and gradual harmonization of the various assistance systems applied by the member countries with regard to exports to third countries. Beyond the transitional period, the common commercial policy would be based on uniform principles.

As mentioned before, the treaty did not set forth a political objective. Nevertheless the question must be asked: Is there indeed such a thing as a political objective of the Common Market? Although the Common Market does not strive toward any immediate political goal, it may be argued that the very existence of the community cannot remain void of political consequences. As evidence of the absence of any immediate political goal, the following arguments can be offered:

1. Signed on the morrow of the failure of both EDC and EPC, the Treaty of Rome could be only a strictly economic agreement; at the time, even the six member countries were far from being unanimous when it came to accepting the idea of a political European union.
2. Fiscal, monetary, and social laws have, to a considerable extent, continued to come within the national jurisdictions.
3. Furthermore, particular care had been taken, when drawing up the treaty, to maintain a balance between legitimate national interests, on the one hand, and the common interest on the other hand.

That it has had political effects cannot be denied, however. The treaty is bound to have political consequences of varying significance both in its immediate implementations and in its subsequent developments. Without going back over the various subjects previously covered, mention should be made, in this connection, of:

1. The supranational character of the executive organs.
2. The compulsory character of all decisions made by the council.
3. The common rules concerning free competition.
4. The relinquishing of sovereignty implied by the customs union.
5. The fact that, as of the beginning of the second stage, the council is prepared to rule on a qualified majority of votes.

Moreover, mere reference to the principal fields of the community's policy will bring to mind their political implications in a more or less distant future. For example, consider the provisions for: harmonization of fiscal, social, and monetary legislation; coordination of economic and commercial policies; and the common agricultural and transportation policies.

When we consider the prospects of closer political ties, there is no way of knowing whether the EEC will one day choose to follow certain tendencies presently favored by the European Council, with which the community stands on excellent terms. Certain facts, however, are obvious: The very first words of the treaty's preamble constitute a declaration of intent full of idealism: "Determined to establish the foundations of an ever closer union among European peoples. . . ." Nor does the EEC spare its efforts in its contacts with the other European institutions and more particularly with the European Council.

That a social policy was also stated in the treaty is not surprising, for social standards and economic welfare have a common core. Equal progress through improvement of living and working conditions is the main object of the social policy adopted by the treaty's signatories. This is evident in the provisions for:

1. Harmonization of Social Systems. The member countries' authority in matters of social progress has been hardly affected by the treaty, whose sole demand is a "close co-operation between the Six, more particularly in matters concerning the right to work, employment, working conditions, professional training, social security. . . ."

2. Bringing National Legislation into Line. Prior to correcting distortions brought about by the more advanced French social system, a certain number of adjustments were to be imposed upon the remaining partners, with a view to obtaining equality of pay for male and female workers as well as a uniform set of rules for paid holidays and overtime.

3. Common Action. Acting on a unanimity of votes, the council was empowered to call on the commission to carry out common measures, more particularly as regards social security and migrant workers.

4. Free Movement of Labor. Free circulation of labor was to be ensured within the community not later than by the end of the transitional period. This implied the abolishment of any nationality discrimination between workers of the member countries.

5. European Social Fund. The mission of the European Social Fund was to promote employment facilities as well as geographical and professional mobility of workers within the community, mainly in order to reduce the inconveniences resulting from technological unemployment. Upon request of a member country, the Fund would cover 50 per cent of the expenses borne by that country or by a public institution of such country, in connection with professional readaptation, resettlement subsidies, and assistance to workers whose jobs had been eliminated or temporarily suppressed. This assistance was to be available as of the date of coming into effect of the treaty.

ECONOMIC POTENTIAL OF THE COMMON MARKET

The six countries signing the treaty had already undergone a long period of rehabilitation since World War II. Pooling their economic potential in an over-all common market was bound to bring about further and important developments. The first of these was in the general economy:

1. Population. The population contained within the area of the Common Market, spread over an area of 449,000 square miles, may be compared to that of the largest countries. The distribution is given in Table 2.

TABLE 2. COMPARISON OF WORLD AND EEC POPULATION
(Millions)

	EEC	U.K.	U.S.A.	U.S.S.R.	World
1952	158	50.4	157	?	2.560
1957	164	51.4	171	200	2.836
1961	171.7	52.9	183	?	3.069

2. National Income of EEC Countries. The average income of the community is the second highest in the world, exceeded only by the United States. The income per capita, computed in terms of actual purchasing power, would prove even more favorable to the EEC. Table 3 presents comparative figures.

3. Economic Activity. The gross national product of the EEC for the years 1952, 1957, and 1960 was $187 billion, $239.5 billion, and $270.6, respectively. For the whole of the EEC, industrial production ranks first among other activities, in spite of the importance of the French, Italian,

TABLE 3. NATIONAL INCOME COMPARISONS

	EEC	U.K.	U.S.A.
Total income (billions of U.S. dollars)			
1952	73.9	35.5	290.2
1957	101.5	49.3	364.0
1961	145.0	60.2	426.0
Per capita (U.S. dollars, official rate of exchange)			
1952	468	748	1,848
1957	635	958	2,129
1959	850	1,019	2,232

and Dutch agriculture. From 1949–1960, the industrial production of the EEC increased by 97 per cent. Table 4 throws some light on the favorable evolution of most of the industrial sectors.

TABLE 4. COMPARATIVE DATA OF INDUSTRIAL ACTIVITY

Industrial Production	Years	EEC	U.K.	U.S.A.	U.S.S.R
1. Coal (millions of metric tons)	1952	239	230	458	215
	1957	248	227	468	328
	1962	227	201	399	517
2. Steel (raw) (millions of metric tons)	1952	42	16.7	85	34
	1957	60	22	102	51
	1962	72.6	20.8	89.2	76.3
3. Iron ore (millions of metric tons)	1952	61.4	16.5	99.5	52.6
	1957	92.4	17.1	107.8	84.3
	1962	92	16.8	73.5	128
4. Nonferrous Metals (in thousands of metric tons)					
Copper	1952	338.7	229.2	1.079	365
	1957	438	207.6	1.467	540
	1962	553.8	237.6	1.340	?
Zinc	1952	527.4	69.8	888	?
	1957	704.5	78	979	365
	1962	761	94.3	821.5	?
Lead	1952	278	77.5	483.6	?
	1957	390	87	548	275
	1962	469	87.6	745	?
Tin	1952	10.8	30	22.9	?
	1957	40.7	34.7	1.6	15
	1962	9.8	24.8	8.6	?
Aluminum	1952	329.6	102.8	1,126.8	?
	1957	509.1	128.3	1,821.6	?
	1962	716.5	151.6	2,036.4	?
5. Crude oil (millions of tons)	1952	2.9	—	309.4	47.3
	1957	8.2	—	353.6	98.3
	1962	13.2	—	354.3[a]	186
6. Motor vehicles (thousands)	1952	1,065	688	5,538	303
	1957	2,492	1,148	7,220	581
	1962	4,631	1,674	8,172	578
7. Electricity (millions of kwh)	1952	146.8	62	462.4	119.1
	1957	219.1	90.9	680.3	209.4
	1962	313.2	141.5	943	369

a 1961 data.

Insofar as agricultural production is concerned, although the EEC has had to cope with a particularly heavy demand, it is one of the most important producers of foodstuffs. The agricultural labor force is steadily decreasing. Unfortunately up-to-date statistics are not available and therefore appropriate global comparisons for the various agricultural products cannot be made.

The second most important development of the Common Market has been the expansion of foreign trade.

This is the backbone of the European economy. The EEC is the first importer in the world and the second exporter. Table 5 gives compara-

TABLE 5. GLOBAL FOREIGN TRADE
(*In Billions of U.S. Dollars*)

	EEC	U.K.	U.S.A.	World
1952	28.9	16.6	25.9	141.5
1957	46.8	20.2	34.—	208.7
1962	69.8	22.7	37.7	254.9

tive data. It should be noted that trade between the six member countries accounts for about one-third of the total of the Common Market's trade.

The third and most outstanding development has been the build-up of foreign-exchange reserves. Official gold and foreign-currency reserves give an important indication of the monetary soundness of the community. Comparative figures are given in Table 6, in millions of U.S. dollars.

TABLE 6. FOREIGN-EXCHANGE RESERVES

	EEC Total	EEC Gold	U.K. Total	U.K. Gold	U.S.A. Total	U.S.A. Gold
1952	3,500	2,350	1,846	1,500	—	23,253
1957	7,700	5,250	2,273	1,600	—	22,857
1962	16,850	11,450	2,806	2,600	16,156	16,057

CONCLUSION

On January 14, 1962, in spite of the complexity of the various tasks that had to be accomplished simultaneously in several fields, the Common Market was able to enter the second stage of its transitional period. Indeed, the council had by then unanimously satisfied itself that the bulk of the objectives set down by the Treaty of Rome for the first stage had been effectively attained. The progressive enforcement of the free circulation of goods had been speeded up twice in succession. Furthermore, the six member countries had agreed to adopt a common agricultural policy. The fears voiced in certain quarters as to the successful launching of the Common Market had thus proved to be unjustified.

Index

Africa, 140–180; agriculture, 142, 146, 159–162; attitudes and institutions, 148–152; capital: accumulation, 151, available for investment, 171, 174, formation, 170–177, 180; colonization and, 143–147, 148–149, 151, 152–153, 179; consumption, 154, 172; economic growth, 148–152, 152–154; education in, 157–159, 180; EEC and, 46, 47, 169–170, 179; foreign capital investments, 174–177; foreign loans and grants, 175, 180; GNP: foreign capital and, 175, trade and, 162–163; government development, 151–152; income distribution, 153–154; labor force, 150, 156, 157; minerals, 142–143, 146; nationalization movement, 140–141, 178–180; natural resources, 141–143, 146; population characteristics, 120, 154–157; production: manufacturing, 162, raw materials, 142, 146; productivity, 156–157, 179–180, agriculture and, 160–161; race problems, 177–178; research investment, 159, 180; savings in, 171–172; slave trade and, 144–145, 153; tax revenue, 172–173; technology, 150–151, 152–153; trade, 162–170; colonialization and, 145–146, 152–153, commodities in, 161, 164, direction, 168–170, exports, 164–165, 171, 180, financing, 164, import pattern, 161, 165–166, 167, GNP and, 162–163, terms of, 166–167; United States and, 176–177

Agriculture; Africa, 142, 146, 159–162; Britain's problems, 83, 85–86, 90; cooperation in problems of, 24–27; economic importance, 242; EEC countries, 39–40, 49–50, 58–59, policy on, 359–361, production, 368; EFTA and, 58–59, 76; Middle East, 187, 190, 196–198, 202; India, 276, investment in, 259, 260, 261, 262, 272, land reform, 268, output, 265; Israel, 223, 230–232; price supports, 25–27; surpluses, 30; trends in, 25; in underdeveloped countries, 29–31; U.S.S.R., 300

Alliance for Progress, 31

Argentina: exports, 126; foreign public debt, 127; in LAFTA, 133; production, 121, 122; social structure, 122; see also Latin America

Associated Overseas Members (AOC) of European Common Market, 73, 169–170, 353

Austria: EEC and, 43, 45; prices and wages in, 70

Balance of payments: in EEC, 363; financing deficits, 329–330; India, 271; interest rates and, 315; international competition and, 8, 9; Israel, 248–250; Japan, 115–116; see also Balance of payments, United States

Balance of payments, United States, 21, 23, 50–51, 303–323; capital out-

Format by Mort Perry
Set in Linotype Baskerville
Composed, printed and bound by American Book–Stratford Press
HARPER & ROW, PUBLISHERS, INCORPORATED